CAMBRIDGE LIBRARY COLLECTION

Books of enduring scholarly value

Egyptology

The large-scale scientific investigation of Egyptian antiquities by Western scholars began as an unintended consequence of Napoleon's invasion of Egypt during which, in 1799, the Rosetta Stone was discovered. The military expedition was accompanied by French scholars, whose reports prompted a wave of enthusiasm that swept across Europe and North America resulting in the Egyptian Revival style in art and architecture. Increasing numbers of tourists visited Egypt, eager to see the marvels being revealed by archaeological excavation. Writers and booksellers responded to this growing interest with publications ranging from technical site reports to tourist guidebooks and from children's histories to theories identifying the pyramids as repositories of esoteric knowledge. This series reissues a wide selection of such books. They reveal the gradual change from the 'tomb-robbing' approach of early excavators to the highly organised and systematic approach of Flinders Petrie, the 'father of Egyptology', and include early accounts of the decipherment of the hieroglyphic script.

Illahun, Kahun and Gurob ~ Medum

A pioneering Egyptologist, Sir William Matthew Flinders Petrie (1853–1942) excavated over fifty sites and trained a generation of archaeologists. The two excavation reports now reissued here together were first published in 1891 and 1892 respectively, written in collaboration with other experts. They outline significant finds at the pyramids of Lahun and Meidum, and at Gurob and Kahun, notably the latter's cache of Middle Kingdom papyri. Petrie and his collaborators describe in detail how they came to make these discoveries, shedding light on developing archaeological practices used towards the end of the nineteenth century. Petrie's professional method of painstakingly recording every find is well demonstrated here, and each report includes a section of valuable illustrative material. Petrie wrote prolifically throughout his long career, and a great many of his other publications – for both specialists and non-specialists – are also reissued in this series.

Illahun, Kahun and Gurob

~

Medum

W.M. Flinders Petrie

CAMBRIDGE
UNIVERSITY PRESS

University Printing House, Cambridge, CB2 8BS, United Kingdom

Published in the United States of America by Cambridge University Press, New York

Cambridge University Press is part of the University of Cambridge.
It furthers the University's mission by disseminating knowledge in the pursuit of education, learning and research at the highest international levels of excellence.

www.cambridge.org
Information on this title: www.cambridge.org/9781108065733

This edition first published 1891 and 1892
This digitally printed version 2013

ISBN 978-1-108-06573-3 Paperback

This book reproduces the text of the original edition. The content and language reflect the beliefs, practices and terminology of their time, and have not been updated.

The original edition of this book contains a number of colour plates, which have been reproduced in black and white. Colour versions of these images can be found online at www.cambridge.org/9781108065733

ILLAHUN,

KAHUN AND GUROB.

1889-90.

BY

W. M. FLINDERS PETRIE,

WITH CHAPTERS BY

PROF. SAYCE, D.D., CANON HICKS, PROF. MAHAFFY, F. LL. GRIFFITH, B.A.,
AND F. C. J. SPURRELL, F.G.S.

LONDON:
DAVID NUTT, 270, STRAND.
1891.

LONDON:
PRINTED BY WILLIAM CLOWES AND SONS, LIMITED,
STAMFORD STREET AND CHARING CROSS.

CONTENTS.

CHAPTER VII.

Ptolemaic Cemetery, Gurob.

CHAPTER VIII.

Ptolemais and late Sites.

CHAPTER IX.

The Greek Papyri.

By Prof. Sayce.

CHAPTER X.

The Hieratic Papyri.

By F. Ll. Griffith.

CHAPTER XI.

The Stone Implements.

By F. C. J. Spurrell, F.G.S.

INTRODUCTION.

1. THE work of the season 1889–90 has completed the exploration of the towns of Gurob and Kahun, which was begun in the previous year. During my absence Mr. Fraser took charge of the place, and succeeded in opening the pyramid of Illahun: and on my return I continued the clearing of the XIIth dynasty town at Kahun, while soon after Mr. W. O. Hughes-Hughes joined me, and took up the excavations at Gurob, to which I could not attend along with the other work. The planning of the town of Kahun required close attention, as over two thousand chambers were cleared; and each required to be measured, and entered in the working plan which was kept, before it was refilled with the earth from other rooms. The most interesting piece of work was the clearing of the Maket tomb. It so seldom happens that a large tomb is found quite undisturbed, and can be entirely cleared in a careful manner, that the details are worth a full record; moreover, the series of added burials in these chambers, the heaping on one side of all the small objects from time to time, and the Phoenician and Aegean pottery found here, are remarkable details. The entrance to the tomb was found late one afternoon; anticipating a long affair, we blocked it with earth, and then opened it next morning. The outer chamber we first cleared, as it only contained broken pottery and some earth: and in this and the rest of the clearance I only allowed the lad Mekowi to be below with me. He was the lucky head of the party who cleared Horuta's tomb; excitable and restless, he always preferred speculative work, and I gave him the business of opening up the foundation deposit of Usertesen's temple. On this tomb being found by two lads who were half afraid of it, Mekowi eagerly offered to share it with them if he might; and as he was very well in hand, and could be quite trusted, I was glad of the change. The outer chamber being clear I began to open the coffins which blocked the door of the main chamber; and as each object was found I recorded it and handed it to Mekowi to lay in the outer chamber. Hour after hour I went on gradually clearing the coffins, until there was hardly any space left in the outer chamber to place the finds. The work was heavy, for not only the weighty coffins needed to be shifted, but a large beam of roofing had broken, and a block of stone lay on the top of the coffins, almost crushing them. This needed to be shifted off, and yet there was no foothold from which to reach it except on the treacherously rotten coffins, so that it made a troublesome delay. Towards evening I finished, and came out, streaming with perspiration, and covered with the black dust of the mummies and wrappings. All the things found were then carefully packed in baskets, and carried over to our house. In these plates will be seen drawings of every object found (excepting duplicates)—even every variety of beads; and it is much to be wished that whenever a tomb or group of objects is discovered undisturbed, a similar index of the whole should be published for reference and study, quite apart from any artistic picture of special pieces.

2. My work at Kahun was finished in January, and Mr. Hughes-Hughes had given up Gurob about the same time. After a brief trip in the Fayum, and packing up all the collections, I left Egypt in March to undertake excavations for the Palestine Exploration Fund. The delays were considerable, owing to an immaterial error in the firman; and at last I only succeeded in getting fairly to work a few days before the miserable month of Ramadan. As the workers came to the work at Tell Hesy from a village six miles off, it was all the more difficult; and only after making a difference in the pay did I force the men to stay all night at the Tell: the women never would stop, but walked each way every day. To drive such a gang,—all of them utterly unaccustomed to steady continuous work,—during Ramadan, was not a happy task. But by repeated weeding out of the laziest I got together at last a tolerable body, which dispersed however like a puff

of smoke when the harvest came on, and not a man could I get to do anything. The six weeks' work however sufficed to clear up the history of Tell Hesy, and—still better—to form a series of dated pottery of the various periods, so laying a foundation for future explorations on a scientific basis. The results of this work having been published by the Palestine Exploration Fund, I need not enter on them here. After thus obtaining a chronological scale I spent a fortnight in visiting various ancient sites, and identifying the periods of the remains from the pottery strewn over them.

3. The costs of the excavations described in this volume have been defrayed by my friends Mr. Jesse Haworth and Mr. Martyn Kennard, in continuation of their liberal assistance of the work which I carried on during two previous years in the Fayum; and the greater part of the objects found have been presented by them or myself to various public museums. While I was absent in England the inspectorship of the Fayum had been transferred to Major Brown, R.E.; but he very kindly permitted me to continue to use the inspection house at Illahun, as Mr. Hewat had done; when so much was being discovered it was most needful to have a lodgement for the antiquities, and but for the use of such a house the work would have been much hindered. After I had worked during October at Kahun, Mr. W. O. Hughes-Hughes came out in November to take up the excavation of Gurob; I could not possibly have attended to this in the time available before I went to Palestine, and it was therefore very fortunate that some regular work could be carried on before the natives finally plundered the place. Of course no sort of guardianship or protection was given by the Government, and it was only by paying guards myself that I could preserve the site until Mr. Hughes-Hughes came. So soon as he left the rest of the town and tombs utterly perished at the hands of the plunderers. We are therefore indebted to his attention for rescuing most of the information on this site which is in the present volume.

Again I am fortunate in having the collaboration of several friends on special chapters here. Prof. Sayce renews his attention to Greek papyri, and Prof. Mahaffy has joined on the subject. Mr. Griffith has begun a study of the series of hieratic papyri: and the demotic will I hope be worked out by Dr. Hess. Canon Hicks has given his special knowledge to the Ptolemais inscription, and Mr. Spurrell has elucidated much about the use of flint implements, with his wide information on the subject. To all these friends my sincerest thanks are due for attending to what neither my own time or studies permitted me to take up.

CHAPTER I.

THE PYRAMIDS OF ILLAHUN.

4. IN the first season at Illahun I had done some months of work toward finding the entrance to the pyramid, but without success. The external construction of the pyramid is peculiar, and unlike any other. It is partly composed of a natural rock, dressed into form up to a height of about 40 feet,—which is misattributed in Baedecker to the pyramid of Hawara. Upon this rock is the built portion of the pyramid core. And this is also unlike any other pyramid in being built with a framing of cross walls. These walls run right through the diagonals, up to the top of the building; and have offset walls at right angles to the sides. The walls are of stone in the lower part, and of bricks above. The whole of the filling in of the pyramid bulk between the walls is of mud-brick.

Much ancient tunnelling has been done in search of the chambers, between the rock and the brick structure; this part is honeycombed with forced passages from the N. side. Much of these I cleared out in search of the chambers, but in vain. Seeing that there was certainly no entrance in the brickwork, I then supposed that the stone lining of the chambers had probably been built in an open cutting in the rock as in every other pyramid that we know of. If so there would be a gap in the rock base, where the passage was built in; and I therefore set about clearing all around the pyramid at the edge of the top of the rock. This was easy enough around most of the circuit, being only a few feet deep. But at the S.E. corner it was very difficult, the rock being there defective, and the bulk being filled up with layers of rubble chips, thrown in and rammed down. Not being able to reach the edge of the rock therefore, I tested it in another way. Clearing a trench in the fragments as low as the rock bed of the pavement, sometimes 15 or 20 feet deep down, and having seen solid rock, we then cut away the stuff above and tracked up the rock, or over the surface of the rubble beds of construction where I could be certain of their being undisturbed. Thus the whole surface of the pyramid core was searched here for the entrance: but yet in vain.

5. The case seemed almost hopeless; after some months of clearances we could not reach the chamber hollow either in the tunnels, on the top of the rock base, nor could we find any sign of an entrance on the outside. I had however made a clearing near the S.E. corner on the ground level, to find the position of the pavement; and having found an edge of rock, part of the pavement bed, I made the men track it along, greatly against their wills. We came on a pit on the S. side, but it was so far out from the pyramid that it hardly seemed likely to be more than one of the many rock shafts of tombs, which abound near the pyramid. As I was just leaving I did not therefore push on with it; but I commended it to Mr. Fraser, when he took charge of the place in my absence, as a possible entrance; or, if not that, a tomb which had better be examined. He opened it, and at about 40 feet down found a doorway on the north side which led up to the pyramid. The mouth of this shaft is very wide and sloping, having been much broken away by use, probably when the place was plundered for stone. We know, from graffiti on the blocks, that RAMESSU II destroyed the temple and the casing of this pyramid for stone; doubtless to build at Ahnas, where I have seen the name of USERTESEN II on a column of Ramessu. Probably therefore the masons removed the pavement of the pyramid; and, so doing, they would find this entrance. To their plundering therefore may be attributed the breaking up of the limestone chamber in the pyramid, and the removal of much of the stone. The well entrance is so dangerous that a Bedawi boy, who was looking about there after it was opened,

fell down the shaft, and was killed on the spot. The survey of the pyramid is unfortunately incomplete. The sepulchre and adjoining chambers, and the sarcophagus are completely measured; the passages are tolerably done by Mr. Fraser's measures, but the south end of the passage and details of the water well are doubtful. The connection with the pyramid above is vague; nothing remains at the pyramid base to define it, and a general survey of the pyramid all over is needed before an estimate of the original position can be made. This incompleteness of the plan arose from some weeks of illness at the close of the diggings, which prevented my doing active work.

6. On referring to the plan of the passages (PL. II) it is seen that the shaft now opened is not at all the main one. Another shaft must exist at the end of the south passage, as the granite sarcophagus is 50 inches wide; the south passage is 54 at the doorway, and the long passage not less than 63 wide, and the entrance to the chambers is 54 wide. So the sarcophagus would pass all these; whereas the doorway at the bottom of the used shaft is but 31 inches. The now-used shaft must therefore have been only a back way, to enable the workmen to pass in and out while the main shaft was blocked with lowering the stonework. At the end of the S. passage is a brick wall broken through; beyond that is a mass of blocks of stone and chips, which seem to turn to the west and to rise upward. Here then is probably the main shaft; but though I cleared much of the ground on the surface, which is encumbered with several feet thick of original banked-up chips, I could not find the top entrance. If it had not been for the second shaft under the pavement, it is probable that this pyramid would never have been opened.

7. The south passage is 734 ins. long; and about 7 feet wide and 4 feet high, but much encumbered with stone, so that it is difficult to crawl along it. The entrance chamber is 132 N. to S., and about 208 to the recess with the water well. This recess is 82 by 102 ins. and the well about 4 feet by 5; it is difficult to reach it owing to a long slope of earth which is above the well. The well itself is full of very salt water up to about the level of the chamber floor. Why such a well should have been made we cannot see. Probably the water level has risen with the rise of Nile deposits, and may have been 15 feet lower when the pyramid was built. The well was therefore perhaps a dry shaft. It may have been either to catch any rain-water running down the shaft above, like the safety wells in the tombs of the kings; or it may have been a water well; or it may lead to some other passages below. It is doubtful even whether all the pyramid passages known may not be a blind, as there is neither a trace of a lid to the sarcophagus, nor of any wooden coffin or mummy in the chamber. On the other hand there are no elaborate precautions for barring the intruder, as at Hawara, and everything was trusted to the secrecy of the entrances. It is unlikely that there is anything of importance beneath this water well, as there seems to have been no care to cover over its upper part.

The passage into the pyramid slopes upward, as will be seen in the section, PL. II. The whole length slopes 6° 46′ from end to end, but the lower part appears to slope rather less, and the upper part more. The axis of this passage is 6° 40′ E. of magnetic N., which shews that it is probably very nearly true north. The limestone chamber was observed as 10½° N. of magnetic W., and if so is 4° askew to the passage, and is so drawn here. The first part of the passage is 648 long on the slope: it is 64 wide, and 74 high on the wall, or 80 in the middle of the curved roof. It is cut in the soft rock fairly well, but the rock is so crumbly and poor that it is merely hard marl, and no smooth face can be made.

The passage chamber is 276 on S., 267 on N., 124 on E., 127 on W. It is heaped up with broken marl from the rock; though where such a quantity has come from it is hard to tell. The upper part of the passage is 894 long, 76 wide, 69 high on the wall, and 79 in the middle. At the top end it is roughly smeared with a thin coat of white plaster, filling up all the roughnesses. It contracts to a doorway 54 wide and 70 high on entering the limestone chamber. Throughout these passages therefore there is no need of stooping, but they are made of full height, like those of the Hawara pyramid.

8. The limestone chamber is cut in the soft marly rock, and lined with blocks of fine limestone. The roof-blocks, and part of the top of the walls, have been broken up, and lie strewing the floor; a damage probably due to the Ramesside masons. The chamber is 123·7 E., 122·8 W., 196·7 N., 195·3 E.; the wall height is 136·2, and the pointed roof rose 37·3 more, according to the piece of the gable end wall which remains, making 173·5 inches in all. The doorway is 5·6 to 59·6 from the E. On the west is a contracted part 81·2 wide; leaving 20·7 on N., and 20·9 on S. side. This is 41·8 N., 41·3 S. length: and contracts to a passage, leaving 5·8 on N., 5·6 on S. This passage is 159·9 long to the granite, and 19·0 of

granite, making 178·9 inches. The width is 69·6 at E., to 69·3. On the south side at 34·5 is a passage 41·3 wide: this is 16·0 long, and then widens to 52 for 413·4 inches. This passage is cut in the marly rock, with a curved top, and is 70 high at sides, 79 in middle. It then turns to the west for 698·6 inches, being 62 high or 72 in middle. Then turns to the north for 783 inches: then to the east for 331, and then to the south for 293, opening into the sepulchre, by a regularly permament doorway in the granite with bevelled edges. This passage is most puzzling, as it has no branches, and merely leads round to within a few yards of where it starts. There is no sign of either end having been blocked up; nor is there any sign of a door or closing of the sepulchre doorway. The sepulchre is all of light-red granite, smoothly dressed but not ground or polished. The sides are 123·1 E., 123·7 W., 206·2 N., 206·9 S. On the east is the entrance 61·1 wide, with 31·0 wall on each side. On the north is the doorway of the passage just named, at 10·1 from the west, and 41·6 wide. On the south is a doorway at 32·3 from the east wall, and 41·1 wide. This is 20·5 long through the granite, and then widens to 45·2 for a length of 89·0, cut in the marly rock. It is 62·8 at side and 72·8 high in middle. It then enters a chamber 126·4 on E., 129·7 on W., 105·4 on N., 104·2 on S. This chamber is 70 high at the E. and W., and rises to 109·6 in the curved roof. In the west wall is a recess 40 by 21 inches, and 20 high. This has been cut later, probably by the Ramesside workmen, as it is not smeared with plaster like the chamber, and is hewn with a pick or chisel 1·1 wide, whereas the pyramid hewer's pick was 55 inch wide and much rounder.

To return to the granite sepulchre. The floor is of granite; and, where the door sill has been broken away, a bed of clean sand between the granite and the rock can be seen. The ceiling is of granite; sloping blocks butt one against the other, and are cut out beneath into a circular curve, which rises 40·8 with a width of 123·3. The upper sides of the blocks are left rough hewn and straight. This construction is exactly like that of the sepulchre of Menkara at Gizeh. The height of the doorway is 81·9; the wall is 72·0 high on N., 72·8 N.W., 71·7 S.: the middle is 110·9 high at E., 111·9 in middle, 112·0 at W. The north door is 51·9 high at the sides, and 59·6 in middle. The south door is 51·0 high at sides. All the doorways have bevelled edges. The sarcophagus stands 10·36 at S., 10·66 at N., from W. wall; and 6·38 at E., 6·58 at W., from S. wall.

9. The sarcophagus is perhaps the finest piece of mechanical work ever executed in such a hard and difficult material. The form is quite unlike that of any other coffin known, having a wide lip all around the top. (See the end view on PL. II.) Another strange peculiarity is that the bottom is of varying thickness; or the inside depth being equal all over, the outside depth slopes down nearly 4 inches from end to end. As the sides are cut square with the top, and the floor is level, the ends all lean over, and the top slants; in short the whole thing is tilted by standing on a sloping bottom. I carefully measured it by stretched threads and plumb lines, with offsets read to a thousandth of an inch. The surface, though not polished, is smooth-ground to an impalpable fineness, and most exquisitely flat. For instance along the top length of 106 inches the errors from a straight line are − 7, + 5, + 17, − 7, − 7 thousandths on E. side; and + 7, 0, − 13, − 3, + 7 on W., or an average of 7 thousandths of an inch of error. On the ends 50 inches long, the errors are − 1, − 3, − 1, + 5, 0; and − 6, + 8, + 5, − 7, average error 4 thousandths of an inch.

The errors of parallelism are also very small; the N. end is 50·053, and S. end 50·073, or a 50th of an inch of difference on 106 inches length. The E. side is 106·100, and the W. 106·116, or a 60th of an inch different. In the lower part of the outside there was not such excessive care, and the average error is 37 thousandths on the distance from side to side, including the errors of forming the planes, and of their parallelism. But even this is fine work on such a scale. The inside is also very parallel; the width at the N. being 26·542 and at the S. 26·552, or only a 100th of an inch slant. The curvature of the planes is almost nothing, over the length of 82 inches; the E. side hollowing 5, and the W. side bulging 2 thousandths, a difference which is probably covered by the errors of measurement, owing to a slight tilt of the sarcophagus sideways. The ends cannot be accurately measured by plumb line owing to the great tilt endways. The skew of the planes of the inside is 5 thousandths on the W., and 7 thousandths on the E., which again may be confounded by the slight tilt of the whole sideways; but it is almost inappreciable in any case.

Lastly, after straightness, flatness, and parallelism, there is the question of ratio between the dimensions, or accuracy of proportions. This is far more difficult, as it requires all the previous accuracies, and in addition a truly divided scale, and an irremediable truth of work, since nothing can be corrected by removing more material. Taking the mean dimensions we see that they are all in even numbers of palms of the usual Egyptian cubit, as follows:—

	inches		palm	cubit	mean scale	error
Length top out	106·116	÷36	2·9477	20·634	106·056	+·060
below	97·165	÷33	2·9444	20·611	97·218	−·053
Width top	50·046	÷17	2·9439	20·607	50·082	−·036
below	41·24	÷14	2·9457	20·620	41·244	·00
Length inside	82·495	÷28	2·9463	20·624	82·488	+·007
Width	26·549	÷ 9	2·9499	20·649	26·514	+·035
Depth	23·56	÷ 8	2·945	20·615	23·568	−·008

The outside height is 36·4 at N. end, 32·6 at S. end; or the bottom varies from 12·84 to 9·04 in thickness.

These variations in scale between the parts are very small. Lumping together all the measures, and taking the average palm, it comes out 2·9460, or cubit 20·622. Then we can find what each dimension should have been on a mean scale, shewn in the last column but one, and the errors of the sarcophagus sides are given in the last column. Thus the mean error from a true scale averages only 28 thousandths of an inch on one dimension; or less than one 2000th of the lengths; that is to say, the scale by which the dimensions were laid out, and the errors of workmanship of size, together do not exceed a hundredth of an inch on the cubit length. This is indeed a brilliant piece of skill in such an untractable material. It would be desirable to level up the sarcophagus, and then measure it more accurately when the planes are as nearly vertical as may be; for doubtless some errors have come in the course of measuring it in its present slanting position.

A few additional measurements may be noted here. The depth of the lip around is 5·977 with a mean error of 22 thousandths. The edges are all bevelled off to a width of ·27 to ·30 of an inch. This bevelling is very neatly done, and the planes of bevel all meet truly in a three-sided pyramid at the corners.

10. In front of the red granite sarcophagus lay the white alabaster table of offerings for Usertesen II (Pl. III). This is of the usual style of the XIIth dynasty altars, and not like the elaborate array on the altar of Ptahnefru ("Kahun," Pl. V); nor are the legs of the animals missing here, as they are on the altar, and on the funeral vases of Ptahnefru and Amenemhat III. The inscription is simple, and of the usual formula. It is beautifully sharply cut, and quite perfect and fresh. Of course it is now in the Ghizeh museum, along with the finest of the other things that I found. It was standing turned up on its end, when Mr. Fraser went into the pyramid; disturbed, but quite uninjured. He had heavy work to get it up from the well, as it weighs four cwt., and is of course a delicate stone to handle.

Beside this some broken pottery was found strewn about in the limestone chamber (Pl. IV, 7, 8, 11) all apparently of the XIIth dynasty, and therefore belonging to offerings made in the pyramid, and not to the Ramesside workmen. Also one fragment of alabaster, apparently the flat brim of a large circular vessel, was found in the passage leading from the limestone chamber round to the sepulchre. This passage was choked by falls of the roof in the N.W. angle of it; but though we moved all that stuff and cleaned the place, no more of this alabaster vessel could be found. Doubtless the Ramesside workmen had carried off the alabaster vessels, though the table of offerings was too bulky for them to pilfer it.

11. Outside of the pyramid a shrine adjoined it on the east. This had been all destroyed by Ramessu II; and the ground was covered with some feet depth of chips. On turning over all this stuff we recovered many pieces of sculpture; some giving the names of Usertesen II, and others shewing the various offerings with which the walls of this chapel has been adorned. The work was beautifully delicate; and the colours are as bright as when first laid on. The largest slab from here with a cartouche of Usertesen, is now at Ghizeh.

On the north and west sides the hill rose up, from the knoll on which the pyramid was built. Here it had been cut away, so as to leave a clear space around the pyramid. The face of this rock scarp is covered with a thick wall of mud brick, which still rises to twenty feet high at the N.W. corner; originally it was probably much more, and retained a bank of chips behind it. Besides this scarp wall there was a built wall along the east side of the pyramid, of which the rock trench of the foundation remains; and also a wall along the south, which served as a retaining wall, being banked up along the inside with chips, so as to form a level platform around the pyramid.

12. These walls were interrupted at the N.E. corner of the area, and extended outward, to include a small pyramid which stood there. This pyramid was of rock in the lower part, like the large pyramid; and—also like that—the chamber is within the rock, without any open cutting above it. The brick part of the pyramid has all disappeared; and when I went to Illahun there was no trace of the pyramid to be seen. But during excavations we hit on the side of

its rock base, and cleared it all round. A shrine had existed on the north side of it, and we found fragments of the painted walls like those of the shrine and of the temple of Usertesen. Also a fragment of an altar of offerings of black granite, but unfortunately no name remaining on it. (Pl. XII, 8.) Among the fragments of the shrine was one which gives apparently part of the name (XII, 6), mentioning a "princess of both lands, Atmu . . . . . ." ; as other princesses of this dynasty have the names of gods compounded with *neferu*, Sebeknefru, Ptahnefru, &c., this princess may be provisionally named Atmunefru. I tried hard to find the entrance to the pyramid ; not only was all the top and edge of the rock core examined, but I also cleared the rock bed of the pavement all around the whole pyramid, for about twenty feet out from the core, but without hitting on the passage. Probably there is a well at some distance away from the pyramid, as in the pyramid of Usertesen. The rock base is about eighty feet square ; and the cutting which marks the extent of the casing, is distant from the rock from 75 to 86 inches. The rock core is distant from the north wall 296, from the wall on the west 246; and from the edge of the pavement hollow on the west 186 to 199. All of this breadth was examined. The only result of the clearance was to find several pits cut in the rock beneath the casing, containing foundation deposits. The most important was at the N.E. corner. Here was a square hole whose corner was 4 ins. N. of N. side and 13 E. of E. side of the rock core. The hole was 36 square at top to receive a slab of stone 7 inches thick ; below that it was 28 square, for a depth of 60 inches. This was filled with clean sand, and near the bottom lay fragments of many vases and saucers (Pl. IV, 1 to 6, 9, 10, 14), with a model brick of mud (13), a few green glazed beads (12), and bones of a calf sacrificed. Of course our hopes were high that we had at last found the entrance to the pyramid, on removing this slab and finding sand filling below it ; but the bottom of the hole was all solid rock. At the N.W. corner another hole was found, very similar to this : the inner corner is 16 W. of W. side, and 9 S. of N. side, thus not lying in the diagonal. The depth is 7 inches and 53 below that ; and it is 35 square above and 30 below. Another rock pit was found at 100 to 130 E. of the W. side, and 160 to 190 N. of the N. side. This contained nothing but sand. And a fourth pit was found opposite the middle of the west side, which contained only one rough vase and saucer. These last two were covered over with mortar, and not with stone. Another pit on the east side had been emptied anciently, and forced at the side toward the pyramid. Though these deposits are rude, and of no value beyond the forms of the vases ; yet they are very interesting in principle, as we did not know before of any foundation deposits being associated with pyramids.

CHAPTER II.

THE TOWN OF KAHUN.

13. Last year only a small part of the plan of Kahun was published, merely five streets of the workmen's quarter. But now we have before us a complete plan of the whole present extent of the town, comprising more than three quarters of all the rooms that ever existed there, so far as we can judge. As this is the first time that the complete plan of an Egyptian town has ever been disclosed, we shall examine it in some detail ; and it is of special interest, not only from the early date and the entireness of it, but from its having been laid out evidently by a single architect on a regular plan.

On first looking at the plan (Pl. XIV) it is seen that the town is of two parts ; the eastern part nearly as long as it is wide, and the western part which is built outside the thick wall, and which is a strip of closely packed workmen's houses. The west part is however of nearly the same date as the other, as such a barrack would never have been wanted here except for the pyramid builders : and its boundary wall is laid out to fit the line of the temple front. The geography of the place explains its outline ; the Nile valley edge runs from S.W. to N.E. along the bottom edge of the town. The buildings are all in a slight hollow, bounded by a rise on the west, running from the temple across to the acropolis, and a rise on the north on which the north wall is built. The highest part of all the ground around is the acropolis, and the town is placed with this as the leading point.

The general divisions of the town are,

- The acropolis and the guard house.
- The five great northern houses on one plan, and one other, along the north wall.
- The three great southern houses on one plan.
- The dwelling houses joining the west wall.
- The store rooms behind the great south houses.
- The workmen's streets „ „ „ „
- The five workmen's streets on the east.
- The eleven workmen's streets in the separate western region.

14. The acropolis has most unfortunately been far more destroyed by denudation than any other region, as a natural consequence of its elevation. On the west the ground falls gently away; on the north it falls irregularly; and on the east and south sides it has been scarped away, and faced with a massive retaining wall, which formed the side of a banked-up platform on which the buildings stood. Thus the grand quarters were well above the roofs of all the other houses of the town. The access to this acropolis was by one entrance at the S.E.; here the doorkeeper's room is first seen on the right hand; then a square entry, out of which three stairways arose. The wider stairway on the east (Pl. XVI, fig. 1), had a separate door to it, and was the front entrance, leading probably to rooms overlooking the town eastwards; while the two lesser stairways (Pl. XVI, fig. 2) probably led to the back rooms. The whole acropolis was occupied with one great house, as its space is exactly the same as that of the other great houses in the same line. Many pieces of brightly painted dado were found here, in the rooms with stone bases of columns. Though the lower part of the scarping is hewn in the solid rock, yet it is all faced with brickwork, plastered over; and even the steps are of brick, and so very little worn away that they shew the place not to have been occupied for long. These stairways were all filled up with fallen walls, and were quite indistinguishably smoothed over in the slope of the hill, until we excavated them: about ten feet of rubbish had to be removed from the deeper parts.

On the south of the acropolis was an open space of ground at the foot of its great retaining wall. In this ground is an isolated building, which from its place before the entrance, was probably a guard house. Doubtless the king would occasionally visit the town, when inspecting the progress of his pyramid and temple; and he would rest in the acropolis, while his guard would have quarters before the door. This building was deserted early in the history of the place, as it was filled up with the broken pottery of the XIIth dynasty, thrown away by those who dwelt in the rest of the town. This agrees to its being an official dwelling, not needed after the pyramid was built.

The five great houses along the north wall are all on one plan, with such very slight modifications that we may ignore them. Four of these houses join in a row; then there is a narrower house of different plan, and lastly one more like the four others. The entrance is from the street on the south; a moderate sized doorway, which had a half round lintel of stone, of which I found a piece lying in one entrance. The doorkeeper's room faced the door. On the left hand we pass along a passage leading to offices, guest chambers, and to the business rooms of the master apparently. Behind these, in the centre of the house is group of private rooms opening on a hall with four pillars. Behind this again is a large space which was probably open to the sky along the northern part with a colonnade along the south side, to give a broad shady place for sitting in the summer time; what is now known as the *mandara* or reception-hall for strangers. There was also a direct access to this *mandara* by a long passage straight from the entrance. Besides this long passage there is another side by side with it: such a duplication would not have been made for nothing, and as the second passage opens on several small rooms, with a separate hall with columns, it is pretty evident that this was the women's side of the house. It had ready access to the front door, a private passage of its own, a hall, and direct access to the *mandara*. The rooms on the other side of the house seem to have been also private, as they open only from the *mandara*. They may have been the private chambers of the master and his family; and containing the best hall, with a tank surrounded by columns, this is not unlikely. In the fourth house these private rooms were cut off, and joined to the women's apartments of the third house. The rooms along the north wall were probably long store rooms and granaries.

Thus there were three ways on entering; to the left to the men-servants' rooms, offices, and business rooms; or straight through to the *mandara;* or thirdly, to the right, to the women's rooms.

The large rooms all required columns to support the roof, as 8 or 9 feet seems to have been the longest roofing beam. These columns were usually of wood, to judge by the large diameter of the marks on the bases: and the lower part of one column, which stood *in situ* in the fifth house on its stone base, was an octagonal one of wood (see Pl. VI, fig. 12). The stone bases were very wide and flat, like those carved in the rock at Beni Hasan, or like the model column found here (Pl. VI, fig. 13). Some of the columns were of stone, octagonal (Pl. VI, fig. 1), eight ribbed (fig. 11) or sixteen fluted (fig. 6). The capitals were either plain abaci (6) or brackets (1) or palm leaf form (7, 8); that the latter was known in the XIIth dynasty is shewn by the ape seated on a palm leaf capital (8), carved in ivory, now at Ghizeh, and dated to Amenemhat II by a cylinder found with it. The best room in each house, the master's private court, had a tank of stone in the middle of the floor; this tank was about 14 inches square, and about as deep, in the middle of a square block, 5 ft. 3 ins. on each side (3 cubits), the tank and its pavement being all one stone. Similar places are found in poorer rooms, with the tank a separate box of stone, and slabs placed around it, sloping towards it. These places seem curiously like Muslim arrangements for feet-washing and ablutions before prayers; possibly the custom is ancient, and the Egyptians may have used these tanks for ceremonial ablution, and stood on the stone slabs. Around the tank-stone were twelve columns supporting the roof; and it seems very likely therefore, as there would be a wide space across the tank, that the middle of the hall was open: thus the arrangement would be somewhat like an *atrium* supported by columns. (PL. XVI, fig. 3.)

The whole size of the block of each house is 138 feet by 198 feet: and this area contained about 70 rooms and passages. The best hall is 29 feet square, and the *mandara* is 63 feet long. Thus these great mansions were by no means scanty homes for the high officials and nobles who had charge of the royal works.

15. We next turn to the three great southern houses. These are of exactly the same size as the northern row, but quite differently arranged. The entrance opens into a vestibule with a column. Thence a short passage leads immediately into the rooms of the house; while a long passage leads away to the back premises. Another long passage led along the opposite side of the house, from the middle of the house to the store-rooms at either end. And against the street wall was a compact mass of nine store-rooms forming a square block, three each way. The plans of these houses have been so much altered by being divided into tenements, and new doorways knocked through, that it is difficult to trace the full details in their present deficient state. We will next notice the dwellings or stores to the south of the acropolis, backing against the thick wall. These blocks are on one repeated plan. The set of copper chisels and hatchets, found in a basket, in the first season, lay in the second block from the south, in a room marked C. A copper dish with a central cup riveted into it, was found in the northernmost chamber next the wall; this is now at Ghizeh. In the same block are two or three rock-cut cellars, the mouths of which are marked by squares on the plan; between three of them is a rock-cut passage, which had been walled across by brickwork. These cellar-mouths were closed by flap doors of stout wood, one of which was still lying in place. The largest of these cellars, with two chambers, was used in the late XIXth or XXth dynasty as a family tomb. The only name found in it was that of the lady Maket; and hence this is called the Maket tomb, and the contents are described as such in Chap. V. The large circles in this district are granaries of thin brickwork. Some of the best papyri of the XIIth and XIIIth dynasties were found in the middle block of these buildings.

Other sets of chambers, to the south of the first southern mansion, were probably store-rooms. They are on a repeated plan, but joined together so that one door suffices for twenty-three rooms.

Behind the other south mansions are some workmen's streets. The separate houses have about seven small rooms each. But in two of these houses some curious wall paintings remain. In the block behind the middle mansion, on a wall marked "paint" on the plan, is a curious subject painted in red, yellow, and white, with some amount of black filling in, on the smooth mud plaster. (PL. XVI, fig. 6.) It shews a large house, with a view of the inside on a level above the outside, a convention known in other Egyptian paintings. The form of the building is interesting. It appears to have been a series of arched chambers; much like some in this town, which were covered by a wide vaulting of brick. The ends of these chambers were walled up in the lower part, and closed with a lattice of wooden bars above. The larger space may perhaps represent the end of a longer gallery, which approached the spectator nearer than the others. In the view of the interior there is the usual group of a servant offering to his master, and various jars placed upon wooden stands. The piles of round objects may really represent a row of cakes on a table, here drawn one above another like the piles of objects on a table of offerings. The white space on the left is indistinct in the painting; but it probably is another building, with an arched doorway next behind the master. In another room in the block of building south of the east mansion is marked "Paint cols," where a columnar building is painted which is here drawn (PL. XVI, fig. 4). This painting is remarkable for the flat curve of the arched roof of the building, the short pillars filling in the tympanum, and the columnar front. This represents a structure more like a later Greek, than an Egyptian, temple; and the forms of the columns (given on a larger scale above) are not like any Egyptian columns so far as we know.

To the east of the southern mansions are several streets of workmen's houses. These were very small and poor, containing only four rooms each. In the second block at "XVIII" on the plan (Pl. XIV), were found two bodies buried with three small but brilliant scarabs of the XVIIIth dynasty. The southern ends of all these streets have been washed away entirely by denudation; and half of the part that is planned here is only a few inches deep, just enough to trace the plan by. At the east wall is a gateway, with a porter's room by it. It seems strange that they should have troubled to make a gate here, if the town lay open to the south. And it would also seem strange if such a stout enclosure wall should have been built for no purpose. I am therefore inclined to suppose that although there is no trace now of a wall on the south side, that nevertheless the town was originally walled all around, and that the south wall and half of the east have been denuded away as completely as the south ends of the streets.

All the streets appear to have had a channel of stone down the middle; such was found in the long E.-W. street, and in several of the small eastern streets, and was therefore probably general. This channel is not deep, but rather a slight curved hollowing of the upper sides of the line of stone, which is about 22 inches wide. Probably therefore the street sloped down to the middle, like an old English street to the kennel; and thus occasional rain, and waste water from the houses, would be led off without making the street muddy. This is far the earliest example of street drainage known; and the system must have been general in Egypt at that age for it to have been used in a labourers' town such as this.

16. Lastly there is the large mass of streets forming the western division. These were evidently workmen's dwellings, at least in the northern part. The houses have four or five rooms each, with steps leading up to the roof. Each house therefore probably had an enclosed court on the roof, like a modern Egyptian dwelling, where fuel and straw could be stacked. Many of these houses contain granaries. The southern part of this region was excavated in the first season, and this part of the plan was published in "Kahun," Pl. XV.

The roofing of the houses was usually made with beams of wood, on which poles were placed, and to these were lashed down bundles of straw or reeds. The mud plastering was then applied both inside and outside, and many fragments of this roofing were found in the rooms. Occasionally a barrel vault of brickwork was thrown across the whole room. The upper part is so generally destroyed that we cannot often find any of the roof; but one large room in the western part of the town, and some of the rooms of the first north mansion (where the wall was preserved against the acropolis), shew us the brick vaulting. There is no evidence about centering being used to build the vault on; and probably where wood was so scarce as in Egypt, it would be a better and simpler plan to fill the chamber with sand, and lay the bricks on the sand until the arch was completed, emptying the chamber by the doorway. All of the doorways, so far as they are preserved, are arched over with semicircular arches, two courses deep of brick on edge. The spacing of the bricks on the outer edge, to give the voussoir form, is done by chips of limestone wedged in.

Rats were as great a plague in the XIIth dynasty as they are at present in Egypt. Nearly every room has its corners tunnelled by the rats; and the holes are stuffed up with stones and rubbish to keep them back.

CHAPTER III.

THE ANTIQUITIES OF KAHUN.

17. In the account of the objects found during the first season's work here, the principal classes of things have already been described, ("Kahun," chap. III). The present account therefore is supplementary to that; and we shall notice the various fresh objects found, without recounting those of the previous collection.

Many more of the incised pottery dishes have been found (see Pl. V), and with fresh designs. The fish with lotus border (3), the lions (5) and other types are noticeable. But the object of these dishes is not at all determined. Their very rough surface seems to make it unlikely that any wet or juicy food should have been put in them. Another curious object is the coop (8) which is made of pottery, pierced with air holes, and fitted with a sliding door. It was not intended merely for a trap, as the number of air holes show: it must have been for retaining animals alive; and it seems very possible that it was for holding eggs in the hatching oven, so that, when the chicks came out they might not stray about, and could be carried away in the warm pottery cage without chilling. Though the modern fowl does not appear to have been known in early times in Egypt, yet artificial hatching was followed in Roman times, and may perhaps have been the custom for duck and goose eggs from a much earlier period. This coop was found broken in the rubbish heap of the XIIth dynasty, north of the town. It had been partly broken while yet used, as a handle is missing from the top, and one hole has been choked with plaster in some repairs to it.

Several pottery stands were found, both of the form for holding dry food on a raised dish (IV, 18), and also for holding the porous water jars. Probably the jars oozed more quickly than the surface evaporated, as jars do now in Egypt; and a pan was needed to catch the filtered water which came through. These stands (IV, 15, 19) with rings set in them would serve this purpose. One piece of pottery has a fine smooth face applied to it, and clouded with black intentionally to imitate marble or serpentine.

The pottery trays of offerings have been again found (IV, 20, 23); and the latter one is unusually complete. The bull's head at the top, the bird, the haunch, and the two jars for wine, are distinct; while below are various flat and conical cakes, and the large radishes so well known still in Egypt. The spaces in front are for pouring out the drink offerings.

Of glazed pottery there is a fine vase (XIII, 19), with a network pattern in purple on a rich blue ground. This was found in one of the long passages of the south mansions. There is also part of a blue glazed doll like those found before (XIII, 20). The fancy beads are also curious (VIII, 14, 15, 18, 19).

18. The most important pottery is that on Pl. I. This is called Aegean in general, without meaning that every piece is necessarily from the Aegean; but the majority are so, to judge by their material and decoration. The term Aegean is used to imply the Greek islands, and the coasts of Peloponnessos and Asia Minor, without the limitations of place and age implied in the name Greek.

We will begin with those pieces which are distinctly foreign. (1) is a black ware throughout, with a smooth surface; on that are bright yellow, red, and white patterns. At the top is the circle of dots and lines in white;* then yellow lines with red across them; then discs surrounded with dots, the regular Aegean design, in yellow; and below that yellow lines with red across. The colouring is very bright, without much binding, and easily rubbed off. It is quite different from any known on Egyptian pottery; and the characteristic disc and dots, and the rest of the pattern, are also quite un-Egyptian. In (3) we see the well-known wave pattern of the Aegean, which is unknown on Egyptian pottery. (4) is a fragment of regular Aegean paste, fine smooth hard brown, with a black iron glaze, and applied lines of red brown and white. (5) is decorated with white on smooth red pottery, like (3); it also appears to be foreign. (6) has the regular iron glaze of the Aegean, with a spiral blocked out by a white ground, and a line of soft bright red applied. (7) is a short spout from a dish, painted with white on an iron glaze. (8) is red pottery stamped in relief, and painted white and red. (10) is another piece of Aegean paste with black iron glaze and applied white. (12) is a similar pottery, part of a peculiar vase without any neck or lip, a round hole being cut for the mouth without even a thickening of the material at the edge. All of these pieces are non-Egyptian; and all were found in the rubbish heaps of the XIIth dynasty. So far we shall be all agreed.

* Where in details the description differs from the colouring on the plate, the latter is in error.

19. But when we come to consider the age of these there is great difficulty. The external evidence seems clear enough, and some very strong proofs will be needed to contradict it. The rubbish heaps where this pottery was found are entirely of the XIIth dynasty. Not only every piece of pottery which I saw there is clearly of that age, but from their position no later people would have accumulated the heaps. The town of Kahun was built by the architect for the pyramid workmen; and when the pyramid and temple were finished the town was mostly deserted, and the people of the XIIth and XIIIth dynasties heaped up their rubbish in the deserted rooms. A large part of the rooms which we cleared were filled up with broken potsherds and rubbish. When therefore rubbish could be shot inside of the town so readily, who would have taken the trouble to carry it outside? The external rubbish heaps must belong to a time when the town was full. And their contents agree to that early age. But this Aegean pottery is found in and under these rubbish heaps, and therefore the evidence unmistakably shews that it must be of the time of Usertesen II. That foreigners were living here at that time is implied by the fact that the greater part of the weights, and two of the three measures, found here are foreign weights and measures of Phoenicia and Asia Minor. And historically we know that the Ha-nebu or "lords of the north," who certainly mean Greeks in the later monuments, were

already known to the Egyptians. The question then rests thus: the external evidence is clear for the dating of this pottery to the XIIth dynasty; the foreigners of the Mediterranean were already known to the Egyptians, and were actually living in this town: and this pottery is distinctly foreign or Aegean. The only difficulty lies in Greek archaeologists objecting to any such early age for such pottery. We will return to the question of age after considering the other varieties.

No. (2) is probably Egyptian, but is of very curious decoration. The dark bands are blackish blue, and are thick body colours like all the others, laid on a massive coarse red pottery. Part of the same vessel was found in the XIIth rubbish heap. The pattern reminds us most of that on the early tomb ceilings, in imitation of woven stuffs. No such pottery is known in any later age. (9) is a bit of an Egyptian cup of XIIth dynasty, with barbaric markings in black and white. (11) is the shoulder of a vase like (16). (13) is a smooth brown pot, lipless, with a black circle joining a black base and black side lines, on either side, and two red lines down by the handle. It is quite un-Egyptian. All of the above were found in the XIIth dynasty rubbish heaps, and have therefore a strong certificate of age.

20. Turning now to other pottery found in the town we notice the curious vessel (14, 15). It is lipless, with merely a round hole for a mouth, like (12 & 13). The handle is like that of (12); and the pattern is evidently derived from that of basket-work. It was found in a chamber alongside of pottery of the XIIth dynasty. (16) is a type of vase which is not uncommon here; (19) belonging to the same, and shewing the pinched spout better; (11) shews the double handle of these vessels; (18) is similarly formed; and (17) though different material has the same handle. This type of (11, 16, 19) is wholly unknown in any later age in Egypt. (18) was found alongside of pottery of the XIIth dynasty in a deep chamber. Lastly there is the black pottery (17, 20, 21) the latter piece being whitened by concretions. This pottery is common at Kahun, many pieces having been found last year (Kahun, XXVII, 199 to 202). It was found also by M. Naville along with scarabs of the XIIth & XIIIth dynasty at Khataneh, deep down in burials which could not have been later disturbed. Its age therefore seems well assured; and it closely resembles in colour, form, and decoration the earliest Italian black pottery.

We summarise therefore that (1) Aegean pottery is found in rubbish of the XIIth dynasty. (2) Black Italian pottery is found in the town of the XII–XIII dynasty, as in graves at Khataneh. (3) Other foreign pottery is found in the town of the XIIth dynasty.

21. Negative evidence in this matter is important. The pottery of the XVIIIth & XIXth dynasty is well known now at Gurob in this same district. Pottery of the XXIInd to XXVth is known in the Illahun graves. Pottery of the XXVIth is exhaustively known at Defenneh. And that of the Greek and Roman periods at Naukratis and Tanis. All these successive periods are well known to us in their manufactures. *But not one piece of these peculiar varieties has ever been found yet in any later period;* nor conversely has any pottery of the later ages been found in the rubbish heaps of the XIIth dynasty.

The main argument for a later date for this Aegean pottery is the fineness of the paste, and the high polish of the surface. No doubt these details appear like those of later times. But there is internal evidence contradicting a late date for these pieces. None are finer or thinner than (12 & 14). Now these belong to a class of vessel which is wholly unknown to myself, or to other students to whom I have referred, as ever having been found in historic pottery. The mouth is a simple hole without a lip, like a hole cut in a gourd. If such a type is unknown in Greek pottery, where can we match it? only so far as I know in the vase found in the Illahun pyramid (IV, 11) and in the earliest Amorite pottery of Syria. There I have found it in the lowest levels of Lachish about the beginning of the XVIIIth dynasty. Doubtless it may have existed before that, only Lachish was not yet built; but it is a type unknown to later ages. This evidence therefore shews that it must be earlier than the Mykenae pottery of Gurob, and not later than that.

22. Another line of evidence may be taken. We know now at Gurob that the style of the earliest Mykenae pottery, the false-necked vase (*bugel-kanne*) with plain bands, belongs to about 1400 B.C. (Amenhotep III). That pottery is highly finished, with a bright polish and fine iron glaze of red or orange. Such was already the development of pottery in the Aegean at that age. Who knows what went before that? No one as yet has found anything to date before that in Greece. What state the Aegean civilization was in at an earlier date we do not know. It has nothing to do with the historic civilization of Greece; it is a branch of the bronze age of Europe, as much so as Hallstadt or Etruria. That this pottery

of Kahun could succeed the Mykenae pottery is in most cases apparently impossible in its very nature. Such pieces as (1, 8, 12 & 14) are all of styles which do not fall into any place in the historic development of pottery from Mykenae downwards, and yet which most certainly came from Greece or Italy.

Finally, on the one hand we have a prepossession to deal with as to what is likely in a period as yet totally unknown, the pre-Mykenaean age. Prepossessions are often valuable, but very risky when dealing with the wholly unknown. On the other hand we have the external evidence of the early age of this pottery in the XII–XIII dynasties; and the internal evidence of extremely early features in it, and of such never being found in later ages, and its not falling into any part of the historic series of known pottery. For the present I feel compelled to conclude that we have here the products of the earliest Libyo-Greek civilization of the Aegean and Italy at about 2500 B.C. Many more of the strange signs scratched on pottery have been found; but as I have not time to prepare copies of them all, I give a hand list of the forms (PL. XV) for purposes of study.

23. Of stonework some curious figures have been found. The dwarf supporting a dish (VI, 9) is remarkable, as we have no clue to the meaning of such figures in Egypt. This is one of the dish-stands, which are generally simple columns; and which, whenever they are found charged, have a cake of dough stuck in the dish. It seems reasonable to suppose that they are stands for household offerings of daily bread. Another such stand (10) is of ruder type, but carefully cut out in pierced work. The two figures back to back recall another rude stand with two figures found last year. Another unusual figure is a torso of a girl carved in a rough and gross style but solely naturalistic, and without any trace of the Egyptian canon; it is painted red, and bears marks of a black wreath around the waist. Another figure of a little girl playing a harp, small and coloured, was also found, and is now at Ghizeh. A rough large figure of Taurt was found, as also a small one last year, shewing that her form was already fixed at this period. And a good statue of a man seated cross-legged, carved in limestone, but without any inscription. The inscribed statues will be noticed under inscriptions.

24. In wood there are some good little carvings. The lion (VIII, 1) and the crocodile (VIII, 2) are each about as fine as they can be. And a most exquisitely carved ivory ape seated on a palm capital may be mentioned here: it is dated to Amenemhat II by a cylinder found with it in a burial: it is of the finest naturalistic work, shewing all the curious puckers of the face, and the half human intelligence of the animal. Of course it is now at Ghizeh. Another bowl with rams' heads was found, like that in "Kahun" (VIII, 3) but rather smaller, and not quite so well worked. The hawk's head in wood (VIII, 7) has garnet eyes inserted; what the use of this was is uncertain. The similar hawk's head in bronze (VIII, 8) has a rectangular hole through from breast to back, as if to fit on to some object. The bases of both these pieces are quite flat and smooth. They might possibly be some pieces for a game. Among glazed objects we notice the star (VIII. 14) the dragon fly (15), the cowry (18) and the cone shell (19) all of blue or green glaze.

25. We now pass on to the tools and fittings. The wooden blocks in which the door-bolts slid have been found and identified: they were let into the door near the edge by a tenon, and fixed with a pin in the edge of the door: the bolt slid through one such block and into the wall, if a single door, or through the two blocks on the edges of a double door. This double door, with a bolt shot, is often seen on representations of a door (see "A Season in Egypt," XX, 13, 20, 21); and a bolt shot through two blocks is the regular hieroglyph *s*. A set of tent pegs was found, cut with heads, and with the ends of palm rope still around them. The fire sticks for drilling fire have been again found, both the lower pieces (VII, 25, 26) and also the upper rotating piece (24). One block (26) is not burnt in the holes, but is very deeply drilled; it suggests that it was a trial block for a learner, who had not yet attained the skill of fire-making. The other (27) is well used, all the holes being charred to a glossy charcoal face; two places have been notched, but not yet drilled. The upper stick (24) is quite charred at the lower end, and ground down with a characteristic shoulder produced by the friction. It is of the XVIIIth dynasty, found with a scarab of Amenhotep III. How these fire drills were rotated we can guess on seeing the common figures of drill bows on the sculptures: such a tool could not be familiar without being used for the fire-drilling. Three examples of drill bows were found, one of which is figured here (22), and also an unfinished drill stock (23). The unsymmetrical form of the bow is to adapt it to hold in the hand by the near end, and the length of it is just suited to the swing of the elbow from the shoulder.

Some more hoes were found of the compound form usual; and also some of the natural hoes, formed of a forked branch trimmed into form (28). These I have not seen in Egypt before, nor on the sculptures; they are the evident prototypes of both the hoe and the adze. The large pointed implement (29) seems to be a plough coulter.

26. Another flint sickle has been found (27) later in development than that of last season ("Kahun," IX, 22), and dated to the XVIIIth dynasty by a piece of pottery with it. This retains three of the four flint saws in position, set in a groove in the wood by black cement, probably of Nile mud and some sticky substance. The tip of this sickle is broken off; and the handle instead of being carved in one piece, as before, is attached with pegs. We now see how much these sickles explain of the use of the toothed flints both of Egypt and Syria; the majority of such flints are just suited to these implements, and shew signs of the wear not extending beyond the edge, i.e. only where the flint was not embedded in the cement setting (5). Several flint tools were found; but as these will be described by Mr. Spurrell (Chap. XI) I need only here notice the classes. (VII, 1) is an adze; (2) a scraper; (3) a hornstone axe, and (4) a flint axe; (5, 5 a) are the corner flints of large sickles; (6) a saw flint; (7, 8) knives; (9) is half of a sharp-edged flint, of a type not seen in others of the XIIth dynasty, and of a different quality; it is therefore probably of the age of some scarabs found with it—the XVIIIth dynasty. (10, 12, 15, 16) are scrapers; (11 and 14) probably knives. A remarkable flint knife is that in a large find of the XIIth dynasty (XIII, 6), having remains of binding with fibre and cord on the handle: flint flakes (4, 5) were also found with it.

27. The copper tools have again been found here; and the recent analyses by Dr. Gladstone, F.R.S., of those found last year have established that the tools of the XIIth dynasty are copper, and those of the XVIII–XIXth are bronze. His analyses are as follow (see Soc. Bib. Arch. 1890):—

XII	Copper	Tin	Arsenic	Antimony	Iron	Total
Hatchet	93·26	·52	3·90	·16	·21	98·05
Chisel	96·35	2·16	·36	..	..	98·87
Mirror	95	some	some	..	little	..
Knife	..	about ·5	..	..	..	..
XVIII						
Hatchet	89·59	6·67	·95	trace	·54	97·75
,,	90·09	7·29	·22	trace	..	97·60

These shew that although small impurities existed in the copper of the earlier times, and were probably valued for hardening the metal, yet these were rather the accidental results of particular ores, than a deliberate mixture, such as the 7 per cent. of tin in the XVIIIth dynasty. The metal tin had been separated, and was known at that later time, as I found a pure tin ring with glass beads of the end of the XVIIIth dynasty at Gurob. In short, copper and flint ran their course side by side, equally in use, down to the close of the middle kingdom; and when the Empire arose in the XVIIIth dynasty flint had almost ceased to be worked, and bronze had replaced copper.

The copper hatchet (VII, 19) and adze (18) were found together. The hatchet is bound around with thread, and sealed twice with a private scarab, impressed on Nile mud: what the reason for this sealing may have been, we do not know; it was not a maker's mark, as the hatchet is worn; but it may have been sealed as a matter of a legacy, or disputed property, or to prevent any person using it. The copper knife (20) is of an unusual shape. Other small knives were found, like those in "Kahun" (XVII, 18–20); and some with the shank rolled up (17), a rude form of handling it. Two round chisels (21) and many fishhooks, tweezers (VIII, 6), needles, and a netting needle (VIII, 3), were also found; beside more of the puzzling knives (VIII, 4, 5) with a hinging back piece, which though previously only known in the XVIIIth dynasty ("Kahun," XVII, 43) are now found to belong to the XIIth dynasty, having been found in the rubbish heaps. Among other tools may be named several plummets of the type found last year ("Kahun," VIII, 19); another shell scoop (K. VIII, 10); and two small shells (Pl. VIII, 16), set in reed handles, the purpose of which is quite unknown.

28. The group No. 9 was the most numerous found in Kahun (see Pl. XIII, 1–18). It was in a house on the south side of the second street from the top, in the workmen's western quarter. The date of the group is not well fixed; but the flint and copper implements, and the forms of the alabaster vases, shew that it belongs to the XIIth or XIIIth dynasty. The mirror (8) is of fine yellow metal, and still bright and clean enough to reflect from the greater part of it; the handle is of hard brown wood, carved with a head of Hathor on either side. The torque (18) is of copper; I do not remember another instance of a torque in ancient Egypt. The spoon (7) is of wood, and has had a little figure at the end of it, of which only the feet remain. Three alabaster vases are of one type (1), one thrice the size here drawn, and two about double of the drawing. Another alabaster vase is of the form (3). A vase of green paste (2) is of the

same form as the alabaster; I have seen also green paste flies on a necklace of the XIIth dynasty. Of tools, there is the flint knife with binding remaining on the handle, made of fibre lashed round with a cord: when first found this was very tender, but by wrapping it in paper I took it home safely, and then toasting it over a stove I dropped melted wax on until it was saturated: thus the binding is now unalterable. This suggests that the other flint knives may have been similarly handled when in use: such a handling would leave no traces on the flint after it had dropped away. Seven flint flakes (4, 5) were found in a leather bag, along with some nuts and some roots, the piece of wood (9) of unknown purpose, one copper piercer (15), and the spoon already described. There was also a broken piece of a flint knife, and a small whetstone (10). The copper tools are the large knife (17); two small chisels or borers set in wooden handles (14, 16); a tapering piercer (12) set in a nut handle; two other piercers (11, 13) without handles; and the small piercer (15) found in the bag. There was also a small wooden box. All of these, except the metal of the mirror and the large knife, were in one chamber; but the mirror handle shewed so plainly the mark of the mirror tang that I had a search for the remainder, and the mirror itself and large knife were in the next chamber.

29. Turning now to inscriptions there is the large stela (PL. XI), of which the upper part was broken away anciently. It had been reused for construction in a deep tomb shaft of the XIIth dynasty, which was re-occupied in the XXIInd; probably it came from the chapel over that tomb. The story of the theft and recovery of this stela has been already given ("Kahun," page 11). It is now at the Ghizeh museum, of course. It recorded the offerings made for a high priest Usertesen-ankh-tef-pen. The dedication to Tahuti and Sokar-asar is not very usual; and the group of festivals of Sokar, Sothis and Khem (or Ames) is interesting. The next largest inscription is on a beautiful seated statue of black basalt, representing a royal relation Se-sebek, born of the lady of the house That (XII, 14). It is quite perfect, and still retains the little original patchings of black clay where the basalt was defective. It was found standing in the corner of a room in the second of the large northern mansions. Unfortunately for me, there were no such statues of the XIIth dynasty in the Ghizeh museum, so this example is now there. The inscription covers the sides, back, and front of the throne seat; it is here given from a hand copy which I made at the time of finding it, checked on the left side by a photograph, from which Herr Spiegelberg kindly suggested some emendations. The identification of the abbreviation for *suten rekh* on the right side is of interest.

The inscription for Antef-aker (XII, 1) is on the lap of a cross-legged figure in hard black serpentine; unfortunately, the upper part of the figure is lost. It adds another to our list of royal officials; but it is curious that a blank is left at the beginning of the last line, as if it had been intended to fill in the father's name; as it is, the mother's name Nebt-tef, "lady of the father," and the grandmother's name Pepi, are given. A small round-topped limestone tablet bears the name of Mera-ankh (2); it seems as if it had been put in a wall as a boundary mark. The stela (3) is very rudely cut, and the names are of curious simplicity; As, son of Hotep, being the person concerned. A seated figure in hard brown limestone has been much knocked about; the upper part is missing, and the throne seat has been broken in three pieces. The inscription is roughly cut (4), and the names are hardly legible; Heshneb is scarcely intelligible for the man's name; and his mother's is even worse, possibly Sebektes - - anf. A small painted stela (5) records Hekekuta. A part of the base of a small green basalt statue (10) gives the name of Apser; and another of a woman (13) has lost part of the name, which ends ... menft, born of Ḥenat; with the addition that it was made by her beloved son, the overseer of her house, Khonsu. The stela (12) is painted, with figures roughly cut in relief; it has the usual inscriptions for a priest Amenisenb, and a lady of the house Mentu. The part of a stela of Anpi (11) is another piece of the side of a stela found last year ("Kahun," XI, 10). The pieces of the shrine and altar of Atmu-neferu (6, 7, 8) have been already mentioned in describing her pyramid. The piece (9) is a part of the list of offerings in the temple of Usertesen; removed, and left in the town, at an early time. The stamp of limestone (15) is very rudely cut, and illegible at present. The wooden stamp (16) is remarkable, as it seems probably to belong to the Hyksos period by the name, if indeed it is not intended for the Hyksos king Apepi himself. The name occurs however as early as the XIth or XIIth dynasty at Assuan ("Season in Egypt," inscr. 219). Some fragments of writing tablets were found; they are beautifully made of wood, faced with a polished surface of stucco, so fine that ink will not soak into it or stain it, but may be washed off quite clean.

30. The scarabs and clay seals found do not call for any particular notice. They shew well the style of such things in the XIIth dynasty. In one case is an enigmatical name (VIII, 36), which is not yet known in the royal lists. The clay sealings (PLS. IX, X) belong almost entirely to the sealings of boxes, vases, and bags: they bear the mark of the vessel, and of the cord which bound it, on their under sides; some grains of resin found with them make it likely that some of the packages contained resin. Nearly all of these sealings were picked up in two or three rooms of the town, by the small boys of the village who used to hunt over the dust and earth, after the workmen had cleared a room; they sometimes thus found little things which were not noticed in the larger work of digging. A most curious article among the small objects (PL. VIII, 17) is a counting stick. It is not intended for doing operations on like an abacus, but apparently for teaching children. It is made from an old piece of furniture; the holes on the left hand being for fastening pegs. It begins with *nefer*, and then dots for 1 to 9; then 10, and dots for 11 to 19; then 20, 25, and 30 to 90; and lastly the sign for 100.

31. Another measure was found at Kahun this year, of the same standard of the double foot of Asia Minor, divided into 7 palms after the fashion of the Egyptian cubit. It is worn away in pointed form at both ends. The divisions are, butt end 0, 2·96, 6·66, 10·53, 12·41, 14·30, 18·22, 22·12, 25·67 inches butt. The palms therefore, excluding the shortened ends, are 3·70, 3·87, 3·77, 3·92, 3·90 inches; the mean is 3·84, and therefore 7 would be 26.88 inches. The measure found last year which was divided in exactly the same way is 26·43 long; but it is more roughly divided than the present example. The various examples of the Asiatic foot would give a double varying between 26·2 and 26·9; and it is of importance to find it with the foreign inhabitants of Kahun, to the exclusion of the regular Egyptian cubit. As being the origin of all our English land measures, the early history of it is particularly interesting.

32. The weights of Kahun are here all stated together, including those of last year (numbered from 4913 to 4920).

No.	Material	Form	Present	Ch.	Ancient	X	Unit
			Egyptian Kat (7)				
4921	Limestone	15	276·2	..	..	2	138·1
4922	Limestone	65	2878·1	..	..	20	143·9
4923	Limestone	79	1439·4	..	1448	10	144·8
4913	Sandstone, br.	44	17675	..	..	120	147·4
4914	Alabaster	63–166	2951·3	..	..	20	147·6
4915	Alabaster	15	151·8	..	..	1	151·8
4916	Limestone	166–171	22235·	625	22860	150	152·4
			Assyrian shekel (3)				
4917	Limestone	62	3708	52	3760	30	125·3
4924	Alabaster	163	3798·6	..	3799·5	30	126·6
4925	Syenite, gy.	10–54	3946·0	..	..	30	131·5
			Attic drachma (7)				
4926	Limestone	cone	1283	..	..	20	64·2
4927	Limestone	cone	133·3	..	..	2	66·6
4928	Limestone	66	3321·5	..	3340	50	66·8
4929	Limestone	cone	263·6	4·4	268	4	67·0
4930	Limestone	cone	540·1	..	..	8	67·5
4918	Syenite, gy.	9	6878	..	..	100	68·8
4931	Limestone	cone	580·4	..	..	8	72·5
			Aeginetan stater (8)				
4932	Limestone	171	19100	..	19180	100	191·8
4919	Limestone	54–66	9625	..	9670	50	193·4
4933	Basalt, br.	64	4869	91	4960	25	199·2
4920	Limestone	171	12040	..	..	60	200·7
4934	Syenite, gy.	9–10	6157	..	..	30	205·2
4935	Syenite, gy.	9–10	6167	..	..	30	205·6
4936	Syenite, gy.	9–10	10340	..	..	30	206·8
4937	Syenite, gy.	9–10	6240	..	..	30	208·0
			Phoenician shekel (19)				
4938	Limestone	57	8302	..	8310	40	207·8
4939	Limestone	cone	837·8	..	..	4	209·5
4940	Limestone	63	25120	..	25220	120	210·2
4941	Limestone	58	8323	100	8420	40	210·5
4924	Alabaster	163	3798·6	..	3799·5	9	211·8
4942	Limestone	171	8536	..	8550	40	213·7
4943	Limestone	82	1960·5	190	2150	10	215·0
4944	Syenite, gy.	9	8609	..	..	40	215·2
4945	Basalt, bk.	169	4489	..	..	20	224·4
4946	Limestone	66	25360	1640	27000	120	225·0
4947	Limestone	cone	902·0	..	..	4	225·5
4948	Limestone	171	8735	300	9030	40	225·7
4949	Syenite, gy.	2	4580	..	..	20	229·0
4950	Limestone	57	56890	1110	58000	250	232·0
4951	Granite, red	44 tall	11650	..	..	50	233·0
4952	Syenite, gy.	9	4685	..	..	20	234·2
4953	Granite, red	65	47290	..	47400	200	237·0
4954	Alabaster	63	480·6	..	..	2	240·3
4955	Alabaster	63	2418·0	..	2426	10	242·6
			Eighty grain (1)				
4956	Limestone	171	3142	..	314·3	4	78·6

Some of these weights bear marks, beside those noticed last year. No. 4924 is entered twice; it is marked IIIIIIIII, shewing that it is 9 units, or 9 Phoenician shekels; but 9 is such an unlikely multiple that I think this is an after attribution, and that it was probably an Assyrian half mina, under which I have also entered it. 4942 and 4948 are both marked ∩∩, and divided by 20 they yield double of the Phoenician shekel, which must have been the unit reckoned. The limestone cones 4926 to 4931 are very roughly chipped, and I was doubtful if they could be weights; but the manner in which they are multiples of one another is far too unlikely to be mere chance, and so most of them appear as of the Attic drachm. Some attributions may be rather beyond the range of the standards here, but are vouched for by similar weights; 4931 cannot be separated from 4930, nor 4939 from 4947. 4954 has 11 on the top of it, shewing it to be 2 shekels. The one example of the 80-grain unit, 4956, was said to come from Kahun, and the form is like other Kahun weights, and unlike those of Gurob; but it is the only instance of this unit before the XVIIIth dynasty. The preponderance of foreign standards is very marked; not a sixth are Egyptian, and even those are all of soft materials unlike Egyptian weights.

33. Lastly we will notice the groups of objects found at Kahun, but belonging to the sparse occupation of the place under Amenhotep III. Only some rooms in the western workmen's quarter appear to have been inhabited then; as only one object of the XVIIIth dynasty has been found elsewhere, except with some few burials in the east part of the town. Everything dated has been of Amenhotep III, except one scarab of Amenhotep II; but there is scarcely any pottery of the XVIIIth dynasty, and the place seems to have only been re-occupied very slightly at this period.

The group of tools on Pl. XIII (21–31) was found in a house at the east end of the fourth street of the western quarter, marked 7 in the plan. It is dated by a papyrus of Amenhotep III, which was wrapped up in cloth, and placed in the pottery cone (XIII, 30). This cone was struck by the pick, and broken across, severing also the cloth and papyrus, which was moreover in a very brittle state. By careful handling I succeeded in getting it home and unrolling it, with only the loss of one or two small chips. The bronze tools are remarkable for being broken intentionally; the hatchet (22) is only half here; the knives (24, 25) are both broken, and the handle of one bent over; the lance head (26) is broken, and several pieces of cut up bronze were found also. The only complete bronze is the chisel in a wooden handle (27). Of wood there were three hoe blades (21), a *nen* handle, a mallet (23), a bent piece, and a strip ribbed ornamentally on each side. A large stone ring-stand, for a jar, was not brought away. Two Egyptian pots were found of coarse brown ware, a pilgrim bottle of smooth polished drab (29), and a Phoenician vase (31) of dark brown with white strips. This last is very valuable as giving us a dated example. The little amulet (28) found with these, is, from its colour and work, doubtless of the same age.

Another such Phoenician vase was found with several large balls of thread and some hanks, wrapped up in cloth, accompanied by a scarab of Amenhotep III; so the age of this pottery is well confirmed.

A third find of this age was in the second north mansion. There one of the rooms of the XIIth dynasty had been refloored at a higher level, on the top of 4 or 5 feet of rubbish; and the wooden tripod cup and scarab of Amenhotep III (VIII, 21, 22) were there found.

The fourth group of this age was in the third street of the western quarter. Here were found together a large lion-hunt scarab of Amenhotep III, of the usual inscription, and fine blue glaze; a lion in wood gilt (VIII, 20) which has been broken from a group in which it stood resting the fore-paws on some object, exactly in the attitude of the celebrated lions over the gate at Mykenae; a glass heart blue, yellow, and white, of the regular style of the middle XVIIIth dynasty; a fire stick with burnt end (VII, 24); a wooden drill head, reel, a piece of unknown use (wider than XIII, 9), and a sickle handle; also a pilgrim bottle of polished drab, and pieces, two flints, and an old alabaster kohl vase of XII dyn.

Three other deposits which are probably of this age were three small fine green scarabs found with a burial in the S.E. streets; a burial in the sixth north mansion with beads, Bes pendants, &c., of the mid XVIIIth dynasty; and a basket with beads and a bronze ring, "Ptah beloved of Ma," found in the 1st (northmost) line of houses in the western quarter. Another burial of the XVIIIth dynasty was described in "Kahun," page 44.

CHAPTER IV.

MEDINET GUROB.

34. In the previous season only a part of this site had been touched; but this season's work has nearly exhausted it. As I was fully occupied with Kahun, I handed Gurob over to Mr. Hughes-Hughes, who was out in Egypt with me. This work then was under his care; and beyond shewing him the ground, and making a plan of the remains after the work was over, I had no responsibility about it. While at work he found the long walls of the southern inner enclosure; but unfortunately the walls of the northern—or temple—enclosure were not traced throughout

during the work, and the western end of it is very uncertain. The columns are marked here in outline by analogy from six bases, found in my first season's work, which are marked solid black. The outer square wall was also traced and surveyed in the first season.

The design of the plan (PL. XXV) evidently was a temple in an enclosing wall; surrounded by a great square enclosure, which also comprised another space similar to the temple area, side by side with that. The only dimensions which appear to be laid out in round numbers are the breadth of the temple area, which is 100 cubits of 20·7 inches, and the length of the forecourt of the temple, which was the same as the breadth. Probably other rows of columns stood in this temple, beside those marked here; but this ground was not exhaustively turned over; and as those lines marked are dependent on only two bases of each row being found, it is very likely that no trace would be left of other lines. The axis is marked by the middle between the walls; but it coincides exactly with the doorway. The southern enclosure may have had other doorways, but only those marked were observed. Nearly all the dwellings of the town are restricted to these two inner enclosures; and most of the square outside of them is bare sand, with only occasional buildings. It will be noticed how the dyke, which protects the Fayum, joins the desert edge almost in a line with the axis of the temple, and the entrance. Doubtless the temple was placed facing the end of the dyke; and a slight displacement of the bank, by re-lining it, accounts for the difference. The end of it has been further diverted to the south in later times.

35. So far as the history of the place can be traced, it is very nearly what I had supposed last season; but we can now be rather more definite. The temple was founded by Tahutmes III; and nothing whatever of earlier kings has been found here. So far as we can judge, all the three enclosures belong to his time. Within forty or fifty years of this, at most, there is evidence of the foreigners being here, Aegean pottery being found under Amenhotep III. Khuenaten cut out the name of Amen in the temple. Probably Tutankhamen was the king who reinserted the name of the Theban deity. Still the temple stood, and the foreigners were here. Then we find the temple nearly all carried bodily away; hardly any of the stones are left, and no chips to speak of; it was not therefore cut to pieces by small workers for miscellaneous stone, or there would be strata of fragments as at the Labyrinth. As we know that Ramessu II carried away the pyramid casing and temples of Illahun to Ahnas for materials, it is pretty certain that this arch-plunderer swept away the temple of Tahutmes III in the same shameless manner. Probably before his time dwellings had invaded the temple enclosure; and so soon as the temple was removed the people soon filled the space with a mass of houses. As we have before noticed, the town was ruined and deserted under Merenptah, the range of kings' names on amulets coming suddenly to an end, doubtless by the expulsion of the foreign inhabitants in the Libyan war. But some slight occupation existed under Ramessu III, as his name has been found in two or three instances.

36. A very remarkable custom existed in this town, which I believe is unknown as yet elsewhere in ancient Egypt. In many instances the floor of a room has been taken up; a hole about two feet across and a foot deep was dug in the ground. A large quantity of distinctly personal property, such as clothing, a stool, a mirror, necklaces, kohl tubes, and toilet vases of stone and pottery, were thrown in, and then all burnt in the hole. The fire was smothered by potsherds laid flat over it; and lastly the floor was relaid. Such was the arrangement of one instance which I examined in detail; and such is indicated by the state of the things in other finds, and the accounts given by Mr. Hughes-Hughes and by the native diggers. It is evident that the objects buried are such as belong to an individual personally, and not to a household. No bones were ever found with the burnt deposits. These were not therefore funereal pyres. Yet we cannot imagine a general custom of burning and burying valuable property, except on the death of the owner. I conclude therefore that there was a custom among the foreign residents of burying the body in the Egyptian fashion, especially as I found light-haired bodies in the cemetery; and that the personal property which would have been piled on the funereal pyre in the Mediterranean home of the Akhaians, was here sacrificed in the house, and so put out of sight. In most instances Aegean pottery was found in these deposits, an evidence of their belonging to the foreigners.

37. We will now notice such groups of these burnt remains as bear a date. On the upper part of PL. XVII is a group of the time of Amenhotep III; it is dated by a kohl tube (20) with part of his cartouch, . . *ma neb*, and that of a daughter of his Hent-taui-neb, who is otherwise unknown. The signs are

inlaid in the violet glaze, in the fashion peculiar to this reign; and from the colour and manufacture, as well as part of the king's name, it would be impossible to assign it to the daughter of Ramessu II, or any later princess of the name. Of pottery there are several types of Egyptian make (1, 2, 5); and one both in form and duplication evidently influenced from Syria (4). There were five examples of the false-necked vases of Aegean ware (3) with iron glaze bands; all of them of this tall globular type. The blue glazed ware has often the pattern but faintly marked (7, 8, 11, 22); but sometimes it is very clear, and thin-lined, as in the pilgrim bottle with a winged Bes (9), and the tubular vases (13, 21). The tube (14) is quite plain. The ring (16) has an eye for the bezel. Of alabaster there were fragments of some dishes like (41); and the complete vase and saucer (6, 10); also ear-studs (17, 18). The two bronze tools (15, 19) are constantly found in these buried groups; almost always the two, and never any duplicates. Dots are here put around the cutting edges. Whether they were used for feeding, for attending to the person, or possibly in the process of embalming, we cannot yet determine. In one case (XVIII, 3) they were tied together, with a needle, by thread bound round them. The gradual change in the form of the lower end of the knife (19) should be noted. Here it is only widened out. Later, under Ramessu II, it became spread into two flanges (XVIII, 3, 38). Lastly, under Seti II, the flanges recurve backward into hooks (XIX, 18). A whetstone (12) is found in each group. A mirror was found with this, as with most other groups; but as no distinction could be traced between the forms during the XVIII–XIX dynasties, they are not drawn here. All these mirrors were of the usual oblate outline, with a tang all in one, to fit into a wooden handle. The beads are all of carnelian or jasper, now burnt (23, 24); the original order is uncertain as the thread was burnt, but as the grass-hoppers are pierced with two holes, a double threading is suggested. This set is now in the Ashmolean, at Oxford.

The next group is dated to Tut-ankh-amen by the delicate little blue pendants (29) found with it. The pottery is foreign; a pilgrim bottle, probably Cypriote (40), and several pieces of false-necked vases of Aegean pottery (28). The blue glazed ware (30, 43, 44) is painted with broader, coarser, lines than before. Three glass vessels were found; one flat bottle (35) with yellow veins on a purple ground; part of one conical bottle with yellow veins on a blue-black ground; and part of a conical bottle (37) with yellow and white veins on a light green ground. The skill of this glass-making is surprising. The veins are completely imbedded, and the surface is as bright and smooth as if polished, entirely by semi-fusion, without confounding any of the finest filaments of colour. Ear-studs (34) and earrings of shell (32), and jasper (33) were here; as well as several stone finger-rings, of white felspar (36, 39) carnelian and haematite (38). The alabaster dish (41) of a fish form was burnt to lime; there was also a bottle (42), and a small cup (31). The beads were in great numbers, of which all the types are shewn here; the little figure pendants (25) in blue, the flat ribbed cone beads (26) of red glaze, and the amulet beads of blue glaze (27). This set is now in the glass department of the British Museum.

The next group is of Ramessu II (Pl. XVIII), dated by a kohl tube with his cartouches (6). From the similarity of the glass to that of Tutankhamen, it is probable that this belongs to the earlier part of the reign of Ramessu. The pottery is mostly open saucers (1, 9, 11), of which there were several. The blue glazed ware is coarser than before (2, 4, 5, 6, 8, 10, 12), and inferior in colour; the imitation shell (12) is however of violet glaze, and looks as if it was an old heirloom from Amenhotep III. The sphinx bowl (Pl. XX, 4) is very curious in its style, as female sphinxes are very rare, the more so with wings. The bowl (2) with the monkey is an interesting bit of caricature; the idea seems to be that the captives were so low that they had to dance to the monkeys of Egypt, instead of the monkey amusing the man. Several blue glazed rings were found, one with a bezel of Bes (14), the other with the cartouche of Ramessu II (20). The glass is of fine quality; the flat bottle and bowl (13, 18) are of almost transparent amethyst glass inlaid with yellow and white; the flat bottle (19) is of blue-black, with yellow veins; the two little bottles are of green inlaid with yellow, white, and black. There is also a heart of violet glass (26). The alabaster is of the types seen earlier (22, 23, 25). The beads are all of stone, jasper or carnelian, but clumsy in form.

The next group is also of Ramessu II, but probably of the end of his long reign, dated by his cartouche and that of queen Nefertari (31). The pottery is coarser and poorer; many of the cups (55) are found, and the coarse jars (57); the three-handled vase (51) appears for the first time, it recurs under Seti II with a shorter neck (XIX, 11), and still taller in the body, under Ramessu VI (Tell el Yehudiyeh XV, 11): the wide jugs of earlier times (XVII, 1, 6) have become narrow and pointed in form (62) as at Tell el Yehudiyeh; the other pottery (45, 54) now appears for the first time. The foreign pottery is of the false-necked vase (52), large, coarse, of Egyptian ware, and evidently an imitation of the real Aegean pottery. The pilgrim bottles (58, 59) have developed; and one is in dark greenish blue glaze (61). A remarkable bronze dish (53) and bucket (60) were found here; both are hammered to a marvellous thinness, with a thickened brim, but both sadly contorted by the fire and pressure. There are also many needles (36, 37), tweezers (34, 35), prickers (33) and two razors (44) of bronze. The alabaster follows the forms of the pottery (43), and is also made into clumsy figure vessels; a girl with a dish (28), and a duck with wooden wings painted (27). Of wood there is a statuette of a queen (42), two polished trays (49), a kohl reed (41), and pin (40), besides a bronze kohl pin (39) and two combs (one nearly burnt away) with a horse drinking (46), carved on the back. The usual jasper earrings occur (29), and alabaster ear-studs (47); the beads are mostly of glass (30), the eye beads of black, white, and yellow being the commonest. The rude pendants of Bes and Taurt (31), cut in stone and blue glazed, first appear here; and that style lasted down to the XXIInd dynasty. The carnelian is cut also into coarse pendants such as the Horus (48). The eye with the cartouches of Ramessu II and Nefertari (31) is broken and worn, so it cannot have been new when buried, but the long reign of Ramessu II would give quite time enough for its deterioration. The large black glass bead, with white and blue pattern (32) is remarkable. The whetstone (50) was probably used for the bronze knife (38).

The last dated group is under Seti II (Pl. XIX), dated by a little tray of black steatite with his name. The pottery is more debased, and most of it like that of the latter Ramessides at Tell el Yehudiyeh. This close connection of the pottery of the Fayum and Delta is of value, as shewing that the same styles, in every detail, were prevalent over large areas, and probably over the whole country, at one period. The pottery is coarse brown (1, 3, 5, 6, 8, 11, 12, 13), and polished red faced (2, 4, 7, 9, 10, 15). Some is of foreign form, such as the false-necked vase (12) but of native ware, and evidently made by a potter who had lost the feeling of the original type. The same may be said of the pilgrim bottle (17). Blue glazed ware occurs, as the pilgrim bottle (14), and the very coarsely painted bowl, (26). Alabaster is of very clumsy forms, (20, 25); and if better (as 19, 27) the type is a mere degradation. Blue finger rings abound, (21, 22); and beads are very coarse, in glass and pottery; or apparently old descended necklaces of jasper (24). The little dish is curious; the sides are roughly engraved with Ptah, the king slaying an enemy before a god, the names of Seti II, and a scarab beetle (23).

38. We will now briefly recapitulate the consecutive changes in various objects, that may be learned from these dated deposits. And though it might reasonably be objected that one dated object might easily last in use for a long time, and be buried with subsequent remains; yet the sequence that can be traced in these deposits shews good reason for assuming that small things lasted in use for not more than a generation, as is naturally the case. The absence of scarabs here before Tahutmes III, shews the same. In the necklaces we may trace sometimes the patched-up sets of two or three earlier periods all put together; but this is not commonly the case. We have noticed the changes in the form of the bronze knives, gradually widening and turning up at the butt. The beads here are entirely carnelian under Amenhotep III, though probably violet and black glass beads were already made; they are of pottery under Tutankhamen; of clumsy stone early in Ramessu II; of glass, and coarse glazed stone, late in Ramessu II; and of very coarse glass, and pottery glazed, under Seti II. The blue glazed vases also deteriorate: the lines are fine and thin under Amenhotep III; coarse but good colour under Tutankhamen; coarse, and poor colour, much green, under Ramessu II; and very rude under Seti II. Glass bottles are as old as Tahutmes III we know from other sources: here they appear under Tutankhamen and Ramessu II. The pottery becomes coarser, poorer, and of exaggerated forms as time goes on. The false-necked vases can now be well traced; beginning in a globular form, of fine Aegean ware, with iron-glaze bands, under Amenhotep III; next flatter in form during the end of that dynasty, with discs surrounded by dots; tolerably imitated on a large scale under Ramessu II; roughly copied in native pottery under Seti II; and of very rude style in native clay, under the later Ramessides (Tell el Yehud.). To displace this dating by a century, every stage of this history would need to be altered; the sequence is quite regular so far as Egypt is concerned; and if the type came down to later times in other

countries, it must be similarly proved by dated examples in those localities.

39. Turning now to the objects found without dates, the blue bowls are shewn in Pl. XX. Nos. 1 and 2 were found together. No. 3 was found with some pottery, Egyptian, and Aegean of the globular form with red bands; a blue glass bottle; two pottery models of trussed fowls, &c. The design is the best drawn of all these glazed objects; the spring of the girl as she poles the boat along to market, with the calf in it, is well rendered, and the dainty turn of the face. The bowl is now brown and black, but was probably violet originally. Another bowl (6) also represents a girl poling the market boat, laden with a bird-cage, and a number of birds on the top; this is of bright clear blue, with dark blue lines, rather faint. The gazelle (5) is drawn with a dry, almost black, line, and great sharpness; the style looks to be the earliest of all those here. The group Pl. XX, 7–15, was found together, and is of the end of the XVIIIth dynasty by the style. Two fine Aegean vases (7, 9) occur: pottery (13, 14): alabaster (8, 15): a small flat glass bottle (11) of blue, green, yellow, and white, with three handles, and originally joined to another at the side: a conical glass bottle (12) with yellow veins on bright blue: a bronze conical vase (broken), and a pair of hinges of bronze, which interlock when closed, by a part of one fitting into the other half, so that the door could not be prised upward; this is just the principle of the blocks on the doors of modern safes. The pottery with this find was of the types "Kahun" XX, 15, 32; XXI, 59; and here Pl. XIX, 2, 4, 6, 7.

Among miscellaneous objects (Pl. XIX) there are of bronze, an adze (28); a spoon (29) said to be found at Gurob, and by its patination apparently of the time of the town, it is not broken, but flat ended; a small knife (30), beside other large ones of the types "Kahun" XVII, 29, 33, 50; a knife with swivel back (33) bound round with thread; two lance heads (31, 32); a supposed razor (40), which it has been suggested is for skinning or flaying, to judge by the place of the edge (dotted around here) and the curve of the handle; also an outline of a goose in bronze (34) with two tags at the back twisted together, perhaps for a brand. A pair of alabaster vessels were found together (41, 42) one with a curiously rough design of dancing goats, which recalls the style of Greek island gems. Another alabaster vase is very clumsy (36). The name of Thii occurs on a knob for a box lid (38), inlaid in light blue on a dark blue ground. The little panel of wood (35) from a box has a lotus pattern, which strongly suggests an original for the so-called "palmetto" of Greek design. The part of a wooden wand (39) is inscribed with the name of "Hu (the god of taste) son of the *ka*s of Urthekau," a rather enigmatical phrase; but as Urthekau was connected with magic, it is possible that these wands were for ceremonial use. The strange figure (43) is from Abusir, in the middle of the Delta; I bought it in Cairo. It is of light drab pottery, hard, and well baked; the lower part is identical with the Greek island figures of marble, and its line divisions are evidently copied from such a figure; but the head bears the Libyan lock of hair. It appears therefore to be a Libyo-Greek product, from the time of the invasions of Egypt by those races jointly, and therefore probably of the age of Gurob, or a little later.

On Pl. XXII are three curious pieces (1, 2, 3) like those found in one class of Cypriote tombs. It has been proposed that they were used by being tied on to one edge of a garment by the middle hole, and then slipped through a small hole in the opposite edge, and drawn back like the swivel of a watch guard; this seems the most likely explanation. The date of them may be put between 1200 and 1400 B.C., being found at Gurob. The rings of blue glazed pottery (4) or of alabaster (6) were sometimes inlaid with small bits of jasper. The charming head (5) is carved alike on both sides of a flat slip; it probably was the handle of a tray. The rings (9, 10) are interesting as shewing that lead and tin were separated as metals thus early; the tin ring was found with glass beads which are probably not later than the end of the XVIIIth dynasty; it has been analyzed by Dr. Gladstone who reports it to be pure tin, without perceptible alloy. The group of jewellery (11, 12, 13, 14) was found together: the little porcelain frog (13) dates it to about Amenhotep III; so the triple ring of electrum (11) set with haematite (?), the haematite (?) scarab in gold setting (14), and the gold eye with Ra on it (12) all probably belong to this age. Of bronze there is a small chisel (7), a pin (8), earring (15), fish-hook (16), weight (17), nail (18), and rivet with two washers (30). The draught men (19, 20) are of glazed pottery, as also the blue plaque of Isis (23). The slip of ivory carved with a vineyard on a wall (21) is probably part of a larger scene, cut down to a netting bone. The ivory slip (22) has been painted in the rosettes. The stud (26) is formed of limestone, faced over with a disc of ostrich egg; such was not uncommon at this period. The bead (27) with the name of Tahutmes III is of opaque blue glass. A spirited rough outline (25) has been scratched on a piece of pottery before baking. The inscriptions (24, 28) are cut on slips of wood, from some inlaying of boxes; (31) is on a separate piece of wood; and (32, 33) were on slips found together, referring to the eastern and western house of Ramessu III in the Fayum, an expression that might refer to Illahun and Gurob as being on the opposite banks of this branch of the Nile.

Of the scarabs and rings (PL. XXIII) there is no need to say much. It is strange that a scarab of Pepi should turn up at Gurob; it is the only one there earlier than the founder of the town Tahutmes III, and this absence of the earlier kings of the XVIIIth dynasty incidentally shews how soon scarabs dropped out of use after they were made. No. 21 is a new variety "beloved of all the gods of the palace." No. 45 is a curious ring with young Ramessu seated on the *nub*, in relief on the bezel. The unnamed scarabs are arranged, as nearly as can be judged, in their order of date.

40. The inscriptions from Gurob (PL. XXIV) are all of the XVIIIth dynasty. They are drawn here on a uniform size of sign; while the actual dimensions of each piece are stated in inches. The large lintel slab of Tahutmes III is from the temple which he built; and which, to judge by this, must have been well decorated. The left hand side of it, bearing hieroglyphs reading in the more usual direction, was done by a skilled sculptor, while the other half was copied by a pupil who shews very inferior ability in both outline and details. This is now in the Adelaide museum. The black granite altar is of special interest. Though roughly cut it seems to have belonged to a class of funerary offerings made for Amenhotep III by his celebrated queen Thii. It follows the usual formulae to Osiris, for the royal *ka* of Amenhotep III, down each side; and then along the base is a line stating that "The great royal wife Thii made her monuments of her brother, her beloved, the good god Ra-ma-neb." The question of the parentage of Thii is one of the most important genealogies in Egyptian history. In every other case that we can prove, the queen through whom the royal descent entailed was herself of royal family. But Thii is stated to have been the daughter of Iuaa and Tuaa. Here however she is the sister of Amenhotep III. Her parents therefore would have been Tahutmes IV and Arat. And she has the title of inheritance, "princess of both lands," on a colossus at Thebes. Either then Iuaa and Tuaa were the familiar names of Tahutmes IV and Arat (as every Egyptian had a great and little name), and Thii was thus sister to her royal husband, as were most of the other queens; or else these titles of sister, and "princess of both lands" were purely formal. It has been claimed as being formal in other cases, but that is very doubtful; unless it can be shewn that a queen was not of the royal stock, her possession of them is no proof of the formality of these titles. So strong does the principle of female inheritance of the throne seem to be in many crucial cases, to the exclusion of male inheritance, that the presumption is that Thii was really the sister of Amenhotep as here stated. The slab from Gurob (9) with the *ka* name of Amenhotep IV is a variant on the known forms; it seems to shew that some large buildings or repairs to the temple were made in his time. Some building also went on in this district under Khuenaten; as in a tomb at Illahun a block of sculpture (10), was found reused, which represented Khuenaten (tattooed with the names of Aten) holding his daughter Ankh-sen-pa-aten; while an offerer in front worships the disc, which is figured as an Asiatic rosette with pendant streamers, and would seem more in place on a Babylonian monument than in Egypt. This block is now in the University of Pennsylvania. The little tablet (11) representing a royal scribe Ra-mes-m-pa-amen adoring Tahutmes III, is probably of the XVIIIth dynasty, in spite of the Ra-mes name.

41. The cubit (12) is of wood, inscribed all along; one end has been broken away about 1·3 inch, at a knot in the wood. The inscription contains the titles of Tut-ankh-amen and his queen Ankhsamen. The dimensions of the cubit are ·94 × ·63 inch, with bevelled edge as usual; in the remaining end is a round hole, ·32 across and ·36 deep, with flat bottom; it seems as if intended to hold a stud to give an accurate terminal to the cubit. The divisions are roughly cut, being at (end) 0, 2·80, 4·16, 5·75, 8·63, 10·08, 10·97, 11·70, 14·70, and 17·77 inches. The palms therefore between the cuts (excluding the butt end) are 2·95, 2·88, 3·07, 3·00, 3·07 inches, which would indicate a cubit of 20·96; or if the butt end lost were of the same length as that remaining the total would be 20·57 which is nearer the probability. No accurate value can be deduced from this therefore.

42. The weights found at Gurob are here stated along with those found last year (numbered 4899 to 4912) so as to give a complete view of the metrology of the place. The arrangement of the table is similar

to that of the previous publication of weights in "Naukratis," "A Season in Egypt," &c.

No.	Material	Form	Present	Ch.	Ancient	×	Unit
		Kat standard (12)					
4958	Syenite, gy.	11	5623	..	..	40	140·6
4899	Syenite, gy.	117·174	1412·0	..	..	10	141·2
4900	Basalt, br.	38–43	1416·6	..	..	10	141·7
4959	Alabaster	86	5682	..	..	40	142·0
4901	Alabaster	79–110	284·6	..	..	2	142·3
4960	Lead	64	142·9	2?	..	1	142·9
4902	Syenite, gy.	2–10	3592·8	..	..	25	143·7
4903	Syenite, gy.	54	5748	..	..	40	143·7
4961	Haematite	2–4	720·1	..	..	5	144·0
4904	Basalt, br.	48–49	1472·3	..	..	10	147·2
4962	Syenite, gy.	2–4	5890	..	..	40	147·2
4963	Haematite	49–52	149·3	..	..	1	149·3
		Assyrian Shekel (7)					
4905	Haematite, bk.	49	363·9	..	..	3	121·3
4964	Basalt, br.	62	2487·1	..	..	20	124·4
4906	Haematite, bk.	52–82	62·7	..	..	½	125·4
4907	Lead	63	2523·2	30	2530	20	126·5
4908	Haematite, bk.	49	127·3	..	..	1	127·3
4965	Calcite	48	63·9	..	..	½	127·8
4966	Syenite, gy.	2–38	2556·1	..	..	20	127·8
		Attic Drachma (5)					
4909	Syenite, gy.	54	2625·8	..	2626	40	65·6
4967	Sandstone	84	2635·6	..	..	40	65·9
4968	Bronze, Pl. XXII,	17	133·1	1·5	132	2	66·0
4910	Alabaster	16	3305·8	..	..	50	66·1
4911	Lead	52–108	415·6	12	408	6	68·0
		Aeginetan Stater (4)					
4912	Lead	108	179·0	16	192	1	192·0
4969	Limestone	56	12180·	..	12181	60	203·0
4970	Syenite, gy.	11	8190	..	8230	40	205·7
4971	Sandstone	84	2081·7	..	..	10	208·2
		Phoenician Shekel (2)					
4972	Syenite, gy.	2	5294	..	..	25	211·8
4973	Basalt, br.	62	1380·2	..	1381	6	230·2
		Eighty grains (2)					
4974	Syenite, gy.	117	1568·8	..	..	20	78·4
4975	Haematite	49	157·0	..	157·3	2	78·6

The foreign character of the weights here is then well maintained by the larger number we have now got. Only ⅜ of all the weights are on the Egyptian standard; and of those nearly half are of the foreign materials, alabaster, lead, and haematite. Thus only a fifth of all the weights are regular Egyptian: and there is not a single example of the typical domed form. The Phoenician weight No. 4973 might at first seem to be a low variety of the uten; but it is marked O IIIIII, 6 units, proving it to belong to the Phoenician system. This is similar to two weights from Gebelen, which are of the same rectangular form, one of 1473·3 marked IIIIII, the other of 14700 marked ∩∩∩∩∩∩; giving units of 245·5 and 245· grains, or the same Phoenician standard.

CHAPTER V.

THE TOMB OF MAKET.

43. This tomb is in the town of Kahun. Many of the houses of the XIIth dynasty there have rock cut cellars, which were closed by massive trap-doors of wood, recessed into a seat and hinging in the stone. One of these cellars became known to people of the XIXth dynasty, and they cleared it, and probably enlarged it, to form a family tomb (see plan in corner of Pl. XIV). The first and last chamber is cut in the rock alone; the middle chamber is roofed and lined with blocks of fine white limestone. One of these roof blocks broke across, and fell on the coffins, somewhat crushing them; this entailed a very difficult matter, of shifting the block weighing many hundredweights off from the coffins, without any firm foothold to stand on so high up (as it lay on two coffins one on the other), and a risk of its falling over on one by the whole mass of half rotted coffins giving way with the weight in shifting it.

The tomb chambers contained in all twelve coffins, beside two boxes for babies. These coffins were mostly stacked two deep, and nearly filled the two inner chambers. When we first opened this tomb I was on the spot watching it; and the entrance to the middle chamber was so blocked by two coffins one on the other that it was impossible for any one to pass. I only allowed the principal lad of the party to come below; and then—half stripped—I set to work on the clearance. Nothing was moved in the whole place, except by my own hands; everything as moved was noted as to its position, and handed into the outer chamber to the lad, who was a trusty fellow, the same who worked Horuta's tomb. Thus there was no confusion, and I worked on steadily nearly all day, opening the coffins and recording all the things as they lay. The burials had evidently been successive, and things had been shifted to make way for the later comers. Each of the box coffins contained several bodies, some holding five or six, piled one on the other. The coffins were in tolerably firm condition; but the bodies and wrappings were all reduced to black powder which crushed up with a touch. The work was hardly cleaner than a chimney-sweep's. I was streaming with perspiration, and coated with black sooty dust of the mummies and cloth. Most of the small objects were found in oval baskets of the Nubian type, with woven patterns on the sides, and a ridge lid. These baskets were all too much rotted to remove : but they sufficed to keep the beads together while I picked them out.

From the positions of the coffins we can trace with tolerable clearness in what order they had been placed here. As they contained in all about 40 or 50 bodies, and as this tomb probably belonged to one family, it must have been added to for a considerable time, perhaps a century. Hence the earlier burials may contain things of a different period to the later. The coffins therefore are here numbered and described in the order of their age, beginning with the oldest.

44. The first must almost necessarily be that at the back of the innermost chamber, and the lowest of the two there. This coffin 1 contained the scarabs XXVI, 1 to 5, and the pottery figure on a couch, XXVII, 12 ; the group of sample beads, 3, is part of a larger number. The general style of these is of the end of the XVIIIth dynasty, and the scarabs 2 and 4 are of the XVIIIth. No. 5 is evidently an old one of the XIIth rediscovered. The black and green beads at the ends of the string are however later, belonging to Ramessu II or after, so that the other things must have been old when buried. This is very probable as the XVIIIth dynasty pendants are rather an odd lot, and not like an original and complete necklace. The back of scarab 2 is formed as the vulture crouched down, and not as a scarabaeus. This coffin on the whole may be of the reign of Ramessu II.

The next is probably that placed in front of it; for though some objects lay on that coffin so that the upper one, 3, could not have been pushed over it, it is likely that they had been replaced there after putting 3 in position, as they were roughly set about. Coffin 2 contained nothing besides the bodies. On the lid of it was standing a basket which had contained a small alabaster jar, (XXVII, 3), which had fallen out and broken ; also the very curious model of a stopped horn, (XXVI, 50) made of green paste ; a flat dish (XXVII, 8), also of green paste ; a quadruple kohl pot of wood too rotted to keep ; and a large round bead of yellow glass.

Coffin 3 was placed on the top of No. 1. It contained nothing besides the bodies. In the N.W. and S.W. corners of this room, and along the S. side, there was Egyptian pottery lying about, of the general character of XXVII, 40, 42, 49, &c. The chair (XXVII, 45,) was lying turned up on its side in the S.W. corner with both of the front legs wholly removed, and not to be found in the tomb ; it had evidently been "killed" before burying it. As it was not strong enough to move in one mass, I took it to pieces (about 40 parts) for transport. Every piece I afterwards soaked in melted wax to preserve it ; this of course darkened it, but prevented further decay.

Coming now to the main chamber, the order of the coffins must have been either No. 4 or No. 5 first ; then the other ; then the figure coffin put in at the back ; then 4 and 5 set to the sides and room made for 6, the coffin of Maket, which must have been last introduced as there is no room to turn a coffin from the door to the side. Then later 8 and 9 ; and probably 10 last of all as it lies on the most important coffin,—Maket's. No. 11 was then put in the passage as there was no room further in ; and lastly 12 was set upon it.

Coffin 4 was roughly painted with Isis and Nebhat at the head and foot of it. It contained a brown serpentine vase, (XXVII, 2) ; and in a basket the kohl pot of brown steatite (XXVI, 48,) with a figure at the side.

Coffin 5 contained five or six bodies, with them was a long walking stick ; a throw stick, (XXVII, 43) ; a folding head rest, (46), which probably had a band of linen to retain the two ends and to serve as a support for the head : a basket containing two pottery vases and an alabaster vase of the early form, (XIII, 1), but coarse and clumsy ; and the black limestone kohl pot on legs (XXVII, 10). On the second body were two hollow gold earrings, (XXVI. 11) ; unfortunately I did not see their exact position, whether on the ears or the hair, as they fell out of the crumbling wrappings as soon as the body was shifted.

Coffin 6 was a figure coffin, roughly cut to the outline, and with a face carved on it, but not coloured. It contained nothing but one body. Behind it lay a small box with slips of ivory on it, rather rotted. And in front of it were two boxes, with double sloping lids, like a roof ridge ; these contained babies, but were much rotted, and could not be preserved.

Coffin 7 was the most important of all. It contained the body of Maket ; with a gold scarab of hollow work (XXVI, 9) ; a silver scarab set in a gold ring, (7) ; and a silver ring, (8) ; all inscribed with name of "the lady of the house, Maket" ; also a scarab set in a ring, (10) ; and a pair of moulded paste earrings with rope edge, (6) ; a bronze mirror, (46), and kohl stick, (49) ; a large reed containing two small musical reed pipes (XXVII, 22, 23, 24) ; a head rest inlaid with ivory studs ; a Phoenician vase (XXVII, 19) ; and the foreign vase, (27), in a basket. There were several other bodies in this coffin also.

The heaps of objects in the S.W. corner must be

of about this period. They probably belonged to the preceding interments, and were shuffled off the coffins when fresh coffins were placed upon the lower ones. The scarabs, &c, in this heap are in PL. XXVI, 12 to 23. A small wooden box contained 12, 13, 14, a green glass plain cowroid set in gold, and some of the smallest beads (15) that I have yet seen; as many as 93 go to a grain weight. Of green paste there are the lions' heads, (18), for forming the ends of a collar; a large number of flat beads, (17), of green and of blue paste, some of which were stuck together in rows, as here drawn. A large number of green ribbed beads, (16), were found, some loose, some in a jar. There were alabaster vases (XXVII 4, 5); brown serpentine vases, (6, 7, 13); a green paste vase, (1); three Cypriote pilgrim bottles, (32, 41); two long smooth red vases, (18); brown Phoenician vase, (17); smooth black Phoenician vases (14, 15, 16, 20); and various small vases, (such as 25 to 38, and XXVI, 45). Also a bronze knife, (XXVI, 43); two whetstones; and two lumps of pumice. All these things were mingled together pell-mell, mixed with rotten and broken basket-work which had held the smaller things, and rotted clothes. It was impracticable to secure everything by hand from such confusion; and the smaller objects (XXVI, 19 to 23), with a plain blue scarab, were found afterwards by sifting the dust. The dark green jasper prism, (19), is of very fine work. In the S.E. corner of the room was also some pottery lying about, but mostly large, (such as XXVII, 40 to 51).

Coffin 8 contained at the north end a small basket with lid inverted, holding a wooden kohl stick, a plaque (XXVI, 24), and scarabs (25, 26). At the south end a basket with fruit, and a broken Phoenician vase, (XXVII 16 type). In the coffin was the Phoenician vase 21.

Coffin 9 had a solid wooden headrest on the top of the coffin. Six bodies were in it, and a small basket with beads (XXVI 30), and a cowroid (33); and the Aegean vase (XXVI, 44) at the south end. At the north end a larger basket with wooden kohl pot (type XXVII, 11), wooden kohl stick; stone kohl pot same type; two dūm nuts; and scarabs (27). The scarabs 28, 29, 31, 32 are also from this coffin.

Coffin 10 was figure shaped, and contained one body with a scarab (XXVI, 34).

Coffin 11, in the doorway, was of the pattern of that of Anentursha ("Kahun" XIX) with the four genii and addresses on the sides; but it was coarsely done and the places for the names were left blank on both lid and sides; all yellow on black ground. There was nothing in it but bodies.

Coffin 12 also contained nothing beside the bodies.

In the outer chamber was a good deal of coarse pottery lying about, much of it broken. In the later sifting and searching of the dust, which was all brought up and examined in sunshine, some more beads and scarabs were found, (XXVI, 35 to 42), the places of which are not known. Also the bronze fishing lance (47), and the cubit, (XXVII, 44) which is the short Egyptian cubit of 17·3 inches, corresponding to 6 true palms, and not to 6 sevenths of the regular cubit of 20·7.

45. We now see how a tomb was continuously used, and how the offerings left for one interment were not taken away, but were pushed on one side to make room for later coffins. The question of the age of this tomb is important, as the Greek and Phoenician pottery was found in it. The broad limits of age are (1) the scarabs which prove the earliest coffin to be after Tahutmes III. (2) The blue glass frog, which is probably of Amenhotep III or IV. (3) The green and black glazed beads, particularly the ribbed ones XXVI, 16, which were not made before Ramessu II, and the ribbing of which shews the first stage of the deep ribbing prevalent in the XXIInd dynasty (XXIX, 57). These belong to the time of coffins 4 to 7; and by the large quantity of them, appear to have been made at the time of those. (4) There is no pottery here like that of the XVIIIth and early XIXth dynasty; no trace of blue paint, no hard white faced ware, no elegant forms; but on the contrary the pottery here is mostly unknown in Gurob, that is, down to the time of Merenptah. These successive evidences bring down the age of the burials here to at least after the reign of Ramessu II, after 1200 B.C. for the earliest limit of possible age.

Now let us take the evidence for the later limit, which is necessarily negative. (1) There are no examples of the well known pottery of the XXVIth dynasty. (2) There are no figures of Bast and other deities which are so common in the adjacent tombs of Illahun in the XXIInd dynasty (PL. XXIX). (3) There are no examples of the light green glazes so characteristic of the XXIInd dyn. (4) There are no stone or shell beads so common in the XXIInd dynasty, nor any scarabs of that age. (5) The coffin 11 is of the style of that assigned to the beginning of the XIXth dynasty at Gurob; and is quite different in motive and colour to those of the XXIInd dynasty. Hence this tomb would be nearer to the XIXth than the XXIInd. (6) The same is shown by the bronze knife, XXVI, 43.

Thus on the one hand we are brought later than 1200 B.C.; at least for interments 4 to 7. While on the other hand we cannot come down to the XXIInd dynasty, 975 B.C. And various things indicate a closer connection with the earlier than with the later limit. As we should probably allow fifty years or a century for the gradual accumulation of these many burials, it seems most reasonable to date them between 1150 and 1050 B.C.; that is during the XXth dynasty. In any case it is a curious feature that the scarabs must have been nearly all old ones when buried. The latest is of Tahutmes III, or 1450 B.C., and probably contemporary with him, by the style of it: whereas the character of the beads, of the pottery, and of the coffin all shew that two or three centuries had elapsed since the scarabs were made. Either then they were heirlooms, though if so it is strange that none of the common ones of Ramessu II should be mixed with them; or else they had been dug up in plundering tombs, and reused. The latter is more likely; and this would agree again to the date of the XXth dynasty, as scarabs were seldom made then, and so no contemporary ones would be likely to be mixed with these.

If then we take 1100 B.C. as a middle date for the Phoenician pottery, and the Aegean vase, it will be reasonable. This consorts well with the dating for other Aegean pottery. The earliest geometrical false-necked vases are about 1400 B.C.; that early style appears to die out about 1200 B.C. (though no doubt coarser imitations may have been made later in the home of such products); and therefore the earliest figure pattern, such as this ivy, may well belong to a century later. This vase is of the same manufacture as two others that were found in Egypt with cuttle-fish ornamentation: they are larger than this but of the same outline (less the handle), and have similar bands and loopy pattern at the top line; one is in the Abbott collection at New York, the other from Erment is in the British Museum.

The value of the objects from the tomb depends entirely on the complete record of its contents, and the evidence which can be obtained as to their relative positions and ages. Unhappily, such records do not exist for more than a very few of the innumerable tombs that have been ransacked in Egypt. A flood of light on the history of the Deir el Bahri deposit would have been obtained, if we knew what were the positions of all the coffins and the minor objects. At what time that hiding place was first arranged; whether the priest-kings had already used it, before bringing in the earlier monarchs; who was originally buried here, and who was imported from elsewhere;—all these questions might have been solved if a record of the arrangement of the tomb had been made.

CHAPTER VI.

ILLAHUN IN THE TWENTY-SECOND DYNASTY.

46. After the fall of the town at Gurob, and the desolation of that site in the XIXth dynasty, a town appears to have risen into importance somewhere in the cultivated land. Kahun had been the town of the great dyke in the XIIth dynasty; after that fell Gurob rose, and was the principal place by the dyke, but at the south of it, instead of the north end; after that fell another town succeeded to the position of the town of the Fayum dyke. Probably this was at the present village of Illahun, or El Lahun, often called simply Lahun by the people. If it had been further off the burial place would have been on the gezireh or sandy rise of Abusir, and not on the western desert. The rise of desert from the north end of the dyke along to the pyramid of Illahun was then riddled with tombs; and the older tomb shafts, sunk deep in the rock around the pyramid, were cleared out and reused for burials of this degenerate time. Not many distinct points fix the age of this cemetery. It certainly comes after the XXth dynasty. It as certainly comes before the XXVIth. But few details help to fix it more precisely. The names which indicate a date are Neter-kheper-ra ("Kahun" XXV, 7) recalling Se-amen of the XXIst: Pima (K. XXV 13) recalling Pimai of the XXIInd: Nekht-bast-ru (K. XXV, 14) probably of the XXIInd: and Amenardus (K. XXVI) which is probably of the XXVth dynasty. The frequent figures of Bast point to the XXII-IIIrd dynasty, when her worship was prevalent; and the only scarab with a royal name is Ra-kheper, (XXIX, 33) which is of Sheshenk IV, XXIInd dynasty. The reinstatement of Crocodilopolis by Usarkon I, points to an attention to this district at that time; and it seems probably that he regulated the water works, and founded the town of Illahun on the dyke to attend to the locks. In any case we may well take the Illahun tombs as being of the XXIInd to XXVth dynasty; not a single object of the XXVIth dynasty has been found in the district. In connection with this period

a large wooden door was found in Kahun; it is 86 inches high, and 43 wide, and 1½ inch thick; the planks are all tongued together. Along the top and bottom a strap of bronze has passed round the hinge, as if to bind the cross bars on to the back-post; this was punched with the cartouches and titles of Usarkon I, and the wood was thus so impressed that it can be read though the bronze was removed. On the middle of the side was a large carved scene 20 inches square of Usarkon offering to Neit and Horus; this has been all scraped and cut away, so as to be hardly traceable. The door was covered with linen, and found lying flat in a chamber of the fourth north mansion at Kahun (see plan, "wooden door"). It must therefore have been removed from some building of Usarkon, and probably sold as old material, having the royal scene erased. Hence some large building of Usarkon I probably stood somewhere in this district. This door was kept for the Ghizeh Museum.

47. The objects from these tombs on PL. XXIX are of about the XXIInd dynasty; and represent well the characteristics of that age. The prevalent colour is pale yellowish green or light blue; the rich blues of the XVIIIth and XIXth dynasties, and the yellows, reds, and violets of the end of the XVIIIth are nowhere seen. But the compensatory quality of the Bubastite school was in modelling rather than in colour. The glazing, though tame and flat in tone, is very skilfully applied; the surface is just sufficiently coated, but not at all disguised, and the most minute details are not choked. The skill of modelling is seen in the delicate smooth figures (XXIX, 12, 14, 20), and the pierced work (21, 22), which is sometimes astonishingly fine (24). Similar open-work rings are found in a cemetery of the XXIInd dynasty at Zu welein, near Tanis.

Amulets we also see here appearing for the first time. On the burials of the XIXth dynasty but little is on the body, perhaps a ring, or a single figure which was valued; and around the body may be a wooden headrest, used in life, a ka-figure, two or three food vessels, and some ushabtis. But in the XXIInd dynasty the placing of funereal amulets on the body seems to have arisen to the exclusion of all else but ushabtis. In a burial which I should assign to the XXIst dynasty (see further on, sect. 49) there are scarabs but no amulets. But on later bodies are found some large coarse amulets; on one was a large plain beryl scarab on the chest, and a large lazuli bead on the neck; and an inscribed scarab of lazuli (*suten du hotep*, &c.) and two headrests of haematite (XXIX, 48) were found in the dust. These early amulets seem to be always coarse and clumsy; and it is not till the XXVIth to the XXXth dynasties that the love of funeral amulets reached such a pitch of development. The grand series of about 120 on Horuta (now arranged in the original order in the Ghizeh Museum) mark perhaps the highest range of the practice.

The scarabs of this period are different from all earlier ones. The designs are poor and rude, kings' names are scarce, and the colours are all of the poor light greens of this age, the glaze generally perishes. The most marked point in them is the use of long straight lines (see XXIX, 7, 35, 44, 46, 47, 50, 55); and the border line, which graces all the early scarabs, is sometimes omitted (as in XXIX, 46, 47, 49). Several classes which are well known in general collections can now be dated from the Illahun examples of the XXIInd dynasty. Such are the rude square plaques (XXIX, 1, 2, 44); the only examples known of kings are of the XXIst and XXIInd dynasties. The solar bark scarabs, (XXIX, 51, 55); the flat pottery ovals with a plain back (49, which has been broken and ground down on the edge); the rude deep-cut figures, (2, 28); and the groups of circles (1, 29), all appear to characterise the Bubastite time. Another peculiarity is in the use of stone beads (XXIX, 17, 26) of alabaster or calcite. The harder stones, carnelian, jasper, &c., seem to have disappeared altogether from use; and only these soft bulky, unsuitable beads are found, in harmony with the poor style of the other work. Strange beads of iron pyrites, and of antimony (XXX, 56), also occur. When made of pottery the larger beads are commonly ribbed, or cut into knobs all over, (57). The smaller glazed beads are very poor in colour; but they tried to make up for that by incongruous uses of them for decoration, threading them into patterns. The mummies of this age are sometimes covered, not only with a diagonal network of beads, but with designs done in coloured beads threaded closely together. The labour of thus producing an ungainly face or scarab must have been immense, and the taste of it is as defective as the colouring. When opening tombs of this age I always cut or drew the pegs, which fastened the coffin lids, as gently as possible. Then, looking in, I saw if there was any pattern beadwork on the body. If there were, the coffin was moved without the slightest shake, as all the threads were rotted out, and the beads lay loose. I then fetched a petroleum stove, and pot of wax; melting the wax down in the tomb I then slopped out spoonfuls of it over all the beads.

If too hot it sinks in too deep, and sticks to all the bandages below; it should be just on the point of chilling. If poured on to the beadwork it runs away in a narrow stream; it needs to be dashed on, sufficiently sharply to spread it, but not hard enough to move the beads. When the coat is laid, and has hardened, it may be lifted up with all the beads sticking together, and then transferred to a tray and fixed in with more wax. This is the only way to preserve these bead patterns when the thread has decayed; only those with firm thread—found in Upper Egypt—have hitherto been brought to museums. The most usual ornament in beadwork is a winged scarab on the breast, joined in—as such work always is—to the diagonal network which covers the mummy. The most elaborate example that I have seen had a diagonal net on the head, a beadwork face on the face joining to a beadwork collar which again joined to a scarab with wings: then a line of diagonal net and a *ba* bird with outspread wings; then three lines of diagonal and a Ma with outspread wings; then more diagonal work, and the row of four genii of Amenti, and some unintelligible patterning below that. The glass beads of plain colours have quite vanished; and the eye beads of Ramesside time (XVIII, 30) have turned into a rather scarce class of blue eye beads, with fine veins of brown and white around the eyes (XXIX, 52, 53).

48. We note also the first appearance of several classes which became very prominent in later times. The Ptah-sokar on the crocodiles (XXIX, 43, backed by Bast, with outspread wings) descended into the large class of Horus on the crocodiles. The head with a wide collar (commonly mis-named an aegis) (XXIX, 16) is very common down to Ptolemaic work. The large *uta* eyes (XXIX, 11, 18, 19), continue to the Roman age. The *menat* counterpoises (22) were often made in the Saite and Sebennyte dynasties. The small glazed figures of deities are very scarce before this time, but abundant in the later ages. Amulets first are found on the mummies now, and hence developed into such a great system in the Saite times. In short, we may go so far as to say that there is a wider gap between the manufactures of the XIXth and XXIInd dynasties—in that space of two centuries—than in any other period of Egyptian art. It is often hard to distinguish between things of the old and middle kingdom, or between the middle kingdom and the Empire; or between the Saites and Ptolemies. But between the XXIInd dynasty and all that went before it there is a profound separation. Whatever was common in that age continued in some form down to the end of Egyptian art, it was the beginning of the end. But all the striking manufactures of the Empire which had descended from earliest ages seem to come to an end with the Ramessides. Why this great separation should have taken place we cannot yet understand. The old schools must have become extinct in the poverty of the breaking up of the Empire. And the new men of the Delta must have obtained their habits from a fresh source.

49. We will now notice two or three special tombs in detail. In one tomb on the hill at the end of the dyke there was a short well leading to a small chamber, and beyond that another chamber. In this lay four coffins. The earliest naturally was that at the back, a lightly made coffin outlined to the figure, but with upright sides; a lid on the top with a coloured head and hands: this contained another similar, and inside that a good cartonnage case covering the whole mummy, and with a slit down the back where it was put in. The inscriptions on these were all real, (and not shams as are most of this age) and are given in "Kahun" XXV, 9, 10, 12. This coffin was banked around by chips of rock which cover the floor of the tomb to some depth. Upon this coffin lay a similar one, containing a cartonnage, also inscribed ("Kahun" XXV, 12). In front of these stood a false sarcophagus.

This style of burial was common in that age; a frame and panelling looking like a sarcophagus stood over the mummy; but it had no bottom, and stood on legs, and the top was all in one with the sides. It was simply set down over the mummy, which rested on the ground below it. This false sarcophagus was inscribed down the middle of the lid for Horuta, son of Au (K. XXV, 16) in blue on yellow; the ends had the old curve top sarcophagus design; the sides were painted in false door panels containing figures; and the edges and corner posts were all painted with inscriptions like that on the lid. Beneath this there lay a white cartonnage covering inscribed around the feet, and with a very deep necklace painted on it covering the body. In front of this was the last burial, a plain white lightly made figure coffin. There were no beads or amulets of any kind with the burials. The bodies and bandages fell to mere black dust when disturbed.

In another tomb which I did not clear out myself, were two sarcophagi; within them two large mummy cases with pink and yellow faces, and inscriptions painted in blue on the raw wood ("Kahun" XXV, 1, 3). They contained two singers of Amen, Ta-rat and Ta-bakem. On one sarcophagus were placed two hawks at the ends, cut in wood and painted; within were three coffins, one in the other; the innermost being stuccoed and gilt all over; but the gilding had all been tarred, and it fell to pieces on exposure. The eyes of all were inlaid with limestone and bronze lids and brows. The inscription (3) was around the feet of the outer coffin. All of these coffins peeled, and were destroyed by exposure to the air. On the mummy was a diagonal bead network, and the scarabs of PL. XXIX, 1 to 10. They were all shifted by moving the mummy case before I opened it. No. 1 is like plaques of Se-amen, XXIst dynasty; and as there is nothing characteristic of later times here, I should assign this burial to that age. No. 3 is peculiar, the design is pretty certainly Ramesside, yet the colour is exactly like that of No. 6. It suggests that there may have been a revival of copying old work for lack of a new style; and No. 6, early as it looks, may be an imitation made in the XXIst dynasty. The great gross Bes scarab, 4, may well be of this age also. Nos. 2, 5, 7, 9, 10, are all of the XXth or XXIst; 5 being an imitation of the Seti I and Tahutmes III scarabs. While 9, though of early style, shews by its colour that it is probably an imitation. Nos. 3 and 6 are set in copper bands.

The other mummy was in similar cases, but with the inscription 1 down the second case. On the body lay a gilt stucco band inscribed, (K. XXV, 2) and two genii, Amset and Kebhsenuf, of the same material. There were many small silver cowries mixed with the shifted beads of the network. The hair had been cut off, and lay in a truss beneath the head; a similar case I noted on a Roman mummy at Hawara, where a long mass of hair had been cut off, and laid down the front of the body under the bandages. At the feet of this burial was a large lot of very rude tiny ushabti, made of rough pressed pottery dipped into a blue wash: others lay by the middle, and a jar at the feet.

50. Another tomb, the finest of all at Illahun, is that of Amenardus; the whole contents of which were taken at the Bulak Museum. The innermost coffin of all had a nonsense inscription. Next to that was a splendid false sarcophagus, with all the inscriptions carved in the wood ("Kahun," XXVI); as it could not be safely moved entire, I took it to pieces, marked the parts, and transported it in perfect condition to Bulak ready to be set up. Beneath it stood a bier, framed of wood, with four lions' feet for legs to it. On that was the wooden sarcophagus, stuccoed white, and finely ribbed all over to imitate drapery. On the mummy was a network of beads, arranged thus; 5½ rows down to the beadwork scarab, 4 lines on each side of that, 1 row to the *ba* bird, 3 rows to the genii of Amenti, 3 rows down to a band, and 15 rows onward to the feet. Outside of this coffin were a jackal and hawk carved in wood and painted, fixed on the head and foot of the false sarcophagus. On another similar burial were the jackal and hawk; and inside a coffin of a woman with the same style of ribbed drapery modelled in stucco. At the head of each of these burials was a square box with a short obelisk standing up on the lid, painted white and red; in the box a quantity of very small clay ushabtis of the roughest kind. By the coffins were two small model false sarcophagi, duly inscribed with white paint along the edges and corners; and containing a large quantity of the same very rude ushabtis. At the sides of Amenardus were two carved and painted wooden Osiris figures. The Osiris Khent-amenti is about two feet high, well executed, and fixed on a tray or hand-barrow, for carrying it, with four handles at the corners. The Osiris Sokar is fixed on a block stand. The last interment was one of Pafui (K. XXV, 17), which was a square coffin, containing a stuccoed figure-case with polished red face. This tomb is perhaps the finest of that age on record; and I hope that in the Ghizeh Museum we may see the various objects placed together, and in their original arrangement, as a complete instance of an interment. The use of giving this detailed description is to illustrate the custom of the time, and to enable curators to understand the age and original purpose of the various stray things without a history which crowd our European collections.

51. To conclude, I will describe the typical details of the burials of the XXIInd dynasty. The coffin thin, straight sloping sides with a slight shoulder, and round head; sides upright. Lid flat board with an edge to it, inscription down the middle, usually nonsense, or the personal name omitted at the end. Head and shoulders in relief, and sometimes the hands; the face a carved block of wood, the head-dress formed of stucco, or more usually of Nile mud; brilliantly painted with red, blue, yellow, black and white; the decoration a wig and vulture head-dress. Inside lies a cartonnage of linen and plaster, modelled to the body form, split down the back, where the mummy was slipped into it. The surface generally white with a band of inscription down the middle: a spread vulture at the top of it sometimes with a ram's head: the face carved in wood

and inserted (hence come the multitude of such faces, as the cartonnages are often rotten or broken up) and the head painted with a wig. Sometimes the cartonnage is painted with scenes of offerings to gods all over it. The body inside seldom has any amulets and is usually mere black dust and bones.

Another type of burial is in the figure coffins carved out of a block; these are generally painted white; with an inscription sometimes down the front, sometimes around the feet. The face is white, or red, or green with a green and black wig. These cases do not contain a cartonnage; but only the body, black dust and bones.

CHAPTER VII.

PTOLEMAIC CEMETERY, GUROB.

52. In a rise of the desert to the north of the town of Gurob an extensive cemetery was formed in Ptolemaic times; and the style of it is so different to that of any other period, that it is worth notice. The usual form of the tombs was a pit about eight feet deep widening on the west side into a hollow scooped out in the sandy soil, in which sometimes as many as a dozen coffins were placed. The coffins were all unpainted; of rough brown wood, and thin. The outline was widening to the shoulders and tapering to the feet, like some bassoon cases inverted. The lids had very deep sides, and the coffins were mere shallow trays, with edges not over an inch high; thus just reversing the proportions of the coffins of the XXIInd dynasty. The only decoration of the coffin was a carved wooden head. These heads are of the most marvellous rudeness; a few are good enough to be grotesque, but others are things of which a Pacific islander would be ashamed. The noses are long triangular ridges, the eyes marked with two scores in the board, and the mouth with a third line. In some the nose is pegged on; and in others a ghastly attempt at improvement is made by painting black and white eyes. Within these grossly rough cases were comparatively fine cartonnages: The separate pieces of cartonnage at this time were the headpiece coming down with a spread on the chest; the pectoral or collar plate, semicircular; the open-work frame with figures of gods; the flat rectangular plate upon the legs, about 4 × 18 inches, with the four genii, and sometimes Isis and Nebhat; and the footcase, with sandals painted on the bottom or two slips separate on the soles of the feet. Sometimes only the head and sandals were used. The earlier heads were tolerably well made, of folds of linen pasted together, and moulded on a block. These blocks were in two parts; the back half, quite smooth behind, which could be withdrawn after moulding; and the front half, with the face in relief, which could be lifted out after the back half was gone. The cloth was pressed on wet, and retains the marks of the junction and carving of the mould. Over the cloth was a coat of stucco, painted dark blue, and often the face was gilt and burnished very skilfully. In later time, about Philadelphos, papyrus was substituted for cloth, and several layers of Demotic or Greek papyri were glued together, covered with stucco and painted; sometimes the face was gilt, sometimes yellow, or else white: the back of the head sometimes has scenes of offering painted on it; and this class of head cartonnage developed into the massive plaster headpieces of the Ist and IInd century found at Hawara, which lead up to the time of painted portraits (see "Hawara," Pl. IX). The later stage of this papyrus cartonnage was under Philadelphos and Euergetes, when they no longer glued together the papyri; but merely soaked them and plastered them one on the other; trusting to crossing them, and a good coat of plaster and glue on the outside, to hold them together.

The papyri recovered from the glued cases are mostly in a bad state; the gluing, the soaking, and separating, and washing, all injure the writing; and the glue has attracted insects, who in most cases have eaten the papyrus entirely away, and left nothing but a hollow double film of stucco. The later cases made with plain wetting are far the best source of papyri; and where a document has been used whole, and put on a flat part (as down the back, or in the pectoral), it may be taken out none the worse for its burial of over two thousand years.

53. Most of the mummies are bandaged, and then covered with a cross bandaging of narrow strips of linen, with edges folded in so as to make a neat band about half an inch wide. These bands overlie the cartonnage; and retain it on the mummy. Exactly the same system of bands is seen on the Roman mummies of Hawara; and there it developed into a regular ornamentation of recessed squares (Hawara, IX, 4) which afterwards had plaster knobs, gilt or coloured, set in the bottom of the hollows. Every stage which leads up to this complicated decoration can be traced.

Some burials were in a different style. Often rush-cases were used instead of wood; they were made with a framework of sticks skilfully covered with rushes to form the sides, and with a hinging lid. Also rush canopies, or baldacchinos, were set up over these coffins, gaudily painted in pink and white: but they were too frail to last.

The only substantial coffin in this cemetery was one made of hard wood, well finished; with figures of Isis and Nebhat, at head and feet, cut in, and filled with green wax; the whole surface was varnished. Inside was a gilt face headpiece, pectoral, Ma, open-work frame, legpiece and sandals. Two other bodies had been thrust into this coffin.

I may note here that the Roman glass (PL. XXXIII) was found together in one tomb at Gurob, excepting Nos. 9, 10, 12, 13, 14, which are later. The main group I suppose to be about the time of Constantine. It is now in the glass department, British Museum. The blue glass vase (13) with white thread on it is probably about the VIIIth cent. A.D. judging by the clothing found with it.

The wood carvings at the foot of PL. XXXII are of about the VIIth cent. A.D. from the cemetery at Illahun. Now at South Kensington.

CHAPTER VIII.

PTOLEMAIS AND OTHER SITES.

54. It has long been a difficulty in the Geography of Ptolemy, that the city of Ptolemais was placed in the Arsinoite nome, some miles south of Arsinoe: and yet it was called a port. The most usual settlement has been by ignoring the connection with Arsinoe and the nome, and placing it on the Nile. It is indeed very possible that such was the original mistake of Ptolemy himself, from supposing that a port must be on the main river, and misunderstanding his materials. Some years ago I pointed out, in "Naukratis," how we must use Ptolemy by extracting from him the original groups of materials, as far as we can; and that we must ignore the cross-references from one line of measurements to another, between which his errors accumulated. Here it is evident that he had a fact of two cities in the Arsinoite nome, the capital and the port of Ptolemais; and he treats in an entirely different part of the two other towns of the Fayum, Bakkhis and Dionysias, naming them along with Lake Moiris, and apparently on the line from Mareotis down to the oases. The position of Arsinoe is beyond question; and therefore the fact which Ptolemy gives is that Ptolemais was 10′ south of Arsinoe, and in the Fayum.

This would lead us to look for it along the canal which skirts the south-east of the Fayum basin. I have walked along all that line; it is impossible for the canal to have followed any other course anciently: the hills rise on the one hand, and the Fayum basin falls on the other. To get water along to the ruined towns and villages about Gharak this present line of canal is the only possible course. It is even now a large canal, which might take boats; and it must have been much larger in Roman times, as a far greater quantity of land was then irrigated than is now under cultivation in this district. It is therefore certain that a navigable canal ran along here in Roman times, and so there is no difficulty in the port of Ptolemais having been on this line. I searched every mound of ruin, but found nothing of any importance,—mostly being Arab sites,—until reaching Talit, the present end of the wide canal, marked as "Ptolemais" on PL. XXX. This position is 12′ from Arsinoe, instead of 10′; which is as near as Ptolemy's precision allows, since he only states the nearest 5′. And it is S.S.W. instead of S., which is tolerably close to the position. The port or end of the navigable canal cannot have been further on, as the ground falls away, and necessitates dividing the water into separate courses. Hence taking only Ptolemy's geography and the configuration of the country we should be led to this site.

55. But a totally separate means of identification exists in the inscription (PL. XXXII), recording a dedication to Nero by the Ptolemaians. This slab was found in the fort which protected the town from the desert. The exact translation of it is not quite settled; and for this point the paper of Canon Hicks, at the close of this chapter, should be considered. This much is clear that the external argument as to the site, is clinched by the internal proof afforded by the inscription.

The ruins of Ptolemais adjoin the side of the canal (PL. XXXI) and cover a space about 1000 feet wide from north to south, and 1300 feet long. This area for a town would contain two to four thousand inhabitants, according to the population of modern Egyptian towns. But the inscription appears to mention 6470 taxpayers, which would imply a population of about thirty thousand. So the persons referred to must have belonged to a much larger area than this town. As the present population of the

Fayum is 150,000, when it was much more widely cultivated in Roman times it may have held 250,000. So that this decree would concern about an eighth of the province, which was probably the size of the district of which Ptolemais was the principal town.

56. At present the ruins have been much dug away for the sake of the earth to spread on the fields; but nothing before the Roman period is exposed, and there is no height of accumulation, so that the city had evidently but a brief history. Some of the streets can be traced, and are shewn on the plan (PL. XXXI); also a raised square area of an important building—now swept away—near the end of the canal. Part of a massive building of red baked Roman brick remains at the south-east; much of it has been destroyed lately, and more waits to be uncovered. At the west side a group of pillars and bases shew where a large building existed, which was probably a Christian church, judging by the capitals with wreaths and crosses of the IVth cent. I carefully enquired for inscriptions or sculptures, but only saw one fragment, which is given here on PL. XXXI. The only other portable antiquity was a bronze steelyard. It had two scales on it, whereby we can recover the unit which it was intended to weigh, although the scalepan, chains, hook, and counterpoise are lost. The unit of it is 7000 ± 200 grains; this is evidently the Attic mina, which was the "common mina" in Greco-Roman Egypt.

The line drawn on the S.E. of Ptolemais is a trench cut in the rock, about 200 yards from the town; it was an ancient work to enable surplus water in the canal to be run off into the low Gharak basin to the south, so as to lower the canal in case of need. It has been lately turned up in some part for the sake of the lining; and other parts could be traced by a dry line on the ground after rain.

57. The fort, a little over a mile to the S.W. of the town, is the place where the inscription was found, so far as I could learn. When the new sluice gates were being built at the end of the canal, the contractor excavated at this fort for materials. Indeed it is a stipulation in some contracts that only ancient bricks are to be used, as they are so superior to the modern native produce. While excavating the ruins, the fragments of this inscription were found built into a wall. The contractor sent them to Mr. Marshall Hewat, the district inspector, who very kindly passed them on to me. From a rough copy which he sent I saw that Ptolemais was referred to, and I took the first leisure time I could to go over and see the place.

The position of the fort is excellent. It stands on the rise of desert nearest to the town, and at the same time it commands a desert horizon at least five or six miles away all along the south. Thus any raid of Bedawin could be noticed in time to repel it. There is a square mass of ruined building and rubbish about 125 feet E. to W., and 150 ft. N. to S. An outer wall enclosed a space 67 feet wide on the east; a rubbish mound is banked against the west face for about 150 feet out; and another lower heap stands about 120 feet away on the north. It is about half a mile from cultivated land; and the magnetic bearings are to canal end 31°, to Hawara pyramid 47½°, to Tutun 65°, to Gharak 338°. But the position of Tutun on the map must be altered to make this possible.

The three patches of ruins between Ptolemais and Medinet Madi are small villages of Roman age; in the furthest I found an Alexandrian coin of the first century. The mound of Medinet Madi I had not time to visit.

58. Before proceeding to describe other sites I should say that the map PL. XXX does not profess accuracy in details of canals, &c. The faultiness of all existing maps is scandalous. Any person with a compass might make a better map than any yet existing of the Fayum. On all the older maps the Birket Kurun is entirely wrong in form and place; the present outline is taken from a government "map of the basins of the Fayum and Wady Rayan"; but the canals are I believe better laid out on the war office map. That is tolerably good in general; but quite wrong on the Birket, and in error as to the positions of villages. It is seldom that a group of cross bearings can be taken that will plot on the existing map without discrepancies being shewn. My present business is merely to fix the ancient sites as well as I can, and I disclaim any responsibility for the errors of this map.

A great feature of the ancient Fayum is the canal all along the eastern side. This originally branched near Hawara, but since Roman times it has been allowed to be breached, and has been dried up for probably all the Arabic period. In consequence a broad band of country has been thrown out of cultivation; and it only needs the reopening of this canal to bring into use again over thirty square miles, or twenty thousand acres, of good land. Probably now the bed of the Bahr Yusuf has been so much eroded by flushes of water that it would be needful to make a new branch canal from the great dyke to feed this old line ; but even that would be a trifling work compared to the cultivation which would ensue.

All along the line of this canal are Roman towns which shew what the populousness of this district must have been. I shall here give notes on this side of the country from Illahun northwards.

On the highest point of the hills N.E. of Illahun, about a couple of hundred feet over the Nile, the ground is composed of rolled blocks (up to three feet long) and washed stuff, which slopes down to the west. And similarly the top of the highest ridge, where the "Mastaba" is marked, on the culmination between the Fayum and the Nile, (some four hundred feet up, I suppose) is all composed of rough pebble beds. These shew that the whole Nile valley has been full of a mass of river gravels up to some hundreds of feet above the present bed; and that all the depth has been cut away by denudation.

59. On the north of the railway the ground is scattered with Roman pottery up to the Kom, No. 1 (PL. XXX), which is a village of Roman age. About ¾ mile N.E. of this is a massive foundation 8 feet thick of stone and cement, which has lately been mined into. About here are patches of sand deposit six feet thick, lying on the general ground of Nile alluvium. How this accumulated is not clear. The Nile mud doubtless accumulated down to Ptolemaic times, when the Fayum began to be dried up below Nile level. It is possible that shallow water lay here landlocked for two or three centuries during the drying, and that thus the blown sand of the desert accumulated here. When once sand falls into still waters it cannot escape either by wind or currents, but it raises the bottom level. A very striking evidence of the old high level of the Fayum lake is seen at the inside of the province, west of Gurob. There a great shingle bank has been formed by a current about 20 feet above the level of the canal there, which would be about the old high lake and Nile level. Between Kom 1 and Kom 2 the old edge of the lake is very distinct, about 30 feet above the present ground there. Kom 2 is all late Roman, a village of some extent. The Mastaba is a landmark of all this part of the country; and can be seen from Hawara, as a white heap on the hill top. It is formed of rough stone blocks laid with desert clay. It was built cumulatively, with successive finished faces, but not finely coated with casing on each. It is about 90 feet square and 25 feet high. A great gash has been cut into it in a murderous fashion on the North side; in the same way that the pyramids of Dahshur Kula, and others have been barbarously mangled of late years. Nothing appears to have been found here, the middle being cleared down to three feet below the pavement level. This is probably a building of the XIIth dynasty; but who lay beneath it we shall hardly find until it is properly explored. The wild hill on which this stands has been trenched in all directions by rainfall, and rises into sharp crests too narrow to stand on, along the top; sloping down to Medum on one hand, and falling in cliffs down into the Fayum on the other. At the west foot of it is a village, perhaps of Cufic date.

60. The Kom 3 is a large town of Roman age; to this belongs the cemetery just behind it in the hill, from whence the collection of portraits was brought which was taken to Vienna a few years ago. This is known as Rubaiyat from the name of the nearest village in the Fayum. The cemetery is about quarter of a mile across. Many chambers are cut in the rock, some with loculi. One square chamber has two ridge roof loculi at each side and the end. Fragments of blue glazed pottery of the IIIrd–IVth cent. A.D. lie about. Another chamber is circular, with eight loculi around it. The road to Kafr Amar in the Nile valley runs through the cemetery. I met here with an enthusiastic agriculturist, Mr. Hugh Main, who is trying to utilise this land by a small canal which waters enough for a farm. He very kindly escorted me up to the cemetery, as some bad thieves were in the neighbourhood; afterwards however I went about this desert for two days alone, without meeting anything worse than two needlessly inquisitive men, and a hyaena.

61. About Kom 4 is a chamber near the canal, of baked brick; and thence the ground is covered with pottery up to the Kom. This town is half a mile across, of Roman age. Much pottery of the IVth and Vth cent. A.D., much green glass, and columns of grey marble, and red granite, lie about here.

The canal then bends round the foot of a slight rise, at Kom 5; the hills being about two miles back here. Just west of this Kom are the stumps of nine old palm trees which shew very plainly in the distance; and further west is a brick wall. About this bend of the canal are some long square blocks of stone upright in the ground. They hardly look ancient, and might be the remains of an allotment of the ground some time when a canal was projected here. But I do not know of any such modern project.

Kom el Akl, No. 6, is a large town, about half a

mile across with high mounds. The surface pottery is of the IIIrd and IVth cent. A.D. and it must have been founded some centuries before that to allow of such accumulation. As it is by the road into the Fayum this might well be an older town of the time before the lake was dried up. I noticed a mass of deep foundation of stone. The tombs east of it are visible for some distance; they are cut in a low cliff facing south; about six or eight chambers; no ornaments or inscriptions.

62. Kom Wezim, No. 7, has been a great town, the most important of all the district. It is about half a mile across, and the top of the mound is about a hundred feet above the plain below, some of which height is artificial accumulation of ruins, about fifteen feet in parts. The most remarkable matter is the number of great weights lying about in the ruins. They are of the round dome-top type of late Egyptian weights. One is 19·8 inches across base, 22·3 across top, sides average 11·9 high, and dome 4·8 high. This will be therefore 5146· cubic inches. The stone is a local shelly limestone; and assuming its specific gravity at 2·3, it would weigh about 2,990,000 grains. It has a mark W on the side, which may be M inverted.

A piece of another such weight, now broken up, lies near this. A third weight has the top broken off; 12 across base, and still 9¼ high. If in similar proportion to the other it would weigh 223 of the larger; so it might be either a quarter or a fifth of it. A fourth great weight is about 19 across base, and 22 across top, 12·2 high on side, and dome 4·0 high, or evidently the same as the first one. The standard of this weight can hardly be settled from one example. If the mark is M it would mean 40 if Greek, or 1000 if Roman: 40 leads to no known standard; but divided by 1000 it yields 2990 grains or the unit of the Nusa, or double uten, which was common at Memphis. (See "Season in Egypt" and "Hawara"). Besides these weights I noted the bases of stone columns, 30 inches across; and a curious slab of stone with a rudely-cut figure of a man in relief on it, arms crossed on breast, but legs not developed. It is quite un-Egyptian, and probably Roman.

Behind Kom Wezim, on the hill to the north, are many tomb chambers and graves, several of which had just been looted before I went there. The meaning of such an important town at this side of the lake seems intelligible on seeing that the present road from the Natron Lakes runs close to this. Before the lake was lowered this would be the port of the road to Nitria, from which boats would sail across the lake and out through the canal into the Nile. Whatever traffic in grain or heavy goods went either way the large weights would be needed for it. In short, Kom Wezim was the port of Nitria in the pre-Roman times.

In the hills, to the N.E. of this, the ground is most curiously weathered into domes, several feet diameter, which stand crowded together all over the surface; at a little distance they appear almost like the dome roofs of a village. The white spot marked is a distinguishing point on the range of low hills in the desert. All this side of the country is utter desert; the eye wanders over miles of undulating sand and rock; gradually rising in steps higher and higher to the north.

The restoration of this district of the Fayum to its former fertility would be a very easy and inexpensive matter; a few miles of new canal, and a clearing of the old bed, is all that is required in order to provide for many thousands of people.

APPENDIX TO CHAPTER VIII.

INSCRIPTION OF PTOLEMAIS.

By the Rev. Canon HICKS.

63. (See the facsimile of the original stone, and the restored transcription on PL. XXXII.) This inscription is a dedication in honour of the Emperor Nero, dated A.D. 60, from the town of Ptolemais in Middle Egypt. The dedication is made by the town at large 'in the person of' or 'by the hands of (dia) the 6470,' and 'by the whole body of men who came to the age of 18 in the 2nd year of the Emperor Claudius' (A.D. 42).

The phrasing of the dedication is very brief, and the meaning of the allusions obscure. Who were 'the 6470'? Why are the ephebeukotes of A.D. 42 so prominently mentioned? And why is that year brought so closely into connection with the seventh year of Nero's reign?

To these questions we may hazard a conjectural answer. In the first place Egypt was one of the chief granaries of Rome. One-third of the annual corn-supply came to Rome in Alexandrian vessels, Mr. Petrie also discovered, from the large number of corn-mills and other indications, that Ptolemais, standing as it did at the end of the Canal, must have been an important lading-place for the corn-produce of Middle Egypt. But moreover, Egypt had to bear under the Romans, as indeed she has always done before and since, a heavy burthen of taxation: her conquerors have always claimed a full share of those fruits which are 'the boon of the Nile.' Every five years, it would seem, the Præfect revised the Egyptian census for the purpose of taxation (Marquardt, *Röm. Staatsverwaltung*, ii. p. 244; Franz, *C. I. G.* iii. p. 319), while the precise strain that the country could bear was nicely calculated every season by help of the Nilometer (Marquardt, *ibid.*; Franz, *ibid.* p. 318). No wonder therefore if we find that some of the most important Egyptian inscriptions deal with the remission of burthens. The Rosetta stone (B.C. 198) is full of this subject. It is the occasion of the important decree of Ti. Julius Alexander, Præfect of Egypt under Galba (Sept. 28, A.D. 68: *C. I. G.* 4957). Accordingly it is not an improbable conjecture that the Emperor Claudius, in whose reign there was a scarcity felt in Rome on more than one occasion, may have granted the inhabitants of Ptolemais some remission of taxation: possibly some poll-tax (Franz, *C. I. G.* iii. p. 318) payable by every adult male of Ptolemais, was either lightened or removed, in return for an increase in the amount of corn shipped from Ptolemais. If so, 'the 6470' will be the adult male population of the town in A.D. 42; and not only were these relieved, but also the young men who attained their ἐφηβεία, *i.e.* the age of eighteen, in that year, were by anticipation brought within the scope of the decree; although they would not be of full age, and therefore (I suppose) not liable to taxation, before the age of twenty. These 6470 *plus* the ephebi of the year A.D. 42 seem to have retained their privilege until the reign of Nero, and therefore are specified thus exactly in this dedication of the year A.D. 60; we may infer that Nero confirmed the privileges granted by Claudius.

The words πόλις (line five), ἐφηβευκότες and (perhaps) πανδημεί (line 12) need not imply that Ptolemais (though its name would imply the præ-Roman foundation) enjoyed any municipal constitution after the Greek pattern. Indeed there is a significant absence of the words βουλή or δῆμος, or of a civic eponymos: with which contrast the dedication to Alexander Severus from the boulē of Antinoe (*C. I. G.* 4705). Strabo mentions it as a remarkable exception in Egypt that Ptolemais in the Thebaid had a communal government (xvii, p. 813). Only three other towns, Naukratis, Alexandria, and Antinoe are known to have been similarly organised on Greek lines; and, of these, Alexandria had no boulē. Augustus and his successors looked upon the Egyptians as a seditious rabble, unfit for any measure of home-rule; the unit of civic organization was the Nome or district, and we may suppose the population of Ptolemais to have been simply merged—for all political purposes—in the population of the Nome. The word polis (line 5) does not tell the other way: Sais is likewise termed a polis (*C. I. G.* 4697 *e*). Nor need ἐφηβεύειν (line 12) involve the gymnasium and the education of the young Greek citizen, and those other interesting associations which the word suggests to the readers of Attic literature: it merely seems here to express a particular age.

The second year of Claudius (line 9) was, to speak exactly, from Jan. 25 A.D. 42 to Jan. 25, A.D. 43. It is noted by Dio Cassius (lx, 11) that in A.D. 42 there was a severe scarcity at Rome, and that this even suggested to Claudius the idea of building the harbour at Ostia. This statement prepares us to believe, what has already been suggested above, that Claudius this year may have given some special encouragement to the exporters of corn from Ptolemais.

The date in Nero's reign (line 14) is noteworthy for a different reason. Mommsen shows (*Staatsv.* ii. 798, note) that in the second year of Nero's reign a new method of reckoning his years was adopted, so that his 'seventh year' does not mean Oct. 13, A.D. 60—Oct. 13, A.D. 61, but rather December 10, A.D. 59—Dec. 10, A.D. 60. If this be the year of our dedication, it is dated a few months after Nero had outraged human nature by the murder of his mother, and had shocked Roman prudery scarcely less by his appearance on the stage. But neither event affected the fortunes or the feelings of these far-off dwellers on the Nile, and when they style Nero the 'saviour and benefactor of the world' (lines 3–5) they are using the commonplaces of provincial compliment. In *C. I. G.* 4699 (from Memphis) he is called ὁ ἀγαθὸς δαίμων τῆς οἰκουμένης.

Next to the name of the site, the most interesting information yielded by the inscription is the name of the Præfect Lucius Julius ——us. Unfortunately his cognomen is lost, but this name is new. He must have succeeded Tib. Cl. Balbillus, who was appointed Præfect of Egypt A.D. 56 (see Franz, in *C. I. G.* iii. p. 311).

CHAPTER IX.

THE GREEK PAPYRI.

By Prof. SAYCE.

64. Mr. Petrie's excavations at Gurob have revived for us the era of the Renaissance. In that exciting period the scholars of western Europe found a new world of ancient Greek literature outspread before their view; manuscript upon manuscript containing the treasures of early Greek thought passed into their hands, and invited them to fresh discoveries and an ever-widening revelation of the past.

But the oldest manuscript at their disposal was of comparatively late date. It was as a general rule separated from the age of the author of the work inscribed upon it by an interval of several centuries. Moreover a time came when the supply of fresh manuscripts was exhausted. The age of discovery seemed past and the age of criticism and collation began.

From time to time, however, more especially since the opening up of the East to European travel and exploration, fragments of classical literature have been discovered, a few of which have contained new texts. Most of them have been derived from Egypt. It was from Egypt, for instance, that the lost oration of Hypereides was brought as well as the hymn of Alkman to the Dioskouroi, and it has been Egypt which has provided us with the oldest manuscripts as yet known of the Homeric poems.

But all that Egypt has hitherto yielded to us is far surpassed by the latest discoveries of Mr. Petrie. That fortunate excavator has disinterred classical Greek papyri of an age of which the most sanguine scholar had not ventured to dream; he has found private correspondence which throws light on the social history of the Greek settlers in Egypt in the early days of the Ptolemaic dynasty, records of wills which will cast a most important light on Greek law, private accounts which inform us of prices and taxation in the Fayoum in the third century B.C., a portion of a lost play of Euripides, and last, but not least, fragments of a precious copy of the *Phædo* of Plato, which must have been written not long after the lifetime of the philosopher himself. When we consider that the earliest manuscript of Plato's writings hitherto known is as late as the ninth century after the Christian era, the value of this copy of the *Phædo* cannot be overestimated. It enables us to test the accuracy of the received text and to determine the extent to which the editors of Alexandria and their successors allowed themselves to correct or modify the texts which they published.

The papyri have been discovered in a way which makes it possible that other early Greek texts may be similarly brought to light, even in the Museums of Europe. At Gurob Mr. Petrie discovered a small cemetery of the Ptolemaic age, where the dead had been embalmed in the Egyptian style and buried in mummy-cases and coffins. These he dug up, and on examining the cartonnage of which the head-pieces and breasts of the cases were composed, came to the conclusion that it was—in many instances at all events—made up of pieces of inscribed papyrus. Practical experiment proved that his conjecture was right, and further showed that the papyri were mostly inscribed with Greek texts, though a large part of them contains demotic texts. An examination of their contents has made it clear that the Egyptian undertaker, before making a mummy case, bought the waste-paper basket of one of his neighbours, and turned the papers that were in it into *papier-mâché* for the particular mummy-case he had on hand. Hence it happens that the papyri coming from a particular mummy all belong to the same collection, the cartonnage of one mummy-case, for example, being composed of letters and documents relating to a certain Kleôn, that of another of the papers belonging to Diophanês, and so on. Of course in some instances the same collection served to produce *papier-mâché* for more than one mummy-case.

The importance of the circumstances under which the papyri have been found will be apparent when we come to discuss the date of the fragments of the *Phædo*. Many of the fragments are dated, and in all the various collections the dates belong to the same period. This is the latter part of the reign of Ptolemy Philadelphus, and the first few years of the reign of his successor. Roughly speaking most of the documents belong to about B.C. 250; none (so far as I know) are later than B.C. 225.

The dated documents are either private letters, or accounts, or the rough copies of wills. They are all of an ephemeral character; there is nothing among them which the owner would have cared to keep for more than a year or two. Their destination was the waste-paper basket as soon as the immediate purpose was served for which they were written.

We may therefore conclude that they passed into the undertaker's hands shortly after the time to which the dates upon them refer. In many cases this would be about B.C. 250, in no case after B.C. 220.

The importance of Mr. Petrie's discovery now becomes evident. Here we have a body of Greek documents considerably older than the oldest hitherto known, older even than the age of the great grammarians and critics of Alexandria and their editions of the earlier classical texts. With the exception of some *graffiti* which I copied on the walls of the temple of Seti at Abydos in 1883 they present us with the first examples of Greek cursive writing as yet met with, and raise the question whether the cursive Greek ostraka from Karnak, which have been assigned by Dr. Wilcken and myself to the reign of Ptolemy Physkôn, do not really belong to that of Ptolemy Philadelphus. These were the only two Ptolemies whose reigns were long enough to allow of certain of the dates met with on the ostraka.

65. If Mr. Petrie's papyri consisted merely of private letters and wills their antiquity would make them sufficiently interesting. But the interest is increased tenfold when we find among them fragments of the works of Plato and Euripides. The Platonic fragments belong to the *Phædo.* They number ten in all, some of them being of considerable size. They form part of a papyrus which must have been of great length since the whole of the *Phædo* seems to have been written upon it, and probably some other philosophical work as well. The average width of the papyrus was 8½ inches, and it was of a fine and carefully-prepared quality. The text was inscribed upon it in parallel columns, each from 5⅓ to 5⅚ inches in length, and averaging from 2½ to 3 inches in breadth. The lines, however, are of very unequal length, as the scribe always ends the line with a word. Between each column a space is left which averages half an inch, though sometimes it is as much as an inch and sometimes as little as a quarter of an inch. At the foot of the papyrus a margin is left a little over 1½ inches in length (4 centimeters); the margin at the top of the page does not measure more than an inch. The text is written in capitals, and the divisions of the dialogue are denoted by a horizontal line drawn between the last word of one speaker and the first word of the next, or else over the first letter (or first two letters) of the following line. Other diacritical marks there are none.

The fragments begin in the middle of chapter xii (67 E of Reiske's edition), and include the first half of chapter xiii. Then there is a break, and they recommence with the last few words of chapter xxvi. They further comprise the greater part of chapters xxix and xxx, about a quarter of ch. xxxi, and half of ch. xxxii, the whole of chapter xxxiii and the first three-fourths of ch. xxxiv.

The text differs in many important respects from the received one, and is distinguished by a consistent neglect of the hiatus and by the use of ἄν with the future indicative. The neglect of the hiatus shows that the received text has undergone a complete recension at the hands of critics who objected to it, and so overthrows the theories that have been based on the supposed observance of the hiatus by Plato. The consistent use of ἄν with the future in so carefully-written a manuscript may be commended to the notice of the authorities on Greek grammar.

More serious are the numerous and important variations of the papyrus from the received text of the *Phædo* which rests on the evidence of one of our oldest and best Greek MSS. (now in the Bodleian Library, and dated A.D. 896). The variations will somewhat shake the confidence of scholars in the purity of the tradition embodied in the texts of the Greek writers which have been handed down to us, at all events so far as regards the texts which go back to a pre-Alexandrine period.

The papyrus must have been a very precious one. Its size and splendour, the extreme care which has been bestowed upon the preparation of the text, and the accuracy with which it has been written, all show that it was of exceptional value. Before any portions of it could have found their way to a waste-paper basket and been handed over to an undertaker to be turned into cartonnage, it is clear that it must already have been some time in use. But if this were the case about B.C. 250 it could not well have been written later than B.C. 300, and is probably of much earlier date. It is thus not only the oldest manuscript we possess of a Greek author, but it is even possible that it may have been written in the lifetime of Plato himself.

66. By the side of the fragments of Plato the two pages of papyrus which contain portions of a lost play of Euripides somewhat pale in interest. But the play was one which was famous in antiquity, and though a few passages from it have been preserved, only one of these is to be found in the portions which have now come to life. The play was that known as the *Antiopê*, and the fragments discovered by Mr. Petrie belong to the concluding part of it. They consist of two pages which may have formed part of a single roll, each page containing two columns of

text. The page was $8\frac{1}{2}$ inches in length, with a margin at the top 1 inch wide and at the bottom $1\frac{1}{2}$ inches wide. The space between the columns averages $\frac{3}{8}$ of an inch. Each column contains 37 lines of text written in capitals. The dialogue is distinguished by horizontal lines drawn over the first letter or two of the line which introduces a new speaker. Unfortunately the fragments are in a bad condition. The majority of the lines are imperfect partly through injury to the papyrus, partly through the obliteration of the letters by the plaster with which they have been smeared.

The first fragment seems to contain a dialogue between Dirkê and Lykos, in which reference is made to the exposure and supposed death of the two sons of Antiopê, Zêthos and Amphiôn. This is followed by a dialogue between the sons and their mother which leads on to the death of Dirkê. In the next fragment the chorus is introduced, and Lykos then appears upon the scene, exclaiming: "Ah me! I am to die, unaided, at the hands of two." To this Zêthos replies: "But do you not lament your wife who is now among the dead?" "How so?" is the answer, "is she dead? 'tis of a new evil that thou speakest." "Yes," says Zêthos, "she is dead, torn in pieces with thongs of bull-hide." "By whom?" asks Lykos; "by you? for I must needs learn this." Lykos, however, is saved at the critical moment by the appearance of Hermês, who orders him to bury his wife, and after burning her bones on the funeral pyre to throw them into the "Spring of Arês," which henceforth should bear the name of Dirkê, and flow through the city, watering the land and saving it from bane. Hermês then turns to the two brothers, who are to provide "the city of Kadmos" with seven gates "in order that it may be holy," while at the same time a lyre made from the shell of a tortoise is given to Amphiôn. Amphiôn is appointed King of Thebes in place of Lykos, he and his brother receiving "the highest honours in the city of Kadmos," and preparations are made for the marriage of Amphiôn with Niobê "the daughter of Tantalos," from among the "distant Phrygians," and to send for her at once,[1] and Lykos concludes the play with a sort of paternal blessing. He yields the throne to his two sons, telling them from henceforth to govern the land instead of himself, "taking the sceptres of Kadmos." He goes on to state that he will fling the ashes of his wife into the spring as had been ordered by Hermês, and concludes with the words, "I put an end to strife and to all that is past."

Among the lines preserved in the papyrus are two, belonging to a chorus, which have been quoted by Stobaios (Ecl. i. 3, 25, p. 118), a writer who flourished in the fifth century A.D. The variations between the text as given by the papyrus and by Stobaios are very considerable, and confirm the inferences derived from the fragments of the *Phædo* that the text of the Greek writers of the pre-Alexandrine period has come to us in a much modified condition. It is needless to insist upon the importance of this conclusion to the scholar.

Another fragment of a classical character is a page which contains two imperfect columns of writing and the ends of lines belonging to a third. It was found along with documents dated in the 39th year of Ptolemy Philadelphus (B.C. 247). The text is written in large capitals but in a schoolboy's hand, and is probably the rhetorical exercise of a pupil to whom it was given to learn by heart. It is a passage in the form of a dialogue from some rhetorical or philosophical work, now lost, which describes the duty of being true to one's friends and draws an illustration from Akhillês, who "tho' deprived even of his armour ran the greatest risks and alone of any who have ever yet been born encountered death on behalf of his dead companion."

67. The classical fragments, however, form but a small part of the collection. This consists mainly of private letters, rough copies of wills, receipts and tax-gatherers' accounts. They throw a vivid light on the social history of the Greek inhabitants of Egypt at the time they were written, on the manners and customs of the Ptolemaic period, and the economical condition of the country. They bear out the conclusion recently arrived at by Prof. Mahaffy in his work on *Greek Life and Thought from Alexander to the Roman Conquest*, that the Greeks were much more widely scattered through Egypt in the age of the Ptolemies than has hitherto been supposed. They were to be found not only in the great centres of political life, Alexandria, Arsinoê Krokodilopolis, Ptolemais and Diospolis or Thebes, but also in the country, Mr. Petrie's papyri showing that the country villages of the Fayoum were full of them. They represented, in fact, not only the modern Greek traders, but also the Turks of more recent days, and constituted the main bulk of the higher official and landed classes. Greek soldiers occupied country-seats where the native peasants worked for them, and

[1] Hermes also declares that Amphiôn and Zêthos shall be "called the white twin-foals of Zeus."

Greek traders carried on a large part of the commerce of the Nile.

That the copies of the wills Mr. Petrie has discovered were merely rough draughts is evident from the numerous corrections which have been introduced into them. The same is the case as regards a good many of the letters. These, too, have been corrected freely, the corrections being written in smaller letters over the line. Like the accounts, therefore, they possessed only an ephemeral value, and hence soon found their way to the waste-paper basket. It is fortunate for us that they did so.

68. The tax-gatherers' accounts throw considerable light on the geography of the Fayoum, and indicate the extent to which the district had been colonised by the Greeks after Alexander's conquest of Egypt. Many of the villages that surrounded the capital Krokodilopolis, now marked by the mounds of Medinet el-Fayoum, received Greek names, from which we may infer that they had in many cases grown up around the farm or country-house of some Greek proprietor. Thus we hear of the villages of Ptolemais, Lagis, Bakkhias, Berenikis, Thesmophoros, Theogonis, Autodikê, Philadelpheia and Theadelpheia, Philôteris, Koitoi ("the beds"), Philagris, Arsinoê Kastammônia, Hêphaistias, Dionysias, Lysimakhis, and Euêmeria, as well as of the village of Arsinoê, "the village of the cowherds," "the village of Athêna," "the town of the ovens" (probably a part of Krokodilopolis), "the harbour of Ptolemais," "the island of Dikaios," "the island of Hêra," "the sacred island of the city" (of Krokodilopolis), and the "island of Alexander." Besides these we meet with Hellenised Egyptian names: Boubastos (to be distinguished from Bubastis in the Delta), Petesoukha, Moukhis, Talithis, Thphôis, Kerkesoukha (a name which helps to explain that of Kerkasôros or Kerkesoura in the Delta, Hdt. ii. 15), Karanis, Malsoutos, Anoubias, Sempathyteus, Tegotys, Tebetria, Psinteôs, Paious and Ibiôn. The most curious name among them is Samareia, which must have been so called by settlers from the northern part of Palestine. The accounts further contain the names of Oxyrinkha (never written Oxyrinkhos), now Behnesa, and Aphroditopolis, now Atfîh, which were included in the province of the Fayoum, as well as those of Lêtopolis, Memphis, Tanis, Sebennytos, Pharbaithos and Pêlousion. But this only means that certain persons who paid taxes in the Fayoum belonged to places in the north. The taxes were paid upon bronze, bricks and castor-oil, and for permission to sell linen, the amount in the latter case depending on the size of the business. It was generally a multiple of 21 silver drachmæ, the most common sums levied being 42, 84, 168 and 336 drachmæ. But we also find 16, 28, and 56 drachmæ paid, and in one case we read: "Of Koitoi, Sokhôtês the son of Phanês 25 drachmæ $4\frac{1}{2}$ obols." The whole amount collected in one instance was 879 silver drachmæ; in another instance it was 780 drachmæ.

The period to which the papyri belong is fixed by the names of the Ptolemies and their sisters which occur more especially in the wills. Thus we read: "In the reign of the deified Ptolemy and Arsinoê in the priesthood of Tlêpolemos the son of [Altibios to the deified] Alexander [1] and to the deified [brothers, . . . being canephoros] of Arsinoê Philadelphia." In the letters and receipts it is usual to give the year only of the reigning sovereign without specifying his name. The dates of the documents I have examined range from the 20th to the 37th years of one king and from the 1st to the 13th year of another, and since the only Ptolemies who reigned more than 36 years were Philadelphus and Physkôn, it is evident that we must see Philadelphus in the one monarch and his son and successor Euergetês in the other.

69. A prominent character in the papyri is a certain Kleôn, who seems to have been the chief architect of the Fayoum in the middle of the third century B.C. One of the letters to him runs as follows (G. 111.)

"Apollônios sends greeting to Kleôn. I wrote to you on the 17th about my position as regards the tithe-collectors before Diotimos concerning the number of slaves and the arranging of the stones, and in what way acknowledgment had been made before Diotimos, and that the slaves who were needed for the placing and arranging of the stones would finish all the work by the time of the new moon if iron were furnished to them; and I wrote to you what holiday ought to be allowed to each, and the amount of work. And now you would do well to order that wedges be provided for each, as enumerated below, in order that we may disregard their excuses (for idleness). For Tekhestheus (we have reckoned) an equal number of slaves and lads, 18 in all, (and) 4 wedges; for Berotheus 15 slaves and lads (and) 3 wedges; for Anamneus 18 slaves and lads (and) 4 wedges; for Paous 16 slaves and lads (and) 3 wedges; for Pepsa

[1] Tlêpolemos son of Altibios was also priest of Alexander and the deified brothers in the 2nd year of the successor of Ptolemy Philadelphus, according to the Louvre papyrus 2438; see E. Révillout, *Rev. Egyptologique*, I. 1, p. 18.

17 slaves and lads (and) 4 wedges; for Phamouneus 12 slaves and lads (and) 3 wedges; for Spsint . . . ."

It is plain that reference is here made to the working of certain quarries in the neighbourhood of the Fayoum, the wedges being required to split the rock. Each gang of quarrymen was under an overseer who was responsible for their work, and kept them employed at it, no doubt with the aid of the lash.

From the same mummy-case has come another fragment of a letter to Kleôn (G. 108). This is addressed to him by a certain Dêmêtrios, who begins by saying that "on the 22nd when I was going down to the works . . . Theokleidês came down again to the doors."

Another letter is addressed to Kleôn by the quarrymen themselves (M. 163). The handwriting of it is very bad, the spelling is defective, and various corrections have been scribbled here and there above the lines. The injuries the papyrus has received add still further to the difficulty of deciphering it. I read it thus: "Greeting is sent to [Kle]ôn by the quarrymen working in Pastôntis, who have received [from] you (the order for) the stones. Choose what has been already hewn in the gypsum (quarries). But now we do no work, because we have no slaves to clear away the sand above the rock [from] the city of Apthi[s] to Eiê. To-day * [from] the day on which they began to work [is an interval?] of two months, and you know that the place is desert; and we have no food, though we want to finish the [work in order that] we may go away. Grant indeed our request quickly in order that we may not desert. Farewell. The 1st year,† the 9th day of Thoth."

A few years previously Kleôn had received another letter from the quarrymen in his employment. It was as follows (B. 31);—"To Kleôn the architect, greeting. We who belong to the original quarrymen from the place of embarcation are being wronged by Apollônios the ganger. He having set us to work at the hard rock and having selected us as against the rest, has shown (us only) the soft rock that he has (in the quarry), and now we are ruined, spoiling (our) iron (to no purpose); therefore we pray you that we may obtain justice; having cut the hard rock . . . . that we be not injured. Farewell." On the back is a note by Kleôn to the effect that the letter was received on the 24th of Phaôphi in the 30th year of Ptolemy (B.C. 255).

It is evident that "Apollônios the ganger" mentioned in the letter is the same as the Apollônios who asked that wedges might be provided for the workmen. Dêmêtrios seems to have been his assistant. A curious letter of the latter has been preserved, which may be translated thus (B. 27):—"To Kleôn Dêmêtrios sends greeting. On a previous occasion also did I write to you about the arrest which I have now undergone. You know also how in former years we have been injured, and how I am at present being injured by being carried off to the prison . . . . you who brought me as your own son out of the prison, not wishing me to suffer harm, [help me] for I am in the prison. Farewell."

* Above is written "on the 10th."

† B.C. 247.

In another fragment Kleôn is appealed to for the repair of a "fortress" the exact position of which is not stated. This is in a letter from Polykratês which begins: "Polykratês to Kleôn sends greeting. As for the southern wall of the fortress, a part of it has fallen, and now that it has fallen the part which looks south is in danger of becoming exposed: about 29 slaves have been farmed out on account of it by Dionysios . . . "

Dionysios is the writer of a letter of which unfortunately only the beginnings of the lines are preserved (G. 115). "Dionysios to Dôros sends greeting. I have sent . . . the copies (of the letters). Keep in good health. The 30th year, the 4th day of Athyr . . . We want an assistant-architect to build the dykes [from] . . . . to Hêphaistis in order that they may patrol the nets . . . and to finish the rest of the design of Kleôn . . . in order that [we may irrigate] the saltish land called . . . "

Polykratês also appears among the correspondents. One of his letters is dated in the 20th year of Ptolemy (B.C. 265). In a second letter addressed to his father he says (A. 2): "Polykratês sends greeting to his father. You do well if you are well and all things else are according to your mind. We also are well. I have often written to you begging you to come and introduce me so that I may be released from my present leisure; and now, if it is possible and nothing hinders you, try to come to the Arsinoite nome. For if you are here, I am persuaded that I shall easily be introduced to the king. And know that I have received from Philônidês 70 silver drachmæ, half of which I have kept for necessary expenses and the rest I have lent out on loan. I have done this in order that we may not have it all at once, but receive it little by little. Write to us on your side in order that we may know how you are, and may not be anxious (about you). Take care of yourself in order that you may be in good health and come to us strong and well. Farewell."

Of the third letter only the first part is left. This reads (A. 1) :—" Polykratês to his father sends greeting. [If you are well] and all things else are to your mind, it would be well. We ourselves are well. Know that I have held the office of inspecting the victims for sacrifice and that I go to the land-surveyor's office. And I have been registered at the custom-house for an estate producing 17 silver drachmæ. In order that we may receive the twentieth of this amount, and not . . . . 70 drachmæ. And they tell us to give way to Herôdês . . . ."

70. The "land-surveyor" is mentioned in another letter (H. 131) dated the 27th of Epeiphi, of which only a portion is left. It was sent from "Athenodôros the land-surveyor," and contains a petition. The writer speaks of himself as "falling down with tears" on behalf of one "who is an old man and of the children," and he goes on to say that "I have acted as steward," "[have gone] to Aphroditopolis with the village-scribes and fellahin," have there visited "the sanctuary" of the goddess, where I was "told that I was in danger," and was "threatened" while "in the priest's chamber in the pylon," out of which I "was able to peep." The person to whom the letter is addressed is told that he had "pitied" the author of it "either because of . . . . or because" he "had served" him ; and mention is then made of "Euêreitos the captain of the guard."

The letter was probably sent to "Diophanês the general," to whom other petitions found in the cartonnage of the same mummy-case were addressed. Here is one of them (H. 123) :—" Moskhiôn sends greeting to Diophanês. Dôrimakhos has brought me a petition, filed against Dionysios, in which it is declared that he considers he should obtain justice. Having therefore summoned Dionysios I made known to him the petition and ordered him to satisfy Dôrimakhos. As Dionysios maintained that there is nothing in the charges brought forward in the petition, I have sent him to you on the 6th of Pharmouthi. Farewell. The 25th year [B.C. 260], the 5th of Pharmouthi." This is addressed on the back in capitals : "To Diophanês," and the date and names of Moskhiôn and Dôrimakhos are written in cursive characters below.

Moskhiôn appears to have been a deputy of Diophanês. The latter is personally addressed in a mutilated petition (H. 125) from " Onêtôr and Asklêpiadês and Mousaios," who inform Diophanês "the general" that they had already "given a petition to the name of the King." The petition relates to a lease of 107 [acres] from a certain Lysander "in the 26th year." The ground they occupied is called a *Klêros* or "allotment," so that they must be regarded as Greek settlers, or (as appears from other documents) retired soldiers, to whom certain lands had been allotted by the government at Alexandria. In another document (M. 172) *Klêrukhs* are referred to, who received 537 drachmæ from the fellahin on their estates upon the produce of the 2nd year (B.C. 246). Onêtôr and his two companions had apparently suffered from bad weather, their "corn had perished on the threshing-floor," some of it had been "taken by the guardians" or police, they had been slandered by "malicious persons," and accordingly they "wanted clean corn" and some alteration in the terms of their lease.

Two more fragments of letters to Diophanês exist. One (H. 124) is from his son Dioskouridês, who remarks that "Asklêpiadês who has given you the letter is sailing up (the river)," the date of the 25th year being written on the back, and the other (H. 129) from "his daughter and [her] children," hoping that "yourself and your son Dioskouridês [are well]," and asking that "he should go to you after being thanked by me."

71. Several letters relate to agriculture. Thus (S. 251) "Diôn the son of Asklêpiadês acknowledged that the vineyard [let] to me has been valued for the 23rd year, including the farmstead of Hêrakleidês, [the value] of the fruit-trees and flowers for garlands [being put] at 12 drachmæ." Another fragment speaks of "the spelt and barley" having been "smitten," and refers to the "place of embarcation," as well as to "the half of the cutting (or trench) at the place of embarcation."

An interesting document on the mode in which retired soldiers were provided for is an I.O.U. from a Thrakian cavalry-soldier (D. 62). "Theotimos the son of Euphrôn, a Thrakian, of those who are under the commander of the cavalry, acknowledges that he engages to pay in full Philip who has received the share for the 2nd year of the district around Philadelpheia, consisting of vineyards and gardens (*paradeisôn*), to the extent of 1 talent and 3000 drachmæ, and to receive from the same (Philip) the vineyards and gardens about Boubastos for 3000 drachmæ, so that the whole shall amount to [two] talents ; in addition to which I mortgage the rights belonging to me and the benefactions I receive (?), and I swear the royal oath which is subscribed according to this bond." The oath is written above, and runs as follows : Theotimos the son of Euphrôn [a Thrakian, swears by the life] of Arsinoê, by the divine Philomêtor . . . and the saviour gods and Sarapis and [Isis who preside over] the contract."

In a mutilated letter written by Hermogenês to Theodôros (G. 117) the writer, after stating that "the copy is not good," goes on to say that he "had hopes up to the 30th of the month Pakhons" (about 23 July) "on account of the waterless part of the district;" as it is, he would "wait until the 10th of Payni" (about 2 Aug.), evidently anxiously watching the rising Nile.

Another mutilated document (S. 251) from Meleagros the son of Meleagros, who bears the curious title of the "champion of peace," declares that he had "valued the crops . . . for the 23rd year, 200 metrêtes; 33⅓ not having been paid (into the treasury) [on account of] excess."

In one year the tax on the gardens and vineyards produced 3 talents 626 copper drachmæ or 104 silver drachmæ and 2 obols, (giving a ratio of 1 : 351 for silver and copper value) the tax on vineyards alone amounting to one talent 617 copper drachmæ, while there was an additional tax on their produce. The fellahin who worked on the estates are called sometimes "agriculturists," sometimes "serfs." Thus (G. 117*a*) on the 3rd of Epeiphi of the 7th year (B.C. 240) Theodôros received a memorandum of Teôs thro' his agent Hermophilos on the back of which he has written the words: "[Let] the work [be] valued equally per serf that it may not trouble us."

Theodôros is called "the steward" in a fragment (G. 116) which reads as follows: "You will do well if it seem good to you to write to Theodôros the steward that he should allow us to draw 100 fathoms as far as the inn." Above are the words: "Memorandum for Theodôros from Petoubastês and Petekhôn," while on the back is written: "The 8th year, the 26th day of Pharmouthi: memorandum from Petoubastês and Petekhôn; mortgage of land to Theodôros."

Another "steward" named Phaiês, who seems to have looked after the royal household, is mentioned in some other letters. One of them (E. 74) is as follows:—"To Phaiês the steward from Ammônios the secretary of Phlyês (know) that when I was present the fellow from the neighbourhood of Oxyrinkha handed in an account to the office; and on the 27th day at the first hour when I was in the office a servant came from Kallôn summoning me. Having put down the books I went out, and when I was at the door of the war-office* the servant ordered (them) to take me away, and now I am in the police-station.† Farewell." The missive is a mysterious one; all we learn from it is that the writer had been arrested and confined, not in a regular prison, but in a sort of "lock-up." The second letter is more explicit, and informs us of the existence of "royal gooseherds," who, however, it would appear, sometimes failed in their duty (E. 75). "To Phaiês the steward from Paôs the son of Petesoukhos and Inarôs the son of Toustotoêtis the royal gooseherds from Pharbaithos, and Paôs the son of Armaios and Amoleês the son of Petosiris the royal gooseherds from Persea Iskhyria. The steward comes to us, ordering us to furnish for the table 12 geese; as we are not able (to do so) we request you, since he further levies upon us the [number] of geese levied for the table upon the gooseherds of the nome, on account of their being half the contribution, to send our account to the office to be inspected; and if it should be correct as we write (it is), that it be done to us accordingly in order that we may be able to deal justly by the king. Farewell."

* Or "general's quarters." † Literally "the day-watch-house."

72. The Fayoum perhaps provided copper as well as stone and the produce of its gardens and farms. Reference is made to the "copper-mines" (G. 113), tho' unfortunately the mutilated state of the papyrus prevents us from knowing where they were situated. Then, as now, moreover, a revenue seems to have been derived from the fish caught in the great canal. At all events this is the most probable interpretation of a document, the key-word to which is half destroyed. I translate it thus:

"The 32nd year, from Theodotos, the account of the [revenue on the fish-pots] in the canal of the harbour of Ptolemais, in the month Thoth, the 3rd day; from the collection* made by Kalatytis 5½ silver drachmæ [less one], i.e. 4;
the 4th day, from Hôros the son of Nekhtheneibis the half of 7½ drachmæ, 3¾;
from the collection made by Komoapis the half of 10 dr., 7 (*sic*);
from the slaves of Sokeus the half of 8 dr. 2 obols, 4 dr. 1 obol;
[the 5th day], from the collection made by Paleuis the half of 6 dr. 2 ob., 3 dr. 1 ob.;
from the slaves of Orsenouphis the half of 2 dr. 2 ob., 1 dr. 1 ob.;
the 6th day, from the collection made by Kalatytis the half of 19½ dr., 14½ (*sic*);
from the collection made by Hôros son of Inarôs the half of 7 dr., 3½;

* The word is that which is used in the New Testament in the sense of a "collection for the poor."

from Hôros the son of Nekhtheneibis the half of 5 dr., 2½;
from the collection made by Solois the half of 4 dr., 2;
the 7th day, from the collection made by Orsenouphis the half of 15 dr., 7½;
from the collection made by Sokeus the half of 12 dr., 6;
from Hôros the son of Khestôytês the half of 11 dr., 5½;
from the collection made by Paeis the half of 16 dr., 8;
from Tekhesyeus the half of 14 dr., 7;
the 8th day, from Hôros the son of Nekhtheneibis the half of 14 dr., 7;
from the collection made by Kalatytis the half of 18 dr., 13 dr. 5 ob. (*sic*);
from the collection made by Paleuis the half of 10 dr., 5;
from Petoseiris, the half of 10 dr., 5½ (?);
from the collection made by Solois the half of 16 dr., 8;
from Hôros the son of Inarôs the half of 8 dr., 4;
the 9th day, from Hôros the son of Nekhtheneibis the half of 11 dr., 5½;
from the collection made by Komoapis the half of 12 dr., 9 (*sic*);
from the collection made by Kalatytis the half of 9 dr. 5 obols, 7 dr. 2 obols (*sic*);
from Orsenouphis the half of 5 dr., 2½;
the 10th day, from Hôros the son of Nekhtheneibis the half of 2 dr. 2 obols, 1 dr. 1 ob."

73. Among the most curious of the papyri are three receipts from a certain Kephalôn a charioteer, written in a somewhat illegible cursive hand. They run thus (F. 81): "The 21st year, the 24th day of Tybi, Kephalôn the charioteer acknowledges the receipt from Kharmas the son of Asklêpiadês [and . . .]los the son of Ar[mai]os at the harbour in Ptolemais, according to the order of Arteutês the overseer of the district, for 5 chariots that have followed him 5 *minæ* (?)[1] and for 3 horses to run together 3 *minæ* (?)[1]; for himself and 7 charioteers, to each of pure bread a quarter of a khœnix,[2] in all 2 *khœnikes*; of oil to each ¼ of a *kotylê*, in all 2 *kotylæ*, of wine to each 4 *kotylæ*, in all 2 *khœnikes* 8 *kotylæ*; and for 13 grooms, of salted bread to each 2 *khœnikes*, in all 26 *khœnikes*, of oil to each ⅛ of a *kotylê*, in all 1 *kotylê* and ⅞; and for a . . . porker, and for a lame (?) horse handed over (to be cured), for the oil 3 *kotylæ*, (and) the wine 3 *kotylæ*; and for singeing, for the candles of castor oil 9 *kotylæ*." The second receipt (F. 82) is injured at the commencement. "The 21st year, the 3rd of Mekhir until the 24th of Tybi or the 3rd of Epeiphi, Kephalôn the charioteer for two chariots and for horses and for 10 grooms. The 21st year the 3rd of [Mekhir, Kephalôn] the charioteer [acknowledges] the receipt from Kharmas the [son of Asklêpiadês and . . . los the son of Armai]os in [Ptolemais at the harbour, for chariots and] two [charioteers] that were left to . . . from the 26th of Tybi to the 3rd of Mekhir, to each (charioteer) per diem of loaves of fine wheat flour 1½ *khœnix*, in all 3 *khœnikes*; of wine 4 *kotylæ*, in all 8 *kotylæ*; of oil a quarter of a *kotylê*, in all ½ of a *kotylê*; and on the 9th day, of bread 7 *khœnikes*, of wine 3 *khoes*, of oil 4½ *kotylæ*; and for four grooms, to each of salted bread 2 *khœnikes*, in all 8 *khœnikes*; of oil, to each ⅛ of a *kotylê*, in all half a *kotylê*; and on the 9th day of bread 1¾ *khœnikes*, of oil 4½ *kotylæ*; and for a lame (?) horse handed over (to be cured) and phlebotomised, from the 26th to the 30th of Tybi, per diem of wine 1½ *kotylæ*, of oil 1½ *kotylæ*; and on the 5th day of oil 7½ *kotylæ*, of wine 7½ *kotylæ*; and for singeing, per diem of castor-oil 7½ (?) *kotylæ*, (and if) he should give any trouble, from the 30th of Mekhir to the 3rd (of Phamenoth) per diem of oil 1 *kotylê*, in all 3 *kotylæ*, of wine 1 *kotylê*, in all 3 *kotylæ*, and for [the horses] that are present . . . ."

Only the last lines of the 3rd receipt remain (F. 81): ". . . a porker and . . . to the 5 chariots 3 *minæ* (?) and an extra horse 1 silver drachma. Sixteen horses: to each for fodder 8 bundles of grass, in all 128 bundles per diem; and from the 1st of Mekhir to the 3rd 384 bundles, and for the 5 chariots that were present on the 3rd 2 *minæ* (?) (and) the 3 horses to run together 3 *minæ* (?); for all the horses, 19 in number, for each, of fodder 152 bundles of grass, and on the 4th day . . . for fodder 280 bundles of grass."

To this is attached the following receipt: "Kephalôn the charioteer acknowledges the receipt from Kharmas the steward of the fodder and what is necessary for the carriages in the house and for the grooms, as well as of what has been stated in the contract."

We have another receipt given to the same Kharmas (G. 112) which reads: "Hôros acknowledges the receipt from Kharmas of necessaries according to the

[1] The interpretation of the symbol is purely conjectural. It looks like a compound of π and ι.

[2] The symbol for "quarter" has been written in the wrong place.

bond; Ptaxas has made the copy by order of Hôros as he himself cannot write."

We gather from a fragment (E 68) that the public deeds and bonds were kept, not in the Fayoum, but at Alabastropolis, a city supposed to be now represented by the Kôm-el-Ahhmar on the eastern bank of the Nile a little above Minieh. The fragment is as follows:—"[The deed] has been registered in the public records by Histiaios. [They] wrote this in Krokodilopolis the 13th year, on the 15th [day] of Payni on account of this keeper of the bonds .... in Alabastropolis."

A minute examination of all the fragments when they have been extracted from the mummy-cases will doubtless reveal many more interesting facts. At present, however, a large number of the fragments are of so small a size as to make it impossible even to guess at their contents. Here and there, indeed, a phrase is met with which throws light on the general character of the document in which it occurs. Thus we have a fragment of a letter (J 132) dated the 4th day of Khoiak and the 25th year, in which we find the words: "but as I have no friends, request Hôros..." As a little above we read: "write to Xanthippos that he pay great attention to me," it is evident that the writer wanted a letter of introduction.

Among all this mass of fragmentary correspondence there is one small square piece of papyrus which contains a complete text, written in a neat cursive hand. It is a memorandum, not about business, but of the appearance of a ghost. This curious relic of a distant past runs as follows (F 88): "A boy appeared to be on the columns in the country-house of Mêtrodôros."

74. The collection of papyri which I have been describing does not by any means include all that have been rescued by Mr. Petrie from the coffins of the Egyptian dead. There is still a considerable quantity which has not yet been arranged for examination, and about which I hope to report next year. A large number of draughts of Greek wills also exist which have been placed in the hands of Professor Mahaffy. They belong for the most part to the military veterans who had received lands in the Fayoum. The veterans were divided into two classes, the older of whom had each a hundred *aruræ* of land allotted to them.

The text of all the papyri will be published as soon as possible in *Hermathena* with a philological commentary.

By way of Supplement I would add to this account of the Greek papyri of Gurob, translations of two papyri found by Mr. Petrie at Howâra. The papyri are of great size and quite perfect. They were discovered in an earthen jar, neatly wrapped round with rags, small sticks being inserted to prevent the rags from injuring the brittle papyrus within. They prove to be contracts relating to the sale of two monasteries by a certain Eulogios son of Joseph, who describes himself as having been formerly a Melitian monk, but "now orthodox." The Melitians or Melêtians, it may be observed, derived their name from Melêtios bishop of Lykopolis (Siût), the rival and antagonist of Peter the patriarch of Alexandria. The deeds are dated in the years 512 and 513 A.D., and throw much light upon the geography of the Fayoum at the time as well as upon legal procedure. I have published the texts in the *Revue des Études grecques* 1890, pp. 131 *sq.*, and M. Th. Reinach has added a translation of them.

No. I. "In the consulate of Flavius Paulus and Moskhianos, the most illustrious, the 10th day of Thoth, at the end (?) of the 6th indiction, in the district (of Arsinoê), in the province of Arkadia. It is agreed by Eulogios the son of Joseph, formerly a Melitian monk, but now orthodox, formerly living in the mountain called Labla in the Arsinoite district, but now dwelling in the monastery called Mikron [Phyôn] in the suburbs of the same city of the Arsinoites, that he has willingly and spontaneously and irrevocably sold and handed over in full possession, from the present for all future time, to Pousis the son of Harpaêsis, a Melitian priest (dwelling) in the aforesaid mountain of Labla, a property belonging to and devolving upon the vendor Eulogios, as he has guaranteed and stated in writing, the sale being made at the risk and charge of the vendor, for just and honourable reasons, conformably to his rights and undisturbed use and possession. (This property) in the aforesaid mountain of Labla (consists of) a monastery in its entirety with all its cells, facing east, together with the ground in front of the cells and all rights over it from the foundation to the whole of the roof, without the reservation of anything to the vendor Eulogios.[1] The (monastery) is bounded on the south by the mountain and the monastery of Saint Andrew the Priest, on the north by the monastery of Naharaos the priest, on the east by the mountain, (and) on the south-west by the public road

[1] Literally "so that nothing whatever throughout (the building) should remain unsold there to the vendor."

on which is the monastery of Peter the deacon. And the vendor Eulogios (acknowledges) that he has received from the purchaser Pousis the full price agreed upon between them and satisfactory to both for the same monastery in its entirety sold by Eulogios to Pousis, viz. 8 pieces of imperial gold [1] current and of good weight and 11200 large pieces of silver,[2] given by the purchaser to the vendor from hand to hand in the presence of the undersigned witnesses. Wherefore, (he acknowledges) that the purchaser Pousis is from henceforth lord and master of the aforesaid monastery [which] has been sold, in its entirety, with all its cells and the ground in front of the cells, with all rights over it from the foundation to the whole of the roof, and that he has power to manage, administer, complete, improve, pull down, rebuild (and) alter in whatever way and fashion he desires, to transmit (the property) to his heirs and successors, to alienate (it) (or) give (it) to others as he wishes, without hindrance. And (it is agreed) that the vendor Eulogios and his heirs and successors shall immediately take action against whosoever shall oppose or lay claim to the whole or a part of the property at their own expense and charges, (in order) to secure the peaceable possession of it to the purchaser Pousis and his heirs and successors; and if they do not do so, they shall pay double the price received by the vendor Eulogios as well as all expenses and charges which shall appear to have been incurred through the improvement or rebuilding of the property, and also any losses judicial or extra-judicial occasioned by it, all these (being paid) double. The deed of sale has been duly drawn up in a single copy, and the vendor Eulogios has guaranteed to the purchaser Pousis by this sale a certain and secure title to his goods present and future, severally and generally, in the matter of security and in regard to mortgage, as by the decision of a court. As to which being questioned by the purchaser face to face +[3]Eulogios the monk, the son of Joseph, aforesaid, has declared: I have voluntarily sold to you, Pousis, a Melitian priest, my property, for just and honourable reasons, in the aforesaid mountain called Labla in the Arsinoite district, viz. a monastery in its entirety, facing east, with all its cells, along with the ground in front of it, and all rights over it from the foundation to the whole of the roof, and I have received from you by hand its price, 8 pieces of imperial gold of good weight and 11200 large pieces of silver, given to me in the presence of the undersigned witnesses; and I agree to all the terms herein contained and I have given a quittance. (Subscribed:) Aurelios Phoibammôn the son of Kyrillos from the city of the Arsinoites, having been requested (to come) have signed on behalf of the vendor who is present but does not know how to write; Aurêlios Paulas the son of Dôteinos a wine-merchant from the city of the Arsinoites, I witness this sale and the payment of the price 8 pieces of gold and 11200 pieces of small coin as aforesaid; Aurêlios Eulogios the son of Euphrôn, from the city of the Arsinoites, I witness the same sale and payment of the price 8 pieces of gold and 11200 pieces of small coin, as aforesaid; Aurêlios Neilios the son of Phoibammôn a land-surveyor from the city of the Arsinoites, I witness this sale and the payment of the price, 8 pieces (of gold) and 11200 pieces of small coin as aforesaid; + Orneiôs Apollônios the son of Eulogios (?) from the city of the Arsinoites, I witness this sale and the payment of the price 8 pieces of gold and 11200 pieces of small coin as aforesaid; Aurêlios Eulogios the son of Neilammôn, a wine-merchant from the city of the Arsinoites, I witness this sale and the payment of the price 8 pieces of gold and 11200 pieces of small coin as aforesaid. (*Monogram of Christ.*) Folded and sealed by me Eulogios."[1]

No. II. "The year after the consulate of Flavius Paulus and Moskhianos, the most illustrious, the 15th day of Epeiphi, at the beginning of the 7th Indiction in the district (of Arsinoê) in the province of Arkadia.

It is agreed by Eulogios, an orthodox monk, of the monastery of Makron Phyôn in the suburbs of the city of the Arsinoites, the son of Joseph and Tlesis, that he has willingly and spontaneously and irrevocably sold and handed over in full possession, from the present for all future time, to Papnouthios the son of Isak and Julius the son of Aranthius, both Melitian monks of the monastery called Labla in the suburbs of the aforesaid city of the Arsinoites, a property belonging to the vendor Eulogios and devolving upon him, as he has guaranteed and stated in writing, at his own risk and charge, with proper and lawful titles, conformably to the rights accruing to the purchase and his undisturbed use and possession. (This property) in the aforesaid monastery of Labla (consists) of a monastery in its entirety, facing east, with all its chambers, together with all rights

[1] The *solidi dominici.*

[2] M. Reinach thinks that the *miliarensia* are meant, the *miliarense* being the 1000th part of a gold *libra*, so that 11200 *miliarensia* would have been equivalent to 800 *solidi*.

[3] Eulogios affixed his "cross" as he was not able to write.

[1] This is written first in Latin and then in Greek letters.

appertaining to it from the foundations to the whole of the roofs, without the reservation of any thing to the vendor Eulogios. (The monastery) is bounded, as is agreed on both sides, on the south by a deserted monastery, on the north by the monastery of Naharaos the priest, on the east by the mountain and the approach and exit of the aforesaid monastery, on the south-west by the public road on which (is) the monastery of Peter the deacon. And the aforesaid vendor the monk Eulogios further acknowledges that he has received and taken in full from the purchasers Papnouthios and Julius what had already been settled, the full price namely that had been agreed upon between them and had appeared satisfactory to both (parties) in return for the aforesaid property which had been sold to them by the vendor in two equal shares, to wit the aforesaid monastery in its entirety, and in return for all rights over it from the foundation to the whole of the roof, (the sum being) ten pieces of imperial gold current and of good weight, given by the purchasers to the vendor from hand to hand, in the presence of the undersigned witnesses. Wherefore (he acknowledges) that the purchasers Papnouthios and Julius are from henceforth lords and masters in two equal shares of the aforesaid monastery which has been sold in its entirety, with all its chambers and with all rights over it from the foundations to the whole of the roof, as is aforesaid, and that they have power to manage, administer, complete, improve, pull down, rebuild (and) alter (it) in whatever way and fashion they desire, to transmit (it) to heirs and successors, to alienate and give (it) to others as they wish, without hindrance. And (it is agreed) that both the vendor Eulogios and his heirs and successors shall immediately take action against whosoever shall oppose or lay claim to the whole or a part of the property at their own expense and charges, (in order) to secure the peaceable possession of it to the purchasers Papnouthios and Julius and his heirs and successors; and if they do not do so they shall pay double the price received by the vendor Eulogios as well as all expenses and charges which shall appear to have been incurred through the improvement or rebuilding of the property, and also any losses judicial or extra-judicial occasioned by it, all these (being paid) double. The deed of sale has been duly drawn up in a single copy, and the vendor Eulogios has guaranteed to the purchasers Papnouthios and Julius by this re-emption a certain and secure title to all his goods present and future, severally and generally, in the matter of security and in regard to mortgage, as by a decision of the court. As to which being questioned by the purchasers face to face, + Eulogios, the orthodox monk, the son of Joseph and Tlesis, aforesaid, has declared to them: I have voluntarily sold to you, Papnouthios son of Isak and Julius son of Aranthios, Melitian monks, my property with proper and legal titles (which is) in the aforesaid monastery of Labla, viz. a monastery in its entirety facing east, with all its chambers, together with all rights over it from the foundations to the whole of the roof, without the reservation of anything whatever to myself, and I have received in full from you by hand its price, 10 pieces of imperial gold of good weight, given to me in the presence of the undersigned witnesses, and I agree to all the terms herein contained; and on being questioned I have made (this) declaration and given a quittance. (Subscribed:) I Phletimotheus the son of Abraham, councillor, . . . of the city of the Arsinoites, have written by request for the vendor who is present but not able to write; Aurelius Julius the son of Phoibammôn, head of the guild of brickmakers, from the city of the Arsinoites, I witness this sale and payment of the price, 10 pieces of gold as aforesaid; Aurêlios Andreôs the son of Apa Ol-trôtêx from the city of the Arsinoites, I witness this sale and payment of the price 10 pieces of gold as aforesaid; Aurêlios Pêktinos from the city of the Arsinoites, I witness this sale and payment of the price 10 pieces of gold as aforesaid; Aurêlios Pousis the son of Joseph, a wine-merchant from the city of the Arsinoites, I witness this sale and payment of the price [10 pieces] of gold. (*Monogram of Christ.*) Folded and sealed by me Eulogios."

75. Rough List of Greek Papyri.

(Numbers omitted are unimportant fragments. *Broken*, signifies that some lines are lost; *fragment*, that the lines are incomplete. The letters shew the individual cartonnages in which the papyri were grouped contemporaneously. *L* shews the number of lines.)

A 1 Letter $5\frac{1}{2}$ l. broken. Polykratês to his father on business. Found along with 20 and 21.

2 Letter 9 l. perfect. Same to same, asking his father to come to him.

3, 3*a* Accounts 14 l. perfect. "Wine at $4\frac{1}{2}$ obols the *khous*, altogether $2\frac{1}{2}$ silver drachmæ; figs one obol" . . . "fruit 1 silver drachma."

4 Letter 7 l. frag. dated Athyr 26th (?) year.

5 Letter 18 l. frag. "To be ambassador" . . . "fond of money" . . . "to Krokodilopolis."

6 Letter 6 l. frag.

7 Account 37 l. broken. Taxes on eel traps (?) in the canal of the harbour of Ptolemais: yr. 32 = 254 B.C.

8 Letter 4 l. fragment. "Write ordering the money and iron to be given."

Aa 9 Letter 14 l. frag. Stone for house building.

10 Letter 5 l. frag. same.

10*a* Letter 1 l. frag. "Agênôr to Theodôros."

11 Letter 20 l. frag. and No. 23 part of same.

12 Letter 3 l. frag. yr. 33 Pamenoth 9.

13 Part of a text (?) 8 l. in three broken columns.

17 Letter frag. to Theodôros.

21 Letter frag. to Kleôn.

22 Letter 16 l. frag. "I have written to you on matters relating to the country," "we are ourselves coming to the place of embarcation."

26 Accounts 13 l.

B 27 Letter 7 l. perfect. Dêmêtrios to Kleôn.

28 Letter 6 l. frag. Apollônios about furnishing "the iron."

31 Letter 7 l. part frag. To Kleôn the architect about stone cutting, yr. 30 Paophi 24.

33 Letter 3 l. frag. yr. 30 Athyr 16.

35 Letter 3 l. frag. Theodôros to Kleôn.

36 Letter 12 l. frag. Copies of two letters from Philotimos.

39 Letter 13 l. frag. yr. 30, Athyr 4.

40 Accounts 35 l. broken.

C 42–59 Accounts Taxes on bricks, bronze, and linensellers, from various persons living in different towns of the district.

60 Accounts 12 l.

D 62 Deeds 5 l. frag. & 7 l. perfect. From Theotimos a Thracian of the cavalry, debtor to Philip for vineyards, in all 1 talent 3000 drachmæ.

64 Letter. 8 l. frag. from Alexander.

65 Accounts 19 l. frag.

67 Letter 3 l. perfect. Heraklides to Androsthenês, naming the house of Hôros.

E 68 Letters 34 & 5 l. frag. yr. 13 Payni 15, naming Alabastropolis.

69 Letters 53 l.

70 Account 18 l. perfect.

71 Letter 9 l. perfect.

72 Letter 16 l. frag., and 3 l. on back, to Hêliodôros.

74 Letter 13 l. perfect. Ammônios, scribe; to Phaiês, steward.

75 Letter 28 l. perfect. Four royal gooseherds to Phaiês, about 12 geese for the table.

76 Letter 8 l. to Phaiês.

78 Accounts 8 l. & 13 l. frag. and letter 2 l. frag. to Nikôn.

79 Accounts 30 l. smudged.

F 80 Receipt 3 l. perfect. To Kharmas from Kephalôn a groom, for fodder and horse expences.

81 Receipt 9 l. and 2 l. broken. Horse expences, and receipt to Kephalon.

82 Letter 2 l. and 18 l. broken. Horse expences. yr. 21 Mechir 3.

86 Letter 2 l. frag. and 12 l. perfect. Horse expences. yr. 21 Tybi 24.

87 Letter 16 l. frag.

88 Memo. 4 l. perfect. Appearance of a ghost in the house of Mêtrodôros.

92 Letter 10 l. and 6 l. frag. Horse expences and acknowledgment of receipt of Hôros from Kephalôn.

G 93 Account 20 l. frag.

95 Account 11 l. broken. yr. 21 Athyr 2.

96 Account 11 l. frag. Taxpayers' list, and No. 107 24 l. frag.

100 Letter 12 l. frag. Horse expences and receipt.

101 Letter 9 l. frag. Charges for wine &c. for grooms.

102 Letter 3 l. frag. Charges for wine &c. for grooms.

103 Letter 11 l. frag. Charges for wine &c. for grooms.

108. Letter 19 l. nearly perfect. Dêmêtrios to Kleôn, about bread for workmen, &c.; yr. 30 (or 1) Khoiak 1. (Writing of No. 185.)

109 Letter 6 l. frag. Horse expences. yr. 21 Athyr 9.

110 Letter 6 l. frag. Fodder expences.

111 Letter 18 l. broken. Apollônios to Kleôn, quarrying expences.

112 Letter and receipt 2 l. broken 4 l. perfect. Horse expences and receipt of Horos to Kharmas.

113 Letter 10 l. frag. naming Harmakheros.

115 Letter 7 l. frag. To Dionysios from Dôros about embankments, naming Kleôn. yr. 30 Athyr 4.

116 Letter 7 l. To Theodôros steward, mentioning 100 orgyae. yr. 8 Pharmouthi 26.

117 Letter 10 l. frag. Hermogenês to Theodôros.

117A. Letter 3 l. frag. Hermophilos to Theodôros. yr. 7 Epiphi 3.

118 Receipt 3 l. broken. Kharmas to Hôros.

119 Letter 18 l. frag. from a steward.

121 Letter 7 l. frag. yr. 21 Tybi 24

122 Account 50 l. frag. List of taxpayers.

H. 123 Letter 6 l. perfect. Moskhiôn, written by a scribe, signed by Moskhiôn, endorsed by receiver. yr. 25 Pharmouthi 5.

124 Letter 6 l. frag. Dioskouridês to Diophanês his father, yr. 25 Phamenoth 11.

125 Petition 22 l. frag. (fine) to Diophanês the general, yr. 26.

128 Accounts 10 l. frag. and back. List of taxpayers.

129 Letter 9 l. frag. from a lady, daughter of Diophanês.

131 Petition 25 l. frag. (fine) sent from Athênodôros a land surveyor.

J 132 Letter 9 + 7 l. frag. yr. 25 Khoiak 4.

K 135 Letter 14 l. frag.

136 Letter 24 l. frag. Mention of feast of Poseidon.

L 138–40 Accounts 30 l. frag. Private accounts.

142 Memos. and accounts 12 + 12 l. frag. with letter on back naming Amolpos.

K 143 Accounts 17 l. frag.

144–6 Accounts 34 l. frag. Travelling expences?

153 Accounts List of taxpayers.

M 163 Letter 12 l. perfect. to Kleôn. yr. 30 Thoth 9.

179 Letter 6 l. frag. "In Ptolemais."

185 Letter 9 l. broken. In hand of No. 108.

187 Letter 10 l. frag.

188 Letter 21 l. frag.

O 189–200 Probate copies of wills. yr. 12.

P 201–220 Same.

Q 222 Letter 8 l. frag. (In hand of Dêmêtrios to Kleôn, No. 108.)

224 Letter 4 l. frag. Polyphrôn to Diogenês.

225–9 Probate copies of wills. yr. 37.

236 Letter 15 l. long.

R. 237–8 Same, yr. 23.

S. 239–49 Frags. of tax-lists with heading.

250 Receipts 14 l. frag. from Isidôros son of Asklêpiadês.

251 Receipt 7 l. frag. Meleagros son of Meleagros.

256 Fragments of the Antiopê of Euripides.

257 Receipts of successive tax payments, 19 l. frag.

258 Letter 10 l. frag.

259 Letter 12 l. frag. Dôrotheos. yr. 3. Epiphi 5.

260 Letter frag. yr. 31.

SUMMARY OF DATES.

Ptolemy II Philadelphos.

Year 21	F F G G G	265
23	R	263
25	H H J	261
26	H	260
30	B B B G G M	256
31	S	255
32	A	254
33	Aa	253
37	Q	249

Ptolemy III Euergetes.

3	S	244
7	G	240
8	G	239
12	O	235
13	E	234
15	O	232
22	O	225

76. [I have been favoured with the following translation of one of the wills, by Prof. Mahaffy.

W. M. F. P.]

"In the reign of Ptolemy, son of Ptolemy and Arsinoe the brother gods, the 22nd year [225 B.C.] . . . rates (? Eukrates or Sokrates) the son of Theogenes being priest of Alexander and the gods adelphi and the gods euergetæ, the Kanephoros of Arsinoe Philadelphos being Berenike the daughter of Kallianax, on the new moon of the month Xandikos, in the city of the crocodiles of the Arsinoite nome, the following testament was made, in his sound mind and right understanding by Aphrodisias of Heraklea, a sojourner about 80 years old, short in stature [word lost] with aquiline nose and bright eyes, curly hair, but rather bald, with long ears.

May it be my lot to keep in health and manage mine own affairs; but should any mortal chance befal me—I bequeath all my goods to Axiothea daughter of Dizoulos the Thracian woman, and I leave nothing to anybody else. But I choose as executors king Ptolemy son of Ptolemy and Arsinoe the brother gods, and queen Berenike sister and wife of king Ptolemy, and their children. Witnesses. Paris the Thessalian, son of Theophilos, of the 2nd settlement, about 30 years old, of middle height, olive complexion, with high forehead and straight hair, with a scar on the middle of his forehead, and a mole beside his right eye. Getas son of [lost] the Koan, of the 2nd settlement, aged about 30, of middle height, olive complexion, and round forehead [word lost] with eyebrows joined, and a scar on each [cheek ?]. Neilon the Libyan, son of Sotairos, of the 2nd settlement, short, olive complexion, with a round forehead and straight hair, with a scar between his eyebrows. Demetrios the Isthmian, son of Demetrios, about 50 years old, tall, olive complexion, rather bald with aquiline nose."

CHAPTER X.

THE HIERATIC PAPYRI.

By F. Ll. Griffith.

77. It seems that some time must still elapse before even a beginning can be made in publishing facsimiles of the hieratic papyri which Mr. Petrie has collected at Kahun and Gurob. The wonderfully varied and novel character of their contents combine with their fragmentary condition to make the task of decipherment a slow and laborious one. Seldom are the strokes of the scribe so firm and clear that the would-be copyist can imitate them with certainty until he has ascertained the meaning of the whole context and identified the signs: nor can the meaning be learnt until the fragments have been sorted over and over and those that belong together united. Gradually during months of effort the handwriting, the state of the papyrus, the arrangement of the fibres have all been made to tell their tale, and assisted by a growing familiarity with the script the student, whose enthusiasm is more than ever aroused, restores one document after another to a definite, though still, alas! incomplete entity. A vast number of the fragments are not larger than an inch square, many are less than half an inch, but thanks to Mr. Petrie's careful packing in "lots" as they were obtained, and to the means of characterisation that I have just mentioned, there is no cause to despair of discovering how pieces join if they *will* join (although one lot may contain 50 or 60 documents of which other parts are sometimes to be found in a different lot); and if they will not join, yet a skeleton-papyrus can sometimes be made up by analogy from more complete examples and prove very instructive. It must be mentioned, however, that to all appearance, quite one half of the papyri of which Mr. Petrie obtained the remains are represented by a single small or even minute fragment. The sources of injury have been various, but here I need only point to the extreme antiquity of those from Kahun, which, though sometimes as fragile as tinder, are far more numerous than the stouter and later papyri of Gurob. Before issuing facsimiles one would wish to make every possible "fit," and to ascertain whatever significance each fragment may possess. A systematic catalogue on which I am now engaged has proved to me the importance and hopefulness of this aim: as one number after another is added to the list, the obscurity that still hangs over this wonderful collection becomes less and less dense, and I hope that a second year will not have passed before some of the papyri of 1889 appear in facsimile.

78. This catalogue is only begun, and it is consequently impossible to give more than an incomplete summary of the classes of documents that will find a place in it.

The first line of demarcation should be drawn between (I) the writings that may be supposed to have emanated directly from the scribe's brain—such as letters, accounts, legal documents and memoranda: these may in some instances be copies; but, if so, they are copies made with the writer's attention alive—and, (II) those that were presumably composed by an earlier scribe, such as literary, scientific, and religious works, school exercises, etc. It is difficult to explain the fact that ridiculous errors exist in such writings, even when the calligraphy shows the skill of a practised scribe and the corrupt passages cannot have presented any difficulty. The cause must be sought in the climate of Egypt inducing extreme carelessness and languor when a more or less dilettante occupation was engaged in by the scribe for his own individual pleasure and profit; while as to matters of business the fear in some cases of substantial loss, in others of an overseer's stick, kept the brain at work. Amuletic writings and papyri deposited with the dead were very faulty for a similar reason, namely that, not having to be read, their correctness would never be put to the test by a second person. Thoroughness, accuracy and orderliness were virtues that met with special praise and recognition in ancient Egypt because of their evident rarity except when brought out by compulsion.

The following remarks on Mr. Petrie's collection as well as the translations are given with all reserve. Further study will doubtless put many things in a new light.

79. I. ORIGINAL WRITINGS.

The legal and official documents may be classed according to their titles: the *amt-per* or deed recording the transfer of property from one person to another either prospectively or immediately, and either with or without benefit to the granter, or as it is technically expressed, with or without *consideration.* A species of will and of marriage settlement would appear to have been commonly committed to writing under this name. Two examples of it exist in the collection and are translated in KAHUN p. 45. A third fragmentary papyrus contained the evidence given that the witness' father had made an *amt-per* exchanging his priesthood of Sepdu for some other benefit which the son might claim.

The *sunu*, apparently the appointment of a government officer, or the engagement of a servant: of the former kind there would seem to be an instance from Kahun: of the latter, one from Gurob (temp. Amenhotep III).

The *aput*, or official list of a man's household, enumerating not only members of his family, but also, if he possessed any, the serfs and slaves in batches as they were acquired. The household might include father, mother, female relations, and young children of either sex. Adult males were probably employed as soldiers, clerks, labourers, etc., and would appear as such in other lists. These documents are drawn up in double columns, red and black, for it appears that generally speaking each Egyptian bore two names, and if he had only one name, in the second column instead of the surname is a kind of "ditto." Two examples, Kahun.

The *am ren f* lists, e.g. of superintendents and workmen engaged in dragging stone. Accounts kept journal-fashion; a fine and hitherto unique example from Thebes of the XIIIth dynasty is at the Gizeh Museum, and was published long ago by Mariette: its decipherment, began by the great De Rougé, was this year (curiously enough) re-commenced by Borchardt in the Berlin Zeitschrift für Aegyptische Sprache, where I shall soon give a résumé of it: it was kept by a scribe of the royal treasury at some period during the XIIIth dynasty, and contains for each day concise and formal notes of the occasions for which several drafts or payments were made, together with names of persons and lists of things paid out or received. At the end of the day the clerk drew up his balance sheet. Small fragments are numerous from Kahun, and good pieces can be restored so as to be intelligible. I may especially note an account of oxen (largely kept in fractions as if several persons might have an interest in an ox, or it may be that it was a butcher's account): also lists of articles in great variety either *stolen* or *withdrawn* from a store.

80. To these may be added memoranda either private or to be sent with letters, and written on small detached squares of papyrus. The letters form a numerous class. They are generally written on one side of a small sheet with the name of the writer and recipient on the back. The communication often exceeded the limits of one side and was continued on the back, but the most perfect specimens in the collection are nearly all of a very formal kind with hardly a grain of information, and this may explain the fact that they were still rolled up and sealed when Mr. Petrie discovered them. The earliest papyrus known is a fragment of a letter from Saqqâreh now at Gizeh. It dates from the Vth or VIth dynasty and was commented on by Borchardt last year: letters of the XVIIIth-XXth dynasties are comparatively common, but none were hitherto known of the intervening periods. A specimen of a formal letter is translated in KAHUN p. 46. Some quaint notes are scribbled on small squares of papyrus: one contains both the note and the reply, the latter in red ink.

81. II. COPIES.

Scientific works: A medical papyrus in three closely-written pages containing prescriptions for the use of midwives: some of these resemble in style the prescriptions contained in the Ebers (XVIIIth dynasty) and Berlin (XIXth dynasty) medical papyri, but there is nowhere any considerable verbal agreement. The prescriptions are very short, and there is only one incantation amongst them.

Fragments of a narrow strip with veterinary prescriptions in linear hieroglyphics, the lines in retrograde order. This is an absolute novelty.

Fragments of two mathematical works with text, I have not yet tried to identify their subjects; one I fear is beyond hope: it was beautifully written in columns, and still contains the most tantalising phrase "multiply by $\frac{1}{2}$ to infinity." Was it the famous problem that "took in" Hercules?

List of the fractions resulting from the division of 2 by the odd numbers from 3 to 21. The Egyptians could express any fraction that had 1 for the numerator, but no others, excepting only $\frac{2}{3}$. Thus $2 \div 19$ is expressed by $\frac{1}{12} + \frac{1}{76} + \frac{1}{114}$. The great mathematical "Rhind" Papyrus published and explained with great acuteness by Professor Eisenlohr in 1887 contains exactly the same table with some words of direction that are omitted from this example. (See Eisenlohr Mathematisches Handbuch, Text p. 36.)

Calculation of the contents of a circular granary resembling and yet differing considerably from that in Math. Handb. No. 43—numerals only without text.

Professor Erman, to whom I communicated this discovery informs me that he has since put together some small fragments of middle-kingdom writing from Thebes, likewise making up a calculation which exists in the Rhind Papyrus. The great Mathematical Papyrus, hitherto quite unique, was copied under a Hyksos king from writings of the time of Amenemhat III, the very period to which the Kahun papyri belong. It is noteworthy that all the known mathematical documents of ancient Egypt date from or can be traced to about the end of the XIIth dynasty.

82. Religious works: I have observed a few fragments from Kahun in linear hieratic. No other early papyri of this class are known, though linear hieroglyphic and hieratic texts have been found painted on coffins and on the sides of stone cists and grave-chambers of the XIth and XIIth dynasties. From Gurob there are fragments of a copy of the Book of the Dead written for Bakenamen. It evidently had good vignettes, but the text is atrocious beyond belief.

Literary works. Several pages of a papyrus containing a remarkable hymn to Usertesen III written on both sides of it. The beginning and end remain, but the intervening portion is of uncertain extent.

Small sheet recording apparently a bricklayer's *bon mot;* but mutilated.

Parts of two pages with a few lines of writing—portion of a strange episode in the mythical contest between Horus and Set, written in the popular dialect.

There are already lodged in museums nearly 1500 lines of literary texts written during the middle kingdom, besides a number of later copies of works produced in that period The following is a list of the middle-kingdom literary papyri.

Five at Berlin, viz.: the story of Sanehat; the story of the Sekhti; a dialogue between a man and his soul together with a fragment of a fairy tale; portion of a second copy of the story of the Sekhti; the Westcar papyrus relating a series of wonderful stories that were told to amuse Khufu, and some marvels that happened hereafter.

At St. Petersburg is a fairy tale about a ship-wrecked sailor (unpublished): at Paris the Prisse papyrus of proverbs. Lastly, at the British Museum are two series of fragments. 1. of the story of the Sekhti, with an unidentified text on the reverse. 2. of the proverbs of Ptahhotep in a different version from that contained in the Prisse papyrus. The latter I had the pleasure of noting for the first time on the day on which I write this list. On the back of it are some remains of accounts.

The general nature of the stories can be gathered from Maspero's deeply interesting volume entitled Contes populaires de l'Egypte Ancienne (Maisonneuve 1889). The Prisse papyrus was discussed by myself in the Proceedings of the Society of Biblical Archaeology vol. xiii. p. 65. And I shall probably write a further account for the same society *à propos* of the new text. Next summer I hope to publish in a separate work the British Museum text of the story of the Sekhti (Histoire d'un paysan) together with a résumé of the other texts.

It is very curious that at the moment when Mr. Petrie was discovering ancient papyri at Kahun Professor Erman of Berlin had in the press his "Language of the Westcar Papyrus" (Sprache des Papyrus Westcar), a grammatical work of the highest importance, as revealing in a really scientific manner one stage in the development of Egyptian speech, and that an entirely new one, being almost, if not quite, the very stage represented so largely at Kahun. From a philological point of view the Westcar Papyrus, which will soon appear in facsimile, has the advantage of being a long clear narrative interspersed with conversations, and thus, as far as its twelve imperfect pages can, it exhibits fully the character of the language: the corresponding Kahun papyri are with a few exceptions terse business documents or letters full of obscure references, and by themselves would give a very scanty idea of its capabilities.

There is still one class of documents to mention and that is *school-literature:* unfortunately Kahun has added nothing to our knowledge of the methods by which children were trained to be scribes. There is no trace of spelling-books, nor lists of signs. The Roman Sign papyrus of Tanis, discovered by Mr. Petrie and published by the Egypt Exploration Fund ("Two Papyri from Tanis") remains absolutely unique.

The only school book or exercise from Kahun is a collection of model letters of the simplest kind, containing little more than repetitions of formulae.

83. Royal names in the papyri. Neferkara, probably the king of the VIth dynasty, favourably mentioned in the "praises of Usertesen III" which forms a section of the hymn above mentioned.

XIIth dynasty. Amenemhat I. He appears as the presiding deity of some locality in the "model letters." Oxen given by him to the temple of

Sebek of the Fayoum are referred to in a papyrus of accounts.

The cartouche of Usertesen II is the commonest of all. The pyramid cities Hotep Usertesen, Kherp? Usertesen, and if I recollect rightly Kha Usertesen (as in the colossus tomb at El Bersheh) are mentioned and are perhaps all to be attributed to this king, whose name often occurs in the letters as that of a presiding deity.

The hymn to Usertesen III may have been composed after his death: a reservoir or garden of this king is mentioned.

Amenemhat III is the first king of whom we may say that papyri certainly written in his reign were found at Kahun.

Amenemhat IV. One letter dated in his reign.

XIIIth dynasty. Sekhem khu taui ra (Sebekhotep I?) the founder of the dynasty: a long *aput* list.

His successor Sekhem ka ra: another *aput.*

(The evidence for the identification of these two names is complicated, but I think will leave little to be desired when published.)

All the above cartouches are from Kahun: the great documentary age there, which can be proved to extend from Amenemhat III to Ra sekhem khu taui, was precisely the period during which the Pharaohs paid especial attention to irrigation: at that time the height of the Nile was frequently gauged as far south as Semneh above the second cataract. The prosperity of Kahun was due not only to the pyramid and temple of Usertesen II but also to the innumerable works involved in building and irrigation schemes thereabouts. Hotep Usertesen, as it was called, was an important entrepôt during the building of the pyramid of Amenemhat III at Hawara, and a scrawled letter speaks of works at three places viz. at Hotep Usertesen, at the tomb-site (hat) of the deceased princess Ptah neferu? and in the city of Aphroditopolis (Atfiyeh).

The transition from the XIIth to the XIIIth dynasty, though marked by Manetho and the Turin papyrus, cannot have been a great revolution.

Sebek nefru (who probably reigned jointly with Amenemhat IV) dying childless like her brother, may have left the kingdom to the representative of another branch of the "sons of Ra;" but this is only hypothesis. Kahun continued to flourish for a time, and the kings of the XIIIth dynasty treated their predecessors' monuments with respect.

Letters came to Kahun from Thebes, Heliopolis, Heracleopolis (Ahnâs), Crocodilopolis (Medinet el Fayoum) as well as from places in the immediate neighbourhood connected with the worship of Usertesen. One of the most puzzling things is to find that Sepdu "Lord of the Eastern desert" is a local God: either we must suppose that the settlers at Hotep Usertesen came from the East of the Delta (or from the Eastern desert), and introduced his worship, or else we must seek an explanation in the original meaning of the word which we translate "East," namely "left." The Egyptians ascending the Nile from the sea had our "east" on their "left." Likewise if they ascended the Fayûm branch from the great lake or sea of the Fayûm, our North would be on their "left." The canal and lake of the Fayûm were of great mythological as well as commercial importance, and I really venture to suggest that they saw so much analogy in them to the main stream and the sea that they considered it most appropriate to place the desert north of the canal under the guardianship of Sepdu "Lord of the left hand desert." The Lake of the Fayûm was sometimes called *uat ur* like the Mediterranean and other seas: and the Fayûm in one of the sacred books is divided up into 24 little nomes as if it were a third land added to the "two lands" of Upper and Lower Egypt.

Kahun furnished also a letter of the XVIIIth dynasty: it was written in duplicate and addressed to "Pharaoh L. W. H. the Lord" Amenhotep IV. Its date of the 5th year is valuable. In the 6th year the king having changed his name to Khuenaten dedicated his new capital city to the Sun's disk or Aten. The letter was written from Memphis and contains no reference to the disk worship: the writer Apii is probably identical with an individual already known by a stela dedicated to Ptah in the museum at Florence.

From Gurob the most important papyri are—

Two small legal documents, *sunu,* found together, and both referring to the same transaction: dated in the 33rd year of Amenhotep III.

One page from a long letter or report presented to a son of Rameses II after the death of that king.

CHAPTER XI.

THE STONE IMPLEMENTS OF KAHUN.

By F. C. J. Spurrell, F.G.S.

84. The stone implements brought by Mr. Petrie from Kahun and proved to be of the date of the XIIth dynasty are an unique collection, and form the first standpoint for a definite knowledge of the subject, in Egyptian history. All are domestic or trade implements. There are amongst them no ceremonial objects specially formed to take a part in religious rites during life or for sepulture merely; and no doubt is experienced when examining them that the style of chipping is of one and the same period. They form a reliable means for establishing a knowledge of the height at which the art then stood when it is considered how numerous are the individual objects from which a conclusion can be drawn, for in this matter any portion of a knife or tool stands for a whole one. [In making the drawings care has been taken to map out the flaking as accurately as possible with a view to displaying the style, but it must be remembered that the equal thickness of the lines is not intended to indicate that the delicacy of working was alike in all, for some are much finer and smoother than others.] Of course these implements do not represent work of the stone age properly considered. Some of their forms have influenced, as might be expected, similar tools in copper, but so have the metallic forms influenced those in stone; and while at the date 2600 B.C. some stone implements may not yet have been superseded, on the other hand others had entirely given place to those of copper.

The flint employed in the fashioning of the implements is truly flint; it is as much flint as that found in the cliffs of England and France, although geologically it is not of the same age. It is as well perhaps to state that there is no reason for giving the flint commonly used in Egypt in ancient times any special or distinctive name, such as pyromachous silex or cherty flint, as has been the custom hitherto; nor are the irregularly coloured stones known as Egyptian Jasper anything more than old river pebbles of flint, rolled and subsequently infiltrated with oxides of iron. As the flint is commonly found in tabular masses from which could be selected pieces more than a foot across and an inch or less in thickness much labour was saved thereby in the process of blocking out, preliminary to the fashioning of long thin blades; while very large and thick masses abound either in the rock or as rolled pebbles, suitable for coarse work and for procuring cores from which flakes of great length could be struck at any moment as required. The flint usually employed was more or less opaque but was apparently more obedient to the operator's will than the translucent and clearer varieties. It was apparently less given to rippling and abrupt change in the direction of the line of separation than in the horny varieties. The edges of the flakes also are tougher and do not splinter so easily. The perfect ability to strike off long, thin, flat flakes extended from the prehistoric ages to Roman times. From deposits of all these ages cores and flakes having an exact similarity of form are gathered. At Kahun most of the carefully formed flakes have been struck off a core by repeated blows, which under a lens are seen to have crushed the end which came in contact with the hammer, rarely however leaving a clear portion of the upper or striking surface attached to the flake by which one can measure the angle it made with the flake intended to be separated. The angles which have been measured reached from 28° to 48°, the latter in one case only. The amount of wind in the flakes was usually very slight.

85. The implements under consideration consist chiefly of the blades of axes, adzes and knives; there are also minor tools and flakes trimmed and serrated.

In the flint axes, the flaking is mostly very bold, and although not neat, is of the kind which comes of that perfect mastery of the material which enables the operator, in roughing out an implement to perfect it at once, leaving it suitable to the work the tool is intended to perform. It should be noted that the time expended is commensurate with the life of the blade; for it is clear, from the portions of hatchets found in the diggings, and miscellaneous gatherings, that the axes very quickly broke up. Some were comparatively slowly consumed until nothing but that which lay within the socket was left, when the cords could be cut and another fitted to the handle. On the other hand large detached portions shew that the whole cutting edge, consisting perhaps of half the blade was sometimes knocked off at the first blow delivered by the workman. In experimenting on the amount and kind of fastening which these blades required, it appeared that although tightness of fit was an advantage, a cord two or three feet in length held the blade in the socket firmly enough for work, without cement. See figs. in Kahun PL. XVI. and Illahun VII. 4. An example of this form or axe blade and its handle is depicted amongst the objects required in a future life, in the interior of a coffin of *Mentu-hetep* in the British Museum, No. 6655; its date is previous to the XIIth dynasty. The axe blades are coloured pale red, but saws and halbert-shaped axes, all evidently of metal, are coloured lemon yellow; and Mr. Petrie tells me that the axe in the tomb sculptures of *Ra hotep* [early IVth dynasty] has also a circular curve and is coloured a bluish-grey, different from the greenish-blue used to express copper. Whether these axes are representations of stone, copper, or bronze is of course uncertain, as colour is rarely to be relied on for the definite expression of a kind of material, though it may be for mere differences between materials; but the circular outline of the blades agrees with no form of copper or bronze implement known to have been found in Egypt hitherto; while the shape is in accordance with the forms of the flint and hornstone axes of Kahun. If these representations and others like them are in any way related to forms of bronze they are of such shapes as are least removed from those of chipped or polished stone, and must represent in the former case a transition type or in the latter an actual survival of an archaic outline.

As to the special use of the hornstone axe, Illahun, PL. VII. 3, with very blunt edges, it is difficult to assign a use other than that of squaring blocks of stone, for which however the use of a coarse adze would be more suitable as admitting of more accurate aim.

An axe blade of the same shape, but much smaller was found; as it was fashioned out of white chalky limestone, it could not have been used for working and must have been a model or toy.

86. The blades of adzes are comparatively rare. When new the cutting edge is carefully trimmed and well rounded. After use the retrimming was in a straight line, see plates Kahun XVI. right and left corners. In both these figures the tang becomes narrow, each however had a little knot at the apex in close resemblance to similarly shaped copper blades also found at Kahun of contemporary age. These knobs were perhaps found necessary in smooth bronze tools to prevent the falling out of the blade when the thongs for attachment had become loose by use. There is another form having a straight edge and broad tang, Illahun VII. 1. The handle suitable for these is figured in Kahun PL. IX. 15. It was a new handle and applicable either to a bronze or stone blade. The shape of the instrument is well known from coloured figures and examples extending from the earliest to Roman times. But it is noticeable that the implement, which is the simplest next to the axe, is very far removed from the neolithic tool of Europe, for no actual examples or hieroglyphs of Nun or Sotep, or pictures, have been found in which the blade is inserted in a wooden socket.

Among the objects of the XIIth dynasty was something intended for an adze blade, six inches long, the clumsiness of whose workmanship, and the failure to produce on it a serviceable edge, suggests the work of a beginner rather than a preparatory blocking out by a skilled workman. A portion of an adze blade is shown in Illahun PL. VII. 9, whose form and workmanship however is not like that of any certainly known to be of the XIIth dynasty. As it was found in a burial with some scarabs of the beginning of the XVIIIth dynasty it is probably of that age.

87. The marked types of knife-like blades are five in number. That figured in Kahun, XVI. [top line last but one on right], is a common variety, the chipping is always rough, it has no good cutting edge and the convex edge is rudely bevelled on one side only. The blade is blunted at the tip. The figure next to the last is another type, and its workmanship is about equal to the former; both these have their free ends downwards. A type not far removed from the last as to shape and style is represented next to the adze blade on the left of the same plate, and a fine example in Illahun PL. VII. 11. By far the most characteristic knife blade however is that represented in Kahun PL. XVI. to the left of the cap of the column and in Illahun PL. VII. 7 and 8. All these examples, and they are numerous, either whole or in portions, are very well chipped in broad flaking, having no attempt at regularity of pattern; but the smoothness of surface and suitability for purposes of cutting are as perfect as in those, with the narrowest ripple flaking so pleasing to the eye, seen on some implements of other periods. In Illahun PL. VII. the fine knives have transverse sections appended. These knives have one edge either perfectly straight or very slightly and gracefully concave. The straight edge was apparently finished off on a stone to get the line even. No signs of hard usage ever occur on this edge in perfect specimens, but on the other edge there is much evidence of rather rough employment, and though generally the splintering is from one side

only it occasionally occurs from both sides. It appears that when these knives got a little blunted they were not retrimmed, but simply used up carelessly. They are smoothed on both edges at the smaller end or tang so as not to cut through a wisp of palm leaf or cloth, which was placed there and bound round with a piece of cord to give a hold for the fingers. One such is figured in Illahun PL. XIII. 6. It is equal in workmanship to the best of these knives. It is notable that of the unbroken blades found in Kahun, this last has suffered more than any from use, it having lost nearly half an inch of breadth from the widest part of the convex edge. None of the knives have evidence of any other mode of hafting. This slight hafting appears to be no mere carelessness. From the nature of flint and the thinness of the blades it is evident that (for instruments not used for thrusting) a handle giving too great a grip might cause the operator to employ too much force in the act of cutting and hacking, if however the blade was delicately held by but two fingers and the thumb, the limited amount of force which the blade could bear was involuntarily secured. There is another form of knife, Illahun PL. VII. 16, of which a whole blade was not found at Kahun. The type of handle is like that found at Arsinoe, Hawara PL. XXVII. 5, though the Kahun example must have had a shorter blade. The very fine Arsinoe example is apparently of the same style of workmanship as those of Kahun and is perhaps of the same date, as it came from disturbed soil excavated from a XIIth dynasty site. The hollowed part of the handle was probably for the reception of two fingers, the thumb being placed above, as before mentioned; and it is noticeable that the larger the blade the more the grasp is limited.

There is yet another form of knife which deserves mention, although no specimen complete enough to figure has been discovered. The workmanship is of the best. One edge is straight and thin. The two flat surfaces do not meet at the outer and slightly convex edge, but are connected by a regular bevelled slope making a right angle in section with one of the sides. The examples found appear to have been used exclusively on the straight edge, which looks as if it had been employed to cut soft material on a board, the thick edge is unworn. The instrument is sharply pointed and has the appearance of a thick-backed knife, the tang is little marked, so that perhaps the knife was held by the middle of the back.

There are four tools figured in Kahun XVI. [to the left of column shaft] which have been adapted from other broken tools. They seem to have been employed as chisels or gouges, though there is no signs of bruising.

One little instrument above the axe in Kahun PL. XVI. is flat and bevelled all round the edge; it must have been mounted as axes were, but may have been employed with others in combination and not used for striking blows.

In Illahun PL. VII. 15 and Kahun XVI. are represented broad flakes with secondary chipping for use as straight edge and scrapers. A small instrument is figured in Kahun PL. XVI., it is U shaped with a straight line at the top (broken at the corners). Its average thickness is $\frac{1}{10}$ of an inch; it is very fairly chipped on the convex surface (the other being flat) of one side only, and very delicate. It will cut with facility pith, wet or dry papyrus—perhaps this was its use.

The employment of mere flakes for use apparently without preparation was of course very common. The art of flaking, if not shared by every member of the community, cannot have been a rare one. But the lack of cores at Kahun is remarkable, none having been found in the houses, nor any special chipping ground. However plenty of well-formed flakes, long, straight and thin were available for cutting, scraping, or boring holes, in short for all the purposes a pocket knife is carried. In one instance, Find No. 9 Kahun, 1890 (Illahun PL. XIII. 1-18) a leather bag was found containing a copper tool or two with other odds and ends, also portions of flint knives and some straight cutting flakes. Many flakes were smoothly blunted along one or both edges. No implements were found in the town suitable for stone facing nor for saws. In the latter case it is impossible to imagine that serrated flakes could be serviceably set as such. Nor were such clumsy saws wanted, bronze or copper having long been in use for the purpose. Some flakes with roughened edges seem to have been used for wood work after the manner we could use the edge of a rasp.

There is little doubt that many knives were made at favourable places and hawked about the country.

88. Besides the numerous flakes which have been slightly modified by secondary chipping or by use, are some which have been found in the town and many more in the miscellaneous gatherings of the neighbourhood. They have long been known to collectors and described as saws. The finding however of a wooden sickle with one of these flints

mounted in it has changed the name hitherto borne to the right one of sickle teeth. Examples of these teeth are given in PL. VII. 5, 5A and 6, and in Kahun PL. XVI. Commonly these teeth are the middle parts of long flakes, either end having been removed in consequence of irregularities. They are more or less regularly toothed or serrated. Occasionally some are found which can scarcely be said to be more than jagged. They vary in length from half an inch to four inches. The average is 1½ inch. Some of the serrations are close without an interval, others with long intervals even as much as a quarter of an inch, and a few have been found apparently unnotched. In experiments made to try the value of notched and unnotched edges, it was found that the plain ones cut at first like an iron blade, but the edge became smooth very quickly, while notched flakes had an incomparably longer life. The sickle found in 1889 is figured in Kahun PL. IX. 22. It must have consisted originally of one piece of wood, for although a fresh tip had been added, probably from breakage, I cannot think that the wood was cut off needlessly in order to put on a weaker tip, as an examination of the grain clearly shows that the wood must have extended much further in the required direction. The broad part was curved during growth, perhaps intentionally with a view to the manufacture of the instrument. Its form irresistibly recalls the form of (half) a lower jaw perhaps of the ox or horse. Were such a jaw actually employed for reaping, certain modifications would be required to adapt it to efficient use, thus as the hand would have a difficulty in grasping the rather short and knobby condyle and coronoid process, they would be smoothed down and a handy piece of wood lashed on; then as the distal end of the body would be occupied by a row of incisors, they would be supplanted by a long stick placed in one of the sockets; and lastly, as the teeth are not very suitable for cutting corn they would have to be knocked out and replaced by a row of serrated flint flakes. In the first found sickle of the XIIth dynasty all these improvements were united, and the bone itself replaced by a single piece of wood, of course a great advance on the crude idea. A groove is cut to hold the notched flints or teeth, which were fine and thin, one remaining in its original position. The groove is filled with a grey brown cement to hold the teeth, formed of clay or mud and gum or glue; a quantity of this cement is smeared over the junction of the wood and the teeth, and resembles and apparently does some of the duty of the gums in an animal. The teeth are partly buried in the groove which in the Kahun examples was cut by metal chisels, and so far as can be seen, the groove did not exceed a half inch in depth. A quarter of an inch of the flake was overlapped by the "gum" and about the same quantity projected. These measures are for the centre of the groove. Towards the point of the sickle the proportions are reduced, at the near end slightly increased. At the latter a special modification of the shape of the end tooth was necessary, of which an ordinary example is given in PL. VII. 5A, on which the parts covered by the socket, by the gum, and free, are indicated by lines. The flakes or teeth at the further end diminished almost to a point and faded into the general contour of the jaw. Taken as a whole the implement has reached perfection, but it is unlikely that sickles were often made as this one, from the difficulty of getting single pieces of wood capable of being worked into the required curves. They were usually made in three pieces, the body, the handle and the point. These compound ones, of which the several parts were separately found in Kahun, always have the "angle" of the jaw very sharp. The handles of all the sickles perfect, or in part, fit the right hand and cannot be employed by the left.

89. That part of the flint teeth left free to cut with is usually brightly polished with the lower margin of polish distinctly marked. Experiments were made with flint (from Egypt) to see whether the sawing of wood, bone, horn, or other such materials would produce it, but without success. The rubbing of flint with sand did not do so; in fact the polish of sand-smoothed flints is very subdued and of a coarser nature, never reaching that obtained by the friction of the fine, organic silica of the stems of cereal grasses. It is often found that the high polish of flakes is in part removed by sand wear, if exposed. The sickle teeth naturally fell out, and were ground down and blunted in the act of reaping. When this happened they were renewed, frequently by the reversal of the same tooth in the groove after the serration of the new edge. Indeed, in anticipation of such an event some teeth were inserted already serrated on the lower edge. On PL. VII. 27 of this volume a compound sickle with three teeth still attached is shewn, its parts differ in no important particular from the parts of compound sickles found in 1889 at Kahun, which belong to the XIIth dynasty; to which date I would have assigned it. But Mr. Petrie on the strength of a piece of XVIIIth

dynasty pot found near it, thinks that the pot and the sickle belong to the same age, and it is also true that the serration of the flakes resembles rather some that were found at Gurob than those from Kahun of the XIIth dynasty.

The use of these sickles I have practically tried in England on various kinds of corn, with a carefully constructed model, which worked well. It works best when the heads of corn have been gathered in the hand and bent backwards, then swept just below the hand with the length of the armature by a rotary twist of the wrist to finish, a saw-like motion being thus imparted. It also cuts well, low down near the ground; but in either case the motion must be *to* the person and slightly upwards. All attempts to cut downwards and away from the reaper proved complete failures, for various obvious reasons; these last were tried in consequence of the attitudes seen depicted in ancient paintings—apparently, too, the requirements of symmetry in the design was the sole cause why a large proportion of the reapers are represented working with the left hand.

90. The forms of sickles as represented in harvest scenes in tombs of the early dynasties are various; some of the variations are obviously mere careless drawing, and some are apparently an attempt to represent sickles like those of Kahun in such a manner as would give a full view of the broadside of the sickle, at the same time exhibiting the implement in action. In reality when the corn stands before the spectator, the reaper would show his back, and the sickle be obscured; or if seen, its horizontal position be represented by a mere line. But such natural views were never drawn, for it was necessary to show the orthodox side views of the man and his tool. In early empire tombs, as at Gizeh and Sakkarah, the forms of some sickles are drawn as nearly like that of Kahun as the style of art permitted. Although sometimes the end of the handle projects some way beyond the hand, in well-executed examples a knob is clearly shewn. The ridge of teeth extended almost to the point, giving the blade a blunt termination; except in instances where a tip is present, when the termination of the row of teeth is marked by an abrupt decrease in the breadth of the blade; the tip is rarely long.

The form of a sickle was taken for the symbol *ma*. This, in the early empire, was represented like the Kahun specimens (without however a very long tip), but always having a sharp "angle." In the tombs of Gizeh of the IVth dynasty the symbol sometimes shews the termination of the row of teeth by the sudden change in the width of the blade, as in the case of the teeth of an ox in the jaw. And in the tomb of Rahotep (early IVth dynasty) the wider part of the *ma* is painted with notch teeth in black, on the shallower edge which represents the projection of the flints. But Mr. F. L. Griffith has pointed out to me that *ārti* in the Pyramid texts, which often have very realistic forms of hieroglyphs, is determined with a sign which is a simple rude picture of an animal's jaw, differing materially from that of *ma*. Therefore it is probable that the symbol *ma* in its earlier known form is really taken from a primitive *sickle*, in which the end of the row of teeth protruded clumsily.

The picture of the sickle and of *ma* are nearest alike in the earliest times, the great vertical compression which the symbol suffers in late times with the absence of the signs of teeth weakens its resemblance to a jaw. The determinative of *ārti* in late examples, though like *ma*, is provided with decided separate teeth.

91. A stone implement not coming under any of the above headings was found in the early town of

Back view.

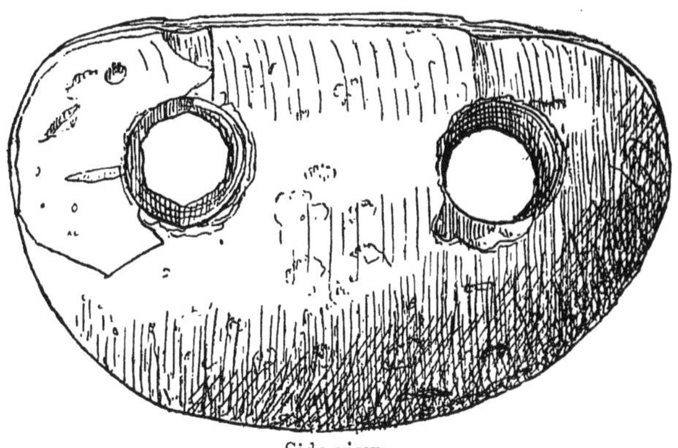

Side view.

Kahun. Its form is ovoid with a straight back. The dimensions are $4\frac{1}{4} \times 2\frac{1}{2} \times 2$ inches. Along the back is a groove $\frac{1}{4}$ inch in width. Two holes are pierced from side to side of the body. They were clumsily drilled, evidently after the implement had received its form. The smaller end of the holes is a little over ½ inch in width, the larger a little over ¾ inch. Shallow grooves are ground across the back connecting the two ends of the holes. It consists of white crystalline nummulitic limestone, and is very hard. It weighs a little under one pound avoirdupois, but must have weighed a little over before it was dismounted, bruised and knocked about in the XIIth dynasty period. The handle must have fitted the back groove well, and been but a quarter of an inch or very little more in diameter at that part. It was fastened on by thongs passed through the holes. A handle to be strong enough with this weight could scarcely have been of wood, but must have been of some tough elastic material to make this weapon serviceable, perhaps it was of rhinoceros horn, or cut from the hide of rhinoceros or hippopotamus. I have not been able to discover the precise form of this club or weapon in any ancient scenes, though one like it apparently of bronze usually with a carved handle and looking as if it had a cutting edge is common. It appears likely to have been a weapon of extremely early date, or one captured from a foreign race, perhaps Ethiopian.

There was also found in the older part of Kahun a white polished limestone mace head of the usual form of mace heads on monuments. The hole through the middle of it was too small to have admitted a wooden stick strong enough to have wielded it by, but as in the case of the club before mentioned it may have been handled with horn or hide.

CORRECTION.

p. 20. The *ka* name is one of those of Tahutmes III and not of Amenhotep IV: hence there is no reason to suppose any building to have been made here later than Tahutmes III.

INDEX.

LONDON: PRINTED BY WILLIAM CLOWES AND SONS, LIMITED, STAMFORD STREET AND CHARING CROSS.

1
2
3
4
5
6
7
8
9
10
11
12
13
14
15
16
17
18
19
20
21
22

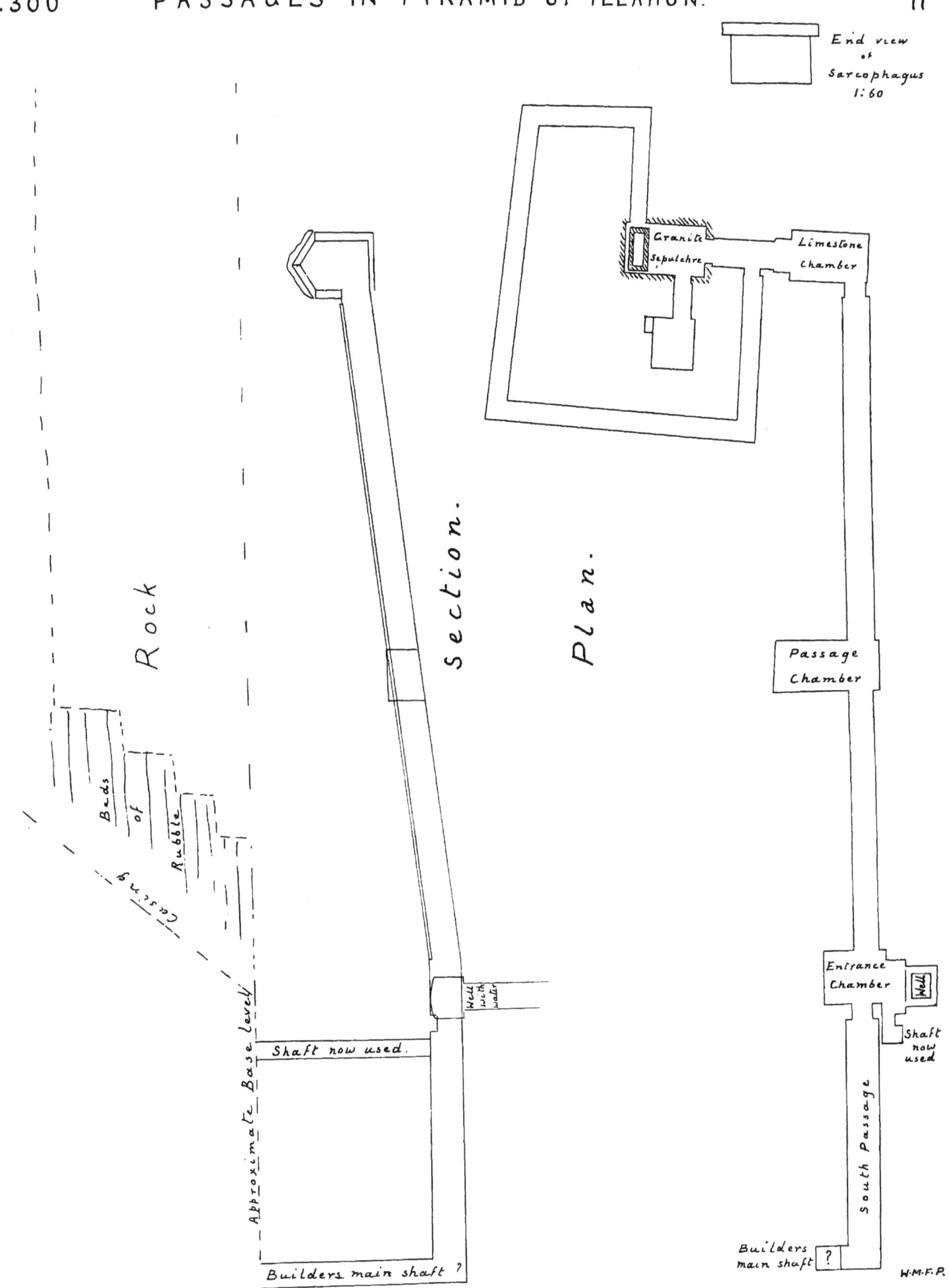
End view of Sarcophagus 1:60
Granite Sepulchre
Limestone Chamber
Rock
Section.
Plan.
Passage Chamber
Beds of Rubble
Casing
Entrance Chamber
Well
Well with water
Shaft now used
Approximate Base level
Shaft now used.
South Passage
Builders main shaft
?
Builders main shaft ?
W.M.F.P.

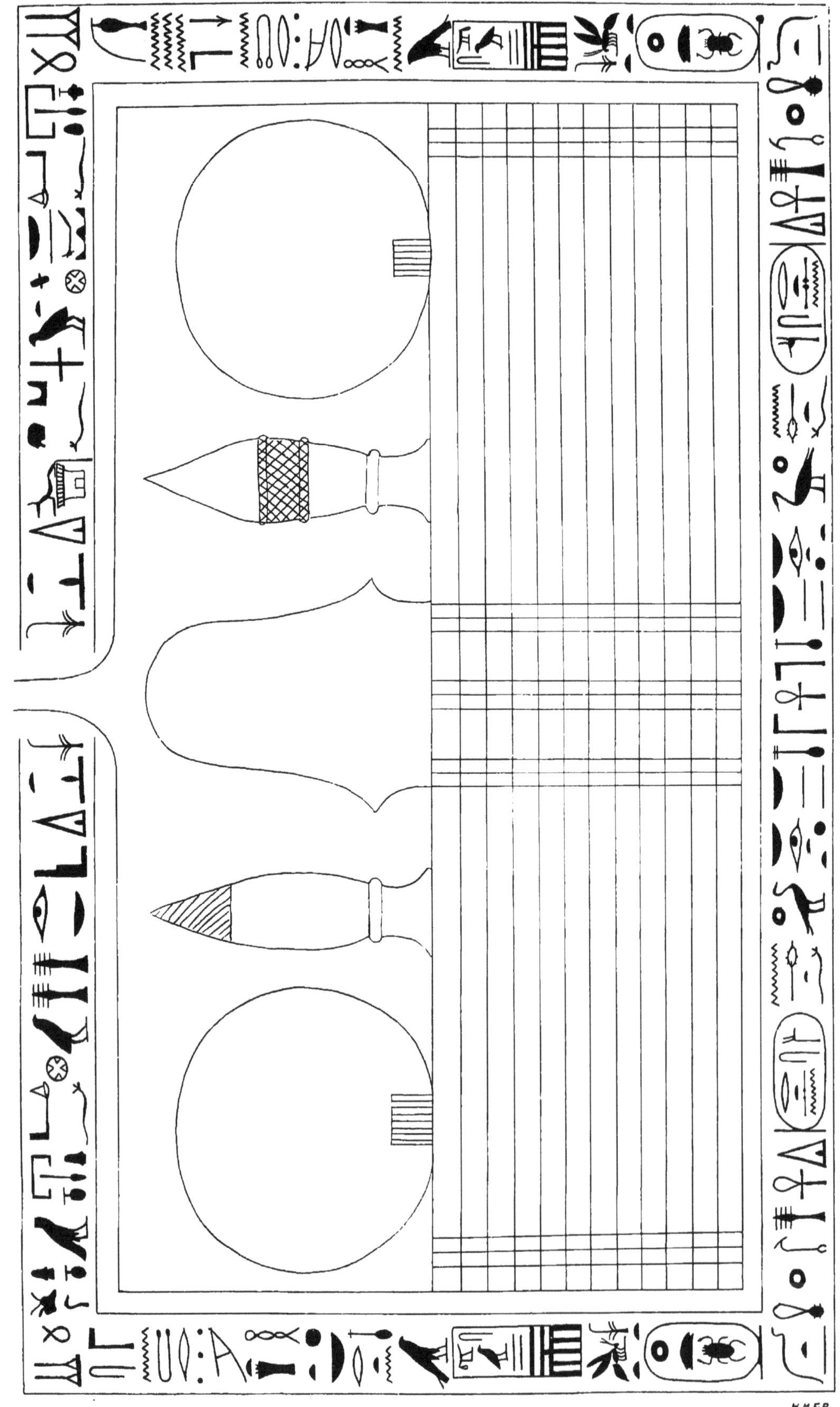

W M F P

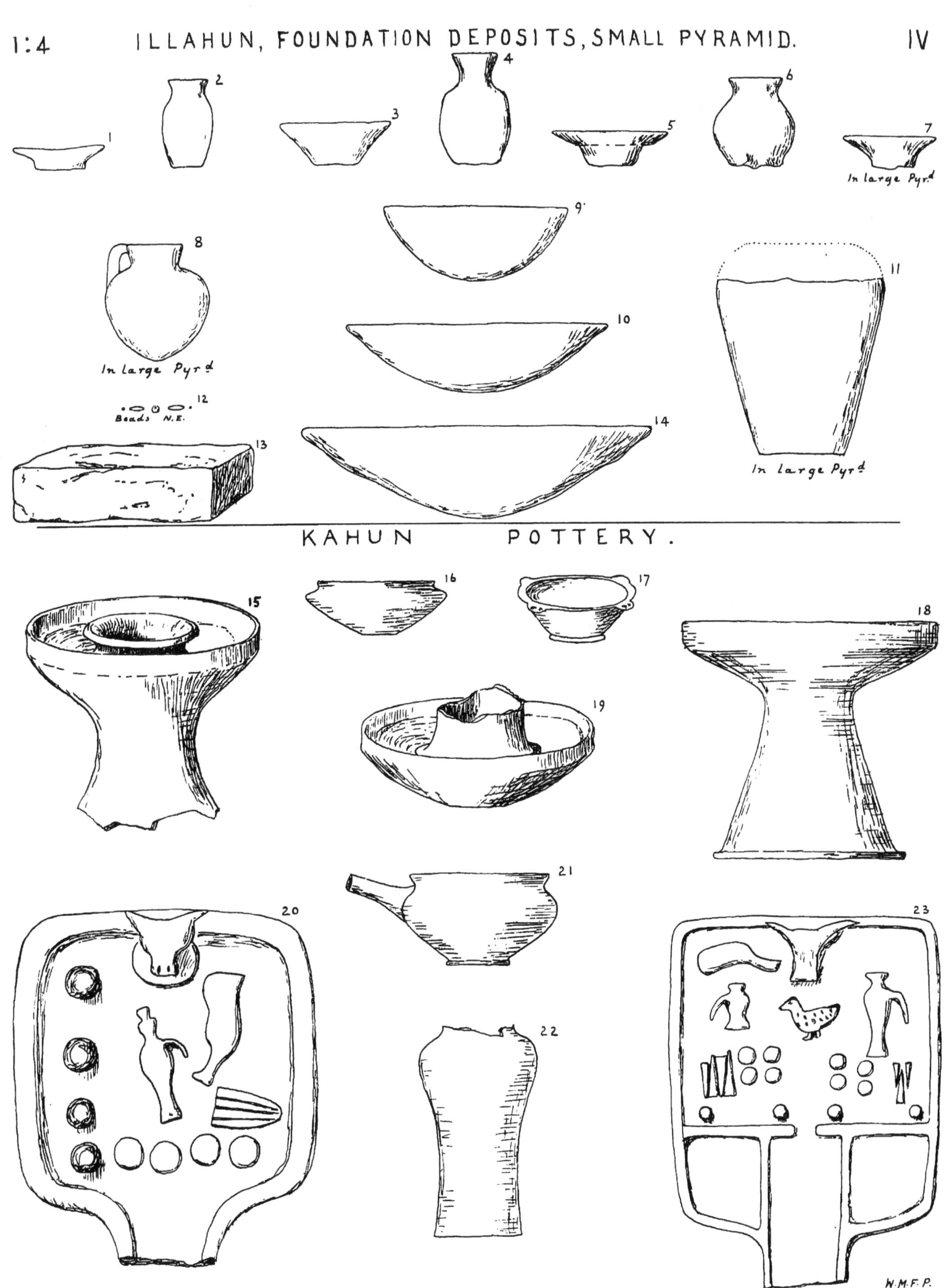
1
2
3
4
5
6
7
In large Pyr.d
8
In large Pyr.d
9
10
11
In large Pyr.d
12
Beads N.E.
13
14
KAHUN POTTERY.
15
16
17
18
19
20
21
22
23
W.M.F.P.

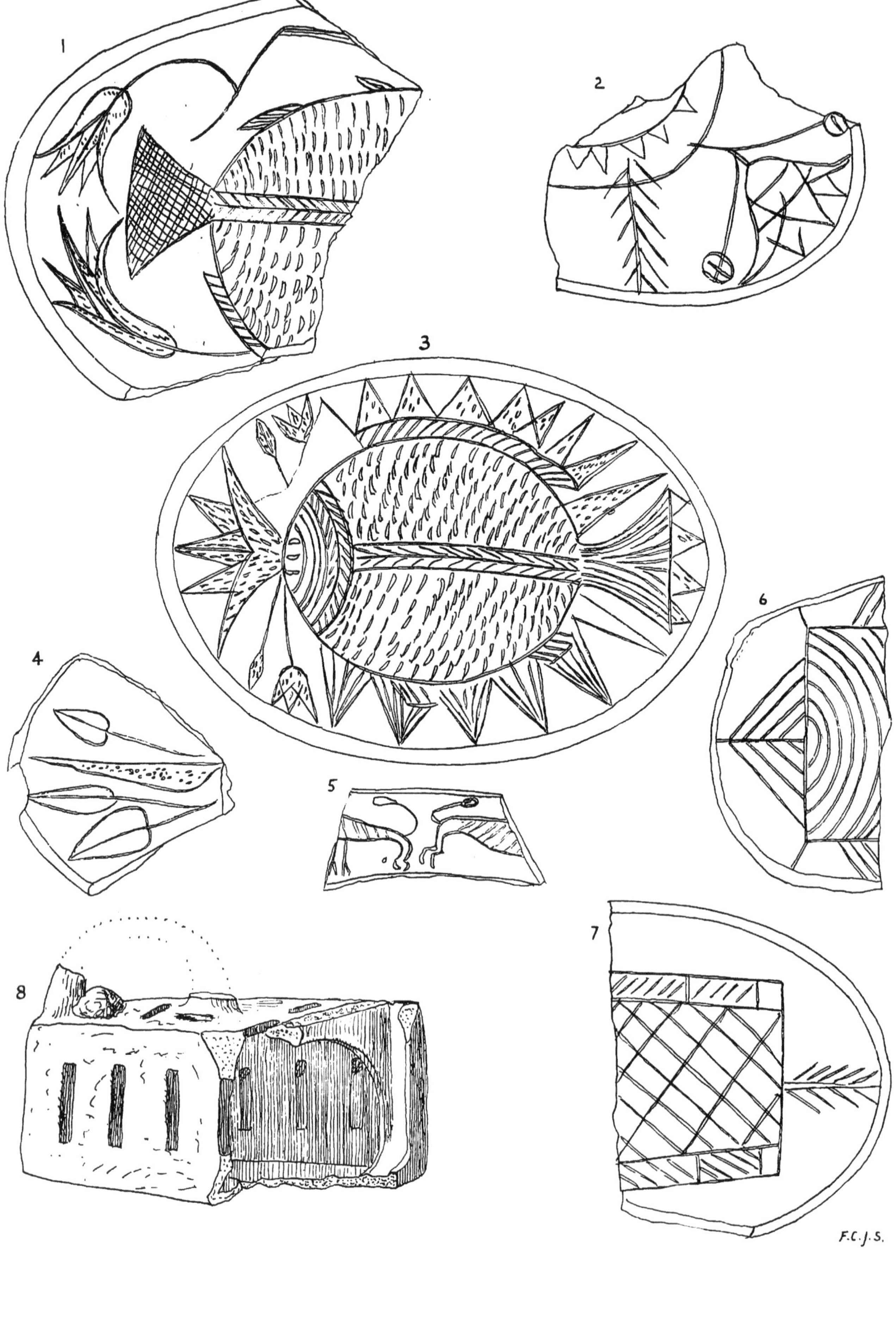

KAHUN. INCISED POTTERY DISHES

1

2

3

4

5

6

7

8

F.C.J.S.

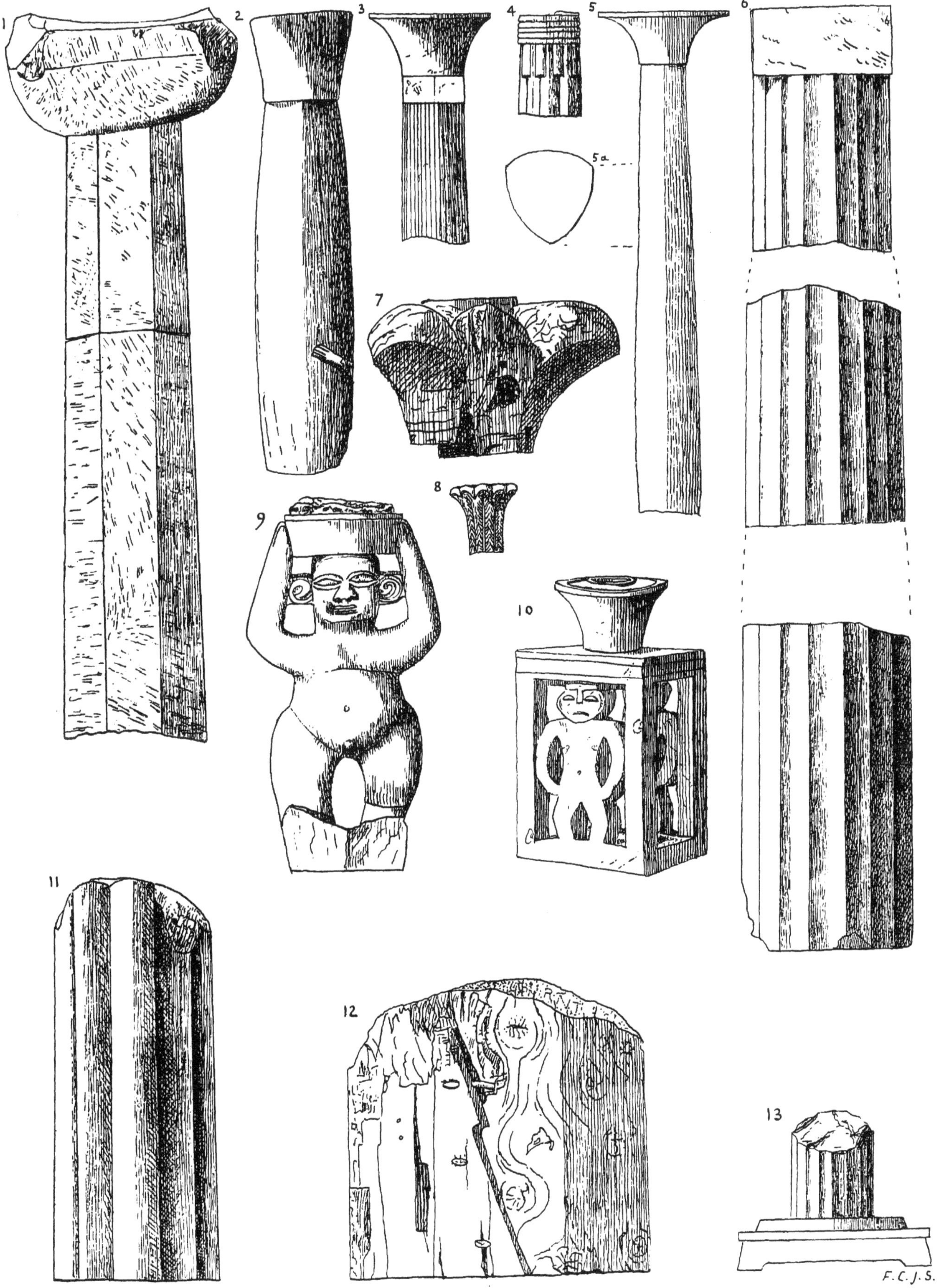

1:5

1 2 3 4 5 5a 6 7 8 9 10 11 12 13

F. C. J. S.

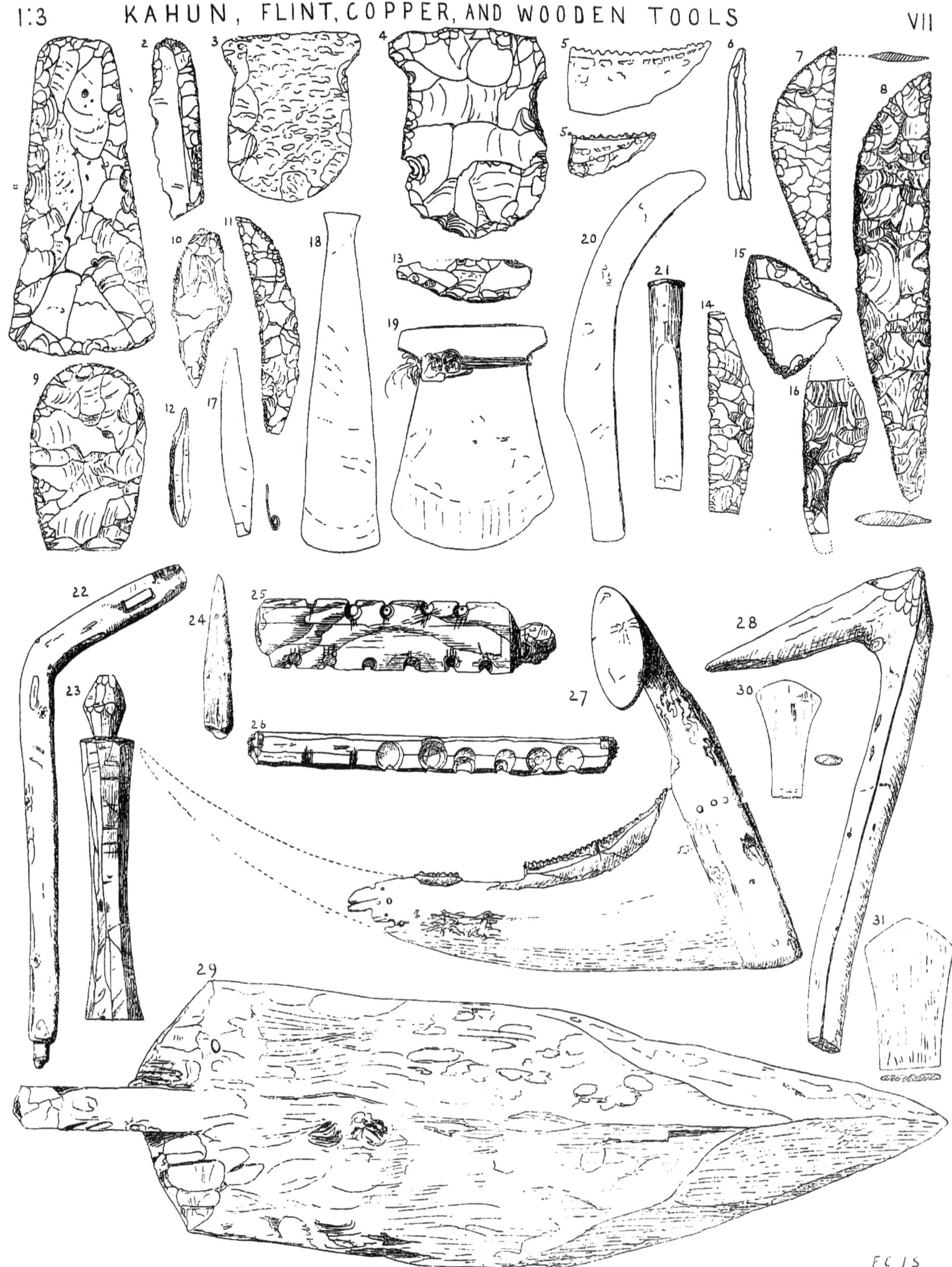
1:3
KAHUN, FLINT, COPPER, AND WOODEN TOOLS
VII
F C J S

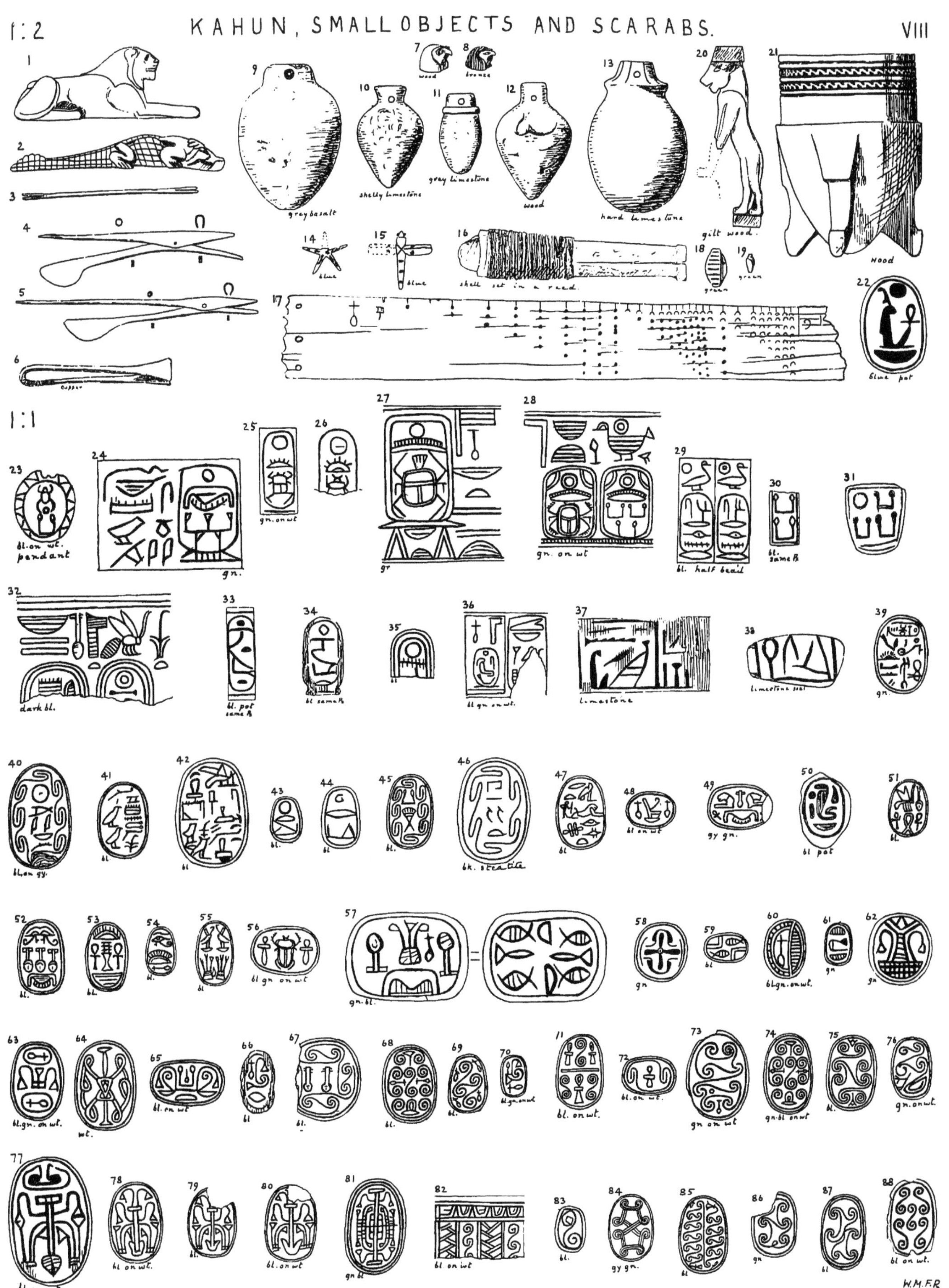
1:2
wood
bronze
gray basalt
shelly limestone
gray limestone
wood
hard limestone
gilt wood
wood
blue
blue
shell set in a reed
green
green
copper
blue pot
1:1
bl. on wt. pendant
gn. on wt
gn.
gr
gn. on wt
bl. half bead
bl. same K
dark bl.
bl. pot same K
bl same K
bl
bl gn on wt
limestone
limestone seal
gn.
bl. on gy.
bl.
bl
bl.
bl
bl.
bk. steatite
bl
bl on wt
gy gn.
bl pot
bl.
bl.
bl.
bl.
bl
bl gn on wt
gn. bl.
gn
bl
bl gn. on wt.
gn
gn
bl. gn. on wt.
wt.
bl. on wt
bl
bl.
bl.
bl.
bl gn. on wt
bl. on wt.
bl. on wt.
gn on wt
gn. bl on wt
bl.
gn. on wt.
bl. on wt.
bl on wt.
bl.
bl. on wt
gn bl
bl on wt
bl.
gy gn.
bl
gn
bl
bl on wt.
W.M.F.R

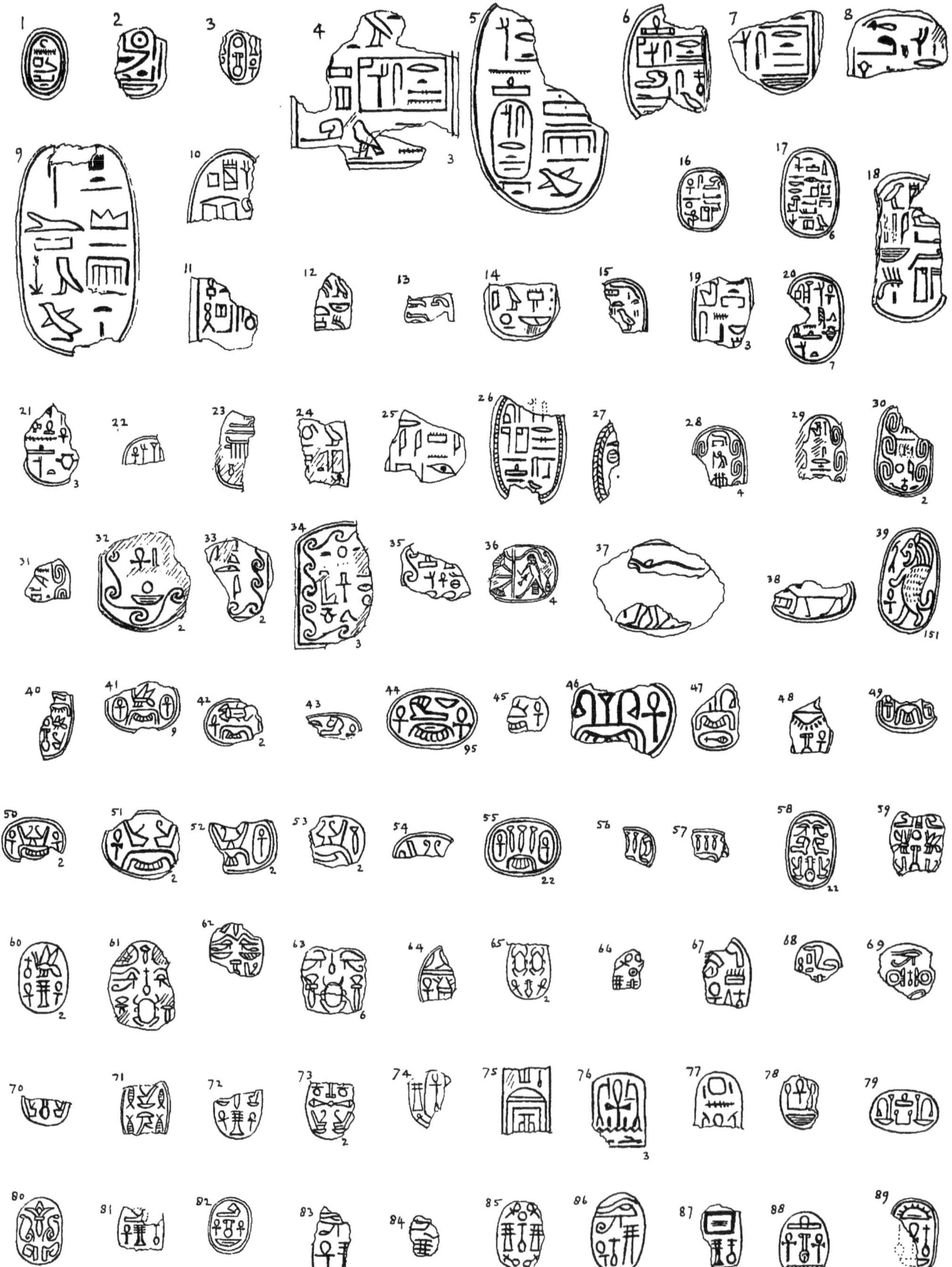
W·M·F·P.

KAHUN, CLAY IMPRESSIONS OF SEALS.

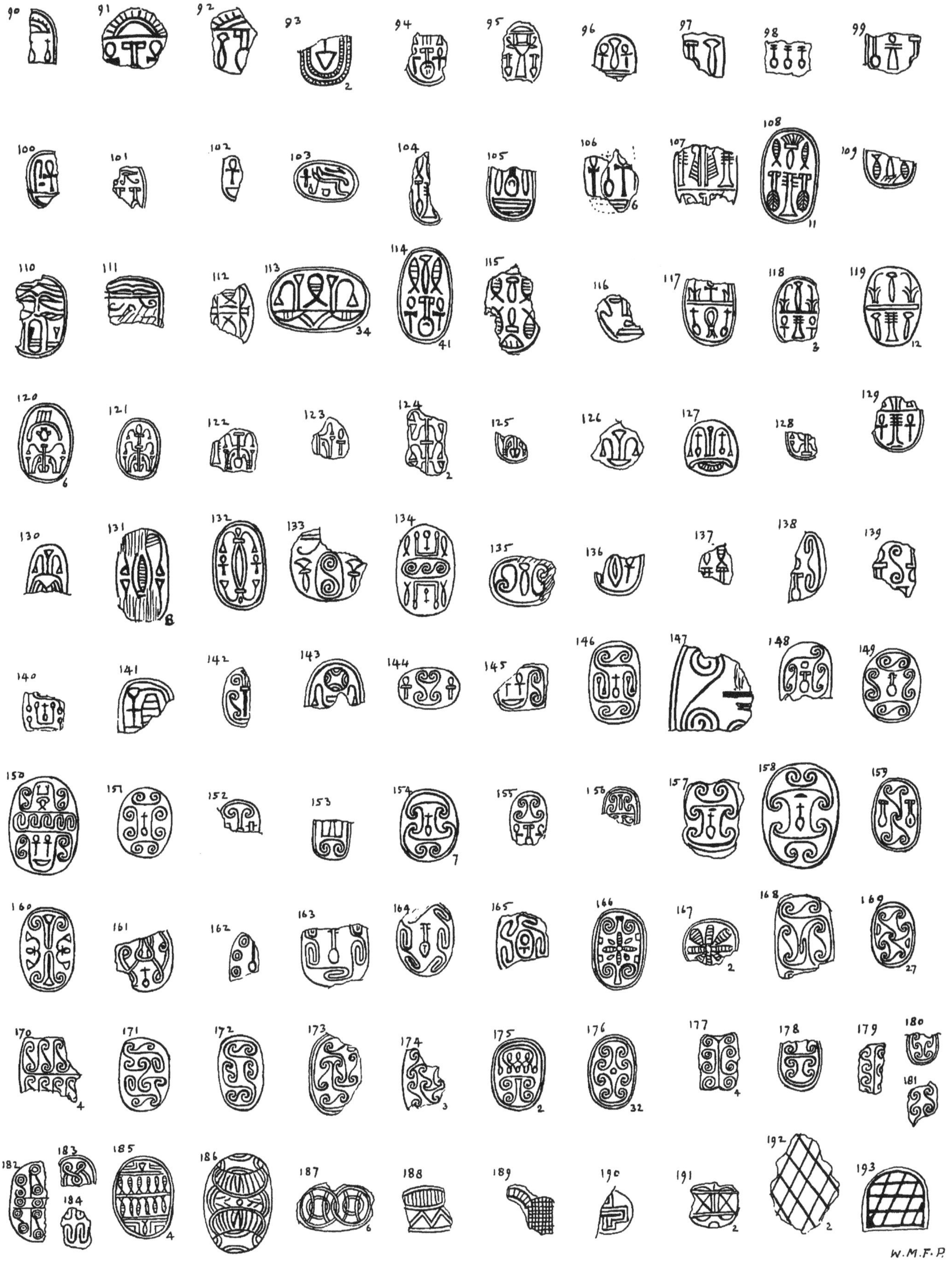

W.M.F.P.

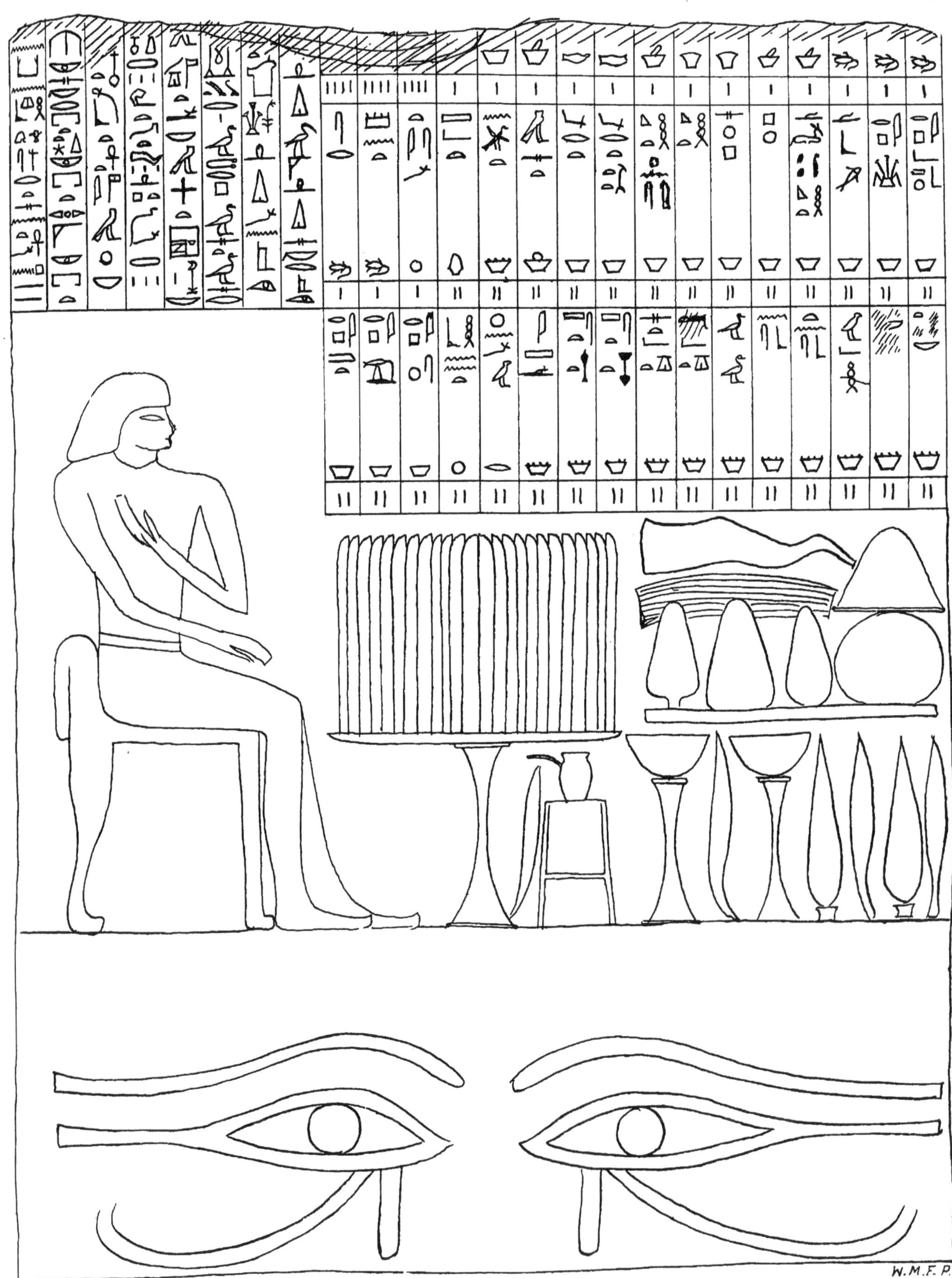

W.M.F.P.

KAHUN, INSCRIPTIONS.

1

blank

Seated figure; black serpentine.

2

Limestone tablet.

3

Limestone tablet.

4

Base of seated figure, limestone.

5

Painted stela.

6

7

8

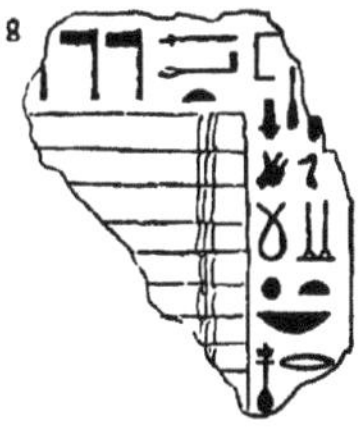

9

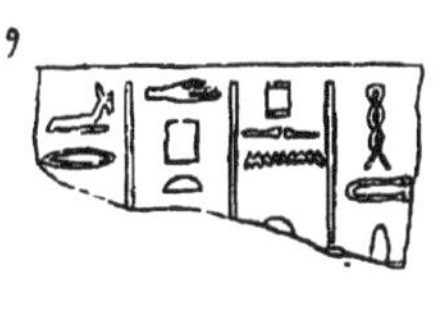

10

Name, — Atmu (nefru?), — offerings & altar.

Temple List.

Base of statue

11

Stela of Anpi.

12

Stela of Amenisenb, painted

13

Base of basalt statue.

14

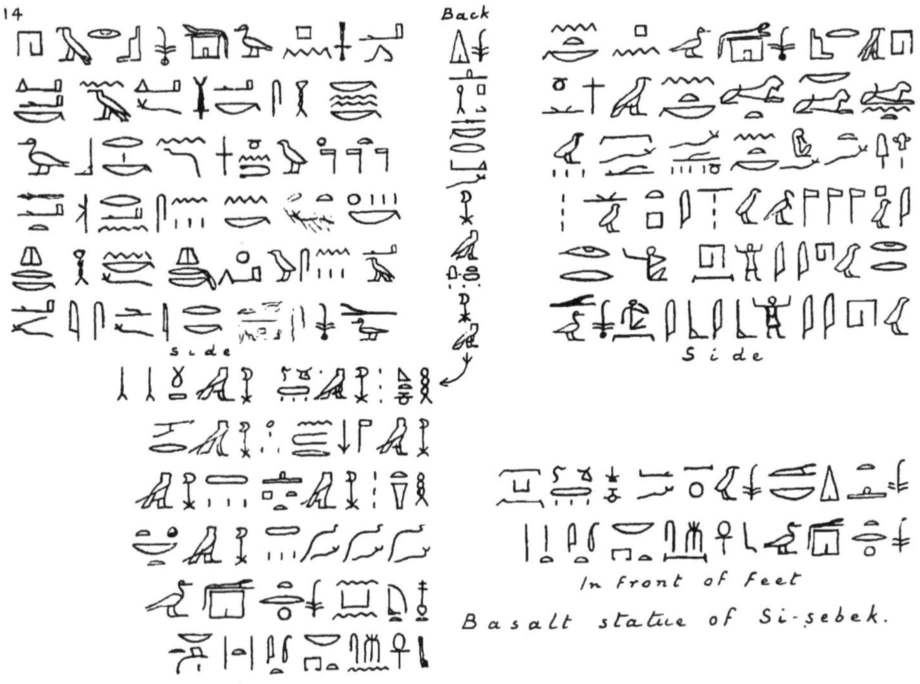

Back

Side

Side

In front of feet

Back.

Basalt statue of Si-sebek.

15

Limestone stamp

16

Wooden stamp.

W M F. P.

1:3

KAHUN. GROUP No 9, XII DYN.

BLUE GLAZE [XIII
XII DYN.

1
2
3
4
5
6
7
8
9
10
11
12
13
14
15
16
17
18
19
20

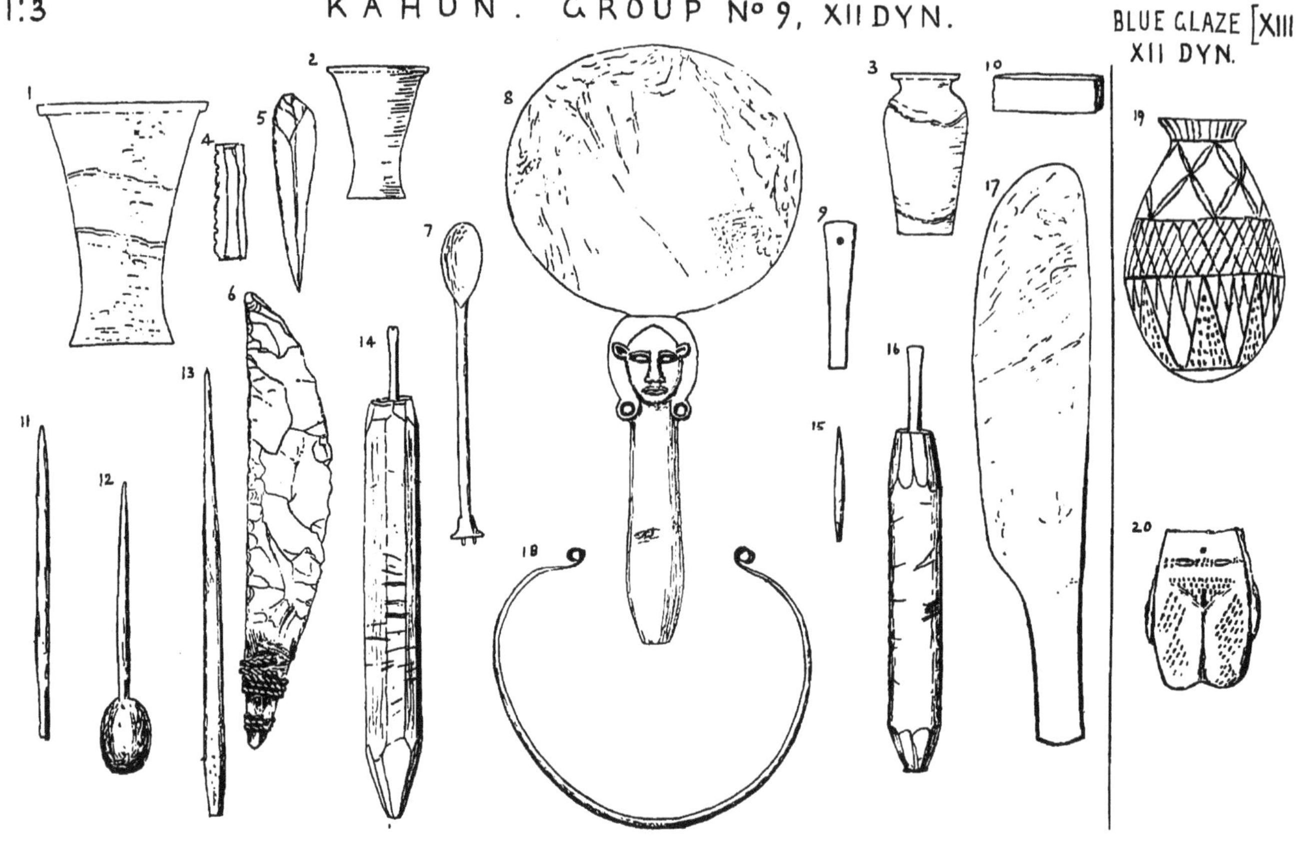

KAHUN, GROUP No 7, AMENHOTEP III

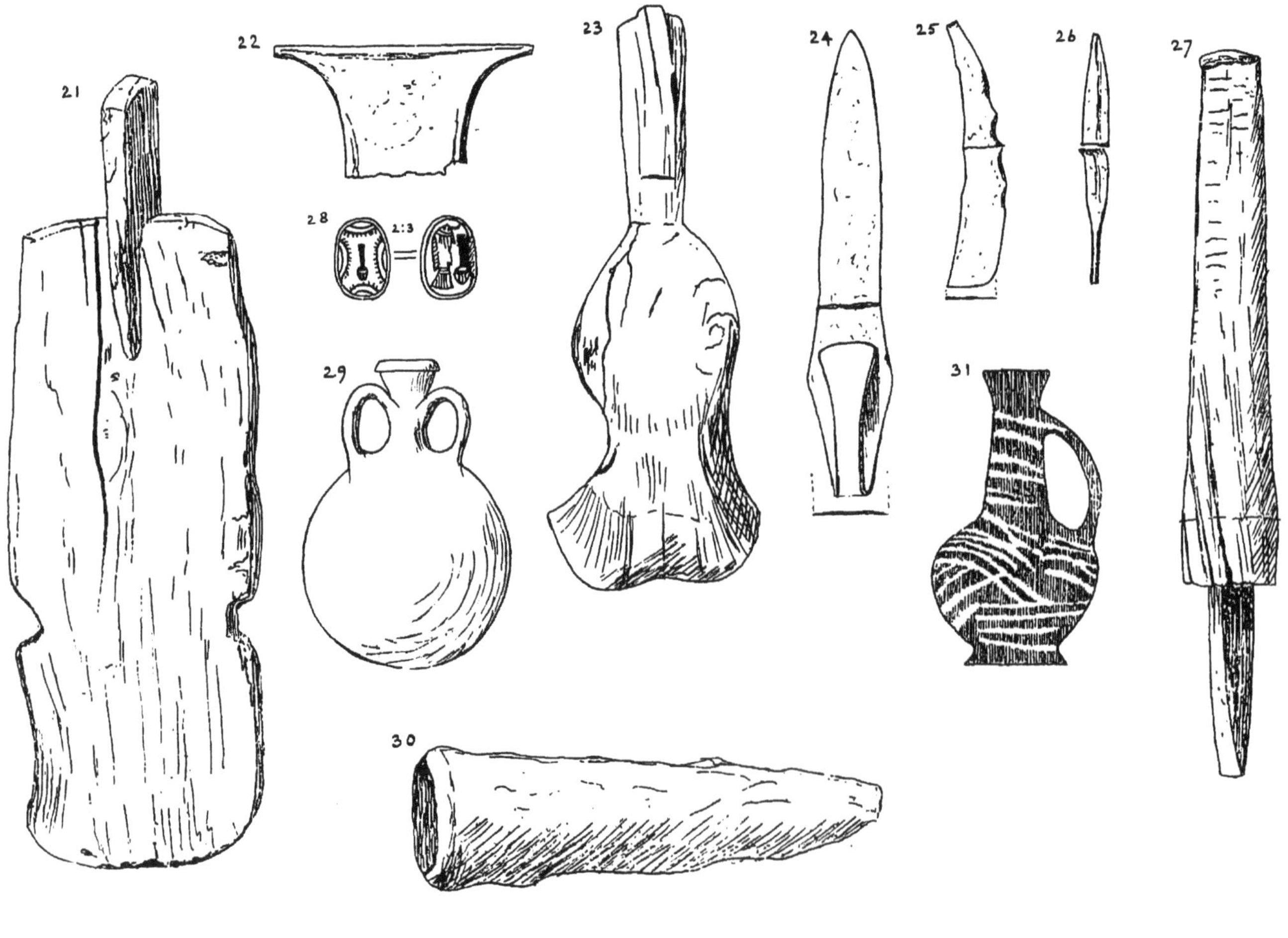

21
22
23
24
25
26
27
28
2:3
29
30
31

1:1500 KAHUN. XIV

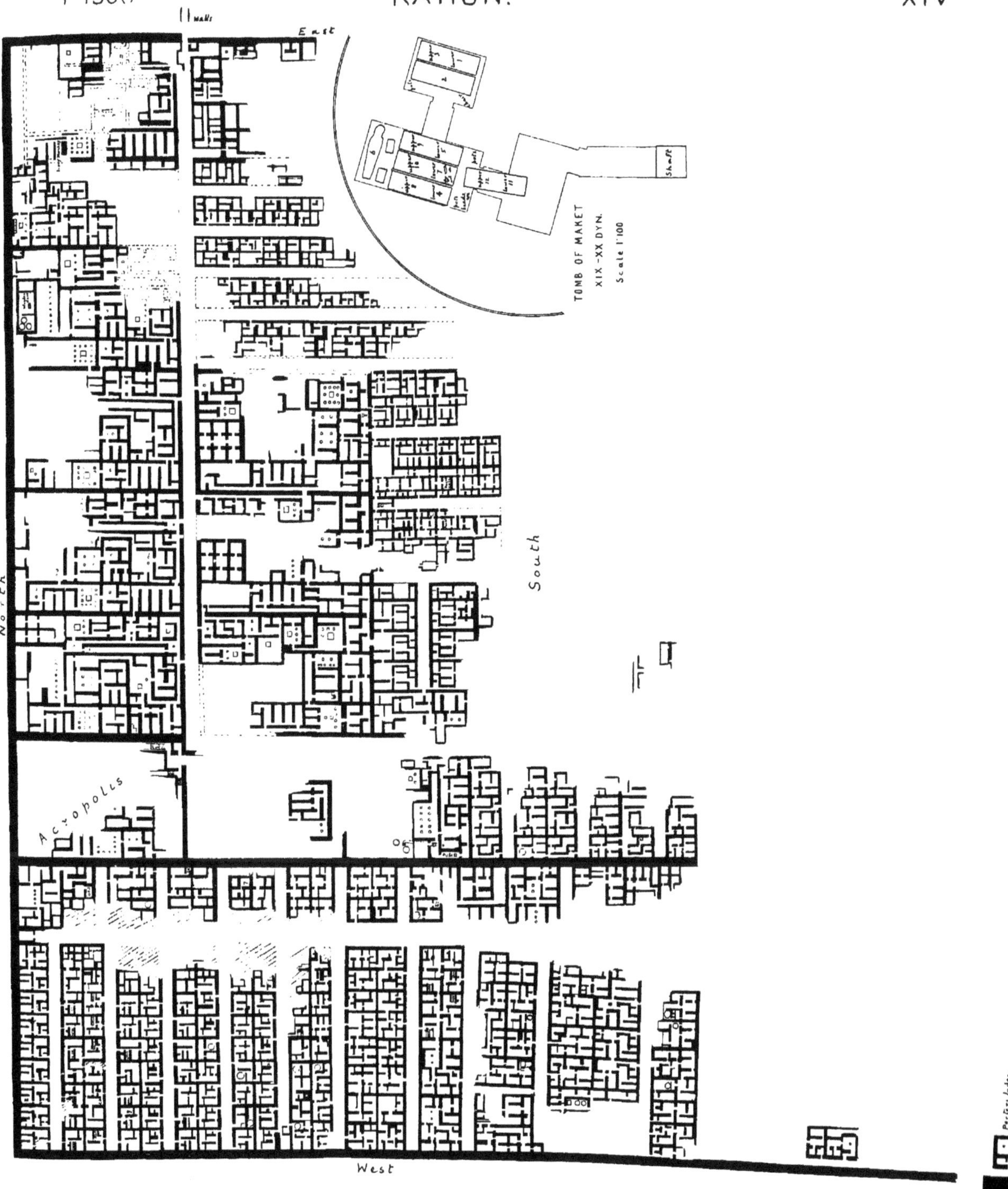

FORMS OF SIGNS ON POTTERY OF XII & XVIII DYN.

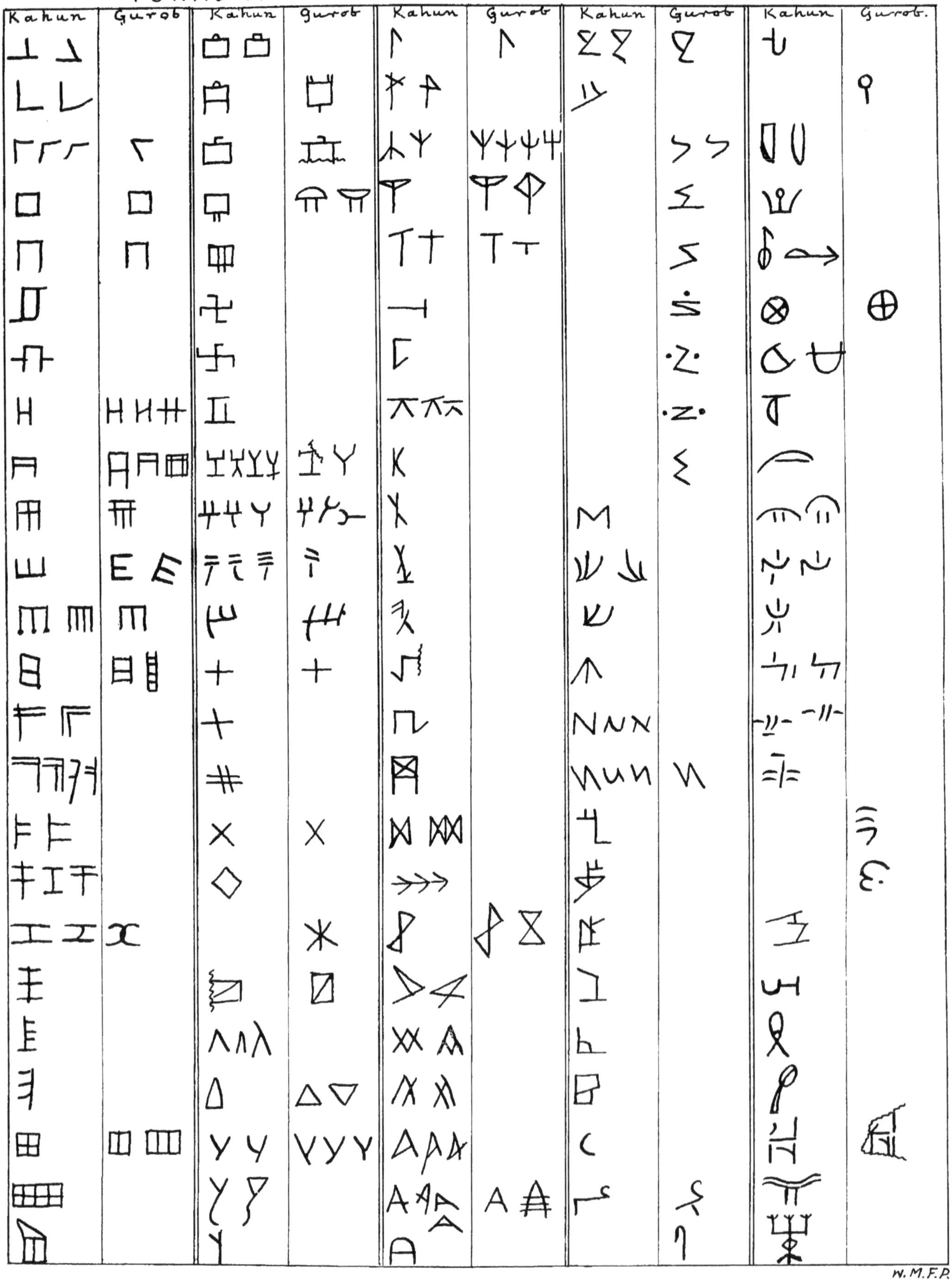

Kahun	Gurob	Kahun	Gurob	Kahun	Gurob	Kahun	Gurob	Kahun	Gurob.

W. M. F. P.

1 Great Stairway up the Acropolis.

2 Small Stairway up the Acropolis.

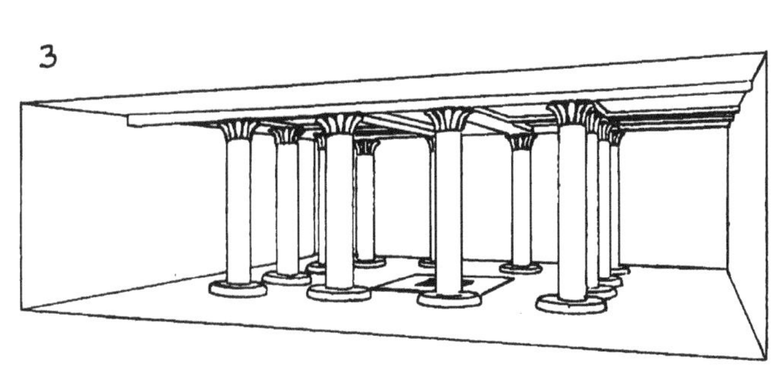

3 Restoration of a Hall.

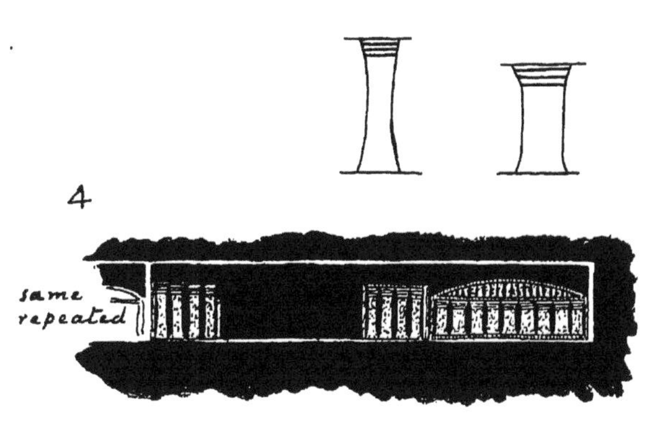

4 Wall painting 1:10

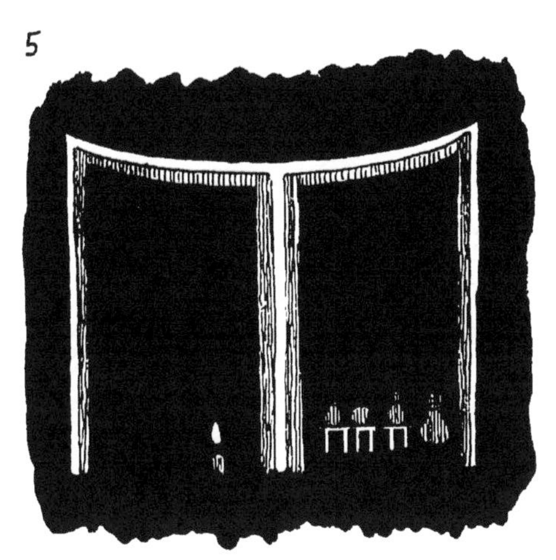

5

6

Wall Paintings 1:10

W.M.F.P.

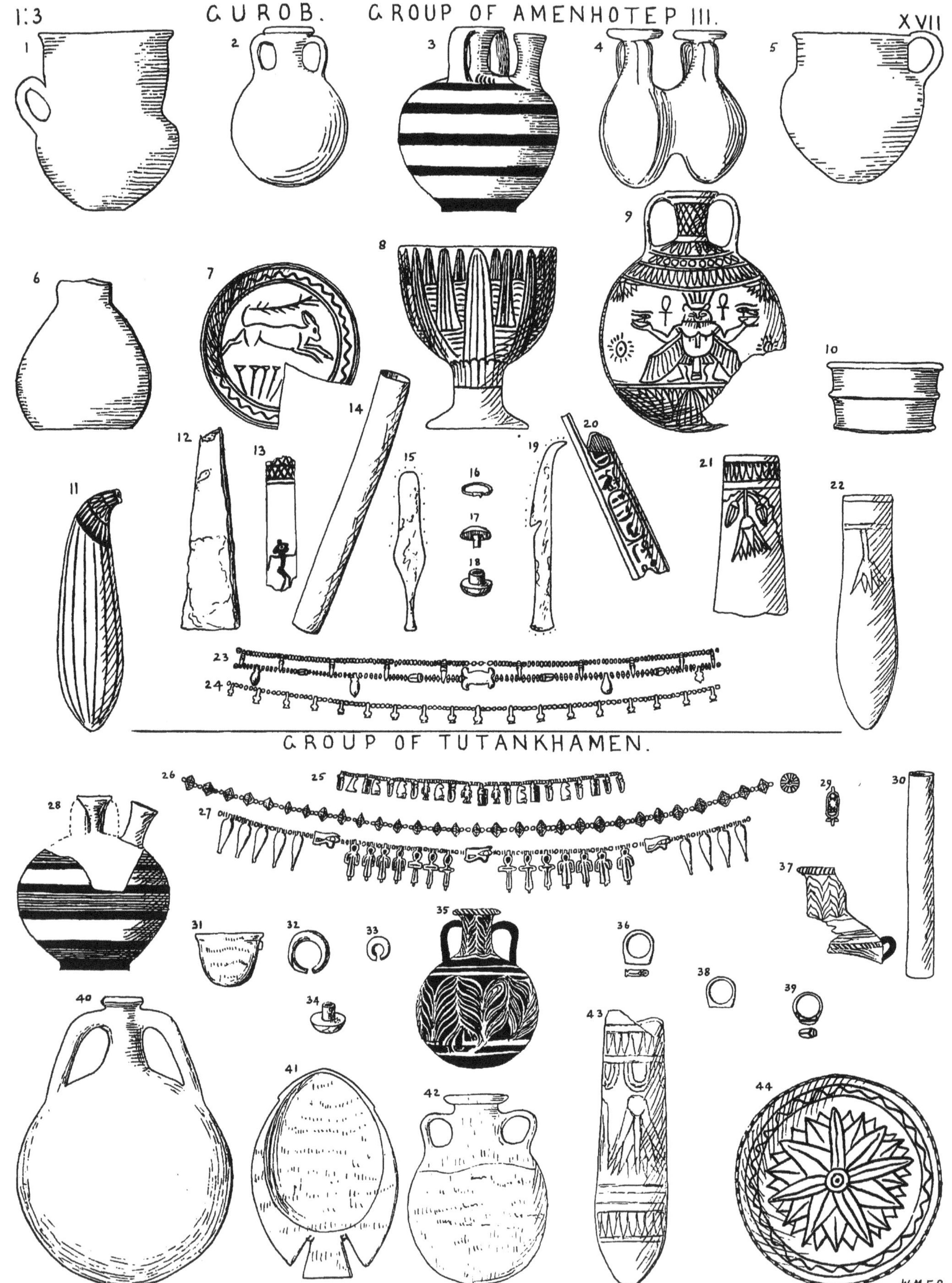
1:3
GUROB. GROUP OF AMENHOTEP III.
XVII
GROUP OF TUTANKHAMEN.
W.M.F.P.

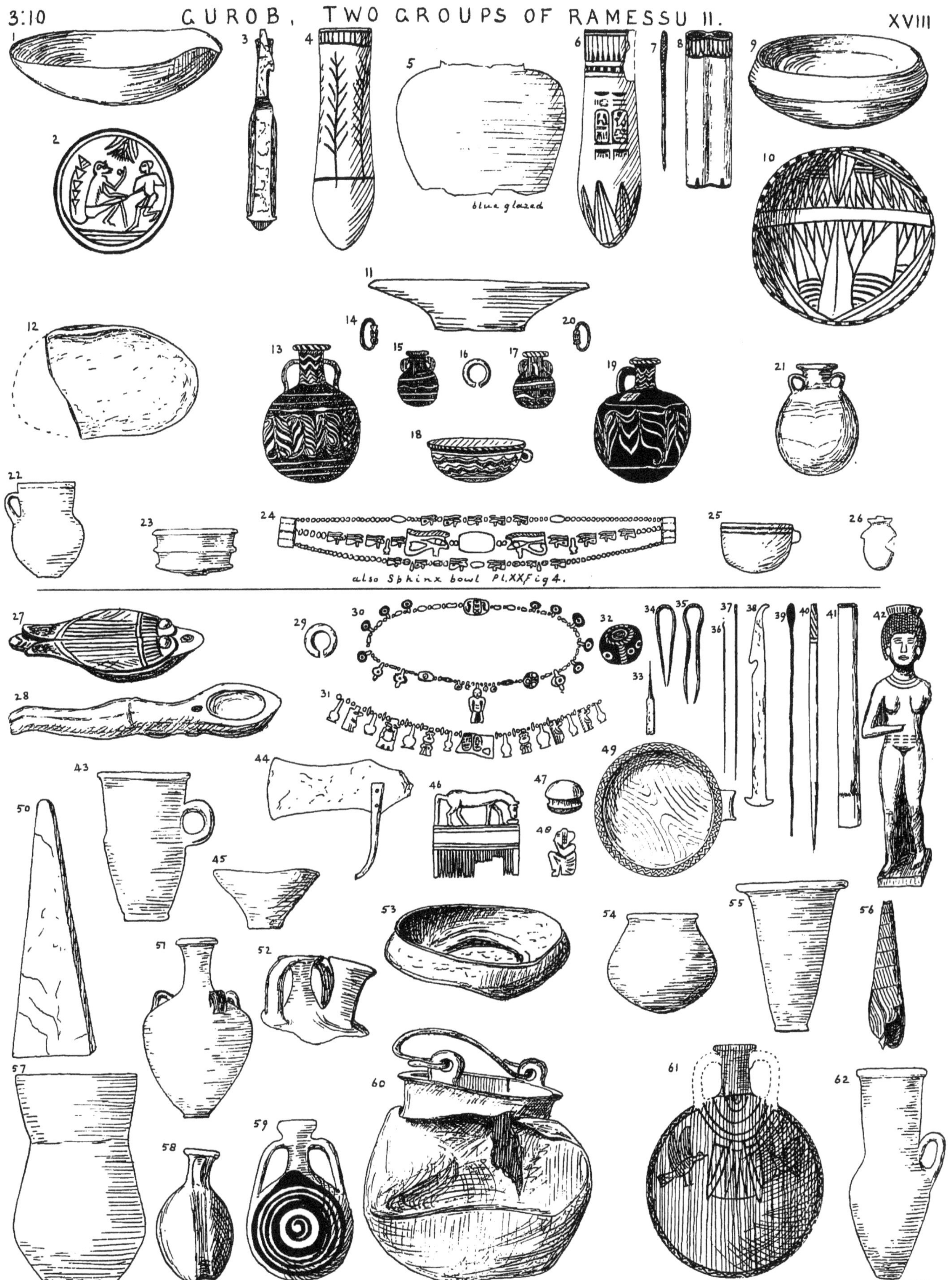
blue glazed
also Sphinx bowl Pl. XX Fig 4.
WMFP

3:10 GUROB. GROUP OF SETI II. XIX

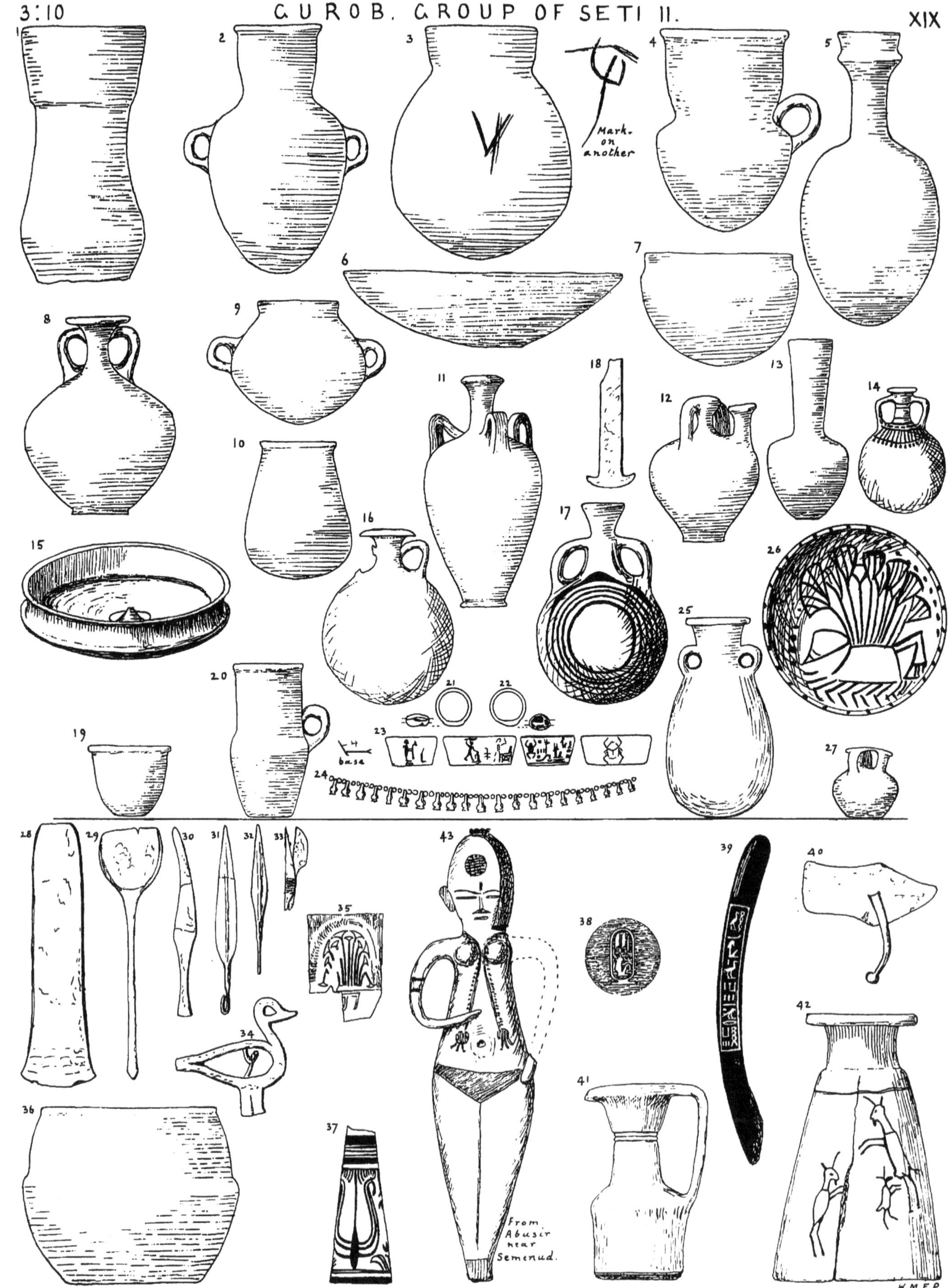

1:2 GUROB BLUE GLAZED VASES. XX

1 Find 5

2 Find 5

3 Group 9.

4 Group 4

5

6

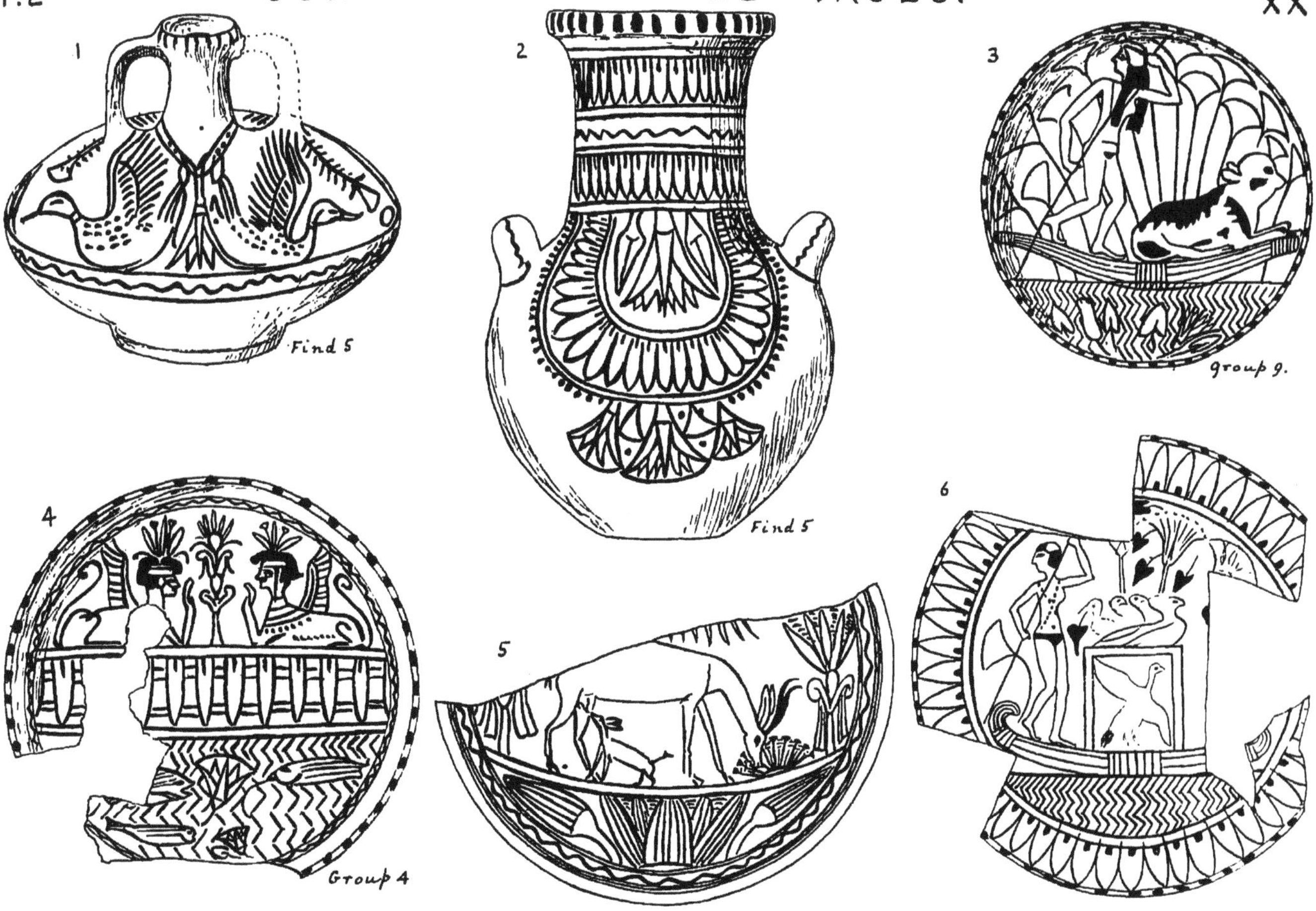

GROUP 7. END OF XVIII DYNASTY.

1:5 GUROB. POTTERY.

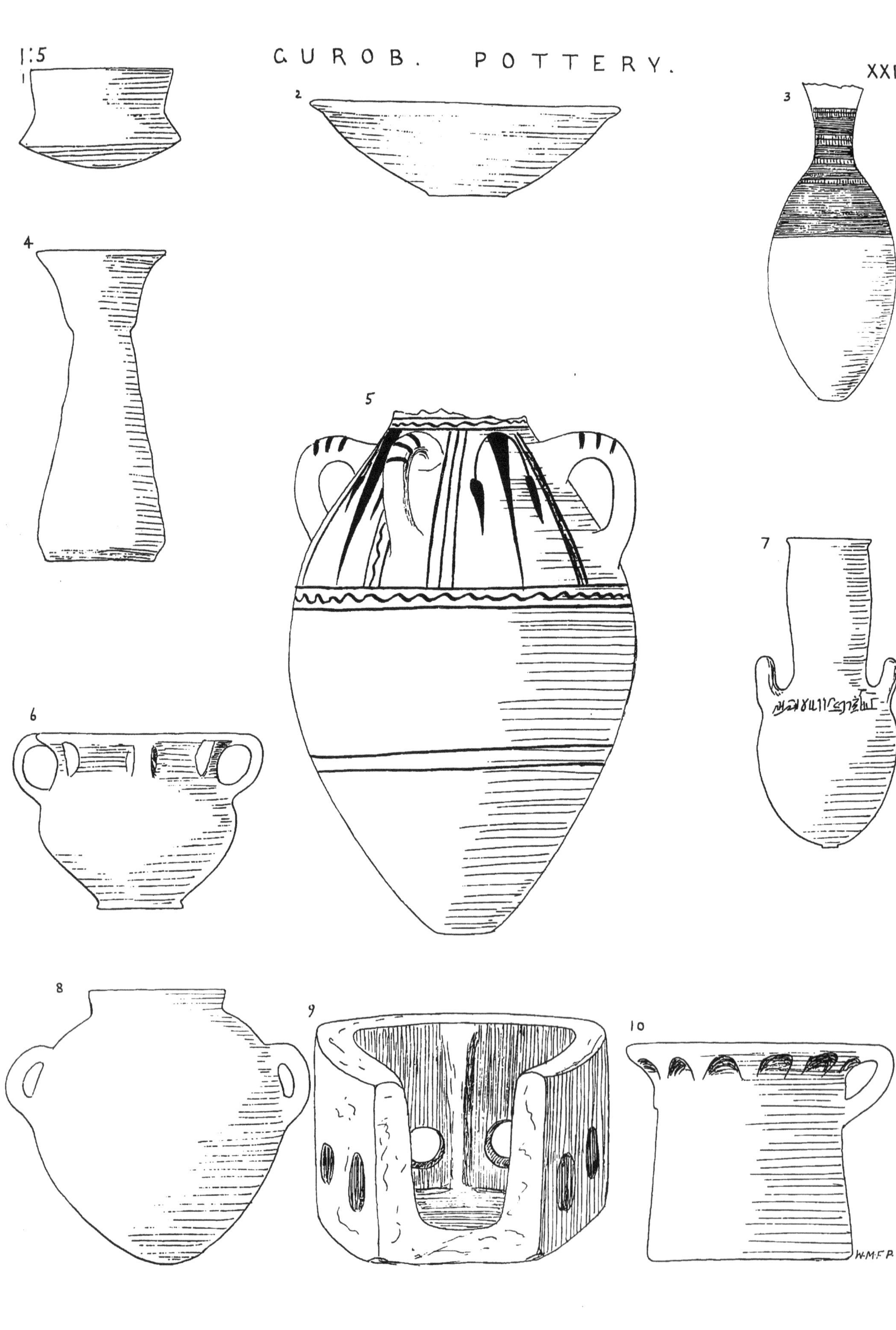

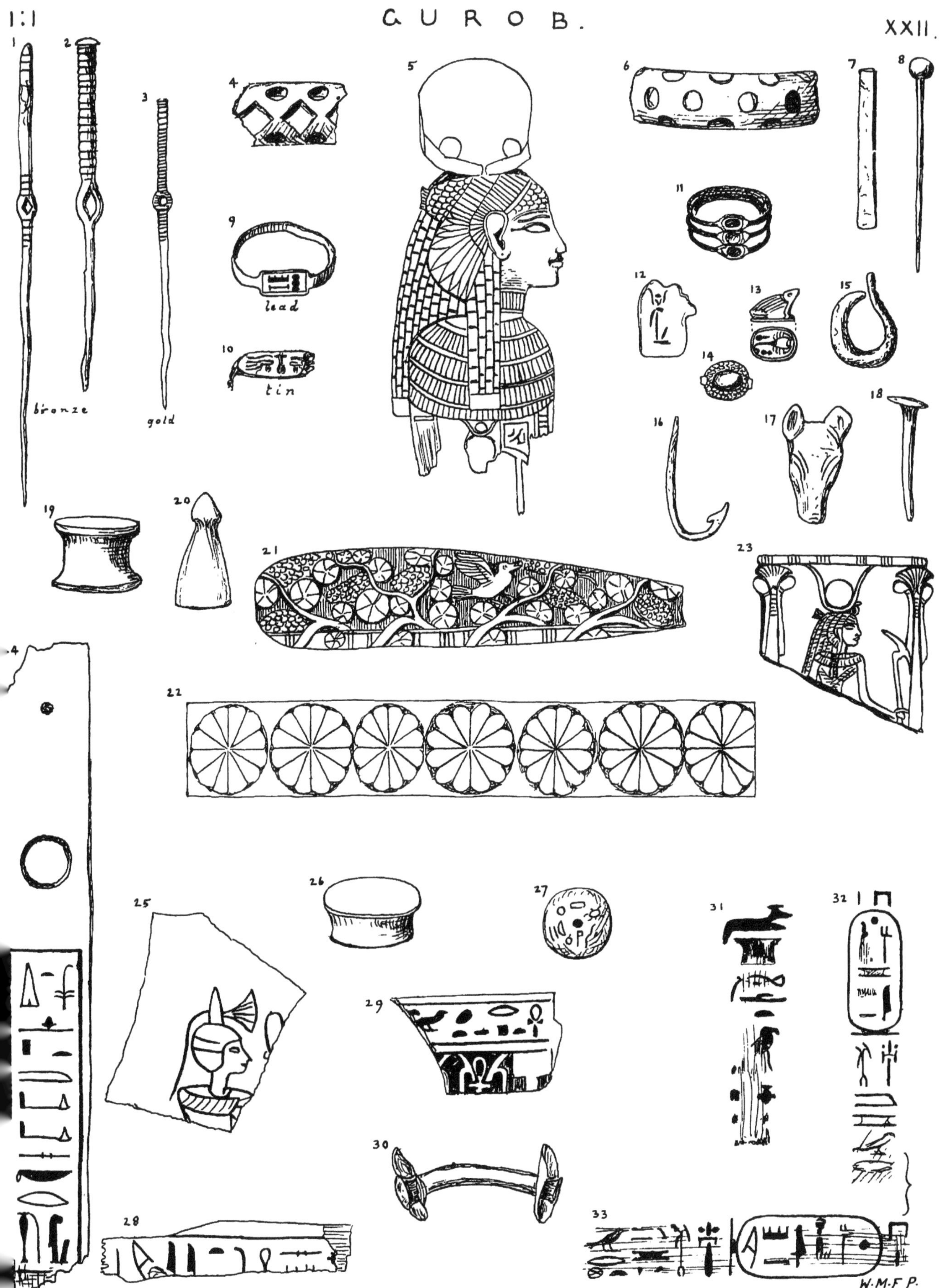
bronze
gold
lead
tin
W.M.F.P.

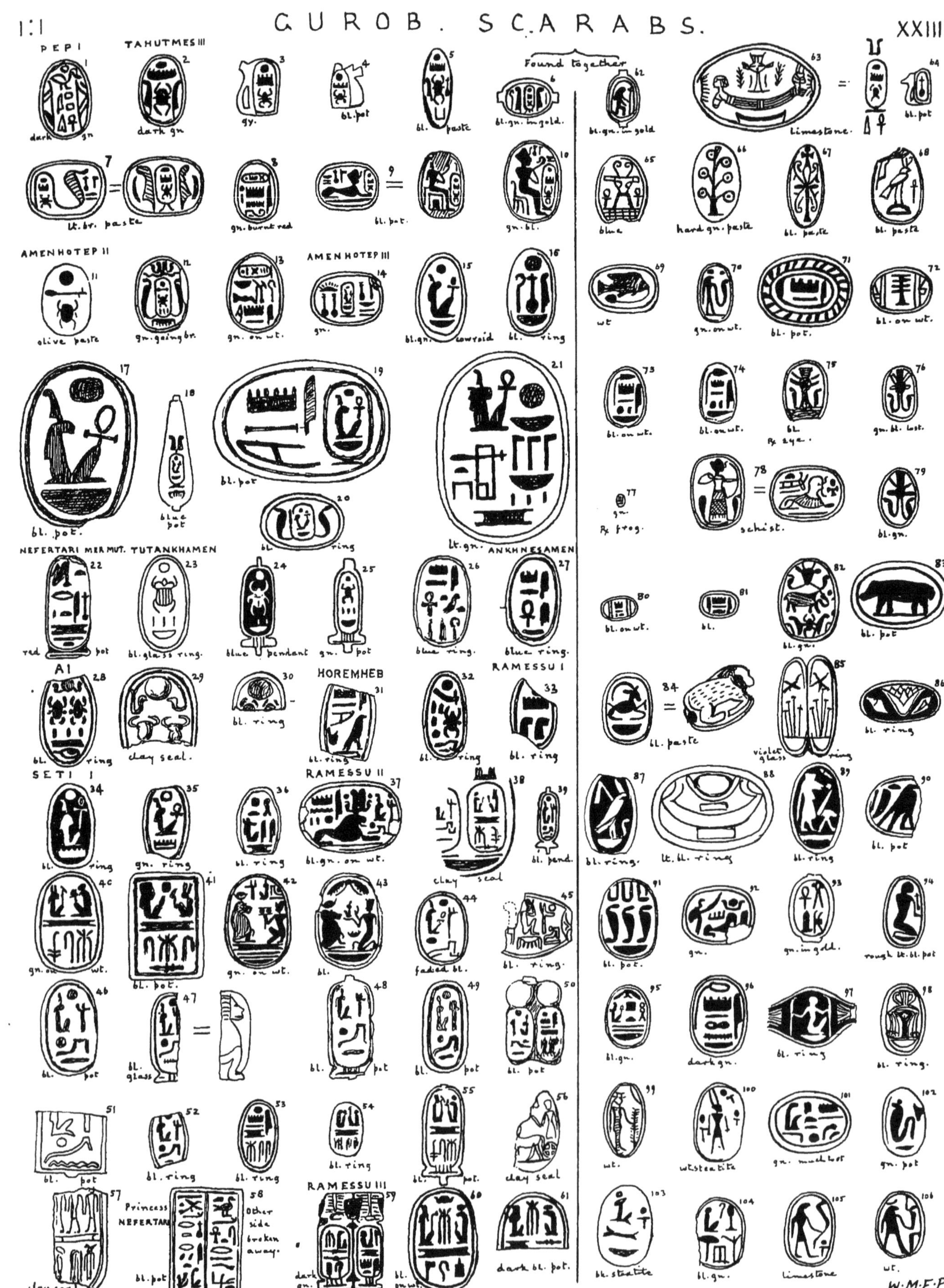
PEPI
TAHUTMES III
Found together
AMENHOTEP II
AMENHOTEP III
NEFERTARI MERMUT.
TUTANKHAMEN
ANKHNESAMEN
AI
HOREMHEB
RAMESSU I
SETI I
RAMESSU II
Princess NEFERTARI
Other side broken away.
RAMESSU III
W.M.F.P.

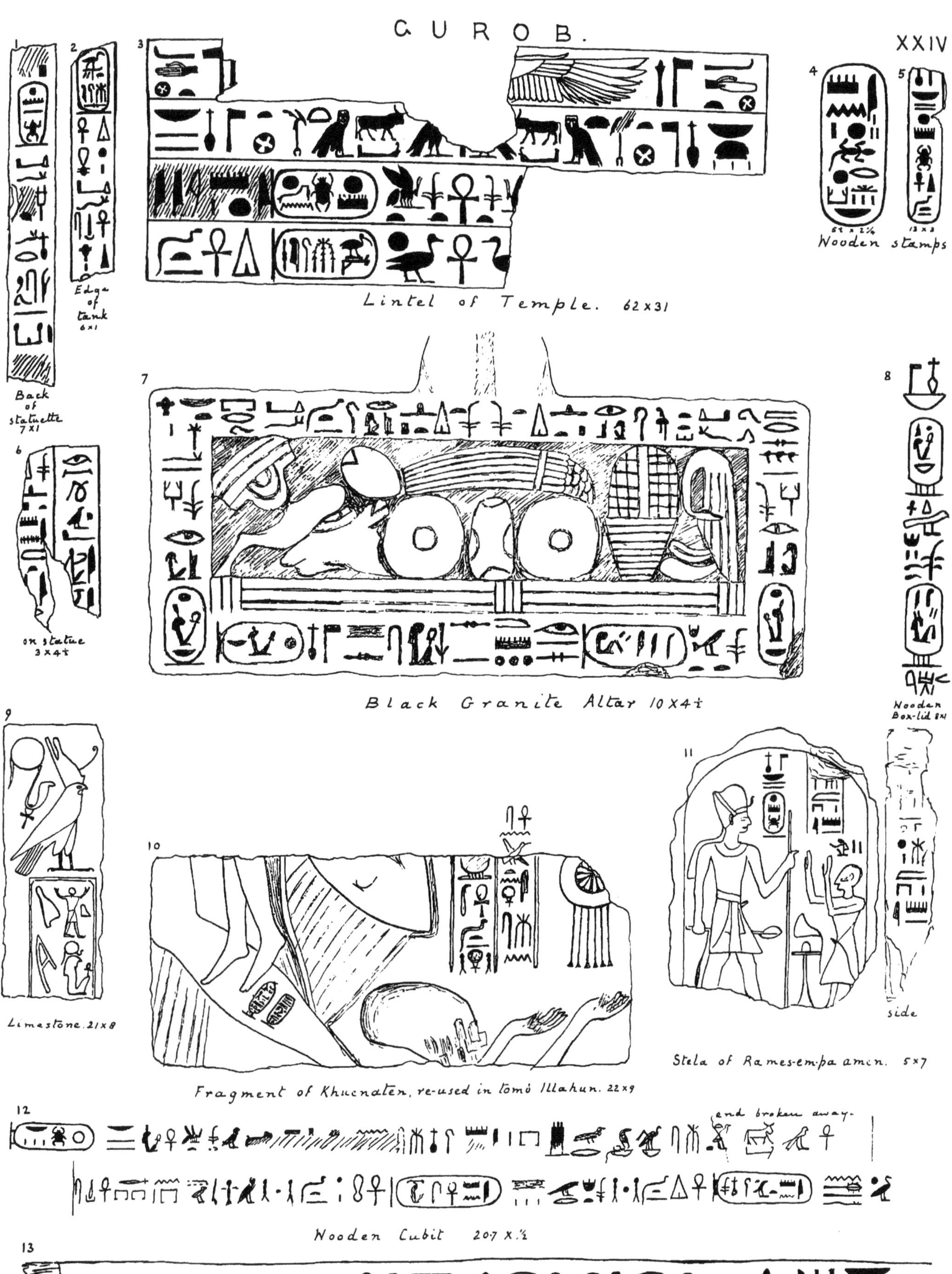
1
2
3
4
5
Back of statuette 7 x 1
Edge of tank 6 x 1
Lintel of Temple. 62 x 31
5¾ x 2½
1¾ x 3
Wooden stamps
6
on statue 3 x 4½
7
Black Granite Altar 10 x 4½
8
Wooden Box-lid 8½
9
Limestone. 21 x 8
10
Fragment of Khuenaten, re-used in tomb Illahun. 22 x 9
11
Stela of Rames-em-pa amen. 5 x 7
side
12
end broken away.
Wooden Cubit 20·7 x ½
13
Side of Coffin. Illahun 43 x 3
W.M.F.P.

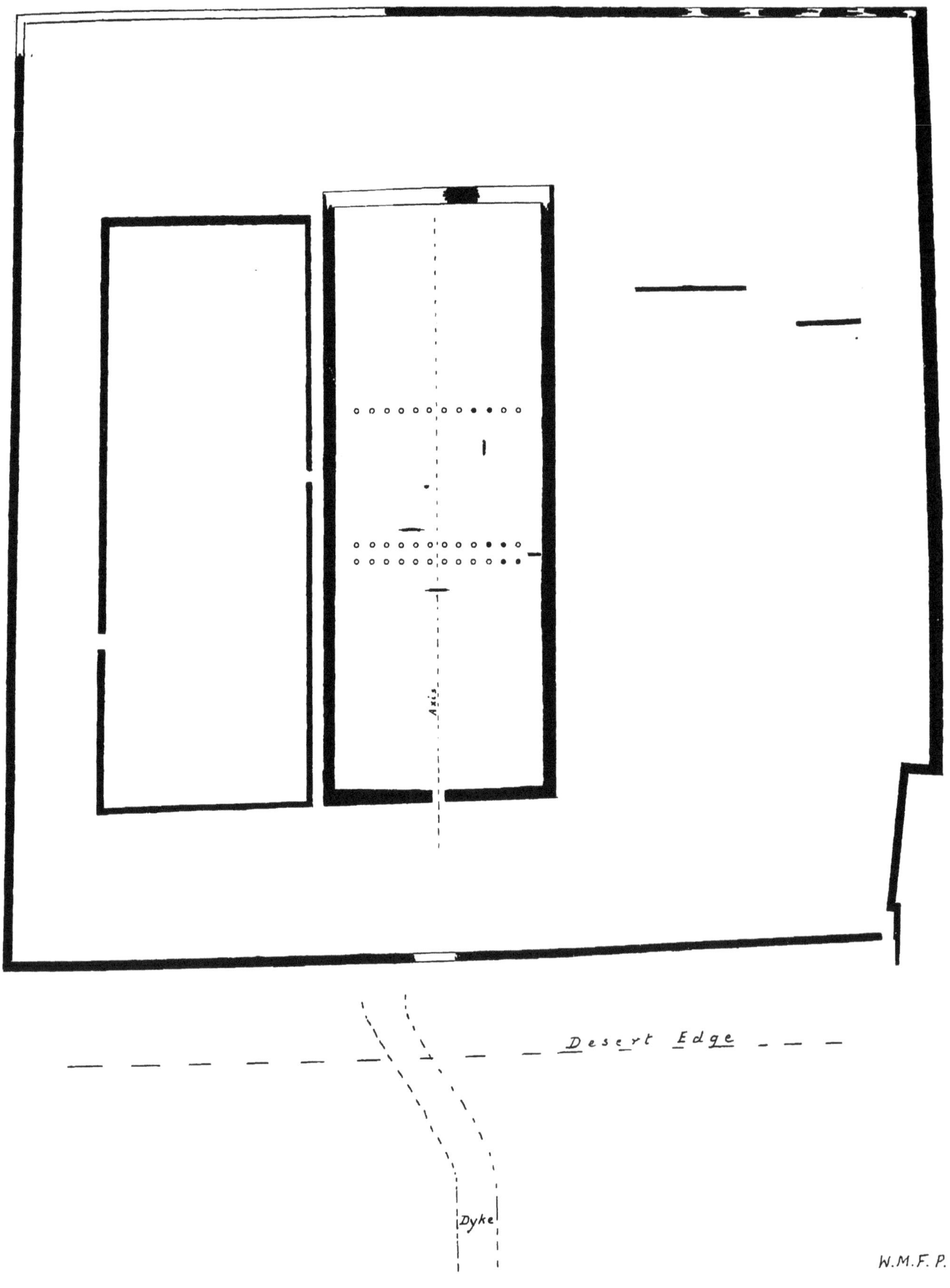

1:1200 GUROB. TEMPLE AND ENCLOSURES. XXV

Axis

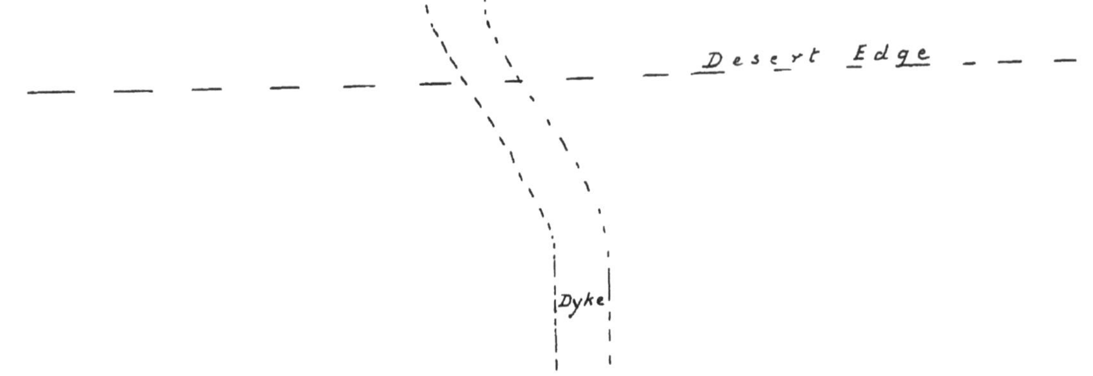

W.M.F.P.

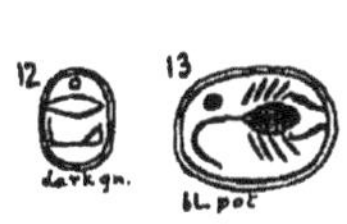

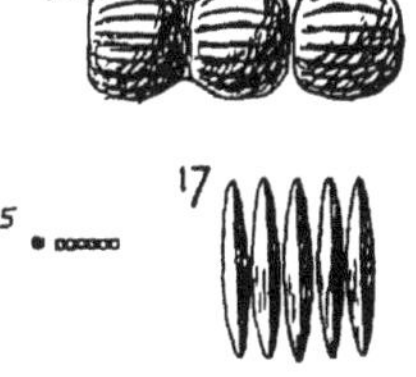

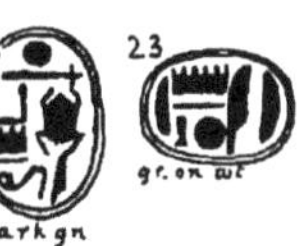

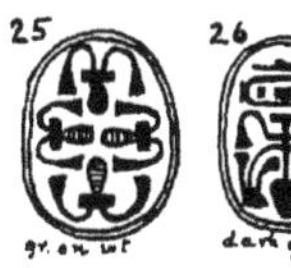

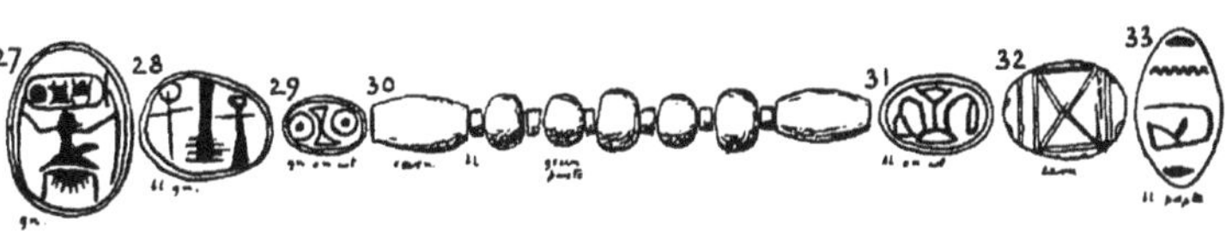

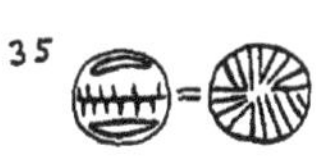

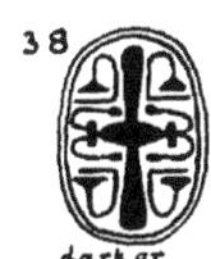

1:2
W.M.F.P.

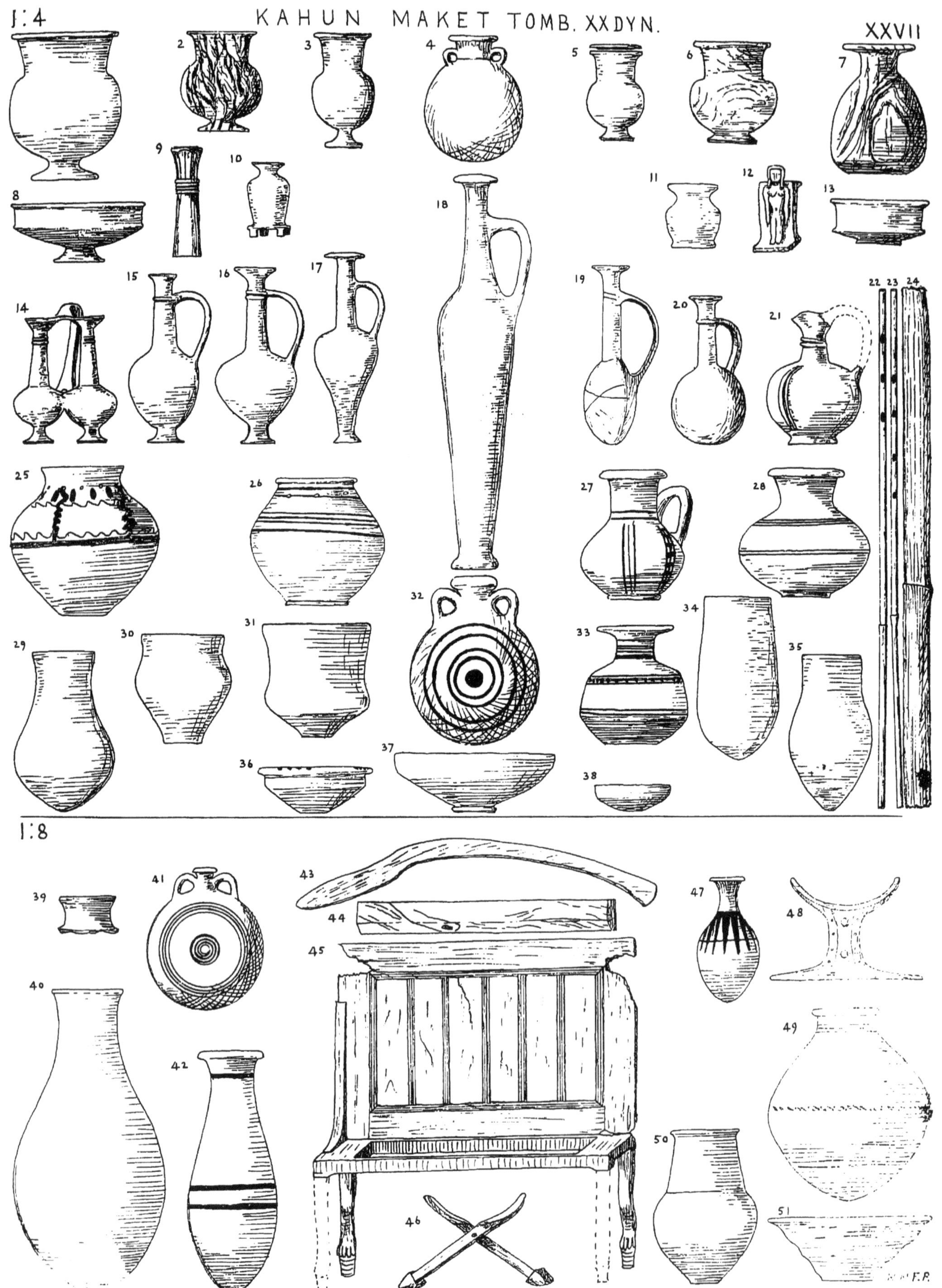
1:4
KAHUN MAKET TOMB. XX DYN.
XXVII
2
3
4
5
6
7
8
9
10
11
12
13
14
15
16
17
18
19
20
21
22
23
24
25
26
27
28
29
30
31
32
33
34
35
36
37
38
1:8
39
40
41
42
43
44
45
46
47
48
49
50
51

COFFIN INSCRIPTIONS.

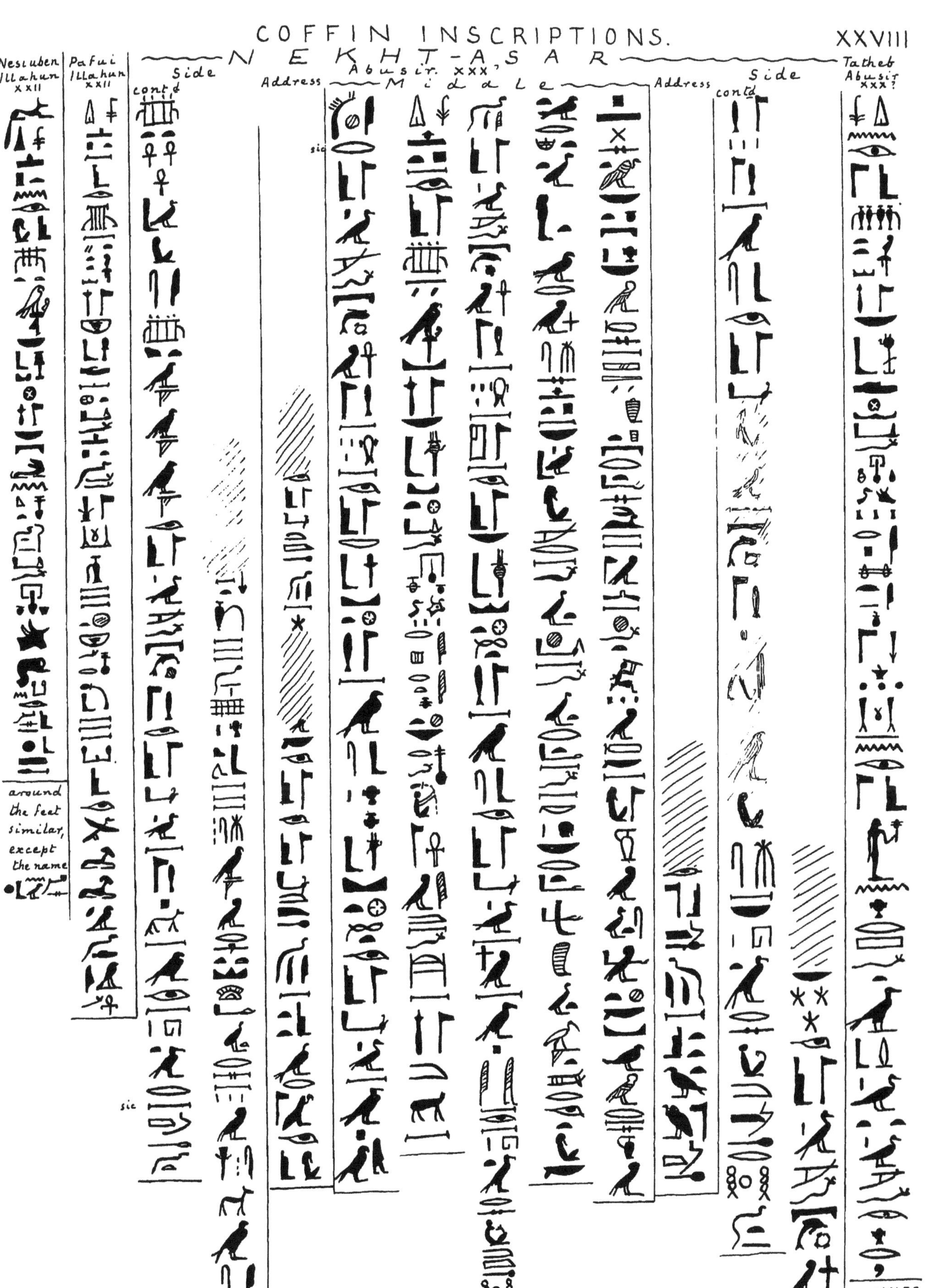

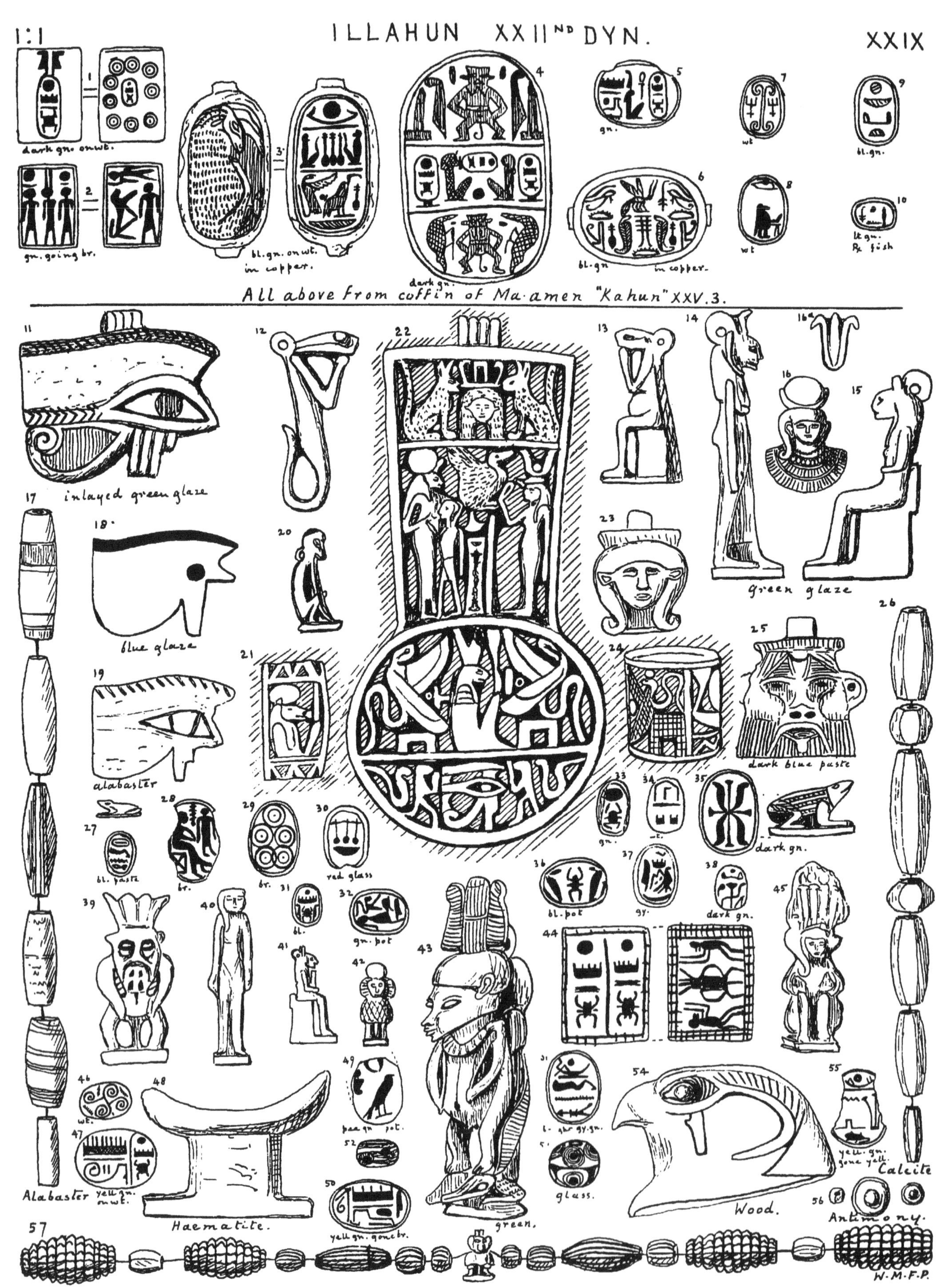
dark gn. on wt.
gn. going br.
bl. gn. on wt. in copper.
dark gn.
gn.
wt
bl. gn.
bl. gn in copper.
lt. gn. Rx fish
All above from coffin of Ma-amen "Kahun" XXV. 3.
inlayed green glaze
blue glaze
alabaster
Green glaze
dark blue paste
dark gn.
bl. paste
br.
red glass
bl. pot
gy.
dark gn.
bl.
gn. pot
green.
glass.
Wood.
Alabaster
Haematite.
Calcite
Antimony.
W.M.F.P.

1:250000 ANCIENT SITES IN THE FAYUM. XXX

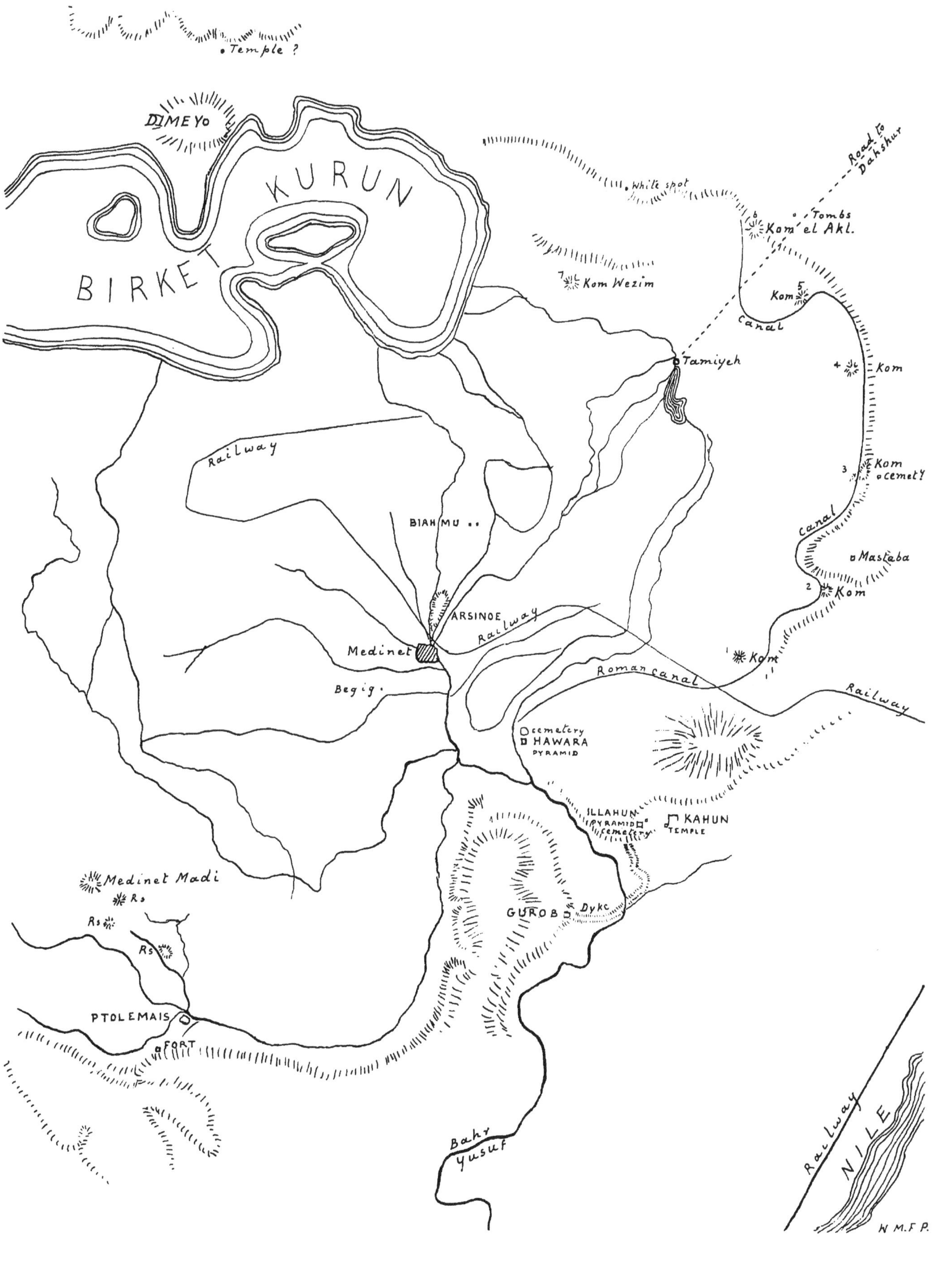

DIMEYO

BIRKET KURUN

White spot

Road to Dahshur

Tombs

6 Kom el Akl.

7 Kom Wezim

Kom 5

Canal

Tamiyeh

4 Kom

Railway

3 Kom

cemet.y

BIAHMU

canal

Mastaba

2 Kom

ARSINOE

Railway

Medinet

Kom

Roman canal

Begig.

Railway

cemetery

HAWARA

PYRAMID

ILLAHUN

PYRAMID

cemetery

KAHUN

TEMPLE

Medinet Madi

Rs

Rs

Rs

GUROB

Dyke

PTOLEMAIS

FORT

Bahr Yusuf

Railway

NILE

W M.F P.

1:2000 PLAN OF TALIT, SITE OF PTOLEMAIS. XXXI

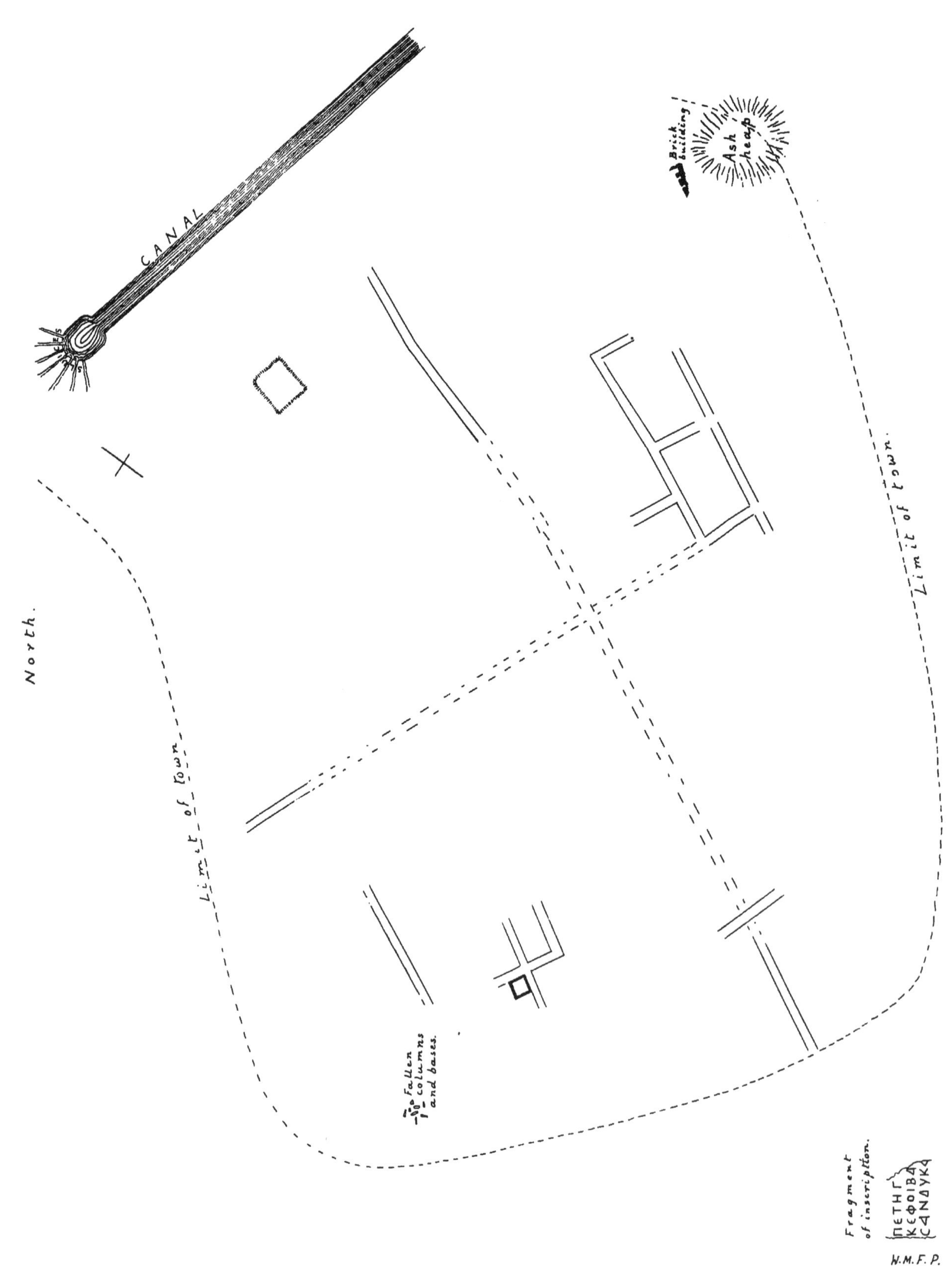

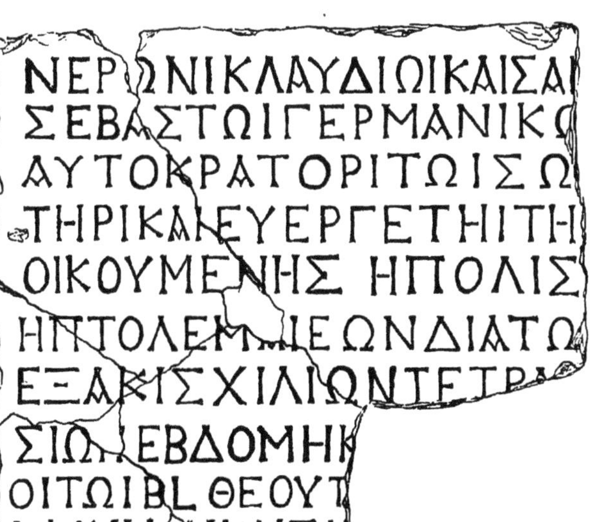

Restoration by Canon Hicks.

Νέρωνι Κλαυδίῳ Καίσα[ρι Σεβαστῷ Γερμανικῷ [ι Αὐτοκράτορι, τῷ σωτῆρι καὶ εὐεργέτῃ τῆ[ς οἰκουμένης — ἡ πόλις ἡ Πτολεμαιέων διὰ τῶ[ν ἑξακισχιλίων τετρ[ακοσίων ἑβδομήκ[οντα καὶ οἱ τῷ β (ἔτει) θεοῦ Τ[ιβερίου Κλαυδίου Καίσαρ[ος Σεβαστοῦ Γερμανικοῦ Αὐτοκρά[τορος ἐφηβευκότες παν [δημεί? ἐπὶ] Λευκίου Ἰουλίου .... ·ου ἡγεμόνος, (ἔτει) ζ [Νέρωνος Κλαυδίου Καίσαρος [Σεβαστοῦ Γερμανικοῦ Αὐτο[κράτορος

W.M.F.P.

1:2 GUROB, ROMAN GLASS. XXXIII

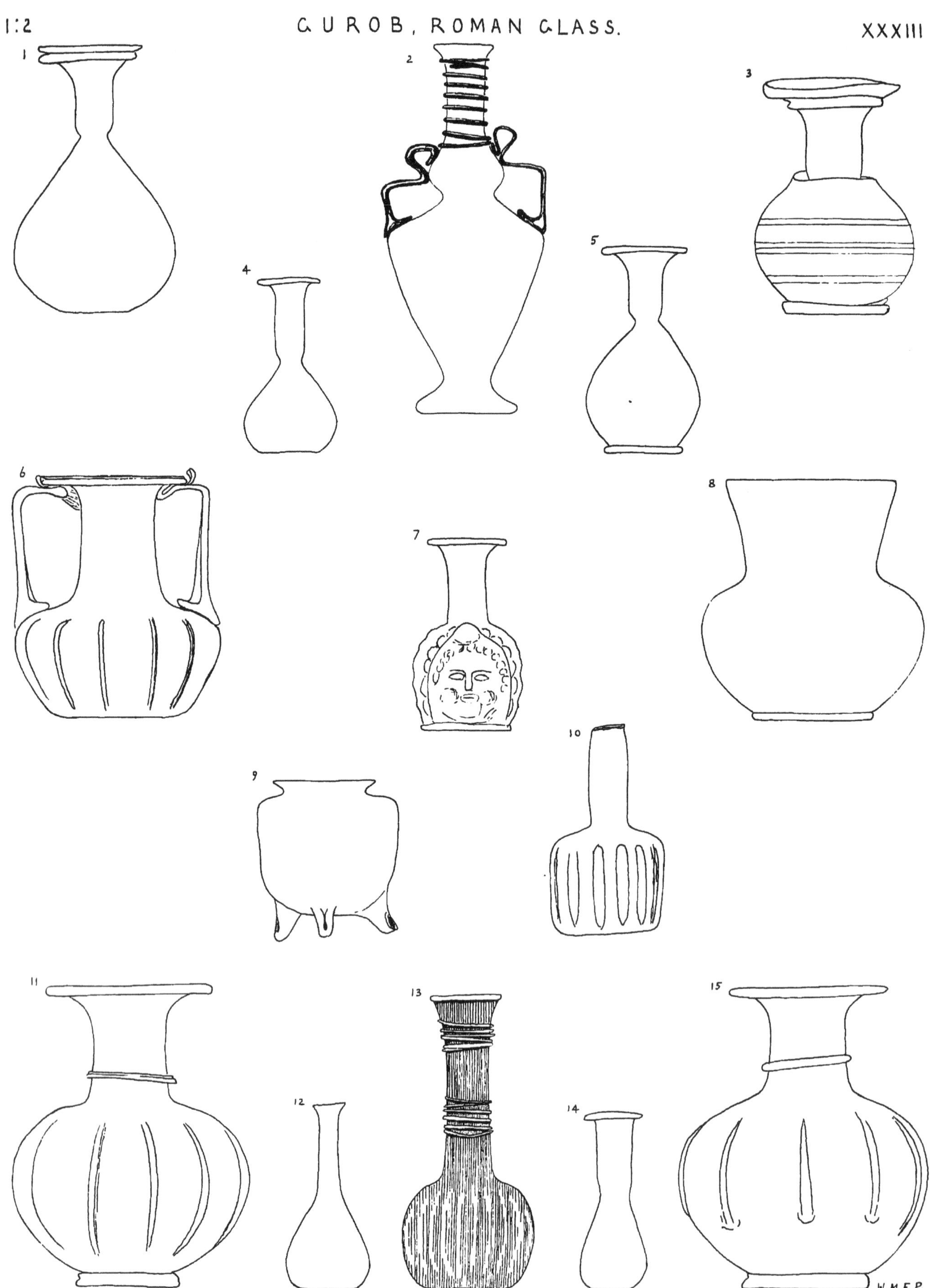

MEDUM SELECTED SIGNS.

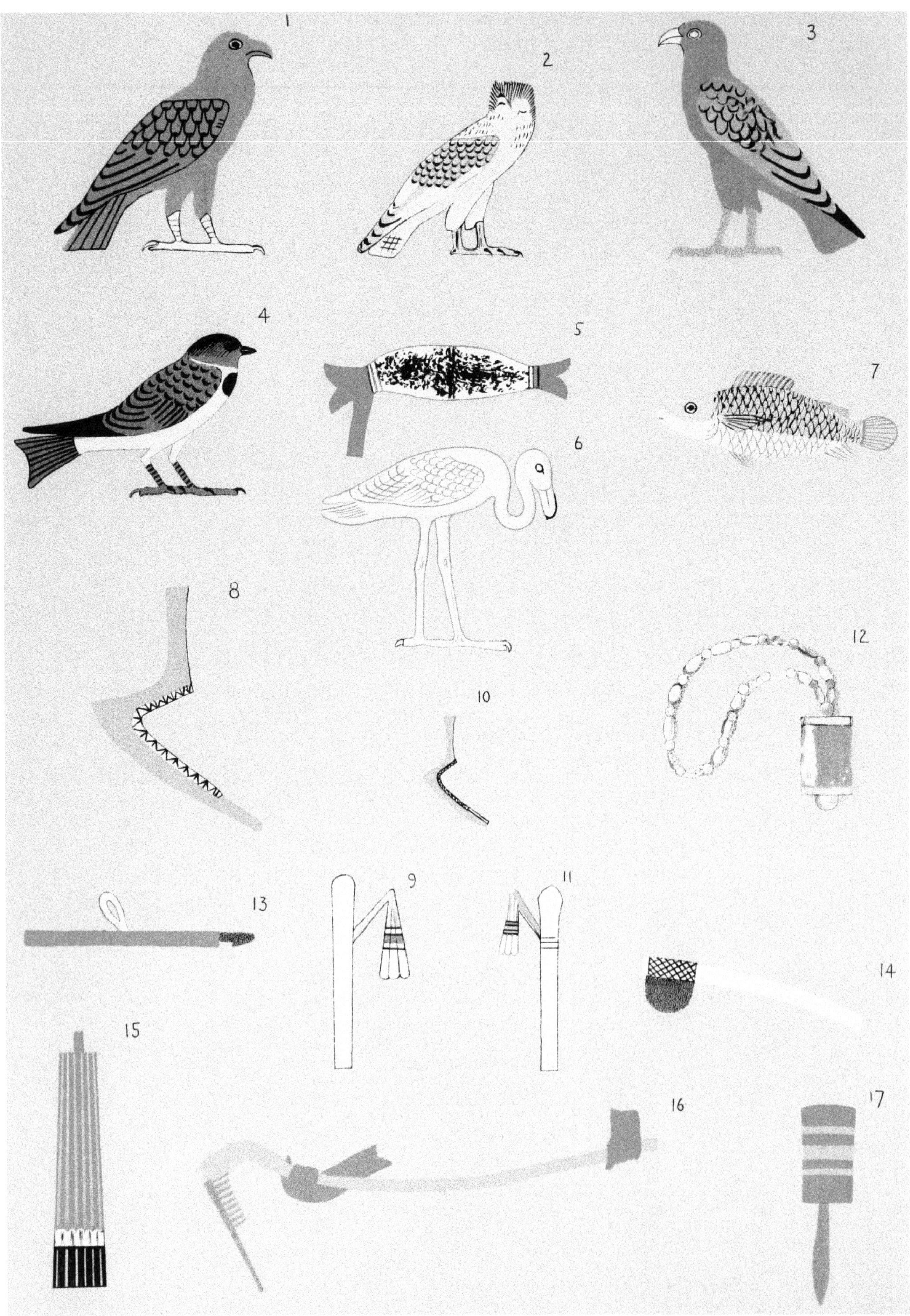

W.M.F.P.

MEDUM.

BY

W. M. FLINDERS PETRIE.

WITH CHAPTERS BY

F. LL. GRIFFITH, DR. A. WIEDEMANN, DR. W. J. RUSSELL, F.R.S.,

AND W. E. CRUM.

LONDON:

DAVID NUTT, 270, 271, STRAND.

1892.

LONDON:
PRINTED BY WILLIAM CLOWES AND SONS, LIMITED,
STAMFORD STREET AND CHARING CROSS.

CONTENTS.

INTRODUCTION.

1. After having explored and described the towns and products of the XVIIIth dynasty at Gurob, and the XIIth dynasty at Kahun, I naturally turned my eyes to what seemed with reason to be the oldest dated site in Egypt, the cemetery of Medum, which was not far distant. Some time was lost before I could begin work, by the attempted imposition of new and onerous conditions; but after a good deal of trouble and discussion I had the satisfaction, thanks to Sir Evelyn Baring, of seeing reasonable terms established for scientific work in Egypt, distinct from the conditions for plundering merely for purposes of profit, which should indeed be wholly prevented. So vast an amount has been altogether lost, that the remainder should be rigidly guarded and reserved for scientific examination, from an archæological and ethnologic point of view, rather than merely for finding inscriptions and bronzes. The present system of allowing native overseers and others to plunder tombs for their private benefit, without the publication of any results, is most deplorable; and it has cost us the loss of all the information that might have been recorded from the cemeteries of Ekhmim, Siut, Mea, and innumerable other sites. Destruction is not the less to be deplored because it is done by legalised agents. Very few Europeans in Egypt, and still fewer natives, would think of spending the needful time to secure details before they are lost in working. To spend one to two hours cramped in a small hole, picking out the tiniest bones of a skeleton from a tomb, and noting its position and any peculiarities, is absolutely needful if we are to understand the details of the race whose works we are studying; and such care has seldom, if ever, been given by excavators.

I began by going over to my old quarters at Illahun to fetch my baggage, and engaged two or three dozen of my old workmen, who were all willing to go with me. They, and others of my older hands from near Medinet, used to walk over sixteen or eighteen miles with a sack of dried bread, work for ten or eleven days, and then walk back for fresh supplies, thus returning every fortnight. These men and boys were as honest and pleasant fellows as I wish to see; they camped in rough huts by my tent, and served as guards by night and workmen by day. I shall not forget the strange astonishment that it was to me when a visitor asked Who protected my things? and If I could trust my people? I never missed any property while I was there; and even if treasures, such as a pocket knife, happened to be left outside derelict, no one disturbed them. The thorough kindly simplicity and good feeling of all the party made it a pleasure to be with them. Where the Egyptian is constantly misunderstood is by applying English standards to him. He has many points in which he is better and pleasanter than an English workman; but he cannot stand long-continued temptation of any sort, nor being "given his head" in any way. He needs "bossing," and he feels the want of a "boss." When I was called away to Cairo, and left my men for a few days, with an ample supply of piece-work to go on with, I found that they had not the heart to do it when not looked after, although the loss was theirs. If constantly encouraged they will earn surprising amounts, by work so hard that any person would cry shame if they were forced to do it. To tempt such people by constantly giving them opportunities of stealing or cheating is extremely wrong; but by guarding against this, and letting them feel that they are always kept in hand and noticed, they prove admirable and industrious workers. Of course so far as possible all my work was piece-work; and though the rate was only from $\frac{1}{2}$ to 1 piastre the cubic metre, or 1*d.* to $1\frac{3}{4}$*d.* the cubic yard, according to the hardness of the ground, yet they usually earned 18*d.* to 2*s.* a day for a man and boy, double the best native wages; 15 to 20 cubic yards was a common discharge for a couple. I also employed many men from Medum and the villages near; and some of them were splendid workers. One couple were nicknamed "The Fiends"; Handawi, the man, was always rampant for fresh ground, and slaved without intermission, and his lad ran to and fro the whole day, carrying baskets of stuff and stones piled on the top, on his back. Where the stuff required to be moved to a distance I used to keep the same rate for the metre, but allow the couple to bring a boy to help them, to whom I paid day wages in addition. These boys then were kept going by their patrons, and gave me no extra trouble; two additional day boys were sometimes given to each couple of metre workers, where the stuff had to be carried perhaps 100 feet distant and 20 feet up. Such a system works very easily, is little trouble, and costs less than any other.

I left Illahun with a couple of camels and a gang of men and boys, and skirting the desert we walked eighteen miles down to Medum, which is about forty miles south of Cairo; there I looked round for a camping-place, where I could be quiet, and not hear the men talking at night. For this end I settled into Nefermat's sculptured chamber for my bedroom, and pitched a tent in the front of it for stores and cooking. Another tent served for a few of the men, and the rest made huts of the bricks of Nefermat, which had been thrown out by the hundred in past excavations there; these, roofed with durra straw, served them for dwellings all the winter, although they found it a cold harbour without any doors, in frosty nights. I had not long been there when I had the pleasure of Mr. F. Bliss coming to join me for three or four weeks, to examine all the details of excavations, before he took up the continuation of my work at Lachish for the Palestine Exploration Fund. I had also several visitors, as Medum was within the range of the private tourist. Since it was needful to close all the tombs the visitors will find less to look at, and probably drop it out of their programmes.

2. After clearing the known tombs, there was a lengthy business in copying them. This could not in most parts be done by wet squeezes, as there was colour on some of the stone, still left after the wet squeezes which had been most shamelessly taken before. I therefore took dry squeezes: holding up a strip of paper, three feet long and one foot wide, against the stone with the left hand, I outlined all the sculpture with my fingers, creasing the paper over the edge if it was incised, or scoring the outline with my nail if it was in relief. To do this accurately needs care; as, if the paper is marked to the outline of the carving the figure will be too wide by the amount of curvature. The mark must be made therefore on the rounding of the edge, guiding the nail by holding thumb and finger together. Having obtained a creased outline the sheet was laid on a board and drawn over by freehand, following the marks and interpreting them by looking at the sculpture. In this way, during six or seven weeks, about 1200 square feet of sculpture was copied in full-size drawing, and notes of the colours marked. After returning to England these slips were matched together, marked, turned over and joined by strips of adhesive, so as to form large rolls, equal to the height of the chambers, 10½ feet, and about 3 to 5 feet wide. The outlines were then all inked in, and the sheets were ready to be photo-lithographed. The joining took over a week, and the inking took a month, beside some kindly done by Mr. Spurrell.

3. After the drawing I worked at most of the mastabas and the tomb pits that I could find. But I found that the old people had had their pickings first, and had plundered every tomb that was worth clearing. The full knowledge of the arrangements that was shewn by the spoilers, is evidence that the attacks were made soon after the closing of the tombs, and while the secrets of their plans were still known. Very possibly some boy employed in the building went there fifty years later, when the place was left deserted, and made use of his memory. In one mastaba were three pits. I first found the central one; it contained absolutely nothing but clean rock chips in the pit and chamber. The next we found contained only some bowls and flints in the bottom of the pit. Both of these were left untouched till I went there; but the third pit, with masonry below it, had been all plundered and wrecked, so that we could not clear it in safety; this doubtless was the sepulchre. In the next mastaba I cleared a large pit, which was untouched; with great excitement we found the stone trap-door; Mr. Fraser, who was there at the time, helped me to shift it out with crowbars, and cut out the stone filling of the passage, only to find that a tunnel had been made from the outside straight to the chamber, which was entered by breaking a hole in the floor. Two mastabas, however, I did not succeed in entering; and it was evident, by the various forced tunnels, that other people had been equally unsuccessful. Possibly no one has yet found those chambers. The common tombs repaid our

labour best, not from objects of workmanship, but from the many complete skeletons of that remote age which I was able thus to collect.

4. The main piece of work was on the pyramid. I went there with the idea of finding, if possible, the temple, as I had found the temple of Illahun. It was soon clear that there was no temple on the desert edge, distant from the pyramid; and I tried pits in the concreted rubbish within the peribolus on the east side, but reached nothing but rock, although I afterwards found that I was within a few feet of the temple door. I hesitated at attacking the great mass of rubbish piled up against the east face of the pyramid. I walked about it, and speculated on it for several days, while we were clearing the corners for my survey. At last I determined to broach it; but it was needful to begin on a large scale, as I knew that I had to descend through over forty feet of more or less loose stuff; and a wide hole was needed at the bottom, to search for the temple. So I marked out a space 70 feet long and 40 feet wide up the slope of rubbish; and, dividing that into strips or stages, I allotted a stage 7 feet wide and 35 feet long to each man and boy. Thus each party delivered the stuff out at the ends of my great hole, the six north stages delivering at the north end, and the south stages at the other. So far we started fairly, and the measuring of the work was simple. But soon we found large blocks of casing and other stones from the pyramid, all lying at the angle of rest in the sloping strata of rubbish; and as we descended these had to be taken out of the way. Then, almost without being able to help it, one big block and then another (which the men detested as hindering their piece-work) slipped off the stage and went bowling down all the other stages, breaking up their regularity. Then the trouble came, whose block was whose? Of course I gave some extra pay for moving out big blocks, but they were a terrible nuisance, and dangerous as well. Two or three times I had to break off all piece-work, and set the whole gang of twenty-four or more to work together at clearing out blocks, arranging all the shifting myself. Though we had dozens of stones so heavy that they needed every man we could get around them to stir them, and tedious crowbar work, yet we happily escaped any accidents beyond scrapes, and a few trapped fingers and toes. As we descended a fresh trouble arose; for the rubbish was much weaker in some parts and could hardly sustain the large blocks left in the steep side of the hole. There were some great pieces which I expected to see drop any hour, but which yet held up to the last.

Of course in cutting a deep hole in a slope the stuff soon has to be lifted out, and so before long it was impracticable to shoot it at the end of the excavation. Then I opened two trenches, leading east from the two sides of the work, which carried off the stuff till we were low down; and finally one deep cut in the middle took out the bottom stuff and left the hole of a T form. Thus by distributing the stuff from different periods of the work at different parts, I avoided raising it up a mountain of rubbish at the last, and left the 6000 cubic yards so spread as to be the least inconvenience. Whenever a large hole is made one of the least obvious—but most necessary—points to consider is, where the stuff shall go; it cannot be annihilated, and before beginning work it is well to fully imagine as one looks at the ground what the hole will be like, and how that amount of stuff had better be placed.

At last we reached the bottom, and there found the sloping casing of the pyramid, and a wall at right angles to it, and the side of a great stele; our hole was a success, but it only shewed where a building existed by revealing one corner of it. We then had to enlarge the pit at the north end, and before we had gone far with that a fresh trouble arose. We had on each side an imminent wall of loose rubbish; on the west it was as high as a London house—sand and chips and big blocks—all sloping in stratification so as to slide off into our hole, from a height of forty or fifty feet. I gave a moderate slope to this face, about 1 in 4, which sufficed to hold it up so long as the weather was tranquil. But soon a raging gale arose; I was in the pit some time that day, and shall never forget the horrid confusion. The air was so full of whirling sand that one's eyes had to be kept longer shut than open; whenever the battering of sand on one's face ceased for a moment, and it was possible to look about, the clouds of dust almost hid the sides of the cutting. And as the sand was blown out from the face of the work, the stones came rattling down in avalanches. The width of the place was enough to enable the men to stand in safety on one side when a rush came, but constant attention was needful. At last, in the midst of a grand howl of the gale, we instinctively looked up through the murky brown cloud in which we stood, and saw nearly all the higher side of our pit coming over in a block; one man only was in front of me; I saw him dash back past me just in time, and knew that they were all safe behind me, when smash came five feet thickness of stones and sand over the greater part of our work. So completely did this disorganise affairs, that it took us a week to get it cleared out, interrupted by continual lesser falls. The scour of the wind constantly undermined the face, and burrowed deeper and deeper into the slightest hollows, until the top overhung, and the face was grooved out, leaving tall slender pillars of loose stuff.

5. After some three weeks of work, from having first seen the building, we again reached bottom, and cleared out the whole of the courtyard. To my surprise there seemed to be no entrance to it, but a continuous wall around it. But as we cleared down we soon found a doorway, and I crawled into the perfect chambers, which had not been touched since the XVIIIth dynasty. To find under all that depth of ruin such a complete building was an entire surprise; all I had looked or hoped for was to trace some foundations, and find some fragments; but here nothing seemed to have been disturbed or injured throughout the whole length of recorded history. Here stands the oldest known building in the world as perfect, except for slight weathering, as it was when even Egypt was bare of monuments. I eagerly looked over the inscriptions on the walls, which I saw were of Tahutmes III. and Amenhotep III.; but my satisfaction was complete when I caught sight of Seneferu's name, and knew that at last there was monumental evidence for an attribution, which had always seemed very probable, but which had been as yet without proof.

The next work was to cut another pit to reach the outer door of the temple; and very glad I was that I had not put all the stuff in front of my great pit, but had so widely spread it; for thus there was not much to move a second time to reach the temple front. I measured it all completely, photographed it, drew it, copied all the inscriptions, and then reburied it as thoroughly as could be desired. To have left it open would have been to ensure its destruction in six months. The pyramid of Medum is the quarry of all the neighbourhood. Large piles of stone are to be seen in the villages, all taken from there. The desert is furrowed with cart tracks in all directions from the pyramid. Every decent Medumi that dies has a stone tomb built of pyramid casing. Expert stone-splitters live there, who know how—with only a hammer—to split up a 6-ton casing block into long bars of stone, as I have seen them do in a quarter of an hour. The great open quarries on the pyramid side are the sign and the scandal of the present order of things. It is only the vast mass of the pyramid that has saved the tombs of Medum from utter ruin, and already one block of the sculptured lintel of Rahotep's tomb is gone. What wonder when no official ever goes to the place to inspect? and even if a native guard was there he would be as capable of selling the stone as of selling the antiquities in his charge. The very tombs of Gizeh are sold for stone to the villagers by the overseer there.

6. Besides clearing the temple I opened up each corner of the pyramid, and found the original casing remaining, even the actual corner casing-stone in one place. This gave the material for an accurate survey of it. I also traced out the peribolus wall all around it, and the causeway which led up to it from the plain, and now runs down under water-level. I also exhaustively cleared the inside of the pyramid to see if there were any other chambers or passages. For though it was opened nine years ago by Professor Maspero, the accumulation of stone and rubbish in it had never been turned over. Every part of the rock, or the flooring, of all the chambers and horizontal passages has now been examined. It is most curious to see the original great logs of wood wedged in at the sides of the shaft in the pyramid; still sound and firm, although saturated with salt. Four months' work at Medum has cleared up most of the questions about it, and recorded its sculptures beyond reach of future loss; though there are still some interesting matters awaiting a future explorer in that place.

7. The same friends as before have continued to help forward this work in various ways. The costs of labour and transport have again been defrayed by Mr. Jesse Haworth and Mr. Martyn Kennard. Mr. Spurrell, I have to thank for continual help with head and hands in the details of the collections, and in special researches of his own. Mr. Griffith has now, as always, rendered every assistance in respect to the inscriptions. And I am indebted to Brugsch Pasha for favouring me with a first and hurried translation of the graffiti, when I had the copies in Cairo. Two chapters here are products of my previous work; the examination of the specimens of Kohl, for the account of which I am obliged to Prof. Wiedemann; and the description of the Coptic papyri, which Mr. Crum has taken in hand. I only now hope that my coming season in Egypt may be as productive of historic results as those which have gone before.

CHAPTER I.

THE PYRAMID AND TEMPLE.

8. The pyramid of Medum is peculiar in construction, and unlike all others, excepting the small pyramid of Rikkeh, and the oblong step-pyramid of Sakkara. These three pyramids have been built cumulatively, that is to say in successive coats each of which bore a finished dressed face; and furthermore two of these pyramids, Medum and Rikkeh, have outer casings in one slope from top to base, like the pyramids of the usual type. The system by which the construction was carried on bears an evident analogy to the building of the great mastaba tombs in the cemetery of Medum. These tombs were rectangular masses of brickwork, or of earth coated with brick, with faces sloping at about 75°, the mastaba angle differing from the usual pyramid angle of 51°. These wide, flat "mastabas," or "benches," were added to during the owner's life by coating them with one or two thick masses of brickwork all around, thereby hiding the sculptured chamber of offerings which contained the statue. And outside of these coats a courtyard was built opposite the chamber of offerings, where the worship of the deceased person took place.

Such a system exactly agrees with what we see in the pyramid of Medum (see PL. II), only it was more fully carried out; the coatings were seven in number, the original mass was carried upward and heightened as the circuit was increased, and lastly a general coat covered over all the steps which had resulted during the construction. The primal mastaba appears to have been 100 cubits square and 25 or 30 cubits high: covering over the sepulchral chamber, which was reached by a passage just above the ground level, on the north face of the mastaba.

The outer casing was largely removed at an early date, probably by Ramessu II; in the middle ages it is described as having five steps, of which the two lower have been removed in modern times; thus leaving the high towering mass isolated in the manner which is familiar to all Nile travellers. Various misconceptions have been written about it by passing visitors, who supposed it to be a tower, and to have had decorations at the places where the steps formerly joined it; but such remarks need not detain us. The needful point to observe is that though this pyramid was built cumulatively, it is no warrant for assuming, as Lepsius did, that all other pyramids were constructed similarly; on the contrary no evidence of such cumulative building occurs except in the three pyramids which I have named, and there is positive evidence that this was not the method followed in the later cases. In short it was a transitional form, when the mastaba had been greatly enlarged, and first began to be smoothed over into a pyramidal outline: that type once arrived at, there was no need for subsequent kings to retain the mastaba form internally, and Khufu and his successors laid out their pyramids of full size at first, and built them up at 51° and not at 75°.

9. The excavations that were needful for making a survey of the pyramid itself were not very large; but the discovery of the temple on the east side was a heavy undertaking. At each corner of the pyramid cuttings were made through 10 or 12 feet of rubbish, to reach the original pavement and casing stones. At the S.E. corner the lowest course of casing remains entire; at the other corners it has been partly removed, and is only found at 20 or 30 feet distant along the sides. Hence at these corners two separate points were determined in the survey, and the corner completed by calculation afterwards. The peribolus wall also required some excavation all along its course, to trace the remaining foundations; for the masonry wall itself only exists where its lowest course is left buried, in the deep mass of chips south of the pyramid. The temple excavations are described in other pages.

Having uncovered the ancient points of construction an accurate survey was needed. As I only had a 4-inch theodolite at the place, I relied more on lineal measure. Four stations were fixed at such a distance from each corner as to be visible one from the other; these were just outside the peribolus wall, except at the north-east, where the big mastaba No. 17 interferes with the flatness of the ground, and the station was nearer in. Then the distances of these stations were measured by a steel tape, suspended and strained by 10 lbs. tension. The points of support were nearly in a level line, and usually at about 30 feet apart; so the whole amount of corrections was in general only $\frac{1}{8}$ inch for differences of level, and $\frac{1}{30}$ inch for catenary curves, on a 100-foot length. Temperature was also noted. Probably the results are correct within ·2 or ·3 inch (= 2° or 3° cent.) on each base measured. The theodolite therefore (which was read to 10″) was only trusted for the angles of the corners, for the short distances from the corners to the casing, and for the observations up to the upper steps. The casing points were observed on from a distance by stretching a string across each excavation, and hanging a plumb-line down the hole to over the edge of the casing; the plumb-line was then observed from the survey corner, and from a station along one side of the measured lines. By measuring each angle, as well as each side, of the survey square, four independent checks were made; as, given four sides and one angle, the other three are mere results. In this way the values for the other three corners were calculated from each corner in succession, and the mean of the four values of the angle for each corner was adopted. The average error of the theodolite measurement was 24″ on each corner, equivalent to about 1 inch on the length of the sides: hence the lineal measures are much the more accurate. The azimuth was determined by Polaris, with Canopus as a time star, taking three observations. Having stated the methods adopted, we will now describe the results. But as it is not likely that any one else will want to proceed on the lines of this survey, I shall omit here all reference to the purely trigonometrical stations, the nature of the station marks (which were only permanent, and buried, at the four corners of the survey) and the coordinates of the calculation of the results, which were entirely worked out on a rigorous basis.

10. The base of the pyramid is built on a pavement, which underlies the casing at every part examined, of both sides and corners. The pavement consists of three courses at the N.W., where the ground was rather low. These courses are not thick, being 17·6, 14, and 14 inches; and they project not far from the casing edge, being 22, 38, and 48 inches out, respectively. The base of the finished casing of the pyramid was on the

N. 5677·2, E. 5694·5, S. 5681·3, W. 5675·0

and the azimuth of the sides was

N. 35′ 25″, E. 20′ 35″, S. 23′ 36″, W. 18′ 3″.

Hence the average length of the base is 5682·0 with an average variation of 6·2 inches: the average error of squareness at the corners is 10′ 11″: and its average azimuth is 24′ 25″ W. of N., or 359° 35′ 35″ in absolute azimuth.

The slope of the face cannot be well measured, as it is only seen for a few courses at the door, and over a very weathered surface discovered on excavating the temple. The latter was so far bad that I did not measure it. At the door the angle was taken as 52° 4′, 51° 54′, 51° 49′, the first being worse than the other two: but on combining the triangulation of the door with that of the base the result would yield 51° 26′. As the latter is dependent on the straightness of the N. base from corner to corner, which was not uncovered or seen, the directly measured angle is much better: I conclude therefore that it was within a few minutes of 51° 52′. Hence the height was 3,619 inches.

This angle, it will be seen, is just that of the Great Pyramid of Gizeh, which was built next after this pyramid. And we have therefore to consider if any of the theories concerning the size of that are elucidated by this. Now the most simple and promising theory is that the ratio of 7 : 44, for that of a radius to a circumference, is embodied by the Great Pyramid height being 7 × 40 cubits and its circuit 44 × 40 cubits; in short, that it was built 7 and 44 times a modulus of 40 cubits. The angle being the same here at Medum the ratio 7 : 44 will of course hold good; the question is if a simple modulus was used here also. The base being 5682·0 inches, it is 7 × 25 cubits in height, and 44 × 25 cubits in circuit; the cubit required being 20·66 ± ·01 inches, or varying from 20·63 to 20·70 according to different sides, which is just the usual range of varieties of the Egyptian cubit. We see then that there is an exactly analogous theory for the dimensions of Medum to that for the Great Pyramid; in each the approximate ratio 7 : 44 is adopted, as referring to the radius and circle; in the earlier pyramid a modulus of 25 cubits is multiplied by these numbers to fix the dimensions; in the later pyramid a modulus of 40 cubits is used.

11. Turning next to the inner surfaces of masonry, of the successive coats of construction, seven such faces may be seen on the concentric masses (PL. II). We cannot at present see any surface within the topmost face visible, as the top of the pyramid is inaccessible: but there is some reason for supposing another surface to exist inside, as, granting that the step would be of the same width as that now existing at the top, the dimension of the central mass at the base, or the primitive mastaba, would be just 100 cubits either way. Such a face is therefore shewn in broken line on the section (PL. II), and is here included in brackets in the list of faces. The angles of the faces are variable; the upper part of the high face is at 73° 20′, the lower part 73° 54′; and the faces now built over, from the outside through to the passage, are at 74° 40′ and 75°. The tendency therefore seems to be for the lower and outer parts to be steeper than the higher. As an average I have used 73° 20′ for reducing the sloping dimensions of the top steps; and 74° 21′, or 100 on 28, for projecting the slopes down to the base. The steps at the top were

observed with the theodolite on the highest complete corners, and the number of courses broken at each corner was examined with a telescope, so as to make allowance for the lost parts. The heights of the courses were noted angularly by the theodolite. The outer coats were measured across where they are broken and accessible, at the top of the rubbish mounds. The results are that the mean sizes of the successive square coats at the pyramid base are as follow:

(2063), 2368, 2673, 3081, 3478, 3879, 4267, 4667 inches, but of course small differences may easily occur owing to the uncertainty of the angle at which these faces are built. The thickness horizontally of the coats which are implied above are, *in* (152½), 152½, 204, 198½, 200½, 194, 200, inches, *out*. And the level of the finished steps above the base are:

top (?), broken, 2576, 2165, 1755, 1246?,
978, 571 inches, *base*.

The steps vary somewhat on different sides. The top step varies from 2221 to 2236 horizontally from the outer base; the second step varies from 1890 to 1937. The lengths of the top edge of the top step vary 1212 to 1231, and azimuth from +8′ to −34′; the second step is 1832 to 1905, at +42′ to −70′. The thickness of the coats also varies, each ranging over 8 or 10 inches, in the parts where they can be directly measured. It is evident therefore that no great accuracy was aimed at in this internal construction, although it was finished off with finely-smoothed faces, well jointed, and of beautiful flatness.

The thickness of the courses varies, but is never very much. The average at the base, by the temple, is 16 inches; in the rough part above the rubbish 20·3; in different parts of the smooth faces 23·6 to 17·8; in the upper face 21 to 16; and in the top 19. The regular system of building was with alternate courses of headers and stretchers, the same as in the brickwork of the Medum mastabas. These blocks, where accessible, average 32 wide and 58 long. The inner masonry, within each of the finished faces is very rough; no attempt has been made to fit the blocks, except by selecting chance adjustments; the courses are approximately equal, but a coarse mortar is largely used to fill the hollows that are left. The stone also is very inferior, brittle, splitting, stained, and weathering badly; the outer faces, on the contrary, are of excellent stone, weathering to a rich brown, and seldom crumbling away, and the smoothness of the faces and of the jointing is very fine.

A line of levelling was carried all round the pyramid, with a discrepancy of only ¼ inch on the 2000 feet length, or 2″. The resulting levels of the pavement surfaces at the corners are:

N.E. + ·5, S.E. + ·2, S.W. + 2·0, N.W. − 2·8 inches.

So in this respect the accuracy is comparable with that of the Great Pyramid, although in size and squareness it is far inferior to that. On the stones may be seen red spots of paint left from the testing by a reddened trial-plate, as on the stones of Khufu at Gizeh.

12. The peribolus wall around the pyramid has been entirely destroyed, excepting the foundation stones in most parts, and the lower course of wall in the deep chip rubbish on the south side. In some parts even the foundations are gone, and their place can only be traced by the hole being filled with sand, against the chip and stone-dust bed which formed a pavement outside of it. Where the wall remains it is 57 inches thick. Its height was probably 70 or 80 inches, judging by a block of the causeway wall described further on. The outer dimensions of the wall were:

N. 8561 at − 30′; E. 9307, + 1′½;
S. 8479, − 27′½; W. 9300, − 29′.

It will be seen (PL. III) that the E. and W. sides are practically equal, and the N. and S. azimuths therefore alike. But the N. side is longer than the S., and the E. azimuth differs from that of the other three sides; an error has therefore been made by the builders, the N. being too long, or the S. too short.

The relation of this enclosure to the pyramid is best stated by the distance of the outside of the wall from the middle of the pyramid base on each side; this distance is

on N. side 2203; E. 1420; S. 1393; W. 1420.

The design for the breadth of the peribolus is pretty clear, as 1420·4 inches is a quarter of the base of the pyramid, so that the enclosure was half as wide again as the pyramid. The space on the south may have been intended to be equal to that at the two sides. But for the extra space on the north side—about 780 inches more than the other sides—I fail to see any reasonable hypothesis. The peribolus entrance was led up to by a causeway; both of which we shall notice in connection with the temple.

A puzzling question is raised by certain groups of pitted holes, on the faces of the inner coats of the pyramid. They are in square groups of five each way, exactly like a modern *siga* board. And they are so high up that they cannot have been reached for some centuries. If they were ever used for gaming-boards, like the many *siga* boards cut by Arabs, it could only be when the stones were lying with the face horizontal, before they were built in. Such is the view of Virchow, and of Reiss (*Verh. Berl. Anthrop. Gesell.* 16 Nov. 1889). On the other hand no instance of this game is known before Arab times; every old game-board that I have found being 3 × 10 square. And it is most unlikely that workmen would be allowed to so disfigure the outer faces of finely-jointed masonry blocks before being built. I must conclude therefore that they were cut in Arab times, though it is hard to suppose that any game could be played on a face sloping at 74°.

13. The temple adjoins the east face of the pyramid. It is in the middle of the side, its axis being 2·1 inch south of the mid line of the face; and this is to be noted, as the east face is 16·7 longer than the mean of the other sides, so that the site for the temple was found by bisecting the face, and not by remeasuring an average half base along it; also it shews that the extra length of this face is not an error of the present surveying. It is built quite independently of the pyramid, not being bonded or joined to it, but merely built against it. The outer mass is plain and rectangular; excepting a slight batter of the outer sides, amounting to 5·5 slope inward on 90 height; and a rounding off of the top edge of the roof in a segmental curve, leaving a slight edge along the front. There is no other ornament, either of moulding, bevelling, or panelling. The whole building is absolutely perfect, roof, stelae, and altar, all but small chips or flaking due to weathering. We cleared it over the courtyard, the interior, the roof of the chamber, and the front from the south corner to the door; but the rest of the front, the north side, and the roof of the passage were not examined. No stone but limestone is used in the whole building and altar.

The temple (PL. IV) consists of a passage, entered at the south end of the face, then a chamber, and lastly the courtyard adjoining the side of the pyramid and containing two steles, and an altar between them.

The door is 67·5 from the foot of the south wall, and is 34·0 wide at top, 34·4 in middle, and flaked below: it is 77·0 high, with a lintel 13·7 thick over it, below the roof slabs. In the passage the doorway is 7·7 to 41·8 from the south end; the passage is 48·0 and 48·5 at south, 45·2 at north, 236·4 east, 237·2 west. The exit door is 6·2 to 40·3 from the north end. The wall between it and the chamber is 42·5 thick at north side of door, 37·4 at top of south, 41·0 at base. In the chamber the east side has been dressed down too much all over the upper part, and left undressed below. The system of building being to lay the stones in the rough, and dress out the faces afterwards; so that each stone turned the corner somewhat when finished, as in the granite temple of Gizeh. The chamber entrance is 5·5 to 39·2 from north end; the sides at north 75·5, south 75·6, east 237·4, west 237·2 at top, 235 below: the exit door to the courtyard is 86·8 to 147·8 from north, or 61·0 wide. The E. wall of the court is 40·0 to 43·0 thick on north, 39·4 to 42·0 on south, being thickest at the base.

14. The courtyard is 237·0 long, and 92·0 wide to the foot of the pyramid; the side walls run on horizontally over the slope of the pyramid face, and so are 174 long on the top. The thickness of the side walls is 56, and of the front of the temple 58. Their top course is rounded in a flattish segment of a circle. The steles are flat-sided, with spherically curved tops, rounding over toward the faces as well as to the edges. The breadths of the north stele are, at base 40·7, at top W. 40·5, E. 41·0; of the south stele, base 41·5, top E. 40·8 to 41·5, edge rounded: the thicknesses of the north at base N. 20·3, S. 20·6, at top N. and S. 20·3: the height is 155·3 to the beginning of the curve, 165·0 to the top. The size therefore was 1 cubit thick, 2 cubits wide, and 8 cubits high, the top ½ cubit being rounded. The sides are dressed very fair and flat, and are set up well in a line, not ¼ inch out of parallel. The distances from the sides of the court are 38·8 at north, 41·4 at south, leaving 74·6 between them. The distances from the east side of the court are 16·3 at north of north stele, 19·0 at north of south stele. These steles stand upon low bases with sloping sides; these bases project 9 to 10 inches from the steles, and are 2·8 high, so they are analogous to the bases beneath obelisks represented in early hieroglyphs, and reinforce the idea that the Mastabat Faraun at Sakkara may have been the base of an obelisk.

Between the two steles stands the altar of limestone, without any sculpture or inscription. It is 25·0 wide, and 54·0 long; the thickness is 10·7, but somewhat sloping and flaked; the spout is 14 long and 11 wide, with a hollow in it, and a groove irregularly deepened out on one side, as if due to corrosion of pouring out drink-offerings of sour wine and beer. The east side is in the east plane of the steles; and the north is 10·5, and south 10·7 inches to the steles.

The courses of the building run the same throughout. At the front the footing is 17 thick, resting on desert pebble and sand, which also filled the space between the footings in the passage and chamber; the courses are 16·4, 32·8, 47·5, 60·9, 77·0, 90·7, 104·7 above the base. In the S.W. corner of the chamber the footing is 17, and the courses 16·2, 32·5, 48·2, 60·8, 75·0, and 90·0. In the north side of the court-yard, which is paved all over, they are 16·3, 33·2, 48·2, 61·5, 75·0, and 90·0. While the pyramid courses are 17·0, 38·0, 56·2, 70·3, 79·0. The stone is left rough in many parts; the excess left on in the chamber has been noted; and the roof edge at the courtyard is all roughly in excess. There is not the fine finish or exactness here which meet us in the later buildings of the IVth dynasty; but, as in the pyramid, the workmanship is solid and sound, though not refined.

15. The peribolus wall has a doorway (PLS. III, IV, VI), in the line of the entrance of the temple carried out parallel to the causeway; that is, $3\frac{1}{2}^{\circ}$ askew to the peribolus wall. The doorway is 62 wide, at 5207 to 5269 from the north end of the peribolus; and the causeway at its head is 118 wide, 5202 to 5320 from the north of the peribolus. The space between the peribolus and the causeway is 180 wide. The thickness of the causeway walls appears to have been 66 at the base, according to the south side, but on the north the foundation is 75 wide. A fallen stone of the top coping of the causeway remains; it is of the whole thickness of the wall, and shews a width of 51·7 at 10·4 under the top, and 49·7 at the top of the face, surmounted by a circular curve 10·1 high; this shews a batter of 1 in 10 on the sides; and hence, if the base was 66 wide, the wall was 90 inches high over all outside. But the causeway was some-what sunk below the ground level in parts, being flat, and independent of the contour of the ground. Its general direction is plainly ruled by its lying in the bottom of a small valley in the edge of the desert; it runs down to the plain, and may go some distance further, but my men were stopped by the water. If this construction were tracked down to its original end it would give us a valuable datum for the rise of the Nile bed during some six thousand years; but such a research would need good pumps.

16. The inscriptions in the temple are none of them due to the builders. The earliest is a scratched graffito (XXXII, 1) on the north wall of the chamber: this is so exactly the colour of the stone, and so uniformly covered with a slight salt coat that I did not observe it until making a final search. It is certainly far earlier in its condition than the two scratched graffiti (XXXII, 2, 3) on the east wall of the chamber. As the latter appear to be of the XIIth dynasty, by their style closely resembling the Assuan graffiti of that age, it seems probable that the earlier one is of the VIth dynasty or before that. All three of these graffiti are within the light from the court-yard, and shew that that was open till after the XIIth dynasty. The other graffiti are all ink-written, facing the front entrance to the temple on the west wall of the passage, and some on the sides of the doorway. They are all of the XVIIIth dynasty: and the reader should refer to their translations by Mr. Griffith in Chap. VI. On the front of the temple are three very rude graffiti of ships by the door.

The temple contained about two feet of blown sand. It was evident that the courtyard had been choked between the XIIth and XVIIIth dynasties, as all the later graffiti were within the light of the outer door, and pieces of burnt papyrus plant strewed the chamber floor, having been taken in by persons wishing to see the blocked doorway into the court-yard, which we found much smoked. In this sand in the passage was an interment of the XVIIIth dynasty, with some beads, two small bronze lance heads, and some pomegranates and nuts. This burial explains why I found the outer doorway carefully blocked with pieces of stone: evidently the passage was looked on as a convenient sepulchre, and the door was blocked, and covered with rubbish. And this heaping-over of it probably finished the hiding up of the temple, which had been nearly covered before by blown sand and fallen pieces of stone from the pyramid. Thus it was mainly out of sight when the pyramid was attacked for stone, probably by Ramessu II, and it was thus saved from being destroyed. Certainly the pyramid was largely pillaged in the XIXth or XXth dynasties, as the burials of the XXIInd dynasty in the rubbish are high above the temple level, some 20 to 30 feet up.

In the sand in the passage were a few objects, probably of the IVth dynasty. Four stone hawks and one in blue glazed pottery (XXIX, 1–5) seem to refer to the worship of "the Horus Snefru," as he is called in the inscriptions here. The most interesting piece is the base of a statuette in hard black serpen-tine (XXIX, 6): several curious points of the in-scription will be seen in the chapter on inscriptions, here we need only note that it is dedicated to the gods of a town called Tat-Snefru by a woman named Snefru-Khati. The lower part of a basalt stand (PL. XXIX, 7) was also found, in the courtyard.

We see then that a statuette, probably almost contemporary with Snefru, was placed here, referring to a person and a place named after him, shewing that he was the genius of the neighbourhood. Next, not later probably than the VIth dynasty, a visitor scrawls up "Thrice good is the name of king Snefru." And in the XVIIIth dynasty, we find that his festival was held here, and all visitors recognised this as his pyramid and temple. Such a chain of evidence gives the final precision to the general inference that the cemetery is of the IVth dynasty, judging by the nature of the pottery found in it.

17. On the south side of the pyramid a strange excavation was partly examined. I observed when first walking round the pyramid that there was a stretch of high ground between the western part of the south face and the peribolus. As it was formed of limestone chips I concluded that some great building had stood here, within the peribolus. Accordingly I began sinking trenches in the site, and found some large blocks of stone, below the level of the peribolus pavement. As the blocks were too large to move in a trench, I then made a wide square clearance, piling up the blocks around it when they were too large to move out or to break. The depth was about 25 feet, through hard concreted chip and lime-dust. I thus found the side of a square pit in the rock, within which a building had been constructed: the building must have been of considerable height, judging by the great mass of chips resulting from its destruction, and also covering a fair area, although I only saw about 15 feet of the pit in each direction. The pit is about eight feet deep in the rock, which is here about six feet under the pavement; and the floor of the pit is flat dressed in the rock. A tunnel roughly cut in the rock leads southward from the pit; but is broken away above, and filled in, at 24 feet from the pit. What the purpose of such a building can have been is doubtful. No temple is known on the south of a pyramid; and neither for that, nor for a small pyramid, would such a rock pit be needed. That it was not solely a subterranean structure is proved by the great depth of resulting chips. It would be desirable to clear it completely; but the depth and hardness of the material, and the absence of a single stone left *in situ* so far as I went, dissuaded me from working further.

18. One detail of the pyramid's exterior, perhaps connected with the position of its chamber, was noticed before I began to excavate for the temple, and influenced my excavation. On the eastern faces of the upper two steps a slight groove or recessing may be seen, especially when the sun is near noon (see PL. II). Judging from below the recess is about an inch deep on the face; and by angular measurements the upper groove is 211 inches wide, and the lower is 195. They are not exactly one behind the other; the distances from the north base being 2991 to 3202 inches for the upper, and 3020 to 3215 for the lower. They are clearly excentric on the faces, and as the temple is centred on the face they cannot be connected in any way with that. But the sepulchral chamber is about 2918 to 3151 south of the north base, which is not far from the position of the grooves, about 60 inches different to the upper groove. As the sculptured chamber with the *ka* statues is often placed in mastabas east of, or before, the sepulchral pit, and as the facade of that chamber always forms a recess on the face, it is not impossible that this shallow recess is a signal of the position of the *ka* chamber, thus carried upward in the building, and repeated on the outer coat, as we find the false door repeated approximately (though never exactly) in front of the inner chamber. If a *ka* chamber exists —and it would be strange if the king had not a better provision in this way than his subjects in their mastabas—it is doubtless on the east face of the innermost mass of the mastaba form, the first block built.

19. Having now described the exterior we proceed to the passages and chambers. The entrance was uncovered, and the passages partly cleared, by Prof. Maspero's workmen in 1882. The floor of the entrance passage begins at 574·8 inches horizontally from the middle of the north base, and 720·7 above the pavement at that point (see PL. II). The passage is 62·5 inches high, at right angles, being built of three courses 21·0, 20·0, and 21·5 high: the floor is 20·2 thick, and the lintel 25·8 thick. The width is 32·2 at top, and 34·3 at base. The entrance was apparently closed by wedges of stone. The block filling the lower course was probably keyed into that of the middle course: this one was secured by the sides of the passage being cut away sloping inward, so that the block could wedge tight; the upper course block was tapered in thickness so that it wedged between the middle block and the roof. Further in, at 326·3 measured along the floor, there is on each wall a joint rising at 75°, the face of the outermost mastaba coat; the remains of a doorway fastening may be seen in this coat; the roof is higher by 7·3, for a length of 48·2; and on each side are two D-shaped holes, 14·6 from the outer face, and 12·7–16·7, and

55·7–59·6, below the roof. These probably held metal bars, against which rested a slab of stone filling the doorway, until the outer coat was finished, and the entrance wedged up. At 516·1 from the entrance is the face of another mastaba coat, also at 75°, on either wall. Below this no joints could be found that were not square with the passage. The whole passage is built of masonry, and never enters the rock, contrary to some accounts. But the salt has so violently scaled the surface of the stone, that it is exfoliated into a circular cavernous form, and it is only by referring to the joints that the plane of the roof can be observed. The upper part of the passage, and particularly the region of the outer casing coat, is of excellent stone, clean and smooth. The tool marks can be plainly seen—short, small adze strokes. And the system may be traced whereby an excess was left on the edge of the face until after the stone was built in, when it was dressed down so as to insure a smooth surface across the joint. The joint thicknesses are very fine, much under $\frac{1}{100}$ of an inch.

At a length of 2247·6 inches the sloping passage ends, and the angle of it, observed from the entrance to more than half-way down, is 28° 48′. Hence the end is 2544·4 from the north base horizontally, and 362·1 below the base. But the floor itself was not seen, owing to the large amount of exfoliated sheets of stone which more than half fill the passage.

20. In the horizontal passages and chambers which follow this, I have had the whole floor cleared and thoroughly examined, a portion at a time, to make certain that no other passages exist below those. The roof drops 2·9, and then proceeds horizontally in one plane until reaching the well which ascends to the sepulchre. The chambers here are 69·5 high. First there is a widening of the passage on the east, immediately it becomes horizontal; thus forming a chamber 82·7 wide (instead of the passage width of 30·7), and 103·3 long. Then for a short way of 21·5 the passage is normal, and afterwards widens on the west into a chamber 83·6 wide, and 103·4 to 104·2 long. These chambers are all lined with masonry. Then a passage, still in the same line, goes south for 146 inches to the well, making a length of 374 in all. The floor of this last piece is broken up, leaving rough rock, with a trench or groove along the middle of it; and the lower part of the well is rough rock, the upper part being lined with stone, which is supported at the sides by large beams or wall plates of wood, still in place, and still sound, though saturated with salt. The floor of the sepulchre is also of rock, covered with a thin paving which is now mostly torn up. Hence the rock rises to about 130 below the pavement, and the lower passages must be built in a trench in the rock.

The well in the lower part is 36·3 on E., and 30·5 on N.; while above it is 46 on E., and 40½ on N. Its height, from the roof of the passage to the pavement of the sepulchre, is 174 inches. The well rises in the extreme N.E. corner of the sepulchre floor, which is 233 on the W. and 104 on the S. side. The E. and W. sides of the chamber close together rapidly upwards in a series of overlappings, formed by the projection of successive courses of stone. This is a standard form in the mastaba chambers of this place, and is seen in the gallery of Khufu's pyramid. These overlappings are at 41, 63, 86, 107, 131, 155?, 180, 204?, and top 225? above the pavement of the chamber; the widths of the chamber being below the laps 104, and then 91, 80, 64, 53, 36?, 20?, 4?, the top space being irregular, and the stones almost touching in parts. That this really was the sepulchre is shewn by our finding thrown down the well the pieces from a wooden sarcophagus, of the early plain style, which had been very violently wrenched open and destroyed. The position of the chamber is 2918 to 3151 from the N. base, or 76 to 309 south of the middle of the pyramid. The azimuth of the passage being 21′ 33″ west of north, it is very nearly that of the pyramid sides, the deviation being about 2 inches: hence the chamber sides would be 42 E. and 62 W. of the middle of the pyramid. The pavement of the chamber is 119 under, and the top 106 over, the north pavement.

CHAPTER II.

THE MASTABAS AND BURIALS.

21. The earliest mastaba of importance appears to be that at the north-east of the pyramid, No. 17 Plan, PLS. I, VI. As it is the largest but one, and the simplest in construction, we will consider it first. Its outside was built of large crude bricks, the body of it is formed of clean chips of limestone, evidently the waste from the building of the pyramid: it is therefore most probably contemporary with the pyramid. It differs in internal arrangement from the other mastabas; and it has no sculptured chamber, opening to the outside, but only a plain stone facade opposite the sepulchre, on the east side. It also differs from others in having been built entire at once, and without any subsequent coating or addition.

The outer faces slope at the characteristic angle of mastabas, 76°, or an angle of 4 vertical on 1 horizontal. And the walls do not rest on a level foundation, but are carried down to reach a rock bed. This was found very markedly on the north side. Seeing that there was a mass of clean chips outside that face, I thought that it might cover an entrance; we therefore began clearing it out, but found the face slope down without any opening until the rock was reached about 20 feet below the ground level. While examining the N.E. corner, in clearing it for the survey, a very curious wall was found outside it, and similar walls were found on searching at the other corners. As remarked, the faces slope down to the rock, and hence it would be very troublesome to lay out the building with sloping faces on an irregular level, so as to bring it to the dimensions required at the ground level.

22. The laying out was therefore most carefully arranged, on a perfectly true principle. Outside of the corners vertical walls were built from the rock up to the ground level of the intended mastaba (see the four "corner walls" on the plan PL. VIII). These walls are of L shape, running in front of both faces at each corner; they are of crude brick, plastered, and whitewashed, to shew up the construction lines. Levelling was then carried around the site, and all the inner faces of the walls were divided by horizontal lines into spaces of a cubit high (see PL. VIII), the deep wall at the N.W. having as many as nine cubit levels still marked on it. Vertical lines were then drawn on the walls, in the planes of the ground lines of the intended faces; *e.g.* on the two northern pieces of wall, at N.E. and N.W. corners, the vertical lines were 2065 apart, the intended breadth of the N. face at the ground level. Then from the intersection of these vertical lines with the ground level, sloping lines were drawn down outwards at the intended angle of the face. Thus at each end of the face was a slanting line defining its plane; and it was only needful to place the eye on one line and sight the brickwork in a line with the line at the other end, to know that it was in the intended plane. Such was evidently the principle, of which the evidences remain at each corner. But for some reason a second sloping line was added outside the first, and the building was thickened out to that. It is impossible to suppose that the ground level was at the intersection of the outer line with the vertical, though possibly that level was marked on the mastaba side now destroyed: and it is equally impossible not to regard the vertical lines as the intended dimension of the mastaba, as the breadth is exactly 100, and the length 200, cubits. So we can only suppose that the mastaba face was built one brick thicker than at first intended.

The construction lines, vertical and horizontal, and the inscriptions referring to them are all in red. The working lines are in black. All the broad lines were marked by two narrow edges, filled in between by brush-work. The faces of the mastaba are exactly in the plane of the outer edge of the outer line; so thus the wide line could be easily seen from corner to corner, while the work could be formed with precision to its outer edge.

Turning now to the details of each corner, at the N.E. the cubit lines are 20·5 apart, and ·3 thick; the black lines are 3·2 wide on the north, and 2·4 on the east; the red vertical is 3·2 on north, and 2·6 on east. The mastaba faces differ from the outer edges of the black lines by being ·3 inside on the E., and 1 on 200 flatter angle on the N. The wall is 17·6 thick; it was somewhat broken down anciently, as the clean mass of stone chips overlies the broken top of the wall; and it seems as if the bricks had been carried off, leaving the plastering projecting alone. This corner is in brilliant condition of colouring.

The S.E. corner wall is somewhat decayed by damp, and the colour a good deal injured, but the same system is quite clear. The red vertical on the east wall has been altered, being re-drawn at 1·6 further out; the black lines evidently belong to the later line. The black lines vary from 1·9 to 2·6 wide, and the red are 2·1 and 2·3.

The S.W. corner is very much decayed by rain; the red cubit lines are mostly effaced; the S. red vertical appears to have been altered like the line in the S.E. corner; and on the west wall no trace of a red vertical can be determined, only a patch of red which by its position may be part of the vertical, but which looks on the spot more like part of a red triangle. The corner of the walls is not continuous, each wall standing separately. The black lines are 2·4 wide.

The N.W. corner is far the most important. The rock bed was here 21 feet below the ground, and a high wall was therefore needed to set out the construction lines. The perspective view of this corner is shewn on PL. VIII, supposing the mastaba corner to be complete at some height above the ground, in order to render it clearer; in reality the mastaba outer face is all broken away above the ground. This corner bears inscriptions relating to the levelling. In the fifth cubit space below the ground level we read at each side, "cubits five under of the *neferu.*" The technical word *neferu* for ground level does not seem to be yet known; but its meaning is clear, and it refers to the "finished" or "completed" surface. Similarly in the eighth cubit space is "cubits eight under of the *neferu*." The walls are not quite true; the west wall projects forward below, thus reducing the breadth of the north wall; and the north wall recedes somewhat at the top part, thus increasing the width of the west wall; hence the crossing corner lines in the diagram. The levelling is marked in certain parts particularly by a red triangle, a sort of bench-mark which is well designed, and may be seen in other Egyptian work. The black lines vary slightly in width, but the average is 2·4 for the inner and 1·6 for the outer lines; the red verticals are 2·5 wide below, and 2·2 above. The level lines were drawn independently on the walls, and differ ·1 or ·2 at the corner; they are about ·2 wide.

23. From these construction lines we have of course a good evidence of the cubit. It is the usual royal Egyptian cubit of 20·6 inches. The heights of the cubit spaces are changed on the walls by the compression of the brickwork, and the plaster is buckled off the wall in parts by its not being compressed in the same manner. The lower parts shew more compression than the upper, and the mean of all is 20·36, varying from 20·0 to 20·5. But, as we have already mentioned, the angle of slope is 4 on 1, and therefore the black lines extend ¼ of a cubit further from the red at every space. Hence there is another set of cubit values, given horizontally, which are independent of the vertical compression. There is no doubt but that they were measured out from the vertical, and probably the outer edges of the red and black lines are the more correct parts to observe. The distances measured are, on the west wall 20·5, 30·6, 41·2, 51·5; and on the north wall 20·3, 30·8, 41·1, 46·4, and 58·0. This last is clearly excessive, but the mean cubit value from the eight other measures is 20·54 inches. Even this is probably somewhat reduced by the contraction of the brick and plaster in very slow drying, as I have found in a tomb the gesso coat of fresco work much buckled off the brick and mud backing owing to the contraction behind.

The best data of all are the dimensions of the mastaba shewn by the distances of the red verticals apart. Owing to the very disturbed state of the ground I could only measure this trigonometrically, and owing to the distance of the stations observed this is not a certain result within a few inches. It yields, however, between the outer edges of the red verticals N., 2065; E., 4121; S., 2063; W., 4,124; and hence a mean cubit value of 20·627 ± ·007 inches, which is very closely that fixed by the most accurate datum in Khufu's pyramid, 20·620 ± ·005. The errors of squareness are considerable in this mastaba, the S.E. and N.W. corners being blunt, and the N.E. and S.W. corners sharp, by about 24′. The average azimuth of the E. and W. sides, which were doubtless those fixed astronomically, is 12′ W. of N., which is only half the divergence of the pyramid azimuth.

The levels of the lines at the corners are related thus: the N.E. is 6·5 high, S.E. is 4·7 low, S.W. is 2·8 low, and N.W. is 1·0 high. There is then an average error of 3·7 inches, which is more than double the error made in levelling the longer base of the Medum pyramid. This shews that levelling was a matter which tried their skill; the error here is 1 in 400, which might occur either by horizon observation, or by plumb line levelling. The bricks had all been splashed with yellow wash, when stacked before being used, in order to prevent any thefts; just like the bricks of Hawara, and the coals in a modern depôt.

24. The interior of this mastaba has not been entered in modern times, and the position of the chamber is yet unknown. On the east face will be seen a stone facade on the plan, near the south end. This has a stone paving before it. It was opened up by Prof. Maspero's workmen in 1882, and left open; consequently nearly all the stone has now been carried away. There was no sculpture, nor even a false door, on it. When I cleared it again I found at the north end of it a forced passage in the loose stone chips which form the body of the mastaba. This I had cleared out for some distance, when it turned downwards, and could not well be worked in, owing to the looseness of all the material, and an old forced well which opened into it, and was full of loose stuff. I had already scraped off the surface of the mastaba on the top all along the middle, down to clean firm chips, to search for a well, but in vain. I then sank a large square pit with winding stairway, in the axis of the mastaba, reaching from about the middle to near the latitude of the N. end of the facade. This pit we carried down to 48 feet under the top—a considerable work; but we neither reached a central chamber, nor any passage leading to the chamber, as I had hoped we might have done. The old forced passage just mentioned was opened out north-west into the pit, for safety of working, and was then cleared of loose stuff, but it proved to have been abortive, as it ceased

in the mass of filling, without reaching the chamber. An indication of the chamber was however reached, as a brick wall was found in the bottom of my pit, with a plaster lining and a red line on it, facing south. This is doubtless part of a guiding wall for the working lines of the chamber, like the walls at the corners of the mastaba. And this shews that the chamber is about behind the facade, and E. of the axis. A long sloping face of dry stone walling rises up above this brickwork, evidently the retaining wall to keep back the upper stuff while working, as this hole is about 20 feet below the pavement. These details were only found in the last week of my work, and I had not time to undertake the heavy task of clearing away another large mass of stuff 48 feet deep to lay bare the chamber. Where the regularly built entrance is we cannot tell: there is no well on the top, nor any passage leading into the chamber from the north, as there is in other mastabas.

The whole length of the east side was laid bare and examined in search of any other facade or false door, but it was all made of smoothly plastered brick. The outside of the brickwork had been a good deal weathered and destroyed down to the ground level, and it was then tunnelled into for graves in about the XXIInd dynasty; the bodies were much swathed, occasionally in wooden coffins without inscriptions, but there were no objects with them, except once or twice a few beads.

25. The largest mastaba of all, however, is No. 16 (PLS. I, V), that of Nefermat and Atet. And first we should notice that in each of the great mastabas here there are two false doors, one near each end of the east face. In No. 8 they are only plastered, and plain; in No. 9 the stonework is nearly destroyed; but in Nos. 6 and 16 we see that the southern door has the master on the panel over it, while the northern of No. 6 has the mistress and master, and that of 16 has the mistress alone, while she is also represented as the main figure of the lintel. Thus it is clear that the northern door was that for the worship of the mother, while the southern is that of the father.

Hence to avoid confusion between the two false doors I have called the southern ones by the masters' names Nefermat and Rahotep, while the northern ones receive the mistresses' names Atet and Nefert. The illustrations therefore of PLS. IX–XV. are all of one mastaba, No. 6; and those of PLS. XVI–XXVII are all of one other, No. 16. The variation of the azimuth of the mastabas from that of the pyramid is verified by magnetic bearings, besides the survey; the Denkmäler plan is therefore in error.

The outer part of No. 16 is of small bricks, and it has been enlarged by a thick outer coat (see detail, PL. VII). The body of it is of layers of Nile mud, poured in and left to harden before a fresh mass was applied. It is thus full of large cracks which extend far in all directions, which conduct currents of warm air out whenever excavations are made, and which form the home of serpents. The top is coated with 3 to 5 feet of gravel and sand, to sponge up the rain, and prevent it penetrating.

I endeavoured to find the well, or entrance to the chamber, during some weeks of work. The top coat of gravel was removed, and the mud body tested from end to end all along the axis; in the middle, around which Mariette's men had made some wide digging, I cut down to about 20 feet deep, and at the northern part in the axis, behind the north door, I also went down 20 feet deep. But only the same layers of Nile mud were found. I also cleared the N. end down to the ground, but found no trace of an entrance. When I cleared the south door I found a forced hole below it, which led into a forced passage; this ran N.W., but ceased before reaching the axis; it was quite empty and clear, 6 ft. high and 3 ft. wide, entirely cut in Nile mud without any sign of other material. At the north door a forced passage has been cut in the south end of the cross space; but as it was choked, and I did not know, before I covered it over, with what skill the plunderers sometimes cut for the point of burial, I did not examine it. It became needful to cover this facade soon after I had cleared it, as the salt in the stone deliquesced with the dew, and was destroying the remaining colours. The burial chambers of this mastaba are therefore at present unknown.

The false doors and *ka* chambers here are facades of stone, with a deep recess or chamber, closely alike, Atet's being slightly smaller. As to the sculpture, that will be noticed in the next chapter. The grand masses of which Nefermat's chamber is formed are striking. The back is all one block, over 156 inches high, 50 wide, and 41 thick, weighing therefore about 8 tons; the sides are 135·5 high, 111 average width, and 40·4 thick, about 20 tons each; and the top is all in one block across, 245 long, 97 deep back, and 41 thick, about 33 tons. These shew a fine mastery in the art of using heavy blocks, and we must remember that they are older than the pyramid of Khufu, and as early as anything yet dated. The chamber thus formed was 95·5 long at top, 137·4 at base, varying according to the slope of the facade; 50·0 wide at back and 56·5 in front, and 135·5 high to the under side of the drum, or roll across the top, or 155·7 to the space behind the drum. These dimensions are not in even numbers of cubits, although the cubit was evidently used in the thickness of the lintel and sides, and depths of the drum. In the plan (PL. VII) it will be seen how the front of the stonework, or facade, is left exposed by a short cross passage, the other sides of which are composed of brick. It seems possible, as a sloping joint is seen on the ends of this passage, that the facade is in the true face of the first body of the mastaba. That was coated over with brick, leaving the facade clear, and a passage to lead to it, which was lined with coloured frescoes. And then a second coat of brick formed the present outside, with a mere niche or false door to indicate the place for offerings. A court was also built in front of this, as we shall notice in the Rahotep mastaba, and this court is analogous to that of the pyramid. The fresco had nearly all perished, and I only saw the lower part of Atet, clad in panther's skin with striped border, and of Nefermat walking in front of her. The fresco over the lintel had fallen from the wall in early times, and part of it was found lying at the foot along with some wood that had formed the roofing of this cross passage. The fresco is shewn on PL. XXVIII.

There is a difference between the brick faces in all these mastabas. The inner is quite plain, white plastered; while the outer is all in panels, or rather a row of small false doors, as an ornament. The angle also differs; the outer is 82° 10′ on the E.: the inner 69° 40′ on E., and 72° 20′ below, 70° 0′ above, on the N. The maximum height is 385 inches, probably 10 cubits (412) originally; and the outer coat rises to 260, but is greatly denuded, so that it probably extended to the top. The panelling on it is in groups; wide niches of 2 cubits (41 ins.) are flanked by a narrower one on each side, and each such group is recessed from the general face, which has three narrow niches between the groups. By the measurements there must be 28 large niches in the length, and 15 in the width, of the mastaba. The inner body is 2474 inches on N. and 2470 on S., 4550 on E., 4554 on W. Probably 120 cubits (of 20·60) and 220 cubits (of 20·69 inches). The outer coat varies in thickness, 97 on W., 101 on S., 115 on N., 119 on E., to the outermost parts, and to the continuous ground level step from which the niches rise.

The chamber of Atet is of less grand blocks, the top being partly compound, and the dimensions being slightly less. The stone has moreover suffered greatly by scaling in the inside. The chamber is 47 4 wide at back, 47·5 at top of front, 46·2 at base: 106·5 long at base: and 127 high to under side of drum, or 148·4 to roof. I should state that Mariette's plans of this and other mastabas are all in error by his confounding the different coatings of the mastabas, and measuring between an inner face on one side and an outer on the other. This is certain, as I found that only one or other face had been discovered on different sides.

26. No. 6 is very similar in design to the above. The body of it is, however, all built of bricks throughout, and is now about 260 high, after most of the gravel top is gone. It will be seen on the plan that it was at first symmetrical; 2060 long, and 1330 wide, with a central pit, two false doors on the E. face, and a second pit nearly behind the north door. The innermost S.W. corner inside this is a division in the mass of brickwork, which can hardly have any designed meaning, as it runs too close to the chamber. Afterwards it was enlarged on the south, and west, and a large addition was made on the north, marked as the "annex." Then a coat was run all round it, making it 3207 long and 1548 wide; and lastly a second coat 97 thick was added over the E. face, to further hide the chambers. The angle of the inner body is 76° 40′, the 1st coat $73\frac{1}{2}$°, the outer coat $73\frac{1}{4}$° on the E. face.

The *ka* chamber (see PL. VII) seems to have been designed after that of Nefermat, as the cross-passage, which was a mere accident of development there, has here become an intended feature, embodied in the masonry, and covered with carving. Within this chamber stood the statues of Rahotep and Nefert, now in the Ghizeh Museum; and the doorway was entirely blocked with masonry cemented into place when Mariette's workmen found it, the chamber being intact. After cutting out the blocking, and removing the statues, and apparently taking wet squeezes from the coloured walls—thus ruining them—the doorway was earthed over by the discoverers. Never being inspected, some traveller chose to unearth it, soon before 1887, which date is written in the tomb; and it has stood open since then, with the result that every face within reach is mutilated, most of the figures spoiled, and all the edges of the stone broken away. I completely reburied it. The sculpture on the side walls is much cut away to insert the blocking, and as similar cutting is seen on Nefermat's walls, it is almost certain that statues of him and Atet existed in his chamber. There is no such trace of blocking in Atet's chamber.

In front of the false door which is in the outermost coat of brickwork a courtyard was built, which contains two steles bearing the inscription on PL. IX, which does not contain the name. Mariette's description is erroneous in stating these to belong to another mastaba built against the E. face of Rahotep's, to which he gives the name of Ranefer as well as to No. 9; the coat of brickwork was mistaken for a fresh mastaba, in this, the only place where it was noticed. These steles are 18·0 to 18·2 thick, 23·2 wide, and measuring from the roughened expansion at the base they are 103⅛ high to the beginning of the curve and 110 to the top, being formed like those of the pyramid temple (PL. IV). In the court of offerings were many small vases and saucers, like those found at the E. of the pyramid and before other tombs here. At the base of the niche of the false door at the back of the chamber is a pit cut in the stone, apparently intended for pouring down offerings. It is so rough that it may have had some fine stone edging now removed.

The false door of Nefert is much less important, being merely a niche, with an unsculptured facade on either side of it.

The central pit of the mastaba had been furiously searched for by Mariette's men; they dug vast holes in the brick body, but never cleared the top; and a trench of theirs cut away one side of the well, without their seeing it. In course of clearing their cutting to examine it my men found the well. It had stood open for ages, and was deeply furrowed with rainfall on the sides. The west side was so rotten that I had to remove a coat of brick from it before clearing the pit. The section of the pit is given in PL. VII. The sides of the pit have a groove on each side to hold a great stone trap-door slid down to the bottom. Some way down we noticed a hollow on the south side, and opening it found a relieving chamber in the brickwork, at the ground-level. The short passage leading to this is curious for having two slight arches built in it (see PL. VII) to relieve the thrust of the overlapping sides. This true arch is important, as it carries the use of it back from the XIIth dynasty to the IVth. This chamber and passage we completely cleared out, but found nothing in them.

Descending further we came on the top edge of the trap-door, which I did not then understand clearly; but suspecting a chamber beneath the relieving chamber, I cleared the well thoroughly first, in order to be able to throw the rubbish from the chamber into it. In the well were 41 blocks of stone, averaging 10 × 10 × 15 inches, about 1 cwt. each; just as much as I or the men could conveniently lift and carry about. These lay loosely and had evidently been the filling in of the passage leading to the chamber. Beneath these was a copper adze in the dust 10 inches over the bottom (PL. XXIX), which must therefore be as old as the first plunderers of the old kingdom; and also the red pottery pan (XXXI, 21) with a spout, in which the men had mixed their plaster when closing the passage with the masonry; for no one would mix plaster down there at a later time. The adze may also have belonged to them.

Then clearing down between the shifted trap-door and the wall we found a mummy interred there later, and the passage leading to Rahotep's chamber. The chamber was quite empty, and all the traces found are some curved wooden bars of the inside of the coffin, and some scraps of fine gauze, like that afterwards found on Ranefer's mummy. The bottom of the sepulchre is rock, and there was about 20 inches depth of large flints, or very coarse desert gravel, laid on it, all of which we turned over. Perhaps this was a substratum to the floor, to serve as a sponge in case of water getting down the pit, so that the body might be preserved dry above it. Alas for the body! —where is it?

A very curious point of construction is the woodwork employed. In the sides of the well are wooden beams occasionally; just as wooden corner beams, and a tie running into the wall, are found on the N.W. corner of mastaba 17. And in the solid mass of brickwork of Rahotep's mastaba are logs of trees built in, nearly upright, and 8 or 10 feet long, to serve to bind the material. So ramifying are some of these that I thought at one time that a whole tree had been built around, but a log was wrenched out one night by the villagers, proving its isolation.

The second well was doubtless that of Nefert, being behind her false door. It had been plundered anciently and a crater surrounded it. For I may say that Mariette's statement that there was no trace of any pits on these mastabas is quite wrong; nearly all shew large pits of successful or unsuccessful plunderers, on the top. We cleared this pit to a great depth, over 40 feet below the crater top, as it is far deeper than Rahotep's. We reached the chamber, but unluckily a snake dropped down, and the boys were afraid to work it, having seen him just under their feet one day. As it was plundered and had stood open for ages, and was in a dangerous condition at the sides, I then did not think it worth much more trouble to proceed with it.

27. The annex is a very unaccountable piece of work. It is certainly contemporary with the other part, as the outer face is continuous; but it is built on to the white-plastered N. end of the mastaba, and is 830 long without the outer coat. On the E. side of it is a false doorway in the brickwork, white-plastered. Above this in the mass of brickwork were two parallel joints, marking where a space or passage had been left (see PL. V), and filled up later with brick. This I cleared out, and found it did not go lower than the top of the false door; and on proceeding inwards the base of this filled space rose upward, and came to the top of the mastaba at about the middle. There was no sloping floor to it, only the parallel joints ended and there was continuous brickwork below them. The lower part of the space was filled with large broken pieces of stone. It certainly seemed as if it would lead to some unopened chambers. However I cleared it completely without any clue. I then cut about all over the top of the mastaba and searched the brickwork everywhere, to see if any filled up pit existed, looking for continuous joints in the brick, and cutting about 6 feet deep all along the axis. Nothing was found. I then sank a pit through the solid brickwork at the end of the blocked space, and in the axis. Nothing but brick was met with above ground. But a round pit was found in the ground, filled up with broken brick and mud. This seemed very promising. It went through the gravels for 13 feet, then soft rock for 2 feet, and then into harder rock, where 3½ feet further it ended, with a flat bottom, rough picked, 39 inches across. There was nothing but brick and rubbish in it, and the object of making such a pit for 18½ feet seems inexplicable. Together with 25 feet of cutting through the mastaba, our pit was 43½ feet deep. Beside the false door there was another curious indication; above the false door, a little to the south was a hollow in the brickwork, 33 inches deep, 29 E. to W., 70 N. to S., and 90 to 120 inches inside the outer face of the brickwork. This hollow was full of sheep's and goats' bones, as if sacrificed and thrown in there. A similar hollow full of ox bones was found near the top of Ranefer's mastaba, a little N. of the N. doorway, about 10 feet back from the back of the doorway. It was there close to a sepulchral pit, and offering chamber; yet in Rahotep's annex no trace of such a pit or chamber can be found.

28. The only other tomb with remaining sculpture is what I have called Ranefer's, No. 9. The portions of figures, PL. XIV, do not yield any such name. But Mariette states "des deux chambres, du sud et du nord, il ne reste que des pans de mur démolis au milieu des quels nous avons pu recueillir le nom du personnage" Râ-nefer. His account is so very incorrect in other points that I do not feel much confidence in this statement; but as much stone seems to have lately been removed from the south doorway, and only small chips are now left, whatever ground there was for the above attribution is now lost. The matter is complicated by Baedecker's account which describes, apparently as being here, a fine complete chamber with very curious and interesting sculptures, lassoing a bull, making of sarcophagi, and an altar of offerings, for Khent and his wife Mara. There is no possible site for such a tomb except at the lately destroyed stonework of No. 9. Yet Mariette says nothing whatever about it, and attributes this to Ra-nefer according to mere chips that were found. Probably this note about Khent and Mara has been entirely displaced in the guide book, and refers to elsewhere.

The plan of the *Ka* chamber, or false door, at the N. of Ra-nefer will be seen, PL. VII: the coat of brick filled up the stone recess, and has another recess in it. The body of the mastaba is, at the base, 1146 on N., 1161 on S., 2161 on E., 2084 on W. The coat of brick on it is 60 to 65 thick on the E. face. On clearing at the middle of the top we found the well, under about 5 feet of gravel. It was wide and quite intact, and took a fortnight to clear out. The stone trap door like Rahotep's was duly in position; and we cut away the side walls and levered it carefully over so as to get behind it, and found a passage blocked with solid masonry. Mr. Fraser, who happened to be visiting me, cut this out with hammer and chisel; when I went down I found only one stone in the way, I wriggled it out, and crawled into the hole, looked over into the intact (!) chamber, only to see a great black hole in the floor. It had been burgled by cutting a tunnel from the back of the south false door straight to the chamber, and breaking away the floor. The plan and section of the chamber is in PL. VII. Ranefer's mummy lay hitched up against the west wall, on its left side, head north, facing east; the head had been broken off by the violators, but carefully replaced, with a stone under it to support it in position. The wrappings on the body were also torn up. The mode of embalming was very singular. The body was shrunk, wrapped in a linen cloth, then modelled all over with resin, into the natural form and plumpness of the living figure, completely restoring all the fulness of the form, and this was wrapped round in a few turns of the finest gauze. The eyes and eyebrows were painted on the outer wrapping with green. The mummy is now in the Royal College of Surgeons. There was no trace of a coffin of either stone, or wood; and certainly none could have been dragged out through the hole. Even if a wooden coffin had been broken up it is unlikely that no bits of it would remain.

In the recess in the south end, similar to that in Rahotep's chamber, there were parts of the internal organs embalmed, forming lumps of resined matter wrapped round in linen, and fragments of such were in Rahotep's recess. Some insect had lived on it for generations, and the place was deep in the cast skins. There was no sign of these organs having been in jars or enclosures; and it seems as if these recesses in the tombs were intended to lay the internal parts on after embalming, before the use of jars for such was introduced.

On making further search a second well was found toward the north, doubtless that of the wife, like the well behind Nefert's door. This had been plundered anciently, and stood open for ages. We cleared it to the chamber, but that was so large and full of rubbish, that—as the well was rather dangerous and time short—I relinquished it.

29. No. 8 is a smaller mastaba, without any coating at the ends, as it stood too close to the others to allow of it. The body is 1607 on E., 1610 on W., 614 on N., 616 on S. In all these mastabas, although the actual base was not exposed at all corners I noted the levels of the points of the sloping face where the measures were taken, and compute the base length by knowing the angle of the face. The E. coat is 93 and 109 thick, and the W. 116 thick. The angle is 80° 37′ on W., 82° 0′ on E., 84° 34′ in S. recess and 88° 18′ at the back niche. The two false doors are both smoothly white-plastered without any decoration. In the southern door was a quantity of ox bones and large goats' skulls, placed there before the outer coat was built over it.

On the top of the mastaba, which is 195 high, are three pits. None of these were found in Mariette's digging, although the eastern side was much destroyed then, and a small tunnel made which went into the middle pit. The diggers could not understand it, and left the place. On crawling in I saw that my head was in a filled up shaft, and dug for it on the top. It was difficult to find the top of the pit, as it was covered with a thick coat of brickwork. About 6 feet down the pit sides were clear, and it was found to be full of clean chips of the soft yellow rock through which the lower part is cut. It had evidently never been disturbed, and our hopes were high. After 30 feet of brick sides we went through 9 feet of rock, and found a short passage leading into a chamber on the south side. But in neither chamber nor well was a trace of any body or buried object to be found, nothing but clean yellow rock chips. I carefully examined all the floor myself and saw that there was no further cutting.

We then tried to the N. of this, and found another well quite untouched. This was cleared down to the level of the top of the doorway on the south side, where objects were found. At this level a mat of rushes had been spread on loose rubbish thrown into the well. Upon this mat were laid 4 alabaster bowls all tied up in cloths (Pl. XXIX, 15); a broken red dish (16) with 28 flint flakes in it tied up in a cloth, a bundle of 50 flint flakes tied up together, 22 more loose on the mat, and 7 at the mouth of the chamber, in all 107: also pieces of thin wood on edge, all quite rotted, with some of the flints between them; and a conical pot of rough hand make like XXXI, 15. Just at the mouth of the doorway was a block of Nile mud 7 × 9 × 8 inches with ribbed outside, ribbing about ·4 inch wide; a red pottery pan broken (Pl. XXIX, 16), three large shells (17) one containing some blue paint made of powdered Chessylite (carbonate of copper), and copper needles, 11 or more thin, and mostly broken, and 3 thicker ones (18, 19). I then went into the chamber and examined it, but not a trace of a body was to be found in either the chamber or the well, nor any objects beyond those lying on the mat at the level of the top of the doorway. The pit is 50 to 57 inches wide, passage 43 wide and high, and chamber 97 on S., 84 on N., 73 on W., roughly cut by a pick 1·6 wide, leaving rounded sides. The flints (20-26) have been carefully sorted by Mr. Spurrell, and rejoined as far as possible to shew their original order and mode of manufacture. They were all struck from only two or three blocks of flint, but were all mingled together before being divided into different lots in the burial; so that the lots as found have no significance. A similar flake to these was found in the debris which filled Rahotep's well, so probably a similar deposit lay there before being exploited.

On further trial a third well was found in the axis

of this mastaba, and this had been opened anciently. We cleared it to near the bottom, but were then foiled by coming on large irregular blocks of stone lying in it. They were too heavy to raise, too large to turn out of the way, and we dare not break them up for fear of shaking down the very rotten and dangerous sides of the well. So risky was it that I abandoned the place, seeing that it had been all disturbed and plundered.

30. We have seen how in these large mastabas the southern false door has a courtyard for offerings before it (see Nos. 6, 11, 16); but a different development took place also, the E. front of the mastaba being decorated by a row of small false doors, and at the south end of it a doorway leading into a chamber in which is a false door, as in Nos. 18, 22; or else a much larger false door at the south, as in No. 13. In all the tombs on the plans, a thick black outline indicates the foundation of a brick wall which is now destroyed.

No. 22 has three small false doors (see Pl. VII), which were painted, and next to these a chamber with a false door, also painted; the E. side was made into a gallery by a wall in front of it, and the S. end of this gallery was walled off, across from the chamber door. This walled part retained fresco painting in a fairly intelligible state, and I made a coloured copy of it which is here reproduced (XXVIII 5, 6, 7) and is described in chap. III. The closed room behind the chamber contained nothing; probably the *Ka* statues stood here, before the tomb was broken up. The well had been plundered, and a burial of the XXII (?) dynasty placed in it.

Mastaba 18 was evidently built later than many here. While No. 17 shews itself to be contemporary with the pyramid, by the whole mass being formed of clean stone chips, with occasional relics of the workmen, No. 18 is filled with whatever could be collected at a later date, much of it the small vases and saucers (XXX, 22 to 27) which were used for offerings in the IVth dynasty. Such a large quantity of these offerings would not be accumulated shortly, and as there is no heap of such by the pyramid otherwise it seems that this was built after the special popular worship of Seneferu was past, and no more were subsequently accumulated. At the pyramids of Gizeh and Dahshur there are similar heaps of these offerings. And they also occur often in private tombs at Medum, as Nos. 4, 6, 7, 11, &c. The number of wells in this mastaba is not original. The primary wells are only the 5th from the N., and perhaps one nearest to the back of the chamber; all the others are secondary, and can be distinguished by being cut through the mastaba, and lined with brick, leaving a belt of hard ground full of chips shewing between the mastaba and the rock. The chamber has a walled up niche or doorway on each side, but it had been so much dug into blindly by Mariette's men that I could not settle it. On each wall are small decorative niches, on N.N.E., 1, on N.N.W. 3, on W.N.W. 3, on W.S.W. 4. These niches are only at 21 to 41 inches (1 to 2 cubits) from the floor. Most of the wells we cleared out; they had all been plundered, and contained a few burials in gaudy illiterate coffins of about the XXIInd dynasty. The strange enclosure S. of the mastaba is of unknown use. The ground plan of it is quite complete, with parallel walls, expanding into a sort of doorway at the south end. Of course I thought we had the entrance to some subterranean place; but all the north end was carefully cleared and examined, and solid rock found under a bed of concreted chips.

31. The third principal type of tomb here is the mastaba with a central well, and sloping passage like a pyramid, leading to the chamber. The above ground part of these tombs has all disappeared: and seeing how solidly the brick mastabas have stood, still 20 to 30 feet high, we cannot suppose that these others were all swept away by denudation down to the last course or so of brickwork. It seems as if they must have been intentionally removed, not for mere destruction as there are no remains about them, but rather for bricks; and this in a very systematic way, and not by mere chance builders. One is tempted to see in this the destructive hand of Ramessu II.; but whoever did it the mastabas seem to have been removed by contract, so that one was completely cleared, before another was touched. A section of one of these passage mastabas is given on Pl. VII. The upper part of the well is brick-work. Then comes a breast-work on the south side, of large courses of stone. At the base a passage slopes down into the sepulchre, which has a recess for the embalmed viscera as in Rahotep's and Ranefer's tombs. The group of destroyed tombs W. of the pyramid (see Pl. I) were probably all of this type, and only shew now as slight hollows in the desert. On trying to clear one of them a wide pit full of sand is found, which requires a long struggle to empty it. Two of these I examined, and others I tested enough to see that they needed a lengthy clearance. Those I saw were plundered, and one had re-interments in wooden coffins of the XXIV–XXVIth dynasty without any-

thing but a few beads. The first tomb of this type which I opened was No. 15, and as the sand hole was very wide and deep, and the well destroyed, and I did not know the type, we had a very long affair with it. The chamber in this was not low and flat roofed, as in those W. of the pyramid, but was like the pyramid chamber, all over-lapping; and at the exposed end one could see of what immense sheets of stone these overlapping roofs consist. A high wind and falls of sand blocked it up before I had made a plan of it. The chamber contained nothing, and the recess in it had been forced out at the end in search of other chambers. From trials that we made and appearances it seems that Nos. 14, 11, 3, 2, and 1 were all mastabas of this type.

32. Having now described the three types of great mastabas we turn to the lesser tombs, which we will notice in order. No. 4 is a small mastaba much destroyed; but the panel over the north false door had fallen in early times, and was found buried; it shews a man named Heknen to have been interred here (Pl. XVI). The work is but rough, though rather different in style to the usual; and we may see in the turned up nose a sign of the aboriginal race, as I have noticed elsewhere. In front of this are the remains of another mastaba which produced nothing.

No. 5 shews just the foundation of the wall, and in the pit we found the fragments of a fine alabaster disc table on a conical foot, and a diorite bowl; these have been rejoined nearly entire, and are now at Manchester. The tomb had been plundered in early times, the large slab placed in front of the entrance to the chamber being left in place and a hole made above it.

No. 7 is a small, well-finished mastaba with a wall along the front forming a passage, and a court in the middle of the wall. The false doors are however at the south end and in the middle. Part of the lintel of the south door was found, and is given in Pl. XVI. It was of the most delicate sculpture, but unhappily was broken into small chips by the action of salt, so that not a single sign could be removed. A copy and a photograph were taken, from which it is here drawn. It shews much the same titles as Rahotep, but there seems to have been a priesthood of Sebek in the Lake; this, and the title "chief of the lake of the crocodile" on Nefermat's tomb, are the earliest mentions of the Fayum. The body of this mastaba is all of stone chips, very likely from the masonry of Rahotep's tomb. No trace of a well could be found, although we trenched three lines all the length of it, down to solid rock. To the west of this is another mastaba of some height; but the tomb had been plundered and left open anciently, like the other tomb pits around here.

No. 10 is mostly denuded away; the pit is a very wide space filled with sand, which we did not clear. No. 11 is a small mastaba; pottery was found in the court of it. The large number of pits to the east of this were mostly separate, with a small brickwork top and sometimes a little niche in the east face of it. They are the poorest class of pit burial, and nearly all the interments were contracted. The chambers below were nearly all on the west side: a space usually about 60 inches long (37–66), 30 wide (28–38) and 28 high (26–30) was cut in the soft clayey rock, the body was placed in it, and the entrance filled by a rude flat wall of crude bricks plastered with mud, which often projected into the pit as much as its own thickness. The pit was filled with earth. In one case the surface brickwork had a slit in it to the N. of the niche, opening into a small *serdab*, in which little vases stood.

No. 12 is one side of a mastaba remaining, and two deep pits. No. 13 is a mastaba for general burials apparently, a sort of undertaker's speculation. The pits are very small, and in rows, as close together as may be. In the southernmost but one was a long wooden coffin, and a wooden head-rest with the body. Many of these common interments had been crushed by the fall of the rock roof or of the brick wall, and though I preserved every skeleton that was complete I could not obtain more than a dozen.

Passing to the Southern cemetery, Pl. VI, the tombs 19, 20, 21 were greatly denuded, only just the foundations being left. The pits had all been plundered: those by 21 were peculiar, being long and narrow. No. 22 has been described already. The pit south of it had water over the entrance of the chamber. In one of these pits about 23 a loose stone sarcophagus was found, very rudely cut; 75 inches long, 24·3 wide, 19 deep inside; 7 to 8 inches thick, and 27 high outside: the head was to the north. No. 24 had water nearly to the roof of the chamber, and the floor could not be reached; the pit had never been opened before. To the S.W. of it was a small pit in the mastaba, built of brick, but not descending into the rock: in this was a large quantity of pottery, two dozen bowls being obtained, nearly all broken (see Pl. XXX, 1 to 8); some of the bowls were wrapped in cloth, and some little clay models of jars (XXX, 7) were found. In No. 27 a similar deposit was found. There the northern pit was very shallow, not 3 feet deep; but just to the S.W. of it was a smaller pit 30 × 32 inches, and 14 deep in the rock, with another deposit of bowls &c. (XXX, 9 to 13). And the southern pit, which is large and had been plundered, had a pit to the S.W. with bones in it. Thus it is evident that a custom existed of forming a small secondary pit into which the offerings were thrown; the bowls were probably wrapped in cloth to retain the food placed in them, and much dark brown organic matter was found saturating this pottery. This helps to explain the pit with bowls in the mastaba No. 8. No. 29 are two small wells with brickwork blocks over them, bearing a small niche on the east face.

33. We now turn to the burials in these tombs. Without giving the details of every skeleton found we may summarise them thus. Thirteen were fully recorded in a contracted posture, while only one burial besides Ranefer was found extended, setting aside those of later age, which were secondary burials. This long burial was in a wooden coffin; a wooden head rest with fluted stem lay by the head. Ranefer (see sect. 28) doubtless had valuable objects buried with him, as pieces of fine diorite and alabaster were found in the second well of that mastaba. On the other hand the contracted bodies very seldom have any accompanying objects, and they are never embalmed. Of the 13, 12 lay on the left side, with the head N., and the face E.; the knees were usually sharply bent, but the thighs were generally at right angles to the body; though sometimes bent up close, so that the knee was only 6 inches from the vertebra. The right arm was usually in front; but sometimes the hand was round the legs, sometimes up before the face. The left arm was generally under the body and legs, with the hand under the knees. The one burial in a different direction was with head W. face N. in a recess on the south of the well. But the motive of the placing in general was not to lay the body looking into the well, as in two other cases the chamber is to the south, but the face is turned to the east. This exceptional burial is also peculiar for having objects buried with it, a walking staff, and a head-rest; it was placed in a box, which is the case as often as not. Only two of the contracted bodies had objects with them; the one just named, and one with three small vases (like XXX, 22) by the head. That this contracted burial was not due to saving space, is seen by many tombs in which the body does not fill the chamber; and in one case the body is doubled up 43 inches long in a coffin 66 long, leaving over a third of the coffin empty. And that the absence of objects with the bodies is not due to poverty is seen by the cost and care of the burials, in these tomb pits, which must have involved some weeks of work, and the frequent coffins of wood, which was always valuable; while even the rough little vases, which might be made in hundreds in one day, are only found in a single case. We are therefore led to believe that there was a distinct difference in beliefs between the people who buried at full length, usually mummified, with funereal furniture, and the people who buried in a contracted form, facing the east with the head north, and without any objects. Such contracted burials have been found at Gizeh, both by Rhind, and also in one case in large jars at the Mena Hotel. Such a difference points to a difference of race, and we see that the contracted posture is only found in very early times. As it died out, and was clearly the custom of the poorer inhabitants, it probably belonged to the aboriginal people before the invasion of dynastic Egyptians; and the extended burial, with its accompanying beliefs, is due to the upper race who founded Egyptian history. Rhind notices that the Nasamones buried in a seated posture (Hdtus. IV. 190); but this does not seem to be a contracted lying position, though it might easily be connected with it. Clothing remained on some of the skeletons, and it was always plain linen, more than a mere kilt or waist cloth, and with a twisted linen girdle in one case.

The coffins that were found, were mere square boxes; only the one with extended body and a head-rest had a framed lid, with large end blocks, and boards inserted in a curve in the end. To shew how far regular the boxes are I give the dimensions of one; outside length 45·6, 45·8; width 22·9, 23·1; inside length 42·8, 43·2; width 19·8, 19·9; depth 19·1. Another was 31·7 × 13·4 × 12·1. A baby was found in an oval basket.

34. A very curious question is raised by the mutilations of these bodies. It should be said that the skeletons lay exactly as placed; sometimes the head had just rolled over, but usually every bone was in its articulation. There was no trace of any rats or other animals having got access to the tombs to disturb the bodies. And the skeletons noted were not crushed, and were fairly clear of any fallen materials. In one instance the whole left leg was missing from the knee: the end of the thigh bone came close to the brick wall, and not a trace of knee cap, leg bones, or foot was present. The end of the bone did not shew any change in the joint surface, so the amputa-

tion must have been shortly before death. In another case the left hand appeared to have been cut off, the end of the arm bone was close to the front wall, without room for the hand, and the nearest wrist bones or others were four inches from it, and those appeared to belong to the right arm, while the left hand bones were under the elbow. The arm bones were not fallen or displaced: so the hand must have been severed in life. In another case, where the arms were both raised, and the hands placed together in front of the face, a wrist bone was found under the leg four inches below the knee, which was quite undisturbed. And in the same body a toe bone was found under the pelvis. This is difficult to account for by any ordinary supposition. Another strange case was where three teeth were found by the pelvis, though I had lifted the skull as carefully as possible, as I always did, to avoid any chance of teeth dropping out. So both from the care in moving, from the skull not being lifted over the pelvis, and from the teeth not being on the top, we must suppose them to have been extracted before burial: possibly they had been swallowed. Four such curious displacements of bones in only 13 skeletons shews that much care must be spent in fixing the positions when such are found in future, in order to clear up the questions involved. All of these skeletons are now being prepared at the Royal College of Surgeons, and will there be studied, with reference to race, and also for the various diseases of the bones which are found in them.

CHAPTER III.

THE SCULPTURED CHAMBERS.

35. The plates IX to XXVII have all been executed by producing full-sized drawings, and from those reducing the present copies by photo-lithography. No doubt it would have been better on the one hand to have reproduced them here on a larger scale, in a few cases the details are too minute or the lines too fine, and a magnifier may be used with advantage to most of these plates; on the other hand a smaller scale would have enabled a more connected view of the scheme of decoration. The advantages obtained here however seem to be the greatest. No wall is divided on to two plates, excepting in the case of the long lintels which spread across the whole length of a tomb facade; these are separated from the rest of the facade, and each divided in two parts. Moreover in all cases the scale is the same throughout, so that the character of different parts can be compared. And the reduction of a foot to one inch enables the whole height of a tomb to appear on one plate.

In the details the greatest accuracy has been aimed at. The individual expression of every face among the farm servants, and other small figures and hieroglyphs, has been observed; the exact shape of the head in all of these, the form of the hands, the relative lengths of the fingers, the number of lines and notches in a wig, and such points, were all attended to individually, and not merely done on a general system. In the forms of the hieroglyphs the same detail has been followed. For instance not only the number of waves in *n*, but also the slope and thickness, have been copied. If a sign is askew, misshapen, or tilted, it has been strictly so drawn. Nothing has been assumed or restored, except in a few cases of a notched or injured line. But although all injuries which destroy the outlines are observed, the forms have been traced as far as possible, and credited with completion wherever the original form was not irretrievably lost. Hence these copies look more complete than are the actual walls. In the many sad instances of disfigurement since Mariette's copies were made (which comprise about 5½ plates out of the 19 here), it might at first seem pedantic not to fill in the parts now lost where those copies shew them. But it will soon be seen on comparing those former copies with the present, that no scientific value can be allowed to their details. The frequent misplacement of signs, omissions, and additions, even extending to inserting a figure and action which does not exist (see top of Pl. XXIII), and the inattention to the real forms of the figures and signs, would make any additions drawn from such a source a serious detriment to these present copies; to say nothing of the doubt as to the very existence of the missing signs. Insertions of dubious character would throw a suspicion over the whole accuracy. To those students who may need the fullest materials a reference to Mariette's plates is not a weighty business; while those who wish to place as much confidence as may be put in human work, can rely on these copies as being equivalent to the original sculptures, for all purposes of study that we can at present contemplate. No doubt but some inaccuracies may have crept in. They will probably be found in slight irregularities of the relative position of parts, due to copying on separate sheets; and possibly a sign might have been omitted, certainly none have been added.

36. The method of work was as follows. Sheets of thin paper, 3 feet high, 1 foot wide, were used. Beginning in a top corner, a sheet was held up by the left hand, and every line of sculpture was outlined by the right hand, a dry squeeze being thus taken. The soft part of the fingers was used or else the nails, according to the form. Then the squeezed sheet was laid on a drawing board, held just below the sculpture, and the outline was pencilled in, following the squeeze, but looking at the stone for all fine details and indistinct points. Thus the accuracy of a cast, and the interpretation of an eye-copy were combined. A minute pencil cross on the stone, at the corners of the paper, insured keeping a correct register of the positions of the sheets. Afterwards—in England—the sheets were joined into large rolls; the outlines were all inked in of a suitable thickness, equivalent to $\frac{1}{400}$ of an inch on the reduced scale; and photolithography did the rest of the business. For the coloured parts proof copies were coloured, and served for the chromo-lithographer to work by. The tints of the colours of each figure had been carefully copied on a key sheet on the spot; and samples of the inlayed colours of Nefermat's tomb, which had fallen out, and were found in the dust, served to give their tints. From much of the surface the colours had entirely vanished; in Rahotep's tomb they had been washed away by wet squeezes being taken in a barbarous way. In such parts the ground tint is made continuous over the figures. Wherever a trace could be found it is noted, but where a wide expanse of colour is without detail, as in faces without eyes, it means that the lesser parts have perished, leaving only a ground-work. In the case of wigs which shew details, they are left in outlines; but in all cases the hair is black. So far as the colours remain enough to give a general combined effect, they are here reproduced; but it did not seem worth the printing to give only a few scattered touches in those plates where the colour had nearly all perished. I have dwelt the more on the details of these copies as I much hope that published copies of all fine work will be made in future on some such system. The very crude method of irregular and inexact hand-drawing, which has been hitherto usual—or even worse, the adopting the style of some period of Egyptian art, on stone or papyrus, and drawing everything in that manner—is responsible for the neglect of Egyptian epigraphy, and artistic detail of styles, and schools, and periods, which is so lamentable. No doubt this exact copying takes time. Altogether these plates have occupied me about four days each, beside the lithographer's work. But such time is well spent, if it opens out a new study of art and history.

37. We will now turn to the separate plates and give some account of them; while the inscriptions will be treated by Mr. Griffith in chap. VI.

PL. IX. The lintel over Rahotep's facade is divided here into two parts, on the upper half of PLS. IX and X. It is less finely carved than the interior, and in very low relief; the separate panels of it are sunk so as to obtain the depth required for the signs. No traces of colour remain upon it. The wall of the tomb front below it is quite plain. The last block of the lintel has been removed in late years; and Mariette's copy shews the remainder of the inscription to have been nearly the same as on the "south side of the recess," PL. XII, ending with the name of Rahotep. The wider panel, first on PL. IX, is over the doorway. The south side of the passage is all in relief, as is the rest of this tomb; it has been defaced near the door, by cutting away the surface to allow of fitting in the closing blocks. We here see Rahotep and Nefert standing watching the chase in the desert, while below—in the lower lands—is the ox led forward, and indicated by three tethers or hobbles formed of a loop of rope passing through two holes in a piece of wood. It seems to be used here as a determination for the place for tame animals, in contrast to the wild ones above.

PL. X. Here, on the opposite side of the passage, Rahotep and Nefert behold their sons snaring birds; and below the fishers coming to shore with the ropes. The titles above contain some of the most important forms of signs; the column *an*, and the columns supporting a roof, with a central pillar *aa*, in the sign *heb*.

PL. XI. This comprises the whole of the wall, through which one enters the chamber; and the inscription on the drum over the door is here turned round to appear in the doorway. Rahotep is standing beholding the boat building: this part is in excellent condition, excepting a large flake which has come off, carrying the head and arm of a carpenter. Below Rahotep are scenes of servants, a cattle-herd, two slaughterers, and bearers of offerings of wine and of sweet palm beer. On the other side are the fishers drawing the net, which has floats above and sinkers below it. The calf-herd and fowler, and six farm servants, fill the lower scenes.

PL. XII. This comprises the south end of the chamber, and the west wall to the south of the recess at the back. The fish-curer seated under the shade of the lotus plants, splitting his fish with a knife, and spreading them out to dry, fills the upper scene. The leaves of the plants are only painted, and not carved. Then the two boatmen who have caught a monstrous fish, which they carry in triumph on an oar between them. The ploughing and 6 farm servants occur below. On the other wall is Rahotep standing in priestly dress with a leopard's skin, as he held more than one high priestly office in the country. The small inscription is from the stelas in front of the tomb; both are alike. It is rather roughly carved compared with the interior work. This is what Mariette ascribes to a separate mastaba which he attributes to a fictitious Ranefer.

38. PL. XIII. The lintel or architrave over the whole west side of the chamber comes at the top. Below this is the recess with its two sides; but as these sides are at right angles to the plane of the lintel and wall, they do not of course appear beneath the lintel actually in this way. The walls really beneath the lintel on each side bear the two large figures of Rahotep on PLS. XII, XIV. The need of keeping the recess all together obliges this separation. The lintel is finely painted, and furnishes some of the best signs selected for the frontispiece. The left wall is covered with lists of offerings many specified as being of the very best, *tep ha*, or A 1. The manner in which the jars are all shewn, with lids fastened down by a cloth band, and bound with string, and sealed, is curiously detailed. In the centre is Rahotep seated, with the usual table before him. The arrangement of the list of offerings is just like that in the earliest tombs of Abusir and Gizeh. Below this is the niche, with the children of Rahotep at the sides; T'etta (or Zedda), Atu, Nezem-ab, Setet, Merert, and Neferku. The damaged part in the centre is given entire by Mariette, the lost signs being *tu* (legs) *u. f.* On the right hand wall are further lists of offerings of the same character.

PL. XIV. Rahotep appears with a slight moustache, as on his statue in Gizeh Museum. On the north wall are wild cattle with their attendants; one of the farm names has been inserted in the lowest of these scenes, and it occurs again in Nefert's tomb on the next plate. The six servants bearing offerings below, of clothing, meat, and drink, fill up the wall. At the side of this plate are given the lower parts of some figures, which are all that remain of the sculptures of Ranefer's tomb, on the sides and back of the recess. The work of this tomb is markedly inferior to that of Rahotep.

39. PL. XV. The tomb niche of Nefert, in the same mastaba as Rahotep's, has a lintel over it, of which the small fragments left shew exactly the same arrangement of titles as on the outer lintel of Rahotep, PLS. IX, X: hence this was not copied. The outer wall below it is blank. On PL. XV is shewn the sides and back of the recess. The lists of offerings occupy the upper part of the sides; and the list of farms the lower part. Of these 12 occur in Rahotep's lists, two here are not in Rahotep's, and one in Rahotep's is not here. They all differ from the farms of Nefermat, so it is certain that these were different families. Much remains to be done in forming property lists of farms, thus tracing the descent of property, and proving genealogical connections by this means. From having this repetition of the names, we can judge whether the matter of the figures being male or female has any significance. We find that of the dozen which recur, four are always male, six are always female, and only two vary, being male in Rahotep's and female in Nefert's. This regularity shews that some intentional distinction, probably in the gender of the name of the farm, is intended. The tombs were not copied one from the other; the spelling of the names varies somewhat, and the order is altogether different throughout; hence the distinction in the figures would not have been maintained if they were purely arbitrary and ornamental in their character.

In the middle are Rahotep and Nefert seated, on the panel; and below that the children occur on either side of the niche, as in Rahotep's. The order varies, so we cannot distinguish their ages, and there is no difference shewn in the ages of the boys, so that the sculpturing of the two tombs must have been nearly contemporary. The distinctions of age shewn in tombs are (1) unclad, pointing to mouth; (2) unclad but occupied; (3) clad with kilt, hands empty; (4) clad, holding sceptre; (5) clad, holding sceptre and long staff; all these may be seen in Nefermat's and Atet's tombs.

40. The decoration of Nefermat's tomb differs entirely from that of Rahotep. The characters and figures of the whole of this tomb, and of Atet's, are incised in the stone, and filled up with coloured pastes, level with the surface; except a few figures down the edge of Nefermat's chamber entrance, which are in relief. This system of colouring was a special device of Nefermat's own, doubtless occasioned by his observing the flaking and washing of colour from painted sculpture. He particularly states (on PL. XXIV) that "He made this to his gods in his unspoilable writing." The sculpture is all hollowed out, with the edges undercut, so that the coloured pastes

with which it is filled should key in. Over wide surfaces special means were adopted. The area was divided into a number of deeper cells in the bottom, divided by cross ridges, of about a third of the height of the whole hollow. Holes were then drilled diagonally beneath these ridges, so as to meet and form bent tunnels for complete loops of the paste to hold in. The details of figures, such as the wig and face, were often cut to different depths, partly to hold the material better, partly as a guide to the artist in paste, to shew where his internal outlines were to come. Very narrow lines are simply graved out in a **V** or **U** form, and filled up. Details of different colour, such as features, or feathering on a bird, are made by cutting outlines in the base paste, and filling them up with a different colour. A base of cheaper colour was often used, and a facing of more valuable paste was incorporated with it. The invention was not a success; extremely tedious, it yet yielded to injury more readily than the painted reliefs. The coloured pastes were very easily picked out and destroyed, and the action of the ever-present salt of Egypt has reduced much of what remains to a mere loose powder, and forced it out of the hollows in the stone, as a rotten mass of dust that will hardly bear touching. Much has been ruined since Mariette uncovered these tombs, and left them to destruction at the hands of every careless Arab and wanton tourist. The colours employed, and the means of fixing them, have been most carefully examined, chemically and microscopically, by Mr. Spurrell; and I have the pleasure of embodying his results in the end of this chapter.

41. PL. XVI. The architrave of Nefermat's tomb is broken in the middle, where it is here divided on the plate; and the right hand end was altogether lost in ages past, while all that remains is deeply weathered by exposure. The titles can be traced out by the list on PL. XX. The portion of a stela, on the left hand, is in relief, and of fine work. It was found lying just in front of the chamber, almost on the ground. Scattered near it were many chips of fine work in relief; these I brought away, as illustrating the use of scraping tools for dressing surfaces. What all these chips and the stela belonged to, and what construction has been here destroyed, we cannot be certain. But as the edges of the chamber door are in relief, it seems not unlikely that the stone blocking of the doorway (of which the traces are seen by the cutting on the walls) had a relief sculpture on it of a false door and panel; and thence, after the destruction of that, came these fragments.

The other pieces on the same plate are miscellaneous. The stela or panel of Heknen was found at the north false door of mastaba No. 4. It is of rough, irregular work, of a primitive style. Now in the Ashmolean Museum, Oxford. The portion of a lintel from mastaba 7, is drawn from a photograph and hand copy. It was so completely shattered by salt that not even a corner of a sign could be moved and kept whole. The titles are much the same as those of Rahotep, and it was perhaps belonging to a son of his, who inherited those offices.

PL. XVII. The south side of the facade of Nefermat is well preserved at the base, as that part was below the evaporating level, and so kept constantly moist; hence the salt has not accumulated in it; and happily Mariette's men did not take the trouble to clear it. The huntsmen carry long bent sticks, or flaps of hippopotamus hide. Two of the sons appear as boys leading tame apes. Below that the leopard is finely drawn with the prowling action; from the position it seems as if he were a hunting animal, and not wild. At the base is a dog hunting jackals. On the jamb of the chamber front is Nefermat, with Atet behind him. Below them are two sons who recur on the back of the chamber (XX) and elsewhere, and four children who do not recur; from *sen* occurring added to two names it may be that they are brothers' children; if not, they may be grandchildren, sons of the sons above them.

PL. XVIII. Here Nefermat stands with a son before him; and Atet is below with three sons. Her robe is of leopard skin, the spots of which are partly in a pattern (each spot is strictly copied); and on the wrists and ankles are bead decorations, shewing how coloured beads were then utilized. The son Khent's title "chief of the lake of the crocodile" is very interesting, as the earliest mention of the Fayum. On the rest of the facade is, at the top, a slaughtering scene; below that, a very curious compound group, a huntsman, a large branching tree, up which a monkey is climbing, and from which a goat is hung being cut up, while a man near stirs the fire by which it is to be cooked. It is very unfortunate that this is so much injured, the surface in parts having been scaled entirely away by the salt. A much scaled group of fishermen comes below; next is only the lower edge of a very curious scene of cattle, among some strange plants, which are inexplicable in form and colouring. A group of bird-snaring, and a pair of ploughmen come below. All the lower part is in excellent state, free from salt, and never exposed until I uncovered it; I soon reburied it.

PL. XIX. This comprises the side of the chamber on the left hand when facing it; the slope down the left of the plate being the sloping front of the facade. As much has been totally effaced here, owing to the insertion of the blocks for closing the chamber, I have brought together the parts of the remaining sculpture, in order to include them in one plate. The top left-hand piece should be about two inches further out to the left, and the lower piece about three inches out on the plate; all the intervening space being blank. The outer figures are all of farm servants, and are in relief, as I have mentioned. Inside Nefermat is standing, beholding the offerings for his tomb; while his sister or daughter Nub, seated on the ground by his side, puts her arm round his leg. The details are all lost, owing to the falling out of the inlayed colouring, but this is the best female head that remains to us in this tomb. Below are two lines of farm servants with the names of the farms. Among these is Methun, which has been considered to be the ancient form of Medum.

PL. XX. This shews the back of the chamber; the lower part of which is all destroyed, except the left hand figure, which is here put at the side.* The arrangement of the list of offerings is the same as in Rahotep's, and the early tombs at Abusir, &c. The granaries in the bottom line but one should be noticed. In the niche below the panel is Nefermat; Atet, his wife, faces him, and five sons can be recognised by their names.

PL. XXI. This is the side of the chamber opposite to PL. XIX. The wall has been similarly disfigured, and the remaining portion of the front part is here brought closer in to the rest. At the top there is a trace of a cartouche of Seneferu in a farm name, as there is on PL. XIX. These mentions of Seneferu are the only cartouches found in any tomb at Medum. Here Nefermat is being borne in a chair of state by six supporters, the front figures of whom have been cut away. Below are two lines of farm servants.

42. PL. XXII. We now pass to the chamber of Atet, in the same mastaba with that of Nefermat. The lintel appears to have been complete in Mariette's time, but it was left exposed then, and before 1882 it was miserably shattered. It is useful therefore to refer to his publication for a fuller view, although not a single point of detail that can be now checked, is accurate in that copy. The scene is of Nefermat closing a clap net, of which only just the top now remains; while his three sons carry birds that have been caught to their mother Atet, who is seated at the opposite end. Below this come the top scenes of the facade, the rest of which appear on PLS. XVII, XVIII. The slaughterer on the left is holding the leg of the ox up, while the head is turned round backward on the ground. The portion of the title *ta sab t'a*, is on a fragment which I found below in excavating, and is here inserted in its place, as I have done with some other pieces found loose. These fragments I of course buried again, putting them at the extreme back of the tomb floor in a heap, with the small fragments behind the larger. The name on the drum is Atet, and not Teta as in Mariette's copy; and it is as well to say that his reading of Nefermat as Nefertma is contradicted both by the sense and by the inscriptions.

PL. XXIII. Down the side of the facade is a series of scenes, cattle at the top, then boat-building, and six children at the base. On the edge of the great monolith of the chamber side, is a figure of Nefermat, in priestly robe, and five children below.

PL. XXIV. This is the opposite side of the facade. The edge of the chamber side forms a slight pilaster, on which is Nefermat standing, and saying that "he made this to his gods in his writing unspoilable." Below him is Atet seated, with two sons behind and four below her. On the rest of the facade is a series of scenes. At the top are servants bearing wine and fruit, *deb* being figs or perhaps pomegranates from the form. Beneath are the tame birds, with the determinative of three tethers; and two tame animals below. This means therefore again the "place of domesticated animals of the tomb" as in PL. IX. The next line shews the "coming out from the marsh," the fowlers in a boat, with the stick, and loop of withy on which the birds are strung, like the object held by the seated figure *sa*. Next come two of the younger sons, in marsh dress, catching birds in a net. And at the bottom a very small boy looking after an ape—who seems to have the better of him—and a monkey in front who cannot resist pulling the bird's tail: the bird's hinder leg is suspiciously raised; as if he was just going to let fly with it right into the monkey's face.

PL. XXV. This is the left side of the chamber when facing into it. The wall is grievously scaled by salt, and not half of the sculpture remains.

* The curious projection on the shoulders of Nefermat is not part of the chair, but is some fitting of the leopard's skin priestly dress, as it is always accompanied by that, either seated or standing.

Nefermat is here standing viewing the boat building; and a fragment remaining at the bottom of the wall shews a wine-press in use.

Pl. XXVI. The back of the chamber is much destroyed, and the figure of Atet seated before a table of offerings (which is shewn by Mariette on the panel) is now wholly smashed away. Nefermat and Atet appear below that, with several sons.

Pl. XXVII. This wall has suffered much in every way. The middle has been much scaled, by salt flaking the stone, while most of the upper part has been broken off in a huge flake, and lesser pieces, by the Arabs since it has been left uncovered. Owing to this shattered state it was difficult to piece it together in the drawing, as the great flake was too large to set up in place. Hence there is some little distortion in this sheet. Nefermat stands with his sister or daughter Nub behind him; for an edge of the sign *nub* remains. He is holding in two hunting dogs by cords, while they are seizing a hare by the neck and a gazelle by the leg. This scene appears to have been designed on a larger surface, and then cut down at the outer edge; in the middle line there are the horns of some animal which is not on the stone; in the top line the hind part of the hare is not included; in the lower line the animal's head is partly off. Perhaps the design was done before the sloping edge was cut, with the intention of a different form of front. The lower part is occupied with tame animals.

43. Pl. XXVIII. The group of geese from Medum, now in the Ghizeh Museum, is justly celebrated. It was found by Mariette's workmen in clearing the tomb of Atet, and was removed by Vassali. When I came to clear out these tombs again, I found in the open passages of Atet and Nefermat various melancholy fragments of what had been fairly perfect paintings twenty years ago. The heads had been chopped out with a pick, and the morsels shewed how barbarously the nineteenth century had treated what had remained to us from the beginnings of history. So ruined were these fragments that only one of them is worth reproducing, No. 2, Pl. XXVIII, representing two fowlers, one drawing the net rope, the other carrying a bird. Some other lesser chips I placed in a recess in the brickwork of Atet's tomb, before I earthed that over. Beside what had been destroyed, I found some portions which had happily escaped the terrible attentions of the previous excavators. In the narrow court in front of Nefermat's facade the ground had not been disturbed at the bottom, since the natural decay of the building. There lay the remains of the blocking of the chamber, carved in relief with a panel, which is in plate XVI. There were also other chips of that work, which I carefully collected, to examine the mode of stone dressing, as they were quite fresh and sharp. Evidently a metal chisel or adze, and a metal scraper were used; for the scratch lines all being sunk, were made by jagged projections of metal. Whereas in Ranefer's stone-work a flint tool was used for scraping (as at Lachish), all the scratch lines being raised, owing to chipping out of the flint edge. The source of this difference is proved easily by experiment. I also found a long length of painted fresco (XXVIII, 1) which had covered part of the mud-brick facade above the stone facade. It had, in course of time, slipped off bodily from the wall, and fallen into the court. Of course it was much shattered, but yet it was fairly continuous. By great care I removed the pieces, but the mud plaster backing was so much rotted (by rains running down into this hollow), that it broke up a good deal in travelling. I therefore removed all the mud back, and transferred the film of painted gesso to slate backing, on which it is now quite safe: this occupied about a week in England. It affords us some details of colouring not otherwise known. The seated figure *sa* is in a banded black and green costume; and the *t'a* sign is curious and inexplicable, and differs from the later forms. This remaining piece opens our eyes to what was the great extent of fresco work in this earliest time. From the arrangement of it, it appears that there was a colossal figure of Nefermat, standing or seated, with his titles and name above his head. He was "Beholding his prosperity," typified by servants leading in oxen, &c., before him. Judging by the relative size of such inscriptions to the figures in Pls. XVII to XXI, this must have been by the average 84 inches high if standing, or 59 if seated; the latter is more likely, according to the length of the inscription. This, with the inscription over him, would require a fresco wall about 80 inches high. The facade below it was about 180 inches high (including a blank space below the sculpture); so that the total required for the court is 280 inches. As the mastaba was probably 412 high, this is quite possible. In the base of this court we found pieces of wooden logs, &c., belonging to the roofing, that had fallen down into the space. It is indeed fortunate that the former excavators did not persevere, and so clear out the whole place, and destroy this evidence twenty years ago.

Another fresco that I found was in a part of the

passage to Atet's chamber. All of this had been finely painted, as Mariette describes, "orné de scènes variées, de chasse et de pêche, peintes avec une grande finesse sur le stuc"; when I cleared it not one piece of all this was left, except behind some of the brick-filling of the passage which the ravagers had not thought worth removing. I there secured the pieces XXVIII, 3, 4. Nos. 2 and 3 are in the South Kensington Museum; No. 4 at Owens College Museum, Manchester. In the passage to Nefermat's chamber I only found remaining a part of Atet in a leopard-skin dress, and the legs of Nefermat. These I left on the wall.

Another example of wall fresco of inferior style, but interesting in detail, I found in the end of the passage of mastaba 22 (see PLS. VI, VII, XXVIII, 5, 6, 7). The master was named Nefer....uu and had the title *Kher heb*. His son, who appears before him in No. 6, had the title *sar*, ruler of the mansion, and companion, but his name is lost. The scene on the west wall No. 5 is the master standing (not copied, as much defaced), before whom are led two pairs of oxen, who have housings, or supports for a litter, upon them. Before the man is the title "overseer of the *Kha*," perhaps a thousand oxen. On the east wall, No. 6, is the master, with three sons, watching the farming scenes, of which two harvesters remain. The white panniers, which they carry on their hips, are to hold the ears as they cut them off. Although no sickle is represented it is seen that only the left hand grasps the straws together, shewing that some implement must be held in the right to cut them. The grain is long-bearded wheat. On the south wall (No. 7) is a fowling and fishing scene. The plants are interesting, as not of the conventional forms; and the fishers, though roughly done, are spirited, the truth of the four men dragging up the net from the water is better than stiff drawings of later times. The remains of two fishes below show what care was given to detail. The sinkers and floats to the net are the same as in Rahotep's tomb. Poor as this tomb is, the paintings are as good as most of those in the great sepulchres of the XIIth dynasty.

44. I have been favoured by Mr. Spurrell with the following results of his careful examination, chemical and microscopic, of the colours employed in the Medum tombs, to which I add my own observations on the local details at Medum.

The coat of colours on the stone sculptures of Rahotep's tomb and Nefermat's doorway has been laid on with a brush, and in some instances apparently rubbed into the stone so thoroughly as to become adherent. The painting of the coloured frescoes, from the passages of Nefermat's and Atet's tombs, is also brush work, and was apparently mixed with a medium which has decayed and left them sometimes pulverulent. In the yellow ochre—on a deer—it appears that something was employed much like albumen in its resistance to water, but the film is too thin to experiment on. These fresco colours are laid on a fine thin layer of gesso, bright and pure, about $\frac{1}{20}$th of an inch thick. The outlines are first traced in faint red, and the final colouring laid over them. The gesso is laid on a coat of lime and gypsum burnt together, and mixed with *tibn* (chopped straw), about $\frac{1}{3}$ to $\frac{1}{2}$ inch thick; and this rests on a coat of mud and *tibn* about $1\frac{1}{2}$ inches thick, which was applied to the bare brick wall, and held up by keying into the joints.

White is a pulverulent efflorescence of gypsum—calcium sulphate—very bright if selected, but creamy in general.

Black is lamp black, and no charcoal or graphite is found. A circular cake of lamp black $\frac{1}{4}$ inch high and $1\frac{1}{2}$ across, slightly concave on top, was found loose in Rahotep's well.

Yellow is yellow ochre with clay, in the best examples it is nearly pure ferric sesquioxide. Much variation in tint was obtained, both by thickness of the film and difference in the earth. Occasionally a faint wash of red hæmatite over the yellow changes the hue to orange. A yellow marl abounds at Medum; it might be used as a pigment alone, but in no case has it been so found. After the removal of the calcium carbonate from it by rain, the fine ochre which would be washed into pockets and seams would give a good colour. Steeped in sour wine the marl gives a superior pigment, identical in colour with most of the yellows. It is noticeable that this deepened colour is not lightened with calcium carbonate, but with sulphate (gypsum), when required by the artist. A greenish grey on the deer (XXVIII, 3) was made by a yellowish earth containing fine brown grains (sand) of some mineral.

Red is red hæmatite ground in water. Coarser and darker reds are from natural deposits of ochreous clays, some of which appear to contain much manganese.

Brown is frequently obtained by a thin wash of hæmatite red over impure black, as for birds' feathers. But it is usually an ochre unburnt, and sometimes laid over a coat of hæmatite.

Green is malachite, and being pure it is remarkably uniform in tint. No traces of green or blue frits have been found in all this early work.

Grey, and neutral backgrounds, often greenish, are made of pale yellowish earth with a little lamp-black, which burns out at a red heat.

Blue is a rarer pigment, and none was found loose for removal, nor on the frescoes brought over. On the walls it appears much of a blue verditer tint, apparently derived from an impure earthy blue carbonate of copper. The shell (XXIX, 17) bore, smeared on the inside, some intensely blue chessylite, very finely ground, and without the minutest trace of malachite. The animal matter of the shell, and the medium of the paint has perished.

45. The colours of Nefermat's and Atet's inlayed work are wholly different in tone, all mixed with more or less white. Their mode of application I have already stated in section 40. These pastes char a little, shewing organic matter, which disappears on burning. No extract by water or alkali could be obtained, nor any smell like albumen or gelatine when burnt. Though some pieces retain their original hardness and polish, most of them are powdery, owing to decay of the medium, and action of salt. This hardness and darkening extends a variable distance into the paste from its face. It is apparently due to rubbing in an oil or liquid turpentine, by which the surface was polished and the colour enhanced. Occasionally the saturated part is not thicker than a visiting card, and by drying has contracted and separated from the mass, which is then seen to be full of bubbles.

There are throughout most specimens many small oval or globular bodies, mainly at the surface. These globules can easily be extracted as they sink in water from the intermixed colour. They are brownish yellow, translucent, easily crushed, and soluble in alcohol: burning brightly with a resinous smell, and moderate smoke. They may be due to grains of resin mingled with the paste before application, or to a collection of the turpentinous polish into the air-bubble spaces of the paste; or—less likely—a segregation of the turpentine originally mixed with the paste. Turpentine may have been liquefied with strong wine.

The colours are,

White, burnt gypsum, more or less creamy.

Black, or rather always grey, of lamp black and burnt gypsum.

Red, in various shades lighter than hæmatite, is an ochreous clay mixed with fibrous gypsum pounded. In one case the red is mixed very intimately with yellow ochreous clay. The painted lines of red are rubbed hæmatite.

Red brown is the same as olivey yellow that is burnt, and it does not alter by further burning.

Yellow. (1) Clear, low tone, yellow; of ochreous clay mixed with powdered gypsum. (2) Olivey yellow; ochreous clay or earth. (3) The same, darker, with brownish stains. None of these contain carbonate of lime.

Green is pure malachite, lightened in some cases by pure gypsum. It is often economised by filling below with yellow, and facing that with the coat of green. This accounts for certain signs which are usually green appearing as yellow in these plates.

CHAPTER IV.

EARLY HIEROGLYPHS.

46. A branch of Egyptology which has been remarkably neglected hitherto is epigraphy. In the limited and arbitrary alphabets of Phœnicia, Greece, and other lands we know that epigraphy is one of the most carefully and scientifically treated subjects. But in Egypt epigraphy should be not merely a study of arbitrary signs, but also of the greatest interest as throwing a light on the civilization; and yet it has scarcely been thought of beyond the mere matter of classifying the signs by their nature. Some variations of forms in different ages are generally recognised, but the question of the earliest forms known has hardly been touched; yet this matter is what explains to us more of the condition of the earliest historic Egyptians than any actual objects that have been found. I propose here to state the illustrative details of the signs that occur at Medum, and also a few which I have noted in the Ghizeh Museum.

47. Following the usual order of classifying signs, we first note the squatting figure holding a long stick on which is a loop; the colour is best seen on the fresco (Pl. XXVIII), but there is a curious variation in three lines radiating from the loop (Pl. XXII); this seems to be the *sa* sign, and when we see the fowler with such a loop of withy, on which they strung their birds (Pl. XXIV) and so carried them by a stick, it seems as if the source of the sign was before us. The Libyan archer appears here (IX) as distinct and characteristic as in any later time.

One rare sign appears, a man pounding in a mortar (XV); and in the old man sign (*aau* XIII, XIV) the stick is forked below; the other human signs (*ur*, *ked* —build—*shep's*, *s* infant, and *menat* nurse determinative) are all as known in general.

Among parts of the body is the nose, which is sometimes alone (XXIV), and sometimes with the eye (XXII). The heart is well shewn (XIII), and is clearly not a vase as it has been classified. It is noticeable that the markings on it, which are constant until late times, are exactly the same as those on the *nefer*; it rather appears that the *nefer* is really the heart and tracheæ, as Mr. Spurrell has suggested to me, and since no trace of strings is ever shewn upon it, nor is the stem prolonged over the round part as in drawings of guitars, we must feel much doubt as to the usual explanation of it. The colour of the parts of the body is not constant; the mouth is mostly yellow but sometimes red, the arm red, the hand yellow, the legs both red and yellow. As red is the male colour and yellow the female these colours are suitable, but are hardly likely to refer to a difference of gender.

Among the animals the hog (XXI) is of rare occurrence, and looks here as if it were wild. The lion's head, *peh* (XIII, XIX), is clearly not a drawing from the animal, but of some object formed like a lion's head, perhaps a draughtman on the top of a staff.

The bird *ur* is unmistakably the wagtail, which is so common in Egypt; the general colouring (Front. and XIII) and the black spot on the breast leave no doubt on the subject. The eagle *a* is very well shewn in coloured examples (Front. and XIII, XIV); and also the owl (Front. XI, XII) which is very true to nature.

The oxyrhyncus occurs here (XIII), which is rare. Of reptiles there is the crocodile, all yellow (XXIII), or yellow with black feet (XVIII), which appears in the interesting title "chief of the lake of the crocodile," the earliest name of the Fayum. The frog also occurs (XVII) yellow. A part of an animal which has been very uncertainly attributed is here well shewn; *Kha* is certainly not a club, nor a part of the human body: the structure shews the mouths of glands (XII, XIII) and can only be referred to the mammæ of some animal. The sign *shed*, which has been classed as a whip, and described as a skin bottle, is here seen (Front. and XI) to be the skin of an animal, yellow, or mottled black or white, flayed off, and rolled up raw, with the fur outside; the red flaps of the inside of the legs and neck skin shew out at the ends, and the roll is tied around the middle, and each end, with a cord. The senses of *shed* (a skin bottle, to pull off, flay, lift up, save, or select) exactly agree with this.

Among plants there are some varieties of tree forms which might be discriminated (XII, XIII, XV, XVII, XVIII, XXIII); and a variety of the *hen* plant (XV), which is clearly a low shrub, and suggests a connection with the Arabic henna. The pod *net'em* (XI, XIII) which is usually called the acacia is hardly of that form; and, from its meaning "sweet," it is more likely to be the sweet pod of the Kharub or locust tree. Coming next to inanimate objects we notice the colouring of the hill sign *du* (XXVIII), which is light red sprinkled with spots of black, white, red, and green, representing the many-coloured pebbles which catch the eye in walking over the desert. In one case there is a strip of green below it for the edge of the green land at the desert foot (XIV).

A sign which has been most absurdly classed as a framework, is the road, *ua* or *her* (IX); this is finely coloured on a slab in the Ghizeh Museum, and explains itself as a red road or embankment, with a blue canal on either side, and green trees growing along the canals in alternation.

It is noticeable that water is always blue, green, or black; the wavy line *n* is black, the tank *sh* and water in a mass are dark blue or green with black ripples. To any one accustomed to the yellow-brown, opaque waters of the Nile such colouring would be unnatural. Does this colouring not seem then to have been fixed by dwellers on the clear, dark waters of the Red Sea?

48. Buildings are the next division; and from the hieroglyphs we learn far more of architecture in the dark period of the first three dynasties, than we can learn by actual buildings until the XVIIIth. Buttressed walls were usual for forts, as the sign is of the same form as the later determinative (XIV, XV). The cornices of the law courts were already crowned with a row of uraei, as shewn in the sign *ta* (XX, XXI). And in the types of columns we see the same highly advanced forms. The sign *an*, which is often called an obelisk, is seen here to be a fluted eight-sided column (Front., X, XIII), with a tenon on the top to fit the lintel, and painted black below, then white with an ornamental edge, and red above. This form is not yet known in the round until the XIIth dynasty. Next the sign *aa*, usually called a spear, is remarkably detailed here (XIII) and is seen to be absolutely identical with the central support of the

roof in *heb* (X), which sign has also octagonal fluted columns at the sides. The *aa* it will be seen has the tenon on the top like the *an*; from its slenderness and general form it was certainly of wood, and it appears to have been the great central pole of a tent or canopy, carved into the form of a lotus plant. This then was the origin of the lotus columns and capitals, with the curious inverted flower or bell, which are so often found in the XVIIIth dynasty. Other forms of columns were also known in the IVth dynasty; I have published a remarkable column with wide capital, apparently derived from the form of a bowl on a stand (Season in Egypt, Pl. XXV), carved in the tomb of Khafkhufu at Gizeh. And another, not dissimilar, is seen on a wall-painting at Kahun in the XIIth dynasty, but with a banded top (Illahun, Pl. XVI). Now on the *dad* (or tat) sign (Pl. XIII) we see a tenon on the top, an evidence of a column; and abstracting for a time the repeated forms of the top, we see that the main body is much like the column drawn at Kahun. What then is the meaning of the multiple top? In representing objects which were not all in one plane the Egyptians used certain conventions, and one of these was that *parts that were behind others were placed above them*; this is seen in the drawings of groups of offerings, the birds, vegetables, &c., being drawn one above the other, to represent that they lay one beyond the other on the table; it is seen in the wall-painting at Kahun (Illahun, Pl. XVI) where the interior with the master and servant is drawn above the front view of the house; and it is the elementary convention of all wall scenes (as Prof. Maspero has pointed out), that the Nile, the cultivation, the near desert, and the far desert, succeed one another up from the base to the top of the wall, in registers one over the other. Regarding this regular convention we can hardly neglect to see that the *dad* is a row of columns one behind the other with the capitals shewn one over the other; the line of columns to support a roof being necessarily particularly stable and firm, and according with the meaning of the sign. From all these we can form some idea of the lost architecture of the first three dynasties; there were octagonal fluted columns of stone painted in bands, columns with capitals of the bowl and stand type, similar ones with capitals of the *dad* type, and slender shafts of wood of the lotus type. Such forms cannot have been introduced as familiar signs in syllabic writing until they were well established as regular architectural members; and we are left in amazement at the fully developed and completed types of decorative architecture which these reveal to us at so remote and unknown an age.

Granaries are shewn in Nefermat's tomb (XX, in list of offerings). The form of the door-bolt *s* is remarkably contracted in the middle, and has a double line along the nick (XIII); such lines usually shew a string, as on the tied-up necks of bags (XIII, XV), and here it seems likely that the middle of the bolt had a string round it, which could be sealed on to the door to prevent it being moved.

49. We next turn to weapons. The axe, *mab*, here (Front., XIII, XIV) bound into the handle, seems from its outline to be a stone hatchet, as both form and colour are much like the blue grey hornstone hatchets which I have found at Kahun of the XIIth dynasty. The dagger in sheath *tep* is of the usual type. The bows appear in a bow case (IX); but it is curious that the *mesha*, archer (IX), is clearly a Lybian in type (? connected with the name Mashuash), and he bears a bow of different form from the Egyptian, in one case (IX) with the string broken and hanging partly from each end. The arrows both of the archer and elsewhere (IX, XIII, XX) are all flat ended, probably tipped with small flints to cut chisel fashion. The *aha* sign of the arms holding a shield and mace, shews that the shield had straight sides, but was either curved (XV) or straight (XII) at the top. The mace is evidently the *het'* sign (which has been classed as a vegetable), and it is well shewn in separate examples (XII, XIII). We recognise the yellow staff, the red binding, and the white stone head, with the yellow staff-end projecting. Such a mace head of very hard white limestone I found at Kahun (XIIth dynasty), and a piece of one of bright white stone (magnesite?) with the names of Khafra, I picked up at Gizeh. The particular whiteness of the heads of those I found, and in the drawings, shews why this was taken to express brightness or whiteness. The harpoon, *ua*, is very well shewn (Front., XIII, XIV); the body being red, probably of wood, the point blue for copper (like the copper cauldrons being blue, see XIII), and the loop is of cord, as is expressly shewn on the tomb of Rameriankh in the Ghizeh Museum.

Among the agricultural implements the sickle, *ma*, is the most interesting. It is always green in the body, with a projecting line of teeth, drawn black on white (Front., XI, XIII). This is explained by the sickles which I have found of the XIIth dynasty; they are carved in wood, with notched flints inserted for teeth; such then was the nature of the sickles of the IIIrd dynasty, though why they should be painted green it is difficult to understand. The obvious origin of this sickle is from an ox's jaw with flints substituted for the animal teeth. Such was a wide-spread implement in the later stone age, as we see from the innumerable flints in Egypt and elsewhere; these are notched on the edge, and shew by their polish that they have been set in a groove socket, and worn on a hard material like siliceous straw. A whole class of matters has been cleared up by these flint sickles which we see drawn in the sculptures. In one tomb-well here over a hundred flint flakes were found. The hoe, *mer*, is of the usual type: but one instance (XV) may be a natural hoe, such as I have found in the XIIth dynasty carved out of a natural branch like perhaps the hoe on XXI. The plough (XII, XVIII) has always two handles, similar to our modern ploughs, and unlike the Roman plough which had a sort of rudder head for guiding it. An article fashioned from a natural branch, with a pole bound on to the fork of it (XII with the pole, and in XIII without the pole), is seen several times; but it is not commonly known, and probably fell out of use in early ages.

Of tools there are several. The chisel *menkh* which became very much corrupted in late times, is well drawn here (Front., and XI) and is unmistakable, as there is both the name and the use of it represented. The handle is of turned wood, with a copper blade inserted. Another form of chisel is the *mer*, often occurring in the title *smer;* it varies in form, sometimes a wide-headed handle with a spike-shaped blade, in others a barrel-shaped handle (XVIII, XX), but most noticeable is the barrel handle with a projection on one side, and the blade excentric (XXIV) and shewing in one case by the side of the handle; this seems to be of the same family as the adze (so familiar in the *sotp* sign) where the blade is not inserted but attached to the handle; here apparently it is secured by a band of metal around it, as the projection is sometimes green; the handle is regularly yellow, being wood, and the blade black. The *nenu* or adze occurs on a grand scale where a carpenter is using it (Front., XI, XXV), and also in the *sotp* sign (XI); the blade is attached to the wood by a long binding. I have much such a blade nearly a foot long, and four inches wide; and I have found the blades in the IVth, XIIth, and XVIIIth dynasties, varying in form. The so-called polisher *t* is always black; such polishing stones are rarely, if ever, found; but black stones of exactly this shape are very common in early times, with a highly worn hole in the flat side; these were doubtless the stone caps for bow drills, and for fire sticks, and we can hardly err in calling *t* the drill head. The *maa* sign (XVI to XXI) which is commonly recognised as a cubit, is long, thin, and square ended, plainly the side view of the cubit; this being confused with the *ta* sign of land, an end view was later adopted, and the bevel, which is characteristic of the section of a cubit, was thus added to the sign to distinguish it. The somewhat variable sign *sem* (XIV), often classed as a knife, is undoubtedly a sharpening stone for whetting knives; it is represented as so used in early tombs, and it is a stone, and not metal (or a steel), as it is secured by a knob at the end and string binding, instead of passing the loop through a hole. The stick for winding string upon (Ranefer XIV) is perhaps what is otherwise known as *ud.* The sledge for dragging stones, *tem*, is of the usual form (XX); and I have found pieces of such sledges, of hard wood, joined by mortise and tenon, among the stone chip filling-in of the pyramid of Usertesen II at Illahun. Two forms of the sign *net* occur, one the knitting-needle (XIII, XV) such as I have found of wood and metal in the XIIth dynasty; the other what is usually called the shuttle, but which is a complex affair, that seems to have handles at the end, and to be bound round with crossing bands (XV); this is the usual emblem of the goddess Neit.

50. Three forms of sceptre are shewn; the *uas* or *t'am* (XIII) has no animal head, as is usual later on, but is merely the natural stick branching from the main stem and subdividing at the tip; the *hek* does not seem to be a crook as usually supposed, but a bent rod, bound around (X, XXVIII, 6); the *kherp* is as usual. The important divine sign, *neter*, is hardly yet explained; that it is an axe is impossible; the later idea of its being a roll of bandages on a stick is not satisfactory, as such an arrangement would be very awkward to use in swathing a mummy. Here there are several varieties. The top is plain with a simple rod (XXIV), or with a rod ending in a ball (stela XVI); the top is divided into two strips in five instances (XV), and into three strips with a cross line in one case (XVI); the colour is yellow, with the lower end of the rod black (XXIV). The ball at the end, the slope at the top, the division into strips, the colour, and the cross bands on the handle, all render it a difficult problem, although it is classed with textiles in the early lists of offerings.

Of personal ornaments three are now explained. The well-known sign of "chancellor" (*sahu*) is now seen to be identical in its two forms, the upright loop and the curved loop (Front., XIII, XIV, XVI, XVII, XVIII, XX); and in the finely carved and coloured example (Front., XIII) it is clearly a string of beads alternately long and round, green and red, with an object attached; this object appears to be a cylinder of dark blue-green, with yellow ends, and a red knob below; and the nature of it suggests a signet cylinder of green jasper, with gold ends, and a central pin with a red jasper knob, to hold it in. It means then essentially the seal, and the title must be the royal seal-bearer, and hence treasurer. The sign *nub* was long explained as a cloth for washing gold; but it is unmistakably a grand collar (XIII) with rows of green, red, and black beads. As gold was probably first used for ornament around the neck, the collar naturally came to be the sign for gold. Another familiar object is the shoulder fastener for garments, which is here identical with the sign *seta* (XII, XIII, XV); the manner in which it was used suggests that it was a spiral coil of sheet metal, into which could be slipped side-ways the thin part of a garment.

The draught-board, *men*, is well illustrated in these sculptures (XI, XIII, XIX). It is regularly divided into 3 squares one way and 10 squares the other; and this carries back the use of this 3 × 10 board to the IIIrd dynasty. As I have found these boards also in the XIIth, XVIIIth and XXVIth dynasties, the game was known for four thousand years. The board is shewn in plan, and the row of pieces in elevation on the upper edge; these pieces are of two sizes, the larger white, and the smaller, some red, some black; or the larger green, and the smaller as before; there were thus three kinds of pieces used, and from the numerals on boards I have found we see that they counted from left to right along the top row of the board. (Kahun, p. 30.)

51. Among the rope and band signs the *t*, *h*, and *shes*, all occur in usual forms. But a point which has not been noticed is that the numerals are all pieces of rope. The unit stroke is not a line, but a piece of rope, with the lower end frayed out to shew it (numbers on stela, XVI). The ten sign is exactly the shape of a rope tether, such as is used to express a tame animal (IX, XXIV). The hundred is certainly a coil of rope. And though the origin of the thousand sign is not clear, and it seems more like a plant, yet it was expressed by *kha*, "to measure," and a "cord for measuring." If then all the system of numeration is derived from rope or cord, we are led to conclude that the primitive Egyptian notation was by a knotted cord. Another remarkable point of notation here (as is also seen in other early tombs) is the sign for a continued series. We write for instance 1, 2, 3, ... 100 to denote all numbers up to 100, or 1, 3, 5, 7 .... 45 for all odd numbers up to 45. So the Egyptian wrote 1, 2, 3, 4, 5, 6, and then drawing a bar divided into a multitude of small parts, he placed 100 below it, to denote all the other numbers up to 100 (stela, PL. XVI). The sign *sa* (back) is here made clearly not like a backbone (XIII), with which it was sometimes identified. The long mid line of it is continuous, and the other loops are attached to that (XIII). It is possible that this is the wide band that goes behind the climber in ascending palm trees; it is most emphatically that which backs or protects him, and as such would be a suitable sign. The package, *p*, is shewn with wavy lines of cord around it in the fresco (XXVIII). The cartouche line, which has not been explained, is drawn on a slab of the VIth dynasty at Gizeh Museum as a rope binding, lashed together at the bottom, and with two bows which form the spread base of it. We can see that rope lashings were used on a very large scale, as the whole of a stone trap-door was girded with no less than 80 turns of rope, in Ranefer's tomb; so this rope lashing of the cartouche, to bind together the group of signs of a royal name, is not an unlikely idea for early times. The sign for a clap net (X, XVIII) is what has been classed as a framework: it represents the two sides of a net. The symbol of life, *ankh*, is shewn with a divided upright (XIV), and in a fine example in Gizeh Museum the side parts are likewise split. It appears (as Prof. Sayce has suggested) to be the fisherman's girdle with the loop passing round the waist, and the loose flaps hanging from it; this is the marsh-dress such as the Nile figures wear, and as we see in the figures of fishers, &c. (X, XI, XVIII). A sign hitherto unexplained is the familiar *hotep*. It is derived by the same system as the sign of the *men* board and pieces; the mat of green rushes lashed together with yellow cross strings is shewn in plan, and above that in elevation is the offering-dish piled up with flour or other food which was placed upon it before the tomb or shrine. The green mat and yellow strings are finely shewn in several cases (XIII, XIV). The reel for winding rope on is shewn in many of the figures of bird catching, at the free end of the rope (XVIII, XXII). Several other signs here remain as yet unexplained, though the detailed colouring of *kher* (XIII) and *t'a* (XXVIII) ought to help us to guess them.

We now see how much light we have gained from

the study of only two tombs; light both on the sources of hieroglyphs, and on the civilisation which filled the unknown age of the first three dynasties. Far more work is needed on the early and fine sculptures to secure their details, and above all to record the colouring before it drops off in the air, or is washed away by some barbarian taking wet squeezes from the walls. Nearly all the colouring in the lower part of Rahotep's tomb was thus destroyed, and Mariette used the squeezes of it.

CHAPTER V.

THE SMALL ANTIQUITIES.

52. The positions of the various objects found have been described in the previous chapters, but here we shall notice the details of the objects in the order in which they stand on the plates.

Pl. XXIX, 1 to 5. Hawks found in the temple of Seneferu. It is not likely that such peculiar offerings would continue to be made on purpose long after the death of the king; we have seen that the offering of small vases and saucers ceased before the mastaba 18 was constructed; and probably as each king died the worship would be transferred to the last deceased. Moreover all these hawks are different, and must have been specially made for offering here, and yet all by different hands; if offered till later times there would probably have been one factory for them, and they would have been all alike. The character of the glazing of No. 3—a clear light purplish blue, with dark purple stripes—is also early, and cannot be of the XVIIIth dynasty, nor hardly of the XIIth. I think probably therefore that these are contemporary with the decease of Seneferu, and the oldest small figures known. The base of a statuette, 6, will be noted by Mr. Griffith in the inscriptions; it is of black serpentine. From both the offerer and the town being named after Seneferu there is a probability of its early date, and it might well be of the IVth dynasty. The lower part of a basalt stand, 7, is evidently a copy in stone of a pottery form, such as XXX, 21. The hole in it is one of three around it, and copied from the hole cut with a knife in the pottery. Both of these seem to have originated in a wooden form, as the hole seems to be the space left between joining pieces of wood; and is not likely to arise as a mere decoration in pottery. It is the regulation type of table stand as seen in the sculptures (Pl. XIII). No. 8 is a potsherd of the XVIIIth dynasty with an hieratic inscription, which was written when it had been broken to nearly the present size. Mr. Griffith will deal with this in the inscriptions. There were also in the temple many blue beads of the XVIIIth dynasty, two bronze lance heads, and dried fruits, from the burial there.

No. 9 is a polished piece of ivory of unknown use; it seems like a toilet object, but the teeth are too small for a comb; possibly it was a skin-scraper.

No. 10 is a horn handle of a mirror, probably of the IVth dynasty.

No. 11 is the adze blade which is certainly of the old Kingdom, and perhaps of the IVth dynasty. The type varies from those of the XIIth and XVIIIth dynasties. The bevel edge is already fully developed; and the thickness of the head suggests that it might be struck by a mallet.

No. 12 is a fragment of a rude saw; the notches do not join, and may have been made with a flint edge. It was broken off anciently, and wrapped up in a piece of linen tied together, to preserve it. I found it among the broken stone and chips, which were thrown in to make the ground level at the north of mastaba 17.

No. 13 is a rude plummet of soft white limestone, hung by a thread passing round it; this was found among the stone chips which form the mass of mastaba 17, which is probably contemporary with the pyramid. Many pieces of linen were also found among these chips; some of it coarse and saturated with ruddle, which may have been used to rub ruddle on stones for colouring, or for masons' marks.

No. 14 is a small bronze chisel of the type of the XIXth dynasty; found low down in the pyramid rubbish it was probably lost by the workmen of Ramessu II when stripping the pyramid.

The find of objects in a well of mastaba 8 has been described. The four alabaster bowls are all alike (15), though but one is perfect. The pottery (16) has a smooth dark red face. The shell (17) contains powdered blue carbonate of copper, as a paint; and two similar shells empty were found with it. The needles (18, 19) shew the thin and thick types. The flints were all kept separate in lots as found, until they were examined; they proved however to have been mixed together after manufacture, and re-divided. Mr. Spurrell examined them and succeeded in restoring the arrangement of seventeen in one block (20, 21), which shews the exact order in which they were struck off with unfailing regularity. The different types of flakes are shewn in 22 to 26. For the first time we have here dated flints as far back as the beginning of historic Egyptian archæology. The three other flints, 27 to 29, were found on the surface, among the desert stones; but as there were a hundred more chances of their being dropped when the place was crowded with workmen in Seneferu's time than since it has stood desert, there is a presumption in favour of their being of the IVth dynasty. The portion 27 is a knife handle of the type of those found at Kahun of the XIIth dynasty.

53. The pottery (PLS. XXX, XXXI) is quite different from that of any later period that I have yet examined. The most distinctive point is the highly polished red face to the bowls, the thinness and hardness of them, and the sharp outlines (XXXI, 2 to 6). This ware I have noticed before (Archæological Journal, 1883, p. 271); it is very fine, and all but equal to the best Roman, far better than what is called "mock-Samian." These bowls are the commonest type of all, and are made both of this fine quality and also coarser; in forms with beaded edge, or turned in or with a lip, (XXX 1–6, 9, 10, 12, 13, 36; XXXI, 2–6). A hard drab ware was also made (XXX, 11), and in some pieces it has been heated until the surface is half fused. It is certainly of the earliest here, as a piece was found in the waste heaps of the pyramid masons. The small cups on stems XXX, 14, 16, are curious, and unlike later forms; the bowls accompanied them, 15 with 14, and 17 with 16. In 15 is a quantity of hæmatite paint. The other pottery with these was of early style. There is some doubt about No. 19; it was found isolated, and is much like some of the XXIInd dynasty. The tray, 20, of very rough red pottery was evidently made to go on a pottery stand such as No. 21. The small vases and saucers 22 to 27 were all found in the filling of mastaba 18, from the offerings at the pyramid. Such are also found in the places of offering at the tombs here, and at the pyramids of Gizeh and Dahshur.

The occurrence of marks on pottery, so far back as the beginning of the IVth dynasty, must be taken account of, in considering the rise and origin of the marks so often found in the XIIth and XVIIIth dynasties. The figures here, Nos. 28 to 34, are all drawn the same way up as on the pottery. 28 and 30 do not occur in the signs I have collected before; 29 may well be a part of the fine pointed star (Kahun, XXVII, 182); 31 is the hieroglyph *as;* and the cross in 32, 33, 34, XXXI, 9, 27, is a naturally frequent sign.

The deep pan 35 of rough brown pottery was found with the fine hard browny white bowl 36, and the rough light brown XXXI, 8; along with the ordinary kinds of red bowls, &c, in mastaba 22.

54. In PL. XXXI the bowl 4 is the only perfect example of the fine polished red-faced ware, though many pieces of this were found, varying somewhat in outline (2, 3, 5, 6, 7). Such pottery I have found at Gizeh of the IVth dynasty; though from some of it being on the surface there, I was inclined to place it to the Roman age as well as the IVth dynasty. No. 9 is one of three large pots found in the E.N.E. mastabas, and bearing a cross on the shoulder and on the bottom; these are roughish red pottery. No. 10 is bright red, not polished. 11 is of rough, thick, soft brown ware. 12 is a curious form of stem, not found in other cases here, and much like late pottery; but its age is certain, as it was found in the stone-chip filling of mastaba 17. No. 13 is of rough, hard, blackish red pot from the filling of mastaba 18, and therefore early. The rude hand-made pottery 15, 17, 19 is very characteristic; it is constantly found in the tombs at Medum, and also in the rubbish heaps of Khufu at Gizeh. The form 15 is that which is shewn in early statuettes of a potter, squatting down and forming a pot with one hand inside and one outside. 17 is a very peculiar shape, the upper part being smooth, and the bottom always rough and irregular. From being always found by tombs it seems as if it were for setting in the sand to pour offerings in. No. 20 is of a hard pale red-brown ware, which is peculiar; it is scraped all over the outside in various directions, and therefore seems as if it was hand made, although very regular. 21 is one of the large pans with a pipe spout, of which pieces occur in many groups here; this is fixed to the date of Rahotep, as it held the mortar used for closing his tomb, and was found in the bottom of his pit. Other forms of spout are shewn in Nos. 22, 23. 24 is a thin bright red pottery; and 25 is rough brown, with a curious ledge round the inside. Many pieces of rough limestone were found in the builders' rubbish about the pyramid, bearing large drilled holes (XXXI, 26). The holes are on both sides in most cases, without any order, often intersecting at the edges. It is certain this is a waste product; and as it was produced by some body rotating under heavy pressure we are led to attribute it to some arrangement for moving the stones. Any fixed crane or lifting machine would pivot on a large stone, or in the rock. But it seems possible that blocks might be moved by lashing them to the short end of

a lever bar, which rested on a pivot near the block; by a gang of men pressing on the long end, the block would be lifted, and could then be transferred by the men walking and rotating the lever on its pivot. Such an arrangement would need a movable bearing to be shifted onward at each lift, and these blocks might well be for such bearings.

The two vases 27, 28 were found in the rock-cut tunnel leading to the building of unknown purpose south of the pyramid. They are intermediate in character between the pottery of the IVth and the XIIth dynasties, and may well be of about the VIth dynasty. The rough implement of black hornstone is one of two found in the rubbish of the destroyers on the east of the pyramid, at some distance from the base. It is therefore certain that these belong to the rude plunderers of stone in the XIXth or XXth dynasties. They are like some implements which I found at Gizeh; those bore signs of having been worked up out of more ancient wrought stone, and in that case also therefore they were not of a primitive age.

55. Dr. Gladstone, F.R.S., has very kindly favoured me with the results of his analyses of the metals which I collected at Medum. His report is as follows:—

"1. The broken piece of an adze. The (freshly) broken face was very uniformly granulated; while the outer surfaces were dark red, as from suboxide of copper. The specimen consisted almost entirely of copper; only 0·38 p. cent. of arsenic was found, with traces of antimony and iron. There is some sulphur, no doubt from imperfect reduction of the ore; but no phosphorus was detected, nor any tin.

"2. The borings from an adze from the well of Rahotep. (Pl. XXIX, 11.) These again were almost wholly copper: 0·54 p. cent. of arsenic was determined, with traces of antimony, iron, sulphur, and probably phosphorus; but again there was no tin.

"3. Piece of cylindrical rod found in mastaba 17. This consists of an internal core, and a dark outer ring. When examined under the microscope the core is found to consist of miscellaneous granules very various in colour; the outer portion is also heterogeneous, containing a red suboxide spotted with green and patches of blue. This was found to contain the large amount of 8·4 p. cent. of tin, with mere traces of antimony, arsenic and iron; no phosphorus was detected. This must, therefore, be looked upon as the earliest specimen of bronze. It is so very interesting that I am making a more complete analysis of the core, which I will send when ready.

"4. The dark filings from a pick found at Gizeh. These were too small in amount to be examined with accuracy. They consisted however of copper with a little arsenic, and a trace of what may have been either tin or antimony."

I should add that the specimen 1 was presumably of the IVth dynasty, or early, from the form, and being found at Medum. No. 2 is certainly of the old kingdom, and probably of early IVth dynasty. No. 3 is the critical matter. It is a bit of rod hammered square with truncated edges, 0·37 across and about 1½ inch long. The ends merely rough; slightly tapering, and hollowed on the end, evidently the result of hammering out. The piece was found low down in the deep foundation filling outside the N.W. corner of mastaba 17 (see sects. 21–23); and, if this position is beyond doubt, it must be of the age of Seneferu, as the chips of the filling are the masons' waste from the pyramid. The only doubt can be on whether it fell in from above during the work, as I did not find it myself. The sides of the excavation were of brick wall, from which it could not come, only the filling at the ends could be in question. The concretions on it are of clean large grains of sand and chips of limestone, quite free from fine wind-blown surface dust, agreeing with its deposit in the bottom of the foundation space. The corrosion on it is very slight, indeed I have seldom seen bronze less attacked, and certainly not where it was in contact with earth: this strongly shews that it cannot have been dropped and lain on the surface exposed to damp and air in later times. And moreover no work was done at this part after the building; no workmen appear to have been about this mastaba: and yet this is plainly a workman's piece, probably for a dowel; and it was not a tool used by people in general. There is then no reason to doubt the evidence of it as being of the IVth dynasty. The presence of bronze in a stray piece, and not in tools, seems to point to some civilisation external to Egypt from which it had come by trade. No 4 is from the tip of a pick, which I found concreted by stalagmite in a tomb at Gizeh never exposed since the pyramid period.

CHAPTER VI.

THE INSCRIPTIONS.

By F. LL. GRIFFITH.

56. PL. VIII. The short inscriptions against the architect's lines read *meh* 5 (and 8) *kher nefru* (or *kher n nefru* and must mean "5 (and 8) cubits (respectively) beneath the ground-level," or possibly "beneath the intersection (of the two lines)." The former rendering, which suggested itself to Mr. Petrie, seems preferable and leads to a good translation for a passage in the Papyrus Abbott (spoliation of the tombs at Thebes) p. iii. l. 12. "It was found that the thieves had violated it (the tomb of king Sebekemsaf) tunneling along the *ground-level? nefru* of its pyramid from the exterior hall of the tomb of Neb-Amen."

57. PLS. IX–XXVIII. The inscriptions of the mastabas.

In preparing this account I have referred to the plates of MARIETTE, *Mon. Div.* PL. 16–20, to the same author's *Mastabas*, pp. 468–487, VILLIERS STUART, *Nile Gleanings*, the notices in Baedeker's Handbook, and other sources of information, in order to ascertain what signs or groups could be recovered beyond those found still in place by Mr. Petrie. It is a pleasure to find that there is not a single sign in the new copy that one can regard with suspicion.

PLS. IX–X. The titles of Rahotep, as given very fully on the architrave, may be compared with those upon the celebrated group of the husband and wife in the khedivial Museum (*Mon. Div.* PL. 20, *Mast.* p. 487). Rahotep, who was a "king's son of his body" (his royal father's name is not stated), must have lived in the reign of Seneferu, or at the latest in that of Chufu. Three of his titles are of known import—"high-priest, *ur ma,* of the Sun at Heliopolis," "member of the Southern tens" (the tens being apparently the name of a council consisting of four tens, making forty members), and "captain of the host." As high priest at Heliopolis Rahotep was certainly one of the leading men in the Egyptian hierarchy, but "captain of the host" is a title that might apply to several military grades, general or local, although I suspect that Rahotep was commander-in-chief: "member of the Southern tens" does not imply a very exalted rank. Of the other titles, fourteen in number, which Rahotep bore, several are partially intelligible: from these, however, nothing of value can at present be deduced, excepting that some appear to denote authority in particular districts.

Turning now to the scenes, we see the king's son Rahotep accompanied by the lady Nefert, a "royal acquaintance." Upon the stela of the outer court (PL. XII) is an inscription which probably is to be read "the royal acquaintance, the king's son of his body, who has attained the reward of merit, Bu-nefer." The name of this individual does not appear in the stone chambers of the tomb, and his connection with it is not explained. A rare peculiarity is that he should be called a "royal acquaintance" as well as "king's son."

Rahotep's children are all designated "royal acquaintances." The sons are Atu, Deda, and Nefer-kau, the daughters Satet, Nedem-ab and Merert (PLS. XIII–XV). It has been reasonably supposed that the term "royal acquaintance" was appropriated to the grandchildren of kings: but there are a few cases in which a "royal acquaintance" or a "true royal acquaintance" is certainly not a royal grandson by either parent, so it is perhaps best to consider the phrase as denoting personal friendship with the king as opposed to mere formal intercourse.

Rahotep and Nefert are "watching the chase" in the upper row of PL. IX. This scene, like all the others, is much abridged: we must imagine, what we can see in later tombs, that a portion of the desert has been fenced in, probably forming a decoy or battue-ground rather than a park. In the lower row "the stock-farms of the house of eternity" are presented to their owners' view. The "house of eternity" of any individual appears to mean the estate settled *permanently* for the construction and service of the tomb.

In PL. X they "watch the netting of waterfowl," in which diversion their sons "Atu" and "Deda" are actively engaged.

PL. XI. "Rahotep watches . . . . . . of the house of eternity" (compare PL. XXV for the same difficult expression). The men are *spt* "lashing" the planks? of the boat together (*spt* is commonly used of binding together bundles of reeds to form rafts and boats), and *mnkh* "using the chisel," perhaps only to tighten the cords by forcing them on to a wider portion of the vessel.

On the right side is the name "bullock?" over a hornless beast, and on the left, behind the oryx, "bringing offerings," while over the animal is *rn*, meaning perhaps "stall-fed." Next *sotept* "cutting off the choice portions" from an ox, and in the last compartment the mysterious expression *per-kheru* for "funereal meals;" the first servant carries "wine," the legend before the second is "bringing sweet things."

PL. XII. In the second row two men are "carrying an *aha* ('fighting')-fish." The accurate representation enables me to identify it as the *keshr* of the Arabs (*Lates niloticus*). This great species of perch attains a length of 5 feet according to Dr. Gunther in his work on the fishes of the Nile (printed in Petherick's Travels), but its extreme length is given as no less than 10 feet in the probably inaccurate account of the Description de l'Egypte, where it is figured (*Hist. Nat.* i. PL. IX). Anyhow the artist at Medum is not guilty of serious exaggeration in allowing its tail to drag on the ground while its lip is raised level with the bearers' shoulders. The fish is named in the great medical Papyrus Ebers, and an argument for a different reading of the sign *aha* has been founded on an erroneous identification of the species, so this marvellous piece of early painting is of importance in more ways than one.

In the next compartment is "ploughing," and below are the domains, some of which we have already passed by in the preceding plate.

In the very earliest tombs the estates of the deceased are named and represented as slaves, male or female according to the gender of the name. Later, in the Vth and VIth dynasties they were all alike symbolised by female slaves, and after the end of the Old Empire they are no longer individually recorded. These names must have had very little stability and probably they seldom survived more than one or two generations, so that the record soon became meaningless. Sometimes the names of the nomes in which the estates lay are mentioned, shewing that they were spread widely over Upper Egypt or the Delta, but at Medum there is no indication of their position. Those of Rahotep and Nefert (PLS. XI, XII, XV and one in XIII) are severally designated as "the temple," "the place of pots," "the red," the "herb-producer," "going-growing (*crescit eundo*)," "entrance-barred," etc., etc.

PL. XIII. In the niche is a prayer to Anubis that the deceased "may come to the West as possessing perfection," the West being the land of the sunset and of departed souls.

Over the table of offerings are the names of "incense, green eye-paint, wine, figs," and other offerings are below. At the side are enumerated various sorts of linen, viz. *neter*, *sunu* and *aa*. In PLS. XVI and XX we see also *dema*, and in XX again *nefer-res*. Of each variety there are different qualities, marked e.g. 100, 9, 5, 3, 2, 1 (the numbers referring perhaps to the strands in the thread) and 1000 pieces of each quality are set down.

At the sides there are wonderfully detailed lists of the furniture, accoutrements, and unguents belonging to the tomb. On the right are jars, perhaps of sacred oils, and vessels and other objects in *uasmu* (gold or electrum) and silver, the former metal preponderating; amongst them is a ewer and basin of *uasmu*. On the left are vessels, also a sedan-chair *utes*, a footstool with sandals? upon it *ma*, and various seats and stools, a table, a box *hen*, writing-case *kher-a* and draught-board *sent*. These named figures will be valuable for reference in the future, but as yet there is not much possibility of illustrating them from other sources. It would appear that most of the names became obsolete soon after the IVth dynasty. The lower half on each side is occupied by things pertaining to the "treasure of the house of eternity." They include a second series of the sacred oils?, and on the right are vessels principally of stône—"limestone?", "blue stone," "granite" and "alabaster."

PL. XIV. The animals are the oryx, stall-fed? *ren*, the addax *nudu*, and the ibex *naa*. The last is led by a figure representing one of the estates, but the name cannot be read. The six figures below are the treasurer? Demd, the butcher? Sen-ankh, Sesa, Dauf, Anta and Sabu.

On the fragment from "Ra-nefer" we see some names or portions of names—Nebef, Rud, Kheft.

PL. XV.; with the offerings of Nefert compare PLS. XI. and XIII. We may note especially that on the right side, top row, below the figure of a man pounding with pestle and mortar there is a clear representation of a pair of corn-mullers with the name *akh*: the same utensils figure in PL. XIII, top line on the left.

PL. XVI. Stela of Heknen, a "royal acquaintance." The confused inscription seems to be "his estate, the royal offerings which it brings daily: (the estates named) Sunu-ta and . . . ta, (the offerings) incense, sycamore-figs," etc. The fragment on the left runs "the ka-servant Persen," who was doubtless represented with an offering.

The lintel of mastaba No. 7 shews a number of titles which, so far as they are preserved, agree with those of Rahotep: the deceased was "captain of the host" and "superintendent of labourers?" and of "transports?" like Rahotep, and a fragment of a new title remains that probably refers to the neighbouring lake of the Fayum under the designation "lake of the crocodile."

On the other hand the titles of Nefermaat, whose inscriptions begin on the same plate, have no single point of contact with those of Rahotep. He must have been a greater man than the latter; he was "eldest royal son, chief justice" and in the hierarchy "priest of the goddess Bastet, of Khentsetet, of Khem, of Thoth and of the Mendesian ram" (compare PLS. XX, XXI). On PL. XX he is said to have "discharged every priestly function:" he was also "superintendent of all works of the king." Nefermaat held the general dignities implied by *rpa*, *ha*, *ari-nekhen*, and royal-treasurer? and it is remarkable that Rahotep had none of these.

PL. XVII. Nefermaat's wife was "the royal acquaintance Atet:" the "royal acquaintance Nub" of PL. XIX was perhaps a second wife. Their children were distinguished. The short titles of the eldest son Henan prove that he enjoyed several offices that were held also by Rahotep: the second, Asu, was *am-a* and priest of some goddess (PL. XXIII), while the other members of this numerous family were called "friends of the king" *semer* or "royal acquaintances" *rekh suten:* their names are Ankherfend, Ankhreshtef, Serefka, Teta, Khent (who appears to be entitled "superintendent of the lake of the crocodile" but the position of the signs makes this doubtful), Uhemuka, Shepseska, Kakhent, Deftsen, Atisen, Ankaf, and a daughter . . . gaut.

PL. XVIII. There is a fragment of a remarkable title in front of Nefermaat which was visible formerly also on the lintel of Atet (PL. XXII). Mariette shews it more complete, and his copy is confirmed by the useful sketch of the niche in Mr. Villiers Stuart's *Nile Gleanings*, PL. G. It may be read perhaps *ud ser neb* "commanding every noble."

PL. XIX. The topmost figure on the left represents the estate called Menat-Seneferu," nurse of the king Seneferu." It is noticeable that a city or estate near Beni Hasan, called "nurse of king Chufu," Chufu being the successor of Seneferu, played an important *rôle* in the early Middle Kingdom. Possibly this Menat-Chufu was an estate of the usual type to which the name clung with unusual tenacity.

Another estate-name on the same plate (bottom row) has been credited with being the earliest form of Medum. It contains the elements *m t w n* (determined by an ox), and the conventional transliteration *metun* has a curious likeness to Medum; but that is *all:* we do not know even whether Metun lay in Upper or in Lower Egypt. The modern name of the place was indeed sometimes written Medun by early European travellers; the ears are often deceived as to *m* and *n* in a new name or word, and Makrizi (Khitat i. p. 112), quotes from an older Arab author a passage referring to the pyramid of Medun (with *n* and short *e*)! but both ancient and modern authorities, Makrizi i. p. 119, the list of villages published in De Sacy's Abdellatif, and the new census of 1882, give Maidûm, corresponding exactly to the modern vulgar pronunciation Mêdûm. Thus writers who are or were familiar with the place agree in final *m;* casual travellers may confuse the two sounds *n* and *m* in a village-name, but natives of the place do not, so that it is useless to compare Metun with Maidum. There is better reason for supposing that Mertum (really pronounced Maitûm) is the ancient equivalent of the name. Ancient *t* is constantly equivalent to modern *d*, and we know the position of the town from the inscription of Piankhi, which places it in this neighbourhood on the West of the Nile. Unfortunately there is no new evidence to shew for this identification, which was proposed long ago.

It must be remembered that the gaps in the scenes here, PLS. XIX, XXI, have been compressed in order to get them into the plate. This circumstance affects especially the list of offerings which must once have existed in front of the large figure of Nefermaat.

PL. XXI. It is unfortunate that the estate-name towards which Nefermaat is being carried is broken away: as Mr. Petrie has pointed out, it was compounded with the name of a king. In the bottom row a boar appears. During the IVth dynasty this animal was domesticated (tomb of Amten, L. D. II. pl. v.), and it is often seen in the earliest hieroglyphs; but from the Vth dynasty onwards it is of extreme rarity.

PL. XXIV. In front of Nefermaat is a statement that has been translated "(the tomb) was made for his gods in writing that cannot be destroyed." Although this rendering may be thought questionable, there is no doubt that the passage contains a reference to the durable nature of the decoration.

In the second column servants are "bringing wine" and "figs": below are the products of the "stock farms of the house of eternity," and in the fourth compartment fowlers are bringing birds? "coming forth from the papyrus-marsh."

PL XXVII. In front of the fallow-deer is the legend "bringing the tribute of the house of eternity."

PL. XXVIII. There is a "stall-fed?" addax in No. 3. The domestication of antelopes in the early periods of Egyptian history is well known.

58. The inscription on the base of a female statuette (PL. XXIX, No. 6) probably begins at the side: "may her name [remain, established] in peace before Uadti mistress of Asheru, Khnumu, . . . ? Neb-Sau? Horus? and the gods (or Neb-sa and the cycle of gods) who are in Dad-Seneferu, for the *ka* of (the lady) Seneferu-Kheti, deceased, possessing perfection." It is a prayer that the name of Seneferu-Kheti, represented by the figure, may remain before various deities of the place, whose titles are somewhat unusual. The chief value of the inscription lies in the place-name Dad-Seneferu. In a collection of wonder-tales, known as the Westcar papyrus, it is related that a magician dwelt there in the time of king Chu Fu. He was 110 years old and yet daily consumed the haunch of an ox together with 500 cakes of bread and 100 jugs of beer. The legendary home of this extraordinary individual who bore the same name as one of Nefermaat's sons, may be fixed with tolerable certainty at Medum.

No. 8 is an ostracon on which were jotted down some accounts: the entries are difficult to unravel. A name Apusenb and the style of the hieratic together point to a date about the beginning of the New Kingdom.

59. In reading the graffiti reproduced on PLS. XXXII–XXXVI, the fact must not be lost sight of that a certain amount of restoration or alteration is allowable. The scribe's pen drawn over an irregular surface may leave a gap where there should be a continuous line or a blot where there should be no ink. Add to these considerations the faintness or complete obliteration of the originals in many places, and a ready explanation is forthcoming for any inaccuracies in the copies, which on the whole are so admirably legible.

On PL. XXXII, No. I. reads "Thrice beautiful is the name of the King Seneferu" (which means "making beautiful").

No. II. "Sebekhotepemsaf," a private name probably of the XIIIth dynasty.

No. III. "The scribe Antifi?"

No. IV. "Ameni."

These early records are true *graffiti*, having been scratched on the stone: the remainder were written in two inks from the ever-ready palette of the Egyptian scribe.

No. V. "Year 41, 22nd day of Mesore, under the majesty of the king Horus Strong Bull, who appears gloriously in Thebes; the wearer of the two diadems, who prolonging his reign like the sun in heaven, the golden (victorious) Hawk who wields might, who prepares glorious visitations, the king of Upper and Lower Egypt, Menkheperra, son of the sun Thothmes III., who lives for ever to eternity upon the throne of Horus (as ruler) of the living.

"Behold his majesty is as a young bull . . . as a goodly youth of 20 years whose equal has not been produced: the god Menthu? formed him for . . . : the god Tum . . . him: the universal lord created him: he is a mighty man very valorous in the field? of [battle?].

"The scribe Aakheperkara-senb, son of Amenmesu the scribe and reader (*kher-heb*) of the deceased king Aakheperkara (Thothmes I.) came here to see the beautiful temple of the Horus (king) Seneferu: he found it like heaven within when the sun-god is rising in it: and he exclaimed, 'The heaven rains with fresh frankincense and drops incense upon the roof of the temple of the Horus king Seneferu.'

"And he says, 'O every scribe, every reader, every priest, who reads this inscription, and all people who hear it, as ye would win the favour of your local deities, transmit your offices to your children, and be buried in the necropolis of Ptah-resanbef on the west (of Memphis), after old age and long life on earth—so say ye May the king give an offering, and may Osiris, god of Busiris the great deity, god of Abydos, and Ra Hru Khuti and Tumu god of Heliopolis, and Amen Ra king of the gods, and Anubis in the shrine, who dwells in the city of embalmment, the god of the west—give offerings, may they grant a thousand loaves of bread, a thousand jars of beer, a thousand oxen, a thousand fowls, a thousand offerings, a thousand provisions, a thousand packets of incense, a thousand jars of wax, a thousand bundles of linen, a thousand herbs, a thousand of every good and pure thing that heaven gives, that the earth produces, that the Nile brings from its source—to the ka of the Horus king Seneferu who has made good his claim? before his father [Os]iris? the great god lord of the sacred land, and to the goddess?-queen Meres-ankh.'"

The complimentary remarks on the temple are stereotyped phrases found also in the graffiti on the tombs of Beni Hasan. They are none too appropriate in either case: the rock-cut tombs had no "roof" exposed to the drippings of heaven, and the bare walls of the Medum temple were but little like the sky at sunrise. I imagine that the expressions were considered the polite ones for admiring or wondering visitors to make on entering a house, at least I see no other explanation for their appearance under such incongruous circumstances.

No. VI. Over the bird a name "Senefer(u ?)."

No. VIII. "Year 26, 21st day of the 3rd winter month under the majesty of the king Menkheperra, son of the sun Thothmes III., living for ever. The scribe of measuring of the king Thothmes I., Aba? . . . came and said . . . the (possessions of the) house of his father . . ." (there follows a list of land and products or offerings. It is unfortunate that this is so much mutilated).

No. X. "The carver (decorative) Fai?"

No. XI. "The sculptor Au ?-senb."

No. XIV. "May the king give an offering, and may the Horus king Seneferu, and Amen-Ra, king of the gods, and Ra-Hrukhuti . . . all things? grant glory? in heaven, might? on earth, drinking water in the mid? stream, breathing the sweet air of the north breeze, to the *ka* of him who follows [the feet] of the master of the two lands, Neter-mesu, who renews life and has obtained the reward of faithful service (*neb amakh*)."

No. XVI. Record of a visitor, "son of Panehsi," shewing traces of the formulæ as in No. I.

No. XVII. "Year 30 under the majesty of the king Neb-maat-Ra, son of the sun Amenhotepu III., prince of Thebes, living for ever to eternity as king established in this whole land. The scribe Mai came to see the very great pyramid of Horus the soul? of king Seneferu."

No. XVIII. "Year 30 under the majesty of the king Neb-maat-Ra, son of Amen, resting on truth, Amenhotep III., prince of Thebes, lord of might, prince of joy, who loves him that hates injustice of heart, placing the male offspring upon the seat of his father, and establishing his inheritance in the land."

This remarkable graffito suggests that the rule of inheritance through the female could be made an instrument of oppression by unscrupulous kings. A male heir would be more capable of defending his rights, and Amenhotep III. may have encouraged male succession as conducive of order: unless indeed the scribe refers only to some personal benefit gained in a suit against a female claimant.

From these graffiti and from a quantity of other evidence converging on the same point, it is clear that the pyramid of Medum belonged to Seneferu. But there are questions still outstanding: this king was most extravagant in the matter of pyrâmids: not only was his pyramid at Medum "very great," but he had built another somewhere! At Dahshur and elsewhere priests of the two *kha*-pyramids of Seneferu are named, and the southern *kha*-pyramid is expressly mentioned. Kha was therefore the name of each, but whether the pyramid of Medum was the southern or northern Kha cannot yet be decided.

One more remark: the graffito No. V mentions the queen Meresankh in such a way as to imply that she was wife of Seneferu. While accepting this provisionally, we must not forget that the scribe of 1500 B.C. may not have known the queens of 3000 or 4000 B.C. very accurately.

CHAPTER VII.

VARIETIES OF ANCIENT "KOHL."

By Dr. A. Wiedemann.

60. The subject of the ancient eye-paint (mestem) was discussed from the literary side two years ago in my *Aegyptologische Studien* (Bonn, 1889, pp. 25–44), with some addenda in the *Verh. der Berl. anthrop. Ges.* (1890, pp. 48–50). Before proceeding to the study of the actual materials here, I may add some details which illustrate the uses of the *kohl.* The substance *uat'*, which often appears along with *mestem*, is named as early as in these tombs of Medum (Pl. XIII) in Leps. *Denk.* II. 3; and both occur in two funereal inscriptions in the Louvre (c. 162, D. 59, in Pierret, *Inscr. du Louvre*, II. 59, 57), and on a coffin of the middle kingdom from Ekhmim (Rec. 11, 142); it also appears in the usual lists of offerings in tombs, the examples of which are arranged by Schiaparelli (*Libro dei funerali*, 11, 342), from the time of Unas to the Roman age. Of the toilet boxes (described *loc. cit.* p. 35) there is an example with four divisions in Leyden (F. 50, Leeman Mon. 11, pl. 32) with the purposes of the various preparations stated. On one is "for opening of the sight," the second "for expelling the tears," the third "for expelling the flower" (*herer*), the fourth "daily eye-paint." Another toilet box is edited by Ebers (*Die hierog. Schriftzeichen der Aeg.* p. 17) from the

Wilbour collection, bearing the inscriptions, "Inundation, for opening of the sight;" "Season when the fields appear, for expelling all evil of the eyes;" "Harvest, for throwing off the waters from the eyes," thus connecting the various cures with the Seasons. This probably belongs to the Middle Kingdom. According to a statement, which is not perhaps worth much, in the inscription of Sehel discovered by Wilbour, line 17, *mestem* and *uat'* were brought from the interior of Ethiopia. With this we come to an end of our literary information at the present time on the ancient *kohl*.

61. But while little advance has been made on this side, we have learned much more about the actual composition of the eye-paints: this is due to the active researches of Mr. Petrie, who in his Fayum excavations has found a long series of examples of *kohl;* with the advantage over previous specimens, from their place and age being known. Mr. Petrie had the goodness to entrust me with 30 examples; and two others (31, 32) also found by him, I have obtained through Prof. Ebers. Dr. Xaver Fischer undertook all the analyses, and will report (in the *Jour für prakt. Chemie*) the results of his careful and exact work, which was carried out in the laboratory, and under the kind superintendence, of Prof. Hilger at Erlangen. With Dr. Fischer's kind permission I now proceed to state those results of his that are of archaeological interest; for the more chemical details the original memoir should be consulted. As that however is not easily accessible to antiquarians, it seemed suitable to give here the results, which are valuable for the customs, and metallurgic and chemical knowledge, of the Egyptians.

The specimens 1–8, 28–31 are from Kahun, 9–10 from Illahun, 11–27, 32, from Gurob. As to age, 6, 7, 31 and perhaps 8 and 27, are of the XIIth dynasty; 32, and probably 28–30, from the XVIIIth; 11–26 of the XIXth (18–22 being from the tomb with amulet of Nefertari); 1–5 of the XIXth or XXth dynasty from the tomb of Maket; and 9–10 of the VIIth cent. A.D., 11–13 were in a quadri-tubular wooden stand, of which one tube was empty.

The general result is that antimony appears very rarely; but galena (sulphide of lead) is very common, both unaltered and manufactured. The powdered sulphide was gently roasted, and left so, or mixed with a slimy vegetable solution (gum), and poured as a paste into pieces of reed. Thus the sulphide slowly oxidised so long as it was kept moist. A rarer paint was pyrolusite (soft peroxide of manganese) which was powdered alone, or in mixtures. As substitutes we find oxide of copper (obtained from roasted carbonate); magnetite (obtained by partly reducing haematite with charcoal); and for a brown, iron ochres were used. The green powders are a mixture of finely powdered silicate (either native, or an artificial glass) with basic carbonate of copper; this was doubtless derived from the natural mixtures that are found in native chrysocolla, such as occurs in Gurob. This green powder (11) was in the wooden tubular stand with ochres in 12 and 13.

The rounded grains of sand, and green and red crystalline chips which occur, are probably accidental. Resin is entirely absent; and fats have disappeared, if ever they were present. Free sulphur which could be extracted probably comes from the galena, which commonly contains some.

The eye-paints were sometimes wrapped in the leaves of dicotyledons; but were usually placed in the stalks of *graminiae*, about as thick as the finger; the internodes were cut just below the knot, and the half-liquid, salve-like mixture was poured into the tube thus formed. Vessels of alabaster or pottery were also used, both for the powders and for the pastes. The rods of paint that may be extracted are rather shrunk at one end, evidently having been slowly dried pastes or salves. The longitudinal streaks on such pieces are produced by the internal form of the reeds used to hold the paste.

62. The following are the various classes of ingredients found. *I. A. Galena (sulphide of lead)*, XIIth dyn. No. 7; XIXth, 14, 16, 18, 22, 24; XXth, 2, 3 ?; Coptic, 10. These are native galena, without sulphate of lead, but with some sand and vegetable remains, oxide of iron, and traces of lime, manganese, and quartz. Nos. 14, 16, 24, also contained carbon. All of these were loose powders, except 24, which was compressed dry in a reed, and had not therefore become oxidised, but is still friable. Two samples were quantitatively analysed, yielding

		No. 18.	No 24.
Galena	$Pb\,S$	91·13	85·16
Peroxide of iron	$Fe_2\,O_3$	3·40	6·77
Carbon	C	..	2·78
Sand	$Si\,O_2$	4·72	4·93
Vegetable matter		·48	..
Manganese	$Mn\,O_2$	..	trace
Calcite	$Ca\,CO_3$	trace	trace
		99·73	99·64

The oxide of iron and some other items were probably associated with the galena, but the carbon is perhaps intentional. The amount of iron points to a native lead ore being used. No. 3 is probably of this class, as lead was found in the few grains available.

I. B. Galena roasted, XIIth dyn. Nos. 8, 31; XVIIIth, 28, 30, 32; XIXth, 20, 23, 25, 26; XXth, 1, 5; Coptic, 9, with molybdenum. In these the sulphide is partly changed by roasting, and by subsequent oxidation while moist. Both free lead, and free sulphur, are found; together with sulphide, sulphate, and sulphite, of lead. The chance impurities are oxides of iron and manganese, ochre, calcite, and chlorides of magnesium and potassium. In No. 5 oxide of copper may be accidentally introduced from another powder. Nos. 20 and 26 are not homogeneous, and are divided here into 20 a, b, c, and 26 a, b. The most interesting are the following:—

		No. 26a.	No. 26b.
Galena	Pb S	30·00 (or 32·00)	trace
Sulphate of lead	$Pb\ SO_4$	53·10	86·22
Oxide of iron	$Fe_2\ O_3$	·38	·68
Carbon	C	3·12	..
Sand and quartz	$Si\ O_2$	3·90	4·13
Chloride magnesium	Mg Cl	1·10	·87
Chloride sodium	Na Cl	2·95	..
Chloride potassium	K Cl	..	3·60
Sulphur free	S	1·75	1·33
Ochre		1·60	1·33
Vegetable matter		..	2·14
Lime and manganese	Ca Mn	traces	traces
		97·90	100·30

The presence of metallic lead, which abounds in other examples, along with the drossy pieces found in some specimens under the microscope, shew that the galena was roasted; the iron and ochre may come from accompanying silicates; the three chlorides may be intentionally added, as "sea salt," for species of natron are named in the Ebers papyrus eye-salves. The lime is a white crust, derived from the alabaster vessels which contained it. Another piece of 26 contained a good amount of metallic lead.

The principal ingredients of the following were determined.

		No. 8.	No. 23.	No 25.	No. 28.
Galena	Pb S	39·43	23·81	29·75	..
Lead	Pb	..	8·09	..	57·
Sulphur	S	..	..	·11	2·35
Sulphate of lead	$Pb\ SO_4$	43·23	37·81	38·70	..
Sulphuric acid	SO_3	..	..	..	2·70
		82·66	69·71	68·56	62·05

The reduced lead in 23 and 28 results from rapid roasting. Nos. 1, 5 and 30 are similar; 5 contained chips of malachite, perhaps strayed. 20 b contained sulphate of lead and sulphuric acid, in all 59·76 of lead. Nos. 31 and 32 are like 26. No. 9 is remarkable as containing sulphide of molybdenum, having lead 58·10, molybdenum 6·01, sulphuric acid 5·06, and sulphur (as hydro-sulphuric acid) 1·22, in 70·39 per cent. But this specimen is of Coptic date.

63. *II. Antimony.* In No. 21, of the XIXth dynasty, there is 32 per cent. of antimony, beside 35 per cent. of matrix and some per cent. of quartz, and other chance impurities such as are usually found in lead powders; but this is completely free from lead, and is antimonious sulphide Sb_2S_3.

III. Ochre. XIXth dynasty, 12, 13, 15, 20 a; XXth dyn. 4. These are more or less mixed with quartz and plant remains, and are strongly ferrous. They are from reeds, and also wrapped in dicotyledon leaves. The green specks in some are perhaps sulphate of iron, oxidised from the pyrites which occurs in clays.

V. Manganese. XIIth dynasty, 6; XVIIIth, 29; XIXth, 26 c. In No. 6 is some oxide of copper, perhaps intended to darken the tint. In 29 is 20 per cent. of $Mn\ O_2$ along with other oxides of manganese, and small quantities of galena, oxide of iron, ochre and silica, so it is a powdered pyrolusite. In 26 c is some lead, perhaps from 26 a.

V. Magnetite. XIXth dyn. No. 19, contains silica 59·64, magnetite ($Fe_3\ O_4$) 26·93, carbon 11·83. Iron 1·49. It is black and strongly magnetic; probably reduced from oxide of iron (haematite?) by heating with charcoal, and mixed with sand and more charcoal.

VI. Copper. XIIth dyn.? No. 27, is oxide of copper, doubtless produced by roasting malachite. XIXth dynasty, Nos. 11 and 17 are malachite (carbonate of copper), with white chips—perhaps artificial glass—and grains of sand. Perhaps the carbonate is artificial, but as it is the only Egyptian ore of copper this is less likely. Fischer points to a note in Zippe that the green patina on some Egyptian bronze is mainly a basic chloride of copper, corresponding to Atacamite. But this is not usual.

64. Of the metals thus found the copper comes certainly from Sinai, where the mines were already worked by the Egyptians in the pyramid period; Fischer points this out in his introduction, which contains a sketch of what was hitherto known on oriental eye-paints. The iron, which is scarce in Egypt, must also have been imported, probably from Sinai, scarcely from Kordofan or India. Antimony and lead are distant products, not being found in Sinai or Arabia. *Mestem* is said in inscriptions to come from the

Arabian coast, but that only proves that the Egyptians received it thence, not that it originated there. Similarly in later times Arabia was named as the home of such products as the cinnamon, which was only conveyed by the Arabs. Thus the lead and antimony were brought by them from India; and probably also the tin which was needed for making the bronze, which starts with the New Kingdom in Egypt. The galena was substituted for the rarer antimony perhaps in Arabia; and the manganese, copper, and magnetite were Egyptian substitutes, either openly or fraudulently; for the true meaning of *mestem* is yet uncertain.

In any case the analyses of Dr. Fischer have taught us something more important than the philological meaning of a word; they have shewn us what materials the Egyptians actually used for eye-paints, and provided evidence as to the primitive relations of trade between Egypt and India. Even if this were but indirect, through the Arabs, yet in conjunction with the apparently Phoenician graves just discovered by Bent on the Bahrein islands in the Persian Gulf, this gives us an entirely fresh insight into the relations of the people of the further east, in a time far before the so-called Greek period.

[The above was kindly translated by Mr. Griffith, and I have with Dr. Wiedemann's sanction incorporated one or two details bearing on the matter. I may add as a personal suggestion that the green *uat'* which accompanies the *mestem* in early times is the green carbonate of copper, which was used around the eyes as we see on early sculptures, and as I found on the mummy of Ranefer. Also I believe that the source of Egyptian tin was from Bohemia, Saxony, and Silesia. That the civilization of Europe was in contact with Egypt before tin appears there, is now certain. That the European civilisation extended to the north is also known from the northern objects at Mykenae. And as tin (in bronze) is found as early, or earlier, in Europe than in Egypt, we must rather suppose that it went from Greece to Egypt, than that it came from the east and was immediately transmitted in large quantity across the Mediterranean to the north. W. M. F. P.]

CHAPTER VIII.

EGYPTIAN COLOURS.

By W. J. Russell, Ph.D., F.R.S.

65. We shall consider here first the colours of purely Egyptian origin, as found in the town of Kahun (XII dyn.) and Gurob (XVIII–XIX dyn.); and then notice the examples of Roman age.

The *red* pigments are all natural products and consist essentially of ferric oxide. The mineral from which they are obtained is commonest at Kahun, and is known as oolitic haematite. Some of the specimens are the mineral in its natural condition; others, from Gurob, are apparently lumps of the same substance after being reduced to fine powder, and probably to some extent purified. A remarkable feature in all the natural specimens is that at least one side is perfectly smooth and curved; had it been a fusible substance the inference would have been that it had been melted and cast in a mould. However, when the surface is carefully examined it is found to be marked with fine lines. These smooth surfaces seemed at first difficult to account for, but I have now no doubt that they were produced by the ingenious way in which the pigment was prepared from the natural product. Instead of pounding or grinding the mineral they simply rubbed it in a curved vessel, or might be a hollow in a rock, with a little water; fine particles were thus abraded, and the water present gradually carried them down to the bottom of the vessel, from whence they could be easily removed. I have tried this way of preparing the pigment, and found it to answer admirably. I took one of the specimens with a curved smooth surface and rubbed it in a large porcelain mortar with a little water, and thus with the greatest ease obtained a wet powder which at once could be used, without addition of any other medium, as a pigment; for it adhered to paper, to wood, and to the fingers, with wonderful pertinacity, and alone it dried up to a powder very similar to some of the specimens found.

No doubt the specimens of haematite were carefully selected; they differ somewhat in texture, but very little in tint. One sample contained 79·11 % of ferric oxide, and another 81·34 %.

The *yellow* pigments are found at Gurob, and are also entirely derived from native minerals, iron ochres. They contain oxide of iron, which is again the colouring constituent, in a hydrated condition and mixed with a certain amount of silica and alumina, and traces of other substances. The colour is very permanent, but varies considerably in different specimens. In some cases it is a light yellow, in others of a much warmer tint.

66. The *blue* pigments are mainly from Gurob, and those of Kahun are inferior: they are by far the most interesting ones, for they are artificial productions, and hence their existence may serve to indicate to some extent the manufacturing skill and knowledge of the producers. They vary greatly in tint; Mr. Petrie having found some of a light and tolerably pure blue, others of a strongly greenish blue, and some specimens of a very fine and slightly purplish blue. All the specimens are of the same character and are what are known as frits, that is a kind of unfused or rather semi-fused glass. The ingredients composing these frits are the same as those found in glass, but the heat to which they have been exposed is only sufficient to cause combination of the constituents to take place, but not sufficient to bring the whole mass into a liquid state.

Mr. Petrie was fortunate enough to find several large pieces of these frits; and in every case they had a smooth and curved surface, exactly similar to the curved and smooth surfaces of the haematite; and again I found that a powder which exactly corresponded to the blue pigment which was used, could with ease be obtained by rubbing the specimen in a large mortar with water. It is to be hoped that some of these vessels where this rubbing of the raw material took place in the preparation of these paints will before long be found.

As before mentioned, there is a great difference in the tint existing in the different specimens, and often the same specimen will have strangely different colours in different parts. Most of the specimens were of the well-known delicate greenish blue colour, a few were of a stronger green colour, and one small specimen was of a splendid rich blue tending towards red, I imagine much the same tint as the so-called Alexandrian purple. This specimen was wholly of this colour, while others had the colour only in part, and none I think were so brilliant in colour as this small piece.

That copper was the colouring-matter in these frits there could be but little doubt; the only question was with regard to the purple one just mentioned. Most of the blues produced by silicates of copper have a greenish tint, but this one was quite free from it, and resembled exactly a frit easily produced by cobalt; but no trace of cobalt was present. There seemed so many points of interest with regard to the production of these different coloured frits, for instance how exactly they were made, what sort of furnace would be necessary, and how it happened that they were at that time, with their comparatively rude apparatus and imperfect knowledge, able to obtain so many different shades of colour,—that I was led to try to imitate exactly the specimens which Mr. Petrie had found. The purple was the most difficult to reproduce, but I have made it, and it is quite equal in colour to the original. The others were, after experience had been gained as to the general method to be employed, readily prepared; and there is no difficulty in considerably extending the number of colours which can readily be obtained by the same process. The colours are all very stable, they do not fade, and are not acted on by even strong acids.

With regard to the necessary appliances for making these frits, judging from the large size of some of the pieces found, we must conclude that considerable quantities of material were acted on at once; and it is certain that the materials to form the frit must have been raised not only to a red heat, but also have been maintained at that temperature for several consecutive hours.

Up to the present time I believe furnaces for accomplishing this have not been discovered. I can only express an ardent hope that before long we may learn in what form of furnace this making of the frit was conducted. The operation was not devoid of difficulty. The materials they used were silica, which was the principal constituent, and formed perhaps 60 to 80 % of the whole mixture; then there was the copper to give the colour, no doubt merely the crude mineral, but almost any salt of copper would produce the same effect. The other ingredients are alkali and lime. The amount of alkali is small; I used in my experiments 10 % of potassium and sodium carbonates. These ingredients have to be well mixed together; and then carefully heated in a crucible of some kind to protect them from the direct action of the gases given off by the burning wood, otherwise the frit would become more or less black. Again, a certain regulation of temperature would be required, for if the fire were not hot enough the necessary chemical changes would not take place, and on the other hand if the temperature became unduly high the materials would fuse, and a hard glassy body would be formed; such a body could not be reduced to powder by the rubbing as above described, and it is of much interest to note that every specimen of the frits that I have seen has been in the friable condition, and not in this glassy state; this shews that they had not been exposed to a high temperature; and also that only a small amount of alkali was used in their preparation. I have found no difficulty in preparing all the imitations of the frits in this friable state, so that on rubbing they can be readily reduced to powder. In certain cases a high temperature would also decompose the copper compounds, and give a more or less black instead of a blue frit. The colour of the frit depends principally, but not altogether, upon the amount of copper it contains. I found I could imitate a very delicate greenish blue frit with a mixture of 3 % to 5 % of copper carbonate: another, and deeper coloured, specimen was exactly imitated by a mixture containing 10 % of copper carbonate: and the imitation of the Egyptian purple was produced when 20 % of the copper salt was used, but the colour is much affected by the temperature at which the heating has been carried on, and also by the length of time of heating. Again, the amount of lime, and presence of small quantities of iron, also affect the colour to a great extent. No doubt the desert sand was used, and I am informed that at different places it can be obtained either white, and it is then free from iron, or deeply coloured, and it then contains much iron: at all events it is certain that a very small amount of iron modifies the colour to a very considerable extent. If the ordinary red sand was used, then there was always a greenish blue frit produced. The most common of the blue pigments are the ones most easily produced, and contain comparatively small amounts of copper, perhaps 3 to 10 %; the ordinary brown sand was probably used in preparing them, and lime in some form was added. The copper compound thus produced very readily and quickly forms, and is not altered even if exposed to a high temperature, or a long continued heat. The green frits, the darker and purer blue ones and the purple ones are not formed quite so easily. The green ones may be produced by the presence of iron, the simplest way of preparing such as I have seen is simply by using a very red sand, and about the same amount of copper as gives the greenish blue frit; but the green colour can also be produced by copper alone, but in this case the quantity must be larger than what is required to produce the light blue frits, and a careful and not excessive heating is necessary. The green appears before the frit has come to its permanent colour, and on continued heating passes away. In some of Mr. Petrie's specimens there is a beautiful mixture of colours; in a small area you find a brilliant blue colour and a delicate but strong green. I have often obtained exactly analogous results, and some of great beauty, in the frits I have made; different copper compounds are formed, their formation arising from accidental differences of temperature or mixture. I have no doubt these effects in the Egyptian specimens are purely accidental, and are produced in mixture made with 10 % or more of copper carbonate. When the amount of copper is increased to 15 or 20 %, and about an equal amount of lime is present, then the purple frits can be formed, but this is a somewhat more delicate operation. The amount of copper present is so much larger that it takes much longer to convert it wholly into silicate, and the range of temperature at which it forms is more restricted than in the other cases, but there is no real difficulty in forming it. At the same time I doubt whether the Egyptians ever made this purple as a sole product, the only piece of frit which was entirely of this colour that Mr. Petrie has found was not so large as the first joint of a little finger, and the other pieces of that colour occur in larger specimens, and are simply local, the rest being of a darkish blue or blue green colour: in a word, its formation in these cases was certainly accidental. With modern appliances I have been much interested in carrying out still further this same process for preparing different coloured frits, and many are the tints in addition to those known to the Egyptians which have been produced. In fact every shade of colour from a pure and very delicate light blue to a very dark indigo blue can be made, and again from a pure blue every shade of green and blue to a strong green; many of these green blues are remarkably forcible in colour and delicate in hue.

[I have since found part of a dish of frit at Tell Amarna, which had been broken and withdrawn from the furnace before complete combination. The pan was of rough pottery, shallow, about 9 inches across; probably covered with a tile to keep off the reducing flame, as the edges are turned black. It was supported by the edges resting on cylindric pots inverted in the furnace. The frit is of a lilac-blue. The uncombined silica is in large translucent splinters, from quartz pebbles, quite white. The mass was blown up while pasty, by about an equal volume of gas, shewing that the lime and alkali were used as carbonates. I have also found many pieces of broken pottery with blue paint in them, suggesting that the frit and probably the haematite was ground in a concave potsherd.—W. M. F. P.]

67. We now proceed to the pigments of the Greco-Roman age, of which samples were found at Hawara. These are of interest, as such colours appear to have been used, mixed with wax, by the painters who produced the portraits discovered there; and they are probably similar to the colours used by the great Greek artists.

These pigments were obtained from six pots of paint found in a burial; the pots had been undisturbed and evidently were just in the same state, as when last used by the owner. In some of the pots but little of the paint remained, but in others a considerable amount. The marks of the brush with which the paint had been removed were still perfectly evident. Mr. Flinders Petrie gave me a small specimen of each of the six pigments; they are a dark red, a light red, a pink, a yellow, a blue, and a white. The specimens being so nearly in the condition in which they had undoubtedly been used as paints, gave them a special interest.

The Dark Red Pigment.—It has precisely the colour of the burnt sienna of the present day, and is identical with it, consisting of ferric oxide. Like the modern burnt sienna it does not dissolve completely in hydrochloric acid, and like it, leaves undissolved flocculent mineral matter and a little silica. No doubt it was prepared from natural iron ochre by heating, and afterwards grinding it; similar operations to those carried on at the present day for preparing this pigment, and in fact this Egyptian colour is indistinguishable from a sample of burnt sienna purchased at the present time.

Light Red Pigment.—This is an oxide of lead, and is known as red lead or minium. It is prepared by heating in the air, to a temperature of dull redness, lead, oxide of lead, or lead carbonate. It is somewhat paler in colour than the ordinary red lead of the present day, but it has some dust and sand mixed with it.

Yellow Pigment.—This is an iron ochre of a light yellow colour. On heating it darkens and becomes of a dull red colour. The dark red pigment, already described, was probably made from this mineral by heating it. This specimen of the yellow pigment has apparently been mixed with some oil or wax, no doubt as a medium, for on heating it white fumes, such as come from organic matter are given off.

The White Pigment consists of calcium sulphate or gypsum. It is very tenacious, but is easily cut or scraped with a knife. It has apparently been ground and carefully prepared for use, and in its present state would work smoothly and well; and as a pigment it could be used for many purposes simply on mixing with water.

Pink Pigment.—This is a most interesting pigment belonging to a different class of bodies from all the others: they are mineral compounds, whereas this pink colour is due to an organic substance. The fact that, even under favourable conditions, an organic pigment should have existed for this length of time is of interest; and I think there is good reason to suppose that it has not only existed, but has undergone little or no change of tint during this long period. On heating this pigment the colour is immediately destroyed, a slight empyreumatic odour is given off, and a white mass remains, apparently equal in quantity to the original substance. This residue is calcium sulphate, the same substance as the white pigment. The colour is therefore due to a very small amount of an organic body which coloured the gypsum, an amount too small to be recognised by chemical analysis. I therefore endeavoured synthetically to determine the nature of the colouring matter which gave to the calcium sulphate its peculiar tint, Madder as a vegetable colouring matter which has been known from the earliest time, naturally suggested itself; and with some madder root I was able to prepare a pigment which agreed in tint and in all its properties with the Egyptian one. It is readily prepared in this simple way; madder is boiled with water; the liquid cooled and strained; and this strongly coloured liquid well stirred up with calcium sulphate. The colouring matter adheres strongly to the gypsum, and if it be allowed to dry, and is then powdered, a substance is obtained of the same colour as the Egyptian pink, the shade of colour depending simply on the strength of the madder solution. Although ordinary chemical analysis could not identify the colouring matter in this case, it seemed to me highly probable that I could confirm this view of the nature of the colouring matter by means of spectrum analysis, for it is well established that the colouring matters derived from madder root are characterised by very definite absorption spectra. As this Egyptian colouring matter appeared to be so little changed, it was quite possible that even the small amounts which I had at my disposal might yield at least the marked and well-defined absorption spectrum of purpurine. I first tried the experiment with some of my imitation pink pigment; it gave on boiling it with alum solution very marked absorption bands which I proved, by comparing them with a purpurine solution, to belong to that body; and on treating the Egyptian pigment exactly as I had treated my imitation of it, it was satisfactory to find similar absorption bands, which leaves no doubt as to the nature of this colour, and shews how little the colouring matter has changed in the many centuries of its existence.

The remaining colour is a blue pigment. It is a frit, or unfused glass, finely ground. The colour it possesses is owing to the presence of copper, like the frits previously described. It is a remarkably stable compound, being practically unattacked even by strong acids, and unchangeable by the action of light.

CHAPTER IX.

COPTIC PAPYRI.

By W. E. Crum.

68. The Coptic MSS. which Mr. Petrie brought, 3 years ago, from the Fayyum, form a collection very similar to those in Berlin and Vienna, though less extensive than either of these. They have in common the same curious anomalies in regard to dialect and the same, as yet insurmountable, difficulties of interpretation. As with all Coptic literature, their monastic origin is evident. Yet even the hypothesis of monasteries with extensive circles of correspondents, seems hardly a satisfactory explanation of the extraordinary dialectual variety discernible in so comparatively small a body of texts. Of the six recognised dialects, four—perhaps five,—are represented, not to mention the several intermediate, local forms which some of the fragments exemplify. One can not but incline to Erman's opinion (*Hermes*, *XXI*,) that supply and demand of modern commerce have been the main cause of the accumulation in the Fayyum of documents which had their origin in widely different provinces.

The only attempt made as yet to deal with the Coptic "Fayyum" Papyri is that of Stern (*Aeg. Zeitschr.* '85); for Krall (*Mitth. a. d. Sammlg. Erzh. Rainer, passim*,) has confined himself to some of the more frequent formulæ, place-names &c. But little light has since been thrown either upon the vocabulary or grammatical forms, which still seem as foreign to those of the "classical" dialects as they 6 years ago appeared.

The material upon which our texts are written is either Papyrus, Parchment or Rag-paper; the first appearing, for all purposes, in a great majority, the second used, (with one exception,) for purposes not merely ephemeral, and the third exemplified only by one or two epistolary fragments of late date. Some of the Papyri are palimpsests; while a number bear two distinct texts, one upon each face. In one instance, half a sheet, of which one side had remained clear, has been employed by a second letter-writer, who ends with the postscript; "Blame us not because I (*sic*) have not been able to find a clean papyrus, worthy of your Honour."

Chronologically the Collection covers probably a considerable period, although not a single date can be cited or inferred. There may be palæographical reasons for placing one of the parchments not later than the 6th century; otherwise the texts would seem to range from the 8th to the 10th centuries; the frequency of the Arabic fragments forbidding an earlier, the rarity of paper a much later boundary.

The following are the Dialects met with in the Collection, in the order of their frequency:—1. Fayyumic; 2. Lower-Sahidic, probably from Memphis and its neighbourhood; 3. Sahidic; 4. Boheiric, with its characteristic guttural letter, which seems not to occur in the Vienna (*v. Mittheilungen II*, 57,) or Berlin texts; 5. Achmimic.* The presence of the fourth only of these can be doubtful, in so far as the two texts in which the characteristic letter occurs, do not exemplify the dialect in its pure form, but bear clear traces of a more southern influence.

69. The documents may be classified, on the basis of subject-matter, as follows:—

A. *Biblical fragments.* One example only, being at the same time the sole instance of the Achmim dialect. A small leaf of thin parchment (4 × 3½ in.), paged ⲱⲓⲏ and ⲱⲓⲑ, bears vv. 17–20 of the Epistle of Jude; while the quarter of a similar leaf has the Epistle of James, iv. 12, 13. These are the only traces, as yet recognised, of the Achmimic New Testament. The text is in single column, and written in so archaic a character,—the 4th plate (de la Zouche) of Hyvernat's "*Album*" may be compared,—that the 6th century would not seem too early a

* Dr. Steindorff points cut that the Graffiti (*Recueil* xi, 145) at Achmim are the best confirmation of the accepted "provenance" of this dialect.

date for these valuable fragments. When compared with the Sahidic and Boheiric versions, our text is seen to stand in close relation to the first, while the second comes, of all, the nearest to the Greek.

B. *Other theological texts.* Part of a parchment leaf has preserved two columns of what appears to be a homily (somewhat in the manner of Jesus Sirach,) upon the domestic virtues of women, and the futility of hoping to atone for their loss by the display of other qualities, if once the husband have ground for mistrust. The dialect is pure Sahidic, and the character an Uncial not unlike that of F. Rossi, *Tre Manoscritti, tav. II.* Upon a fragment of Papyrus, of late date, can be recognised the remnants of the story of Athanasius and Arsenius, bishop of Hypsele, whose hand the former was accused of cutting off and using for magic purposes. The groundlessness of the charge was proved at the Synod of Tyre. (See Hefele, *Conciliengeschichte,* I. 458, 464. I have to thank Prof. Harnack for this identification.)

70. C. *Letters.* This section embraces so large a majority of the fragments, that the remaining texts may be looked upon merely as exceptions. Unfortunately there are but few of the letters which approach completeness in preservation, and none which do not present great difficulties to the translator. They are for the most part in the Fayyum dialect, and, of course, in a character much more cursive than that of the texts described above. Ligatures are nevertheless not so frequent as in Sahidic MSS ; many of the fragments are wholly free from them. In one instance a Papyrus letter, of not more than ordinary importance, is written in a very fine uncial script, the same being the case with the only letter in the collection upon parchment.

The correspondence is wholly monastic; individuals being rarely mentioned without the title Monk, Brother, Deacon, Apa, or Presbyter. Other ecclesiastical dignitaries, such as Bishop, Archimandrite, Hegemon, also occur. Yet there does not appear to be any monastery named which might help to localise the writers; while but few of the place-names which do occur, can, as yet, be identified. Almost all the letters begin with a formula of greeting; "In God's Name! (var. With God!) First of all I greet and enquire for (var. embrace) the health of thy God-loving Fatherhood (var. Brothership, Sonship,) and thy whole company (or, all the Orthodox). Further, I inform thee, &c." In some cases this is more elaborate and mentions by name the various inmates of the cloister whither the letter is directed, adding in a Postscript, such as may have been overlooked. The matters dealt with appear to be chiefly commercial or financial affairs in which the writer or his monastery are concerned. They are often dispatched very summarily, a single short letter referring to half a dozen points, each with its introductory ⲗⲓⲡⲟⲛ (*λοιπόν*).

The following may serve as a specimen of the style and form usually adopted by the correspondents. Great uncertainty as to the meaning of several words, added to the incompleteness of the text, make a fuller translation very difficult.

"With God! I greet and embrace the well-being of my god-loving, reverend Lord Brother . . . and I greet the whole company, that is to say, the Elders. Repose thy saintly Spirit in the Lord Jesus Christ, . . . from God. And now (lit. Thereafter) my Lord Brother, behold, (here is) the Deacon, Apa Cyrus, (and) I have sent thee the —— ? (cargos ? or salt ?), namely those with which thou art used to favour me. Send the Deacon, Apa Cyrus that he may lay them before Apa Jacob, till the Deacon Pisynthius comes and takes them . . . An answer, if thou desire it afterwards, . . . I greet my Lord Brother fairly, (ⲕⲁⲗⲟⲥ *sic,*) according to God's will. Farewell in the Lord!"

71. D. *Accounts, Lists, &c.* Though few in number, the examples of this class are of considerable interest. The most remarkable is a large fragment which bears, in double column on both faces, the names of workmen and others and the sums paid them during the "Inundation" and summer months. Among them appear Gardeners, Agricultural labourers, Shepherds, Camelherds, Bakers, Carpenters, Potters, Smiths, Washermen, Messengers, Watchmen. Several persons receive payment, although the services rendered are not stated. Some of those employed are monks; "the Deacon Georgios, the Carpenter," "Apa Petros, the Gardener." Several bear, moreover, the names of their villages, and from these we see that the monastery was not confined, for the supply of its needs, to the immediate neighbourhood, since the localities identifiable range from Lake Moeris to the Bahr Yusuf. This document has striking similarity with a Papyrus in Oxford, brought from Sohag, but probably originating, (as its place-names and dialect indicate,) in the Fayyum.

Another Papyrus, in a very fragmentary condition, seems to bear monastic accounts in which the measure of value is throughout ⲕⲟⲩⲣⲓ, the identification of which with the Greek measure of capacity *κοῦρι, κόρος, χόρ*, I owe to Professor Wilcken, who adds that it is frequently to be met with in Greek MSS., especially in connection with wine. Although the latter repeatedly occurs in our Papyri, as an article of commerce, there is, in the present text, no trace of it, ⲕⲉⲣⲁⲙⲓⲁ (*κεραμεία*) and ⲃⲓⲧⲧⲓⲛⲁ (?) being the only words, still legible, to which the figures might be supposed to refer.

Upon another fragment the Catalogue (ⲗⲟⲅⲟⲥ) of a monastic library is partially preserved. It has included the canonical books of the New Testament, in several copies and in Greek as well as Coptic; the Psalter, also in both languages, besides theological works such as "The Rules of Apa Petros," both Coptic and Greek "Mystica," works (?) of Syrianus, as well as "Reading Books" (presumably *κατὰ μέρος*, lectionaries). Some of the books are of Parchment (ⲙⲉϥⲣⲱⲛ *sic*), others of Papyrus (ⲭⲁⲣⲧⲏⲥ). Others are followed by the epithets ⲡⲉⲧⲁⲗⲟⲛ or ⲁⲧⲡⲉⲧⲁⲗⲟⲛ, the exact meaning of which it is difficult to determine. Prof. Wilcken suggests that they perhaps serve to distinguish Books consisting of *leaves* and Rolls of papyrus.

Of the Proper names which occur, little need be said; they are those which we are used to find borne by the Copts, e.g. Ⲟⲩⲉⲛⲁⲃⲉⲣ (*'Οννωφρις*), Ⲡⲓⲥⲩⲛⲧⲓ (*Πεσύνθιος*), Ⲃⲓⲕⲧⲱⲣ (Victor), ⲭⲁⲏⲗ (*[Μι]χαήλ*), Ⲙⲁⲣⲕⲟⲥ; less common are Ⲙⲟⲩⲥⲉⲑⲁⲣⲓ,* Ⲏⲓⲗⲁⲙⲙⲱ, Ⲫⲱⲣⲉ. The Place-names, on the other hand, are of interest, and, in some cases, recognisable still in their Arabic forms. Arsinoe, under its Greek form, does not appear. It seems, in one instance, to be represented by ⲡⲓⲁⲙ, the name which otherwise designates rather the district than its capital (but v. Quatremère, *Mêms.* I, 391). Elsewhere the same town is referred to merely as ⲡⲟⲗⲓⲥ, "the City." Ellahun—ⲗⲉϩⲱⲛⲓ is met with several times. Among the less important localities one need scarcely hesitate to identify Ⲧⲟⲩⲧⲱⲛ with the modern طوں (Schweinfurth, "Tutûn"). Ⲡⲟⲩⲁⲉⲓⲍ may be compared with بويط (de Sacy, *Abdallatif*, p. 685, note), Ϣⲏⲛⲁⲣⲱ with سينرو (ll. 683).

* Here masc., but see Wilcken, *Sitzungsber. d. Berl. Akad.*, 1883, 904.

ⲕⲉⲣⲕⲉⲥⲟⲩⲭⲟⲥ is already known from Greek sources (v. *Aeg. Zeitsch.* '83, 162). Further, the names ⲧⲁⲛϣⲉⲉⲓ, ⲡⲉⲗϭⲓⲥⲱⲕ, ⲡⲥⲁⲃⲉⲧ ("the Wall"), recur sufficiently often, either in this collection, in Berlin or in Oxford, to establish their existence, although their identification be not easy.

[NOTE.—Mr. Petrie gives the following details as to the above localities. "Tutûn is 10 m. S.W. of El Medînet; Bawît is 7 m. W. of Derut (27° 39′), and has large Coptic ruins; Tansâ is 18 m. S.E. of El Medînet." The last may represent our Ⲧⲁⲛϣⲉⲉⲓ. Sênru should not be confounded with Senûres, lying some 8 m. to its N.E. All the MSS. come from El Hamâm near Ellahun.]

POSTSCRIPT TO CHAP. III. p. 27.

I AM desirous of making a correction to § 45 consequent on a more careful and extended examination of the inlaid colours than time allowed before Mr. Petrie left England. I found the globular grains of gum in all the specimens but the white. The gum being insoluble in water, was probably pounded, mixed with the paste, and heated to boiling point in the endeavour to dissolve it; but no more could thus be accomplished than to bring it to the half melted globular form. The gum comes nearest to Mastick by tests, and especially imitative preparations. It was doubtless new at the time of using, but changed very much since, as it will no longer soften in boiling water, as it must once have done. It is probable that it was used instead of gum arabic, or ignorantly mixed with it. Some of the pieces of colour, which had not been examined, were very hard. These yielded an animal matter, which answered completely to gelatine, precisely as the extract does from some of the bones from tombs of the same age. I therefore conclude that the gum used having been found incapable in places of retaining the pastes, gelatine or size in some form was applied to the surface of the paste, which it penetrated to varying depths, thus overcoming the difficulty in part. The whole process was evidently experimental.

F. C. J. SPURRELL.

INDEX.

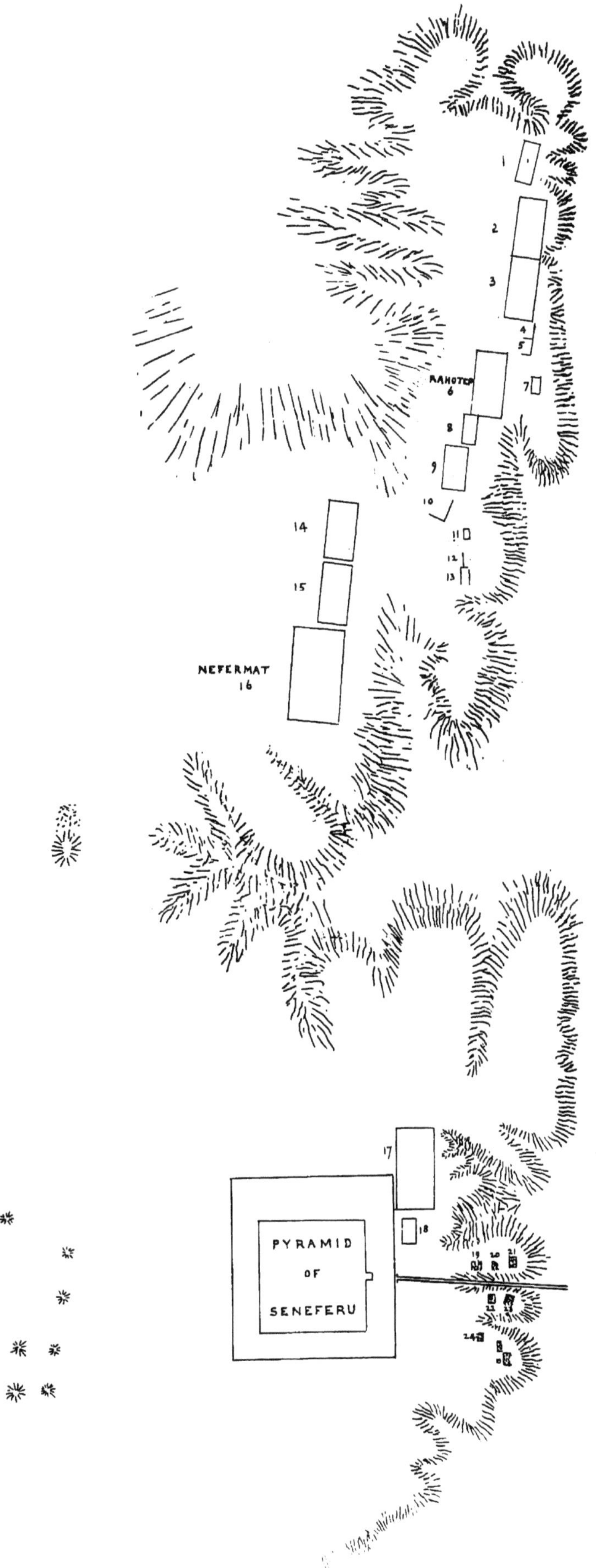

1
2
3
4
5
RAHOTEP
6
7
8
9
10
11
12
13
14
15
NEFERMAT
16
17
18
PYRAMID
OF
SENEFERU
19
20
21
24

W.M.F.P.

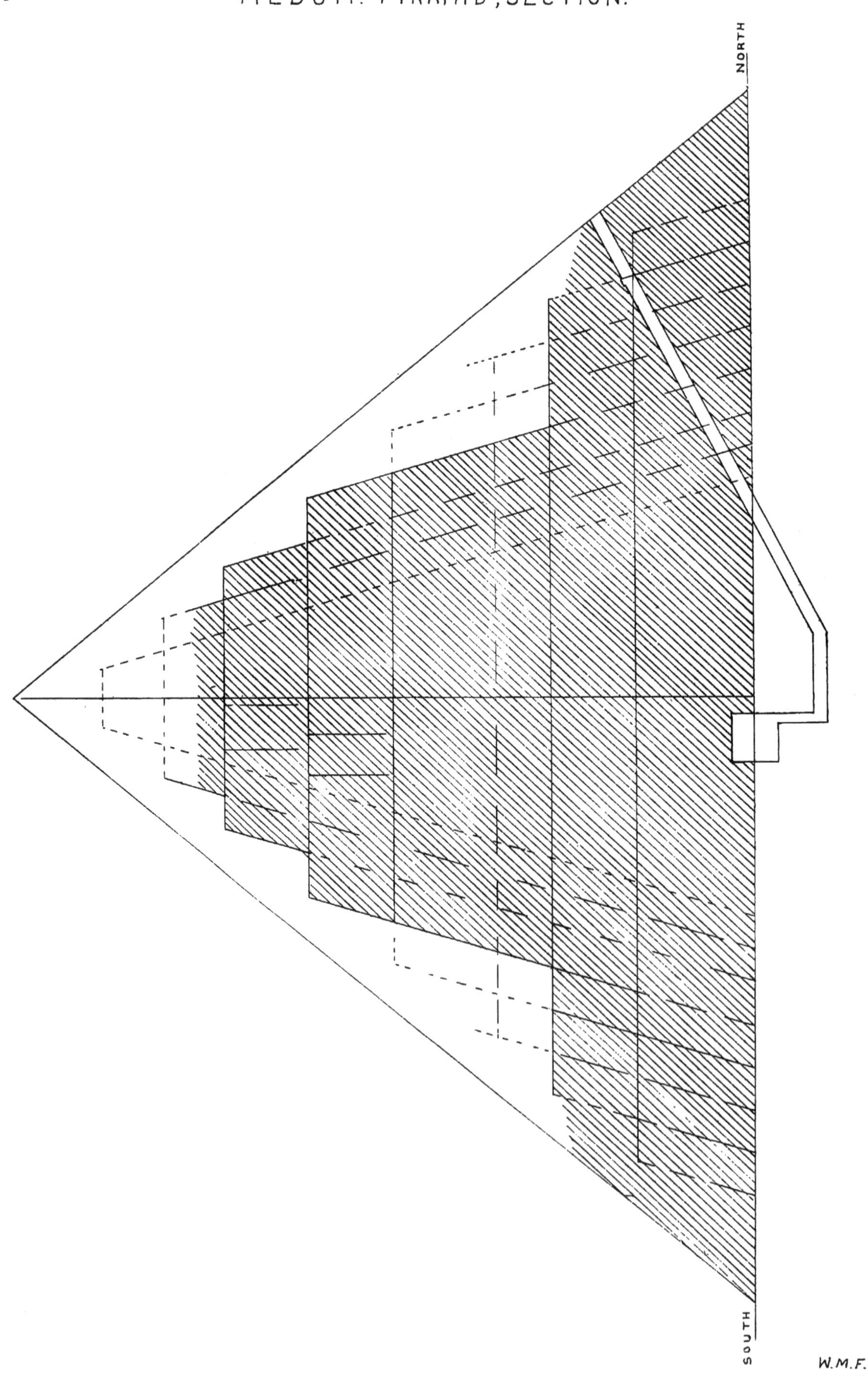
NORTH
SOUTH
W.M.F.P.

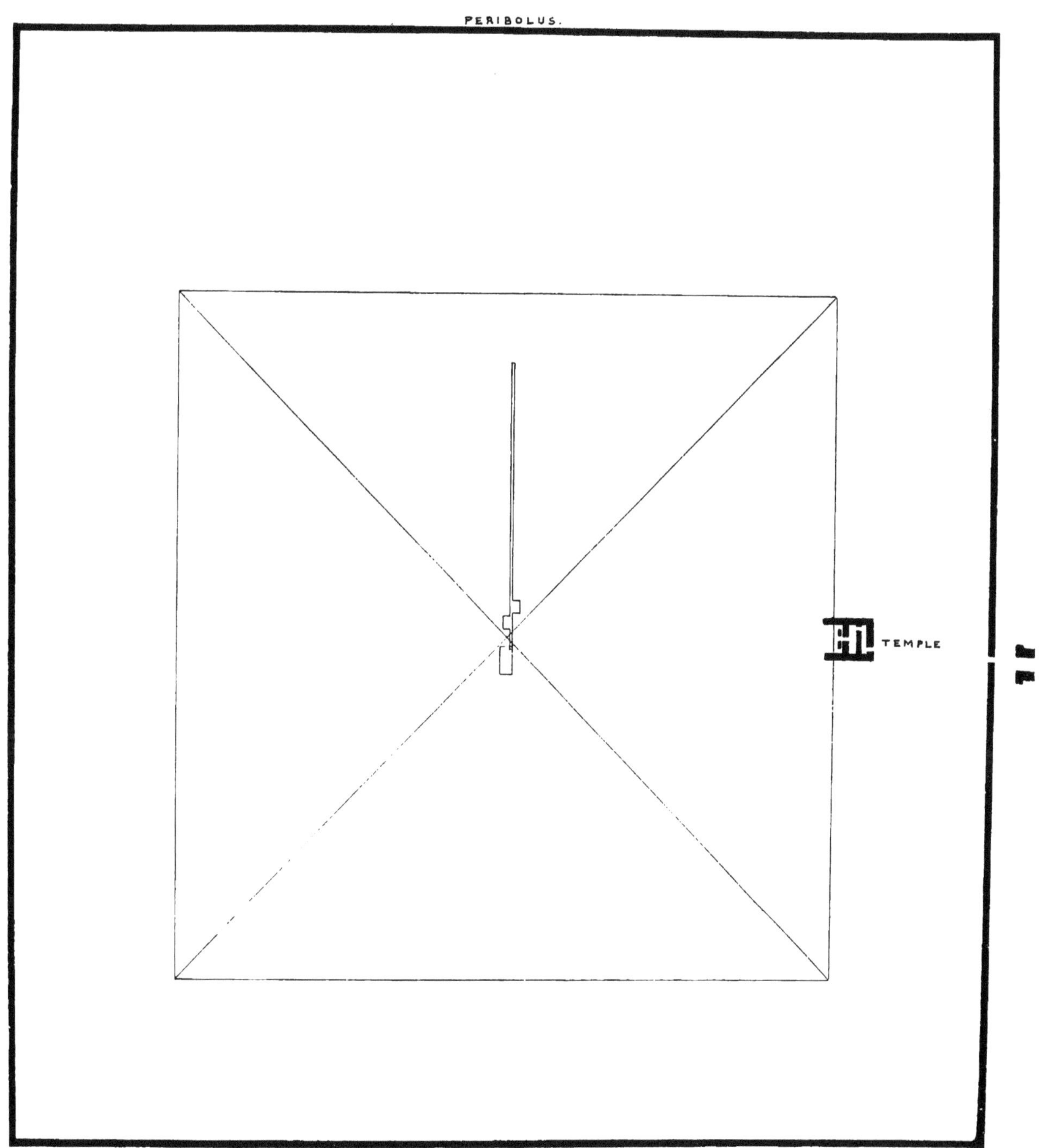

W.M.F.P.

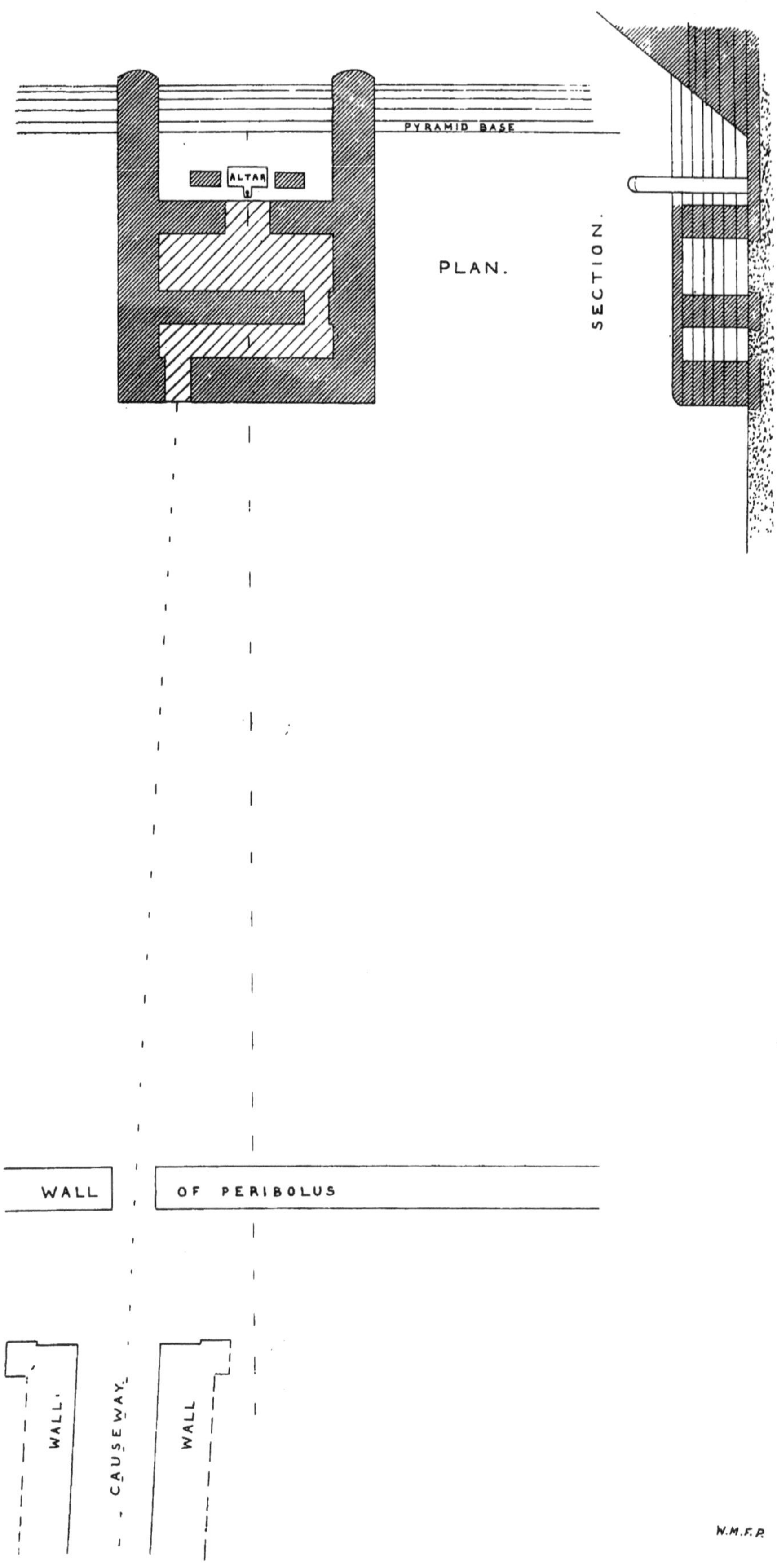
PYRAMID BASE
ALTAR
PLAN.
SECTION.
WALL
OF PERIBOLUS
WALL
CAUSEWAY
WALL
W.M.F.P.

1:3000 MEDUM, NORTH CEMETERY. V

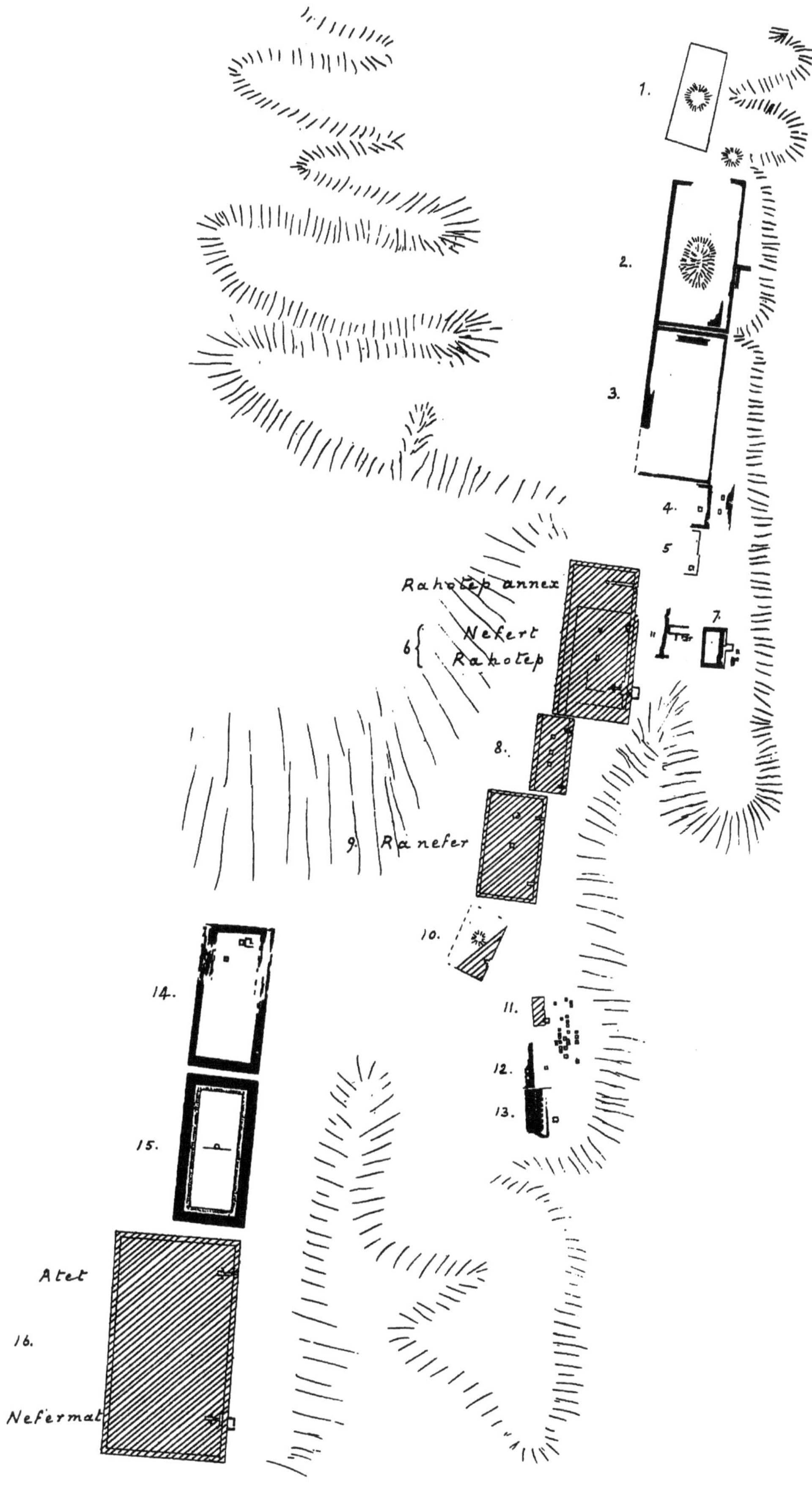

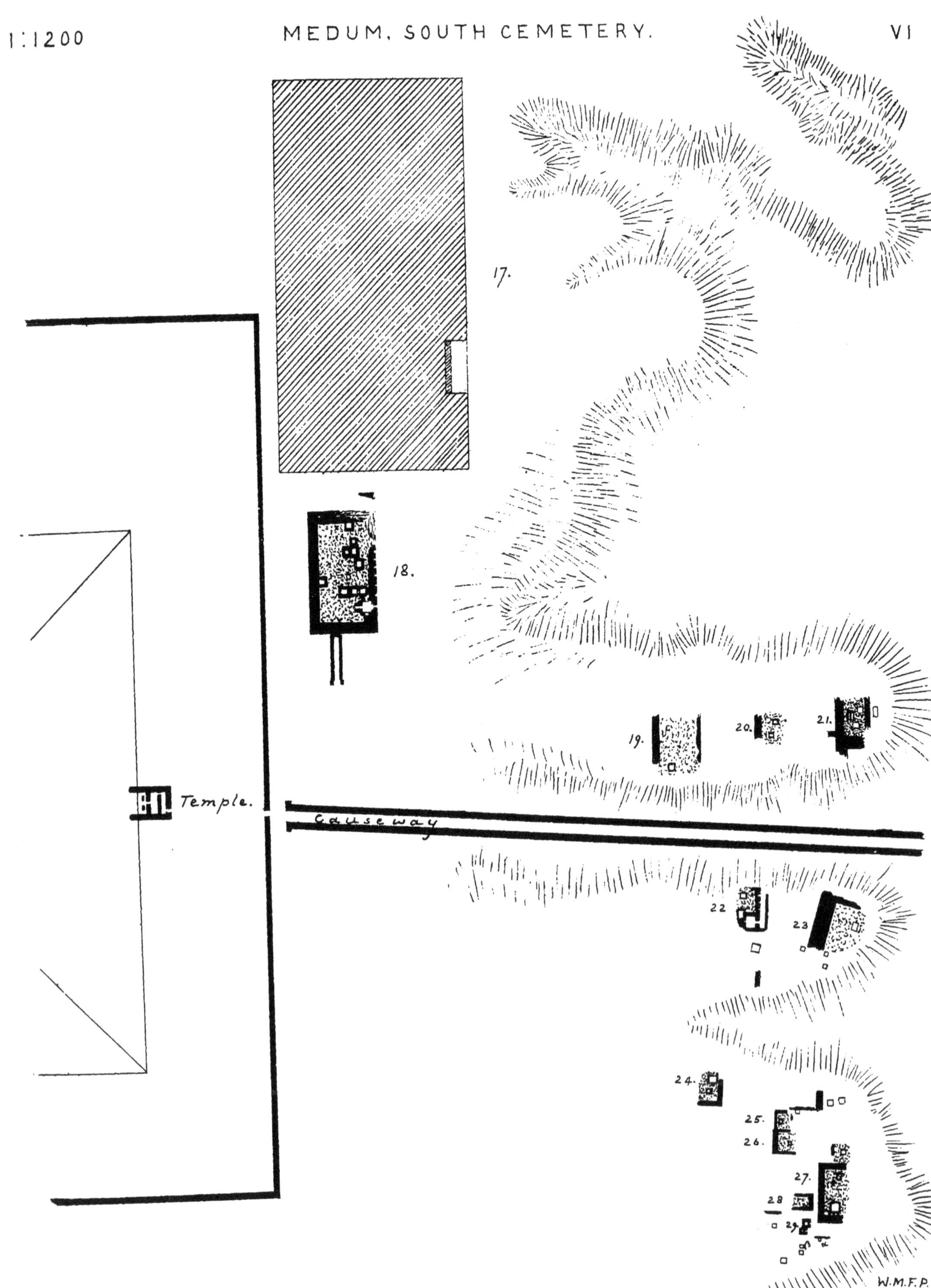
17.
18.
19.
20.
21.
Temple.
Causeway
22
23
24.
25.
26.
27.
28
29.
W.M.F.P.

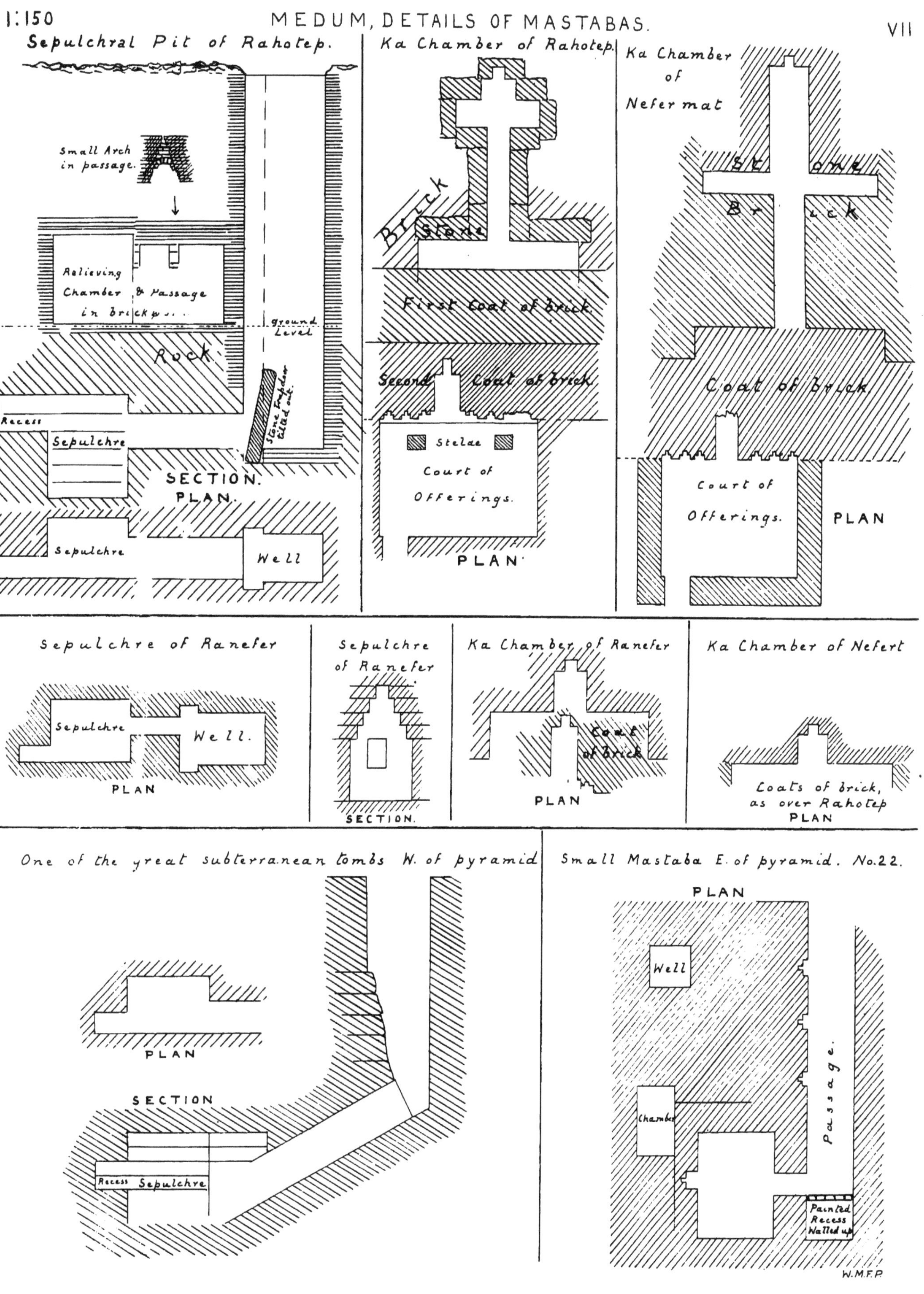

Sepulchral Pit of Rahotep.
Small Arch in passage.
Relieving Chamber & Passage in brickwork
ground Level
Rock
Stone trapdoor tilted out.
Recess
Sepulchre
SECTION.
PLAN.
Sepulchre
Well
Ka Chamber of Rahotep.
Brick
Stone
First Coat of brick
Second Coat of brick
Stelae
Court of Offerings.
PLAN
Ka Chamber of Nefermat
Stone
Brick
Coat of brick
Court of Offerings.
PLAN
Sepulchre of Ranefer
Sepulchre
Well.
PLAN
Sepulchre of Ranefer
SECTION.
Ka Chamber of Ranefer
Coat of brick
PLAN
Ka Chamber of Nefert
Coats of brick, as over Rahotep
PLAN
One of the great subterranean tombs W. of pyramid
PLAN
SECTION
Recess
Sepulchre
Small Mastaba E. of pyramid. No.22.
PLAN
Well
Chamber
Passage.
Painted Recess Walled up
W.M.F.P.

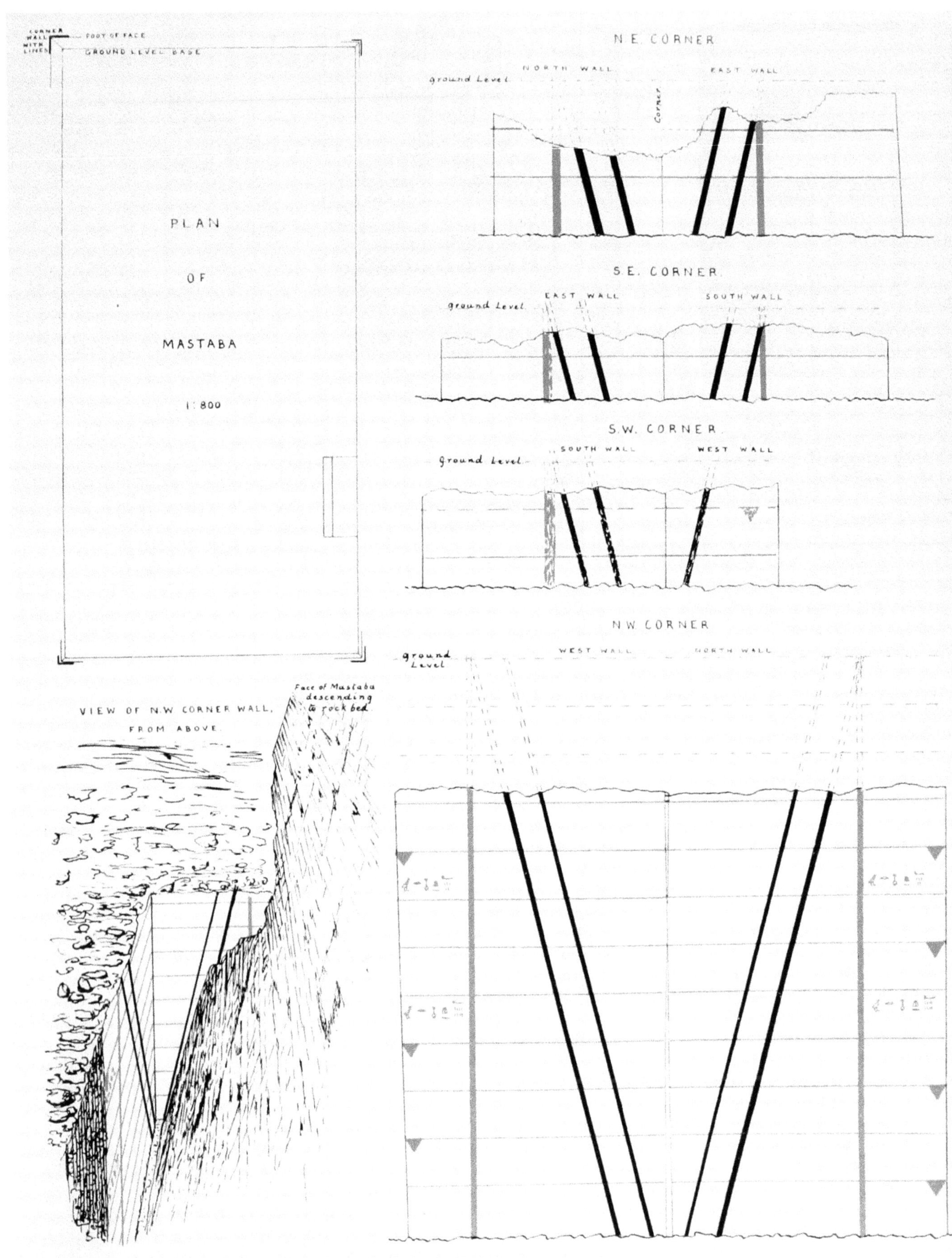
CORNER WALL WITH LINES
FOOT OF FACE
GROUND LEVEL BASE
PLAN
OF
MASTABA
1 : 800
N.E. CORNER
NORTH WALL
EAST WALL
ground Level
Corner
S.E. CORNER
EAST WALL
SOUTH WALL
ground Level
S.W. CORNER
SOUTH WALL
WEST WALL
Ground Level
N.W. CORNER
ground Level
WEST WALL
NORTH WALL
VIEW OF N.W. CORNER WALL, FROM ABOVE.
Face of Mastaba descending to rock bed

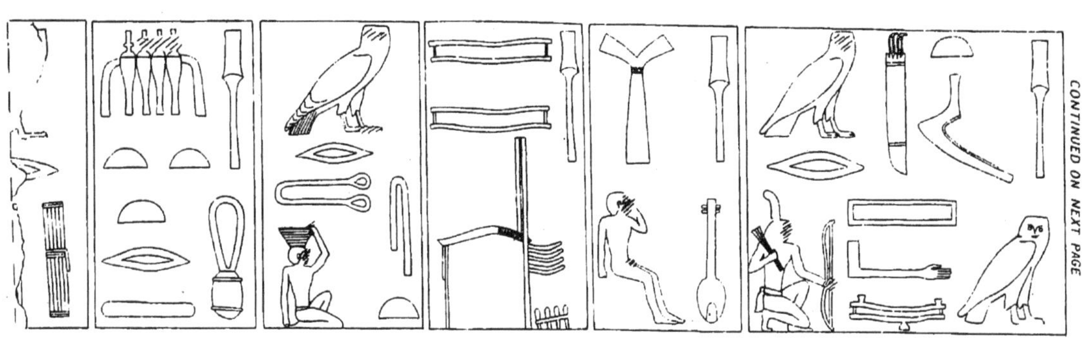

CONTINUED ON NEXT PAGE

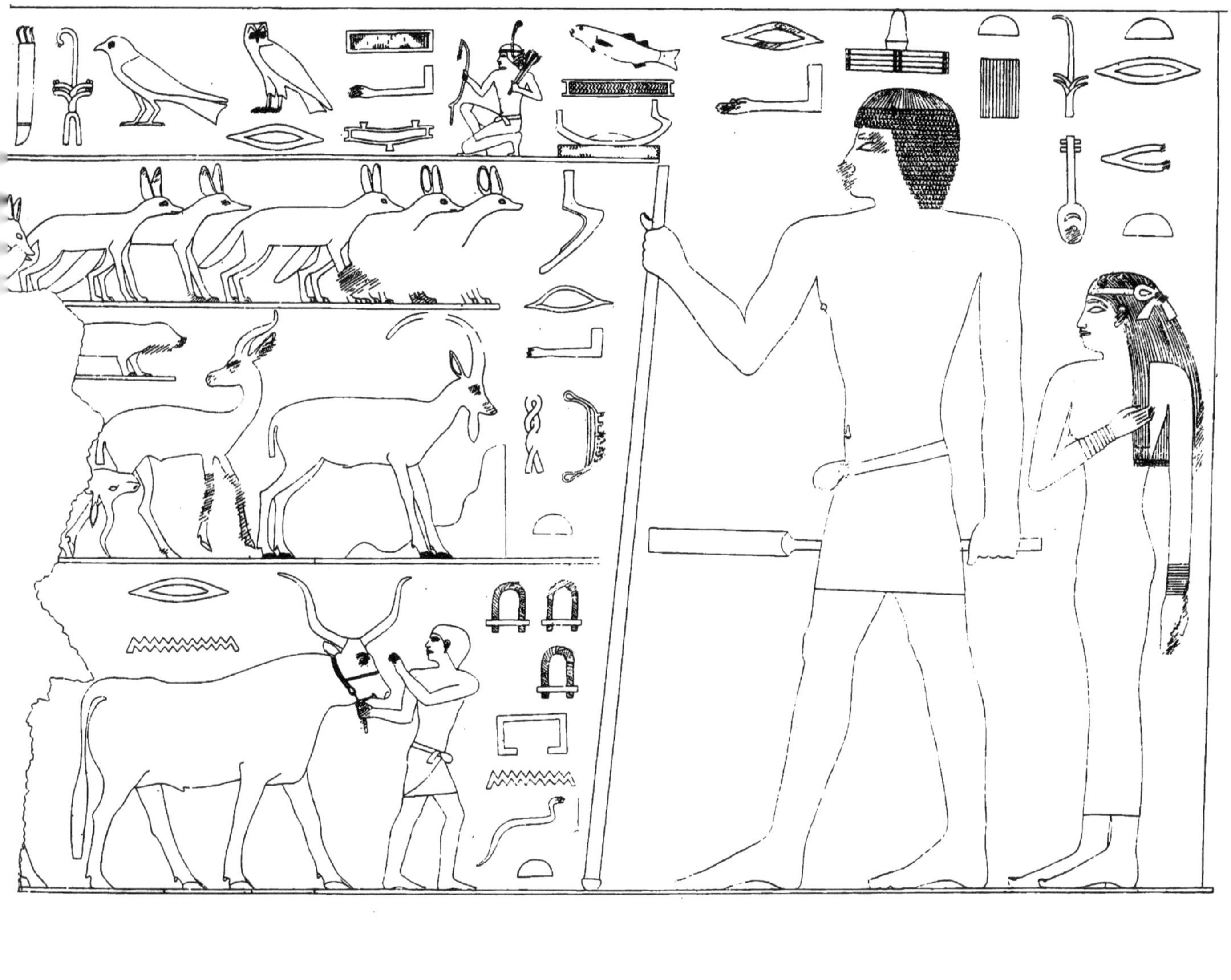

1:12 MEDUM. RAHOTEP. N. HALF LINTEL AND PASSAGE SIDE X.

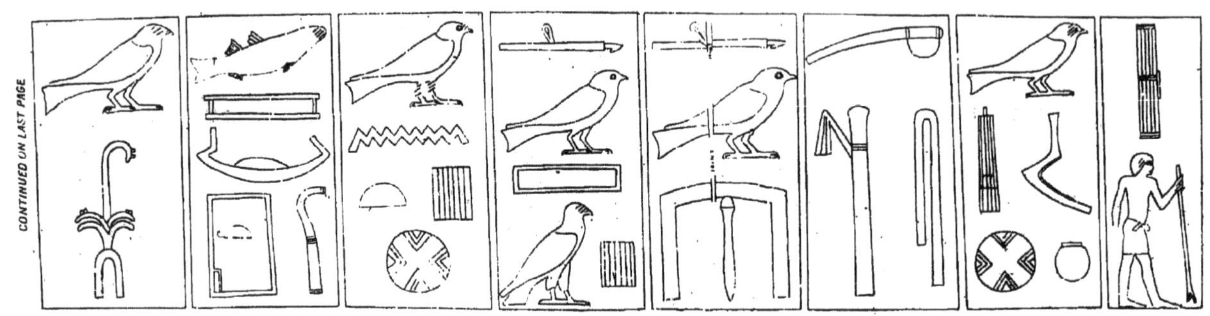

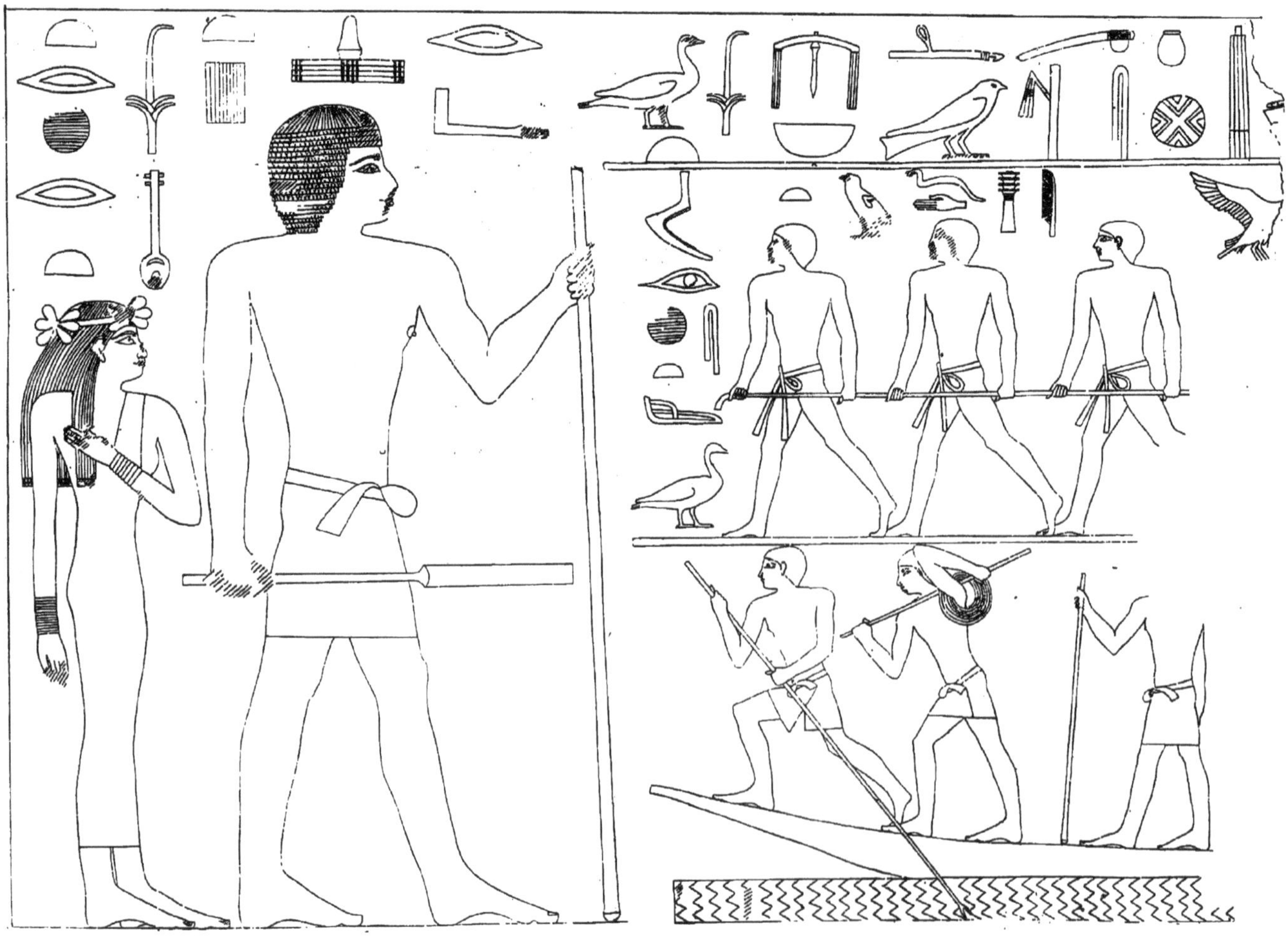

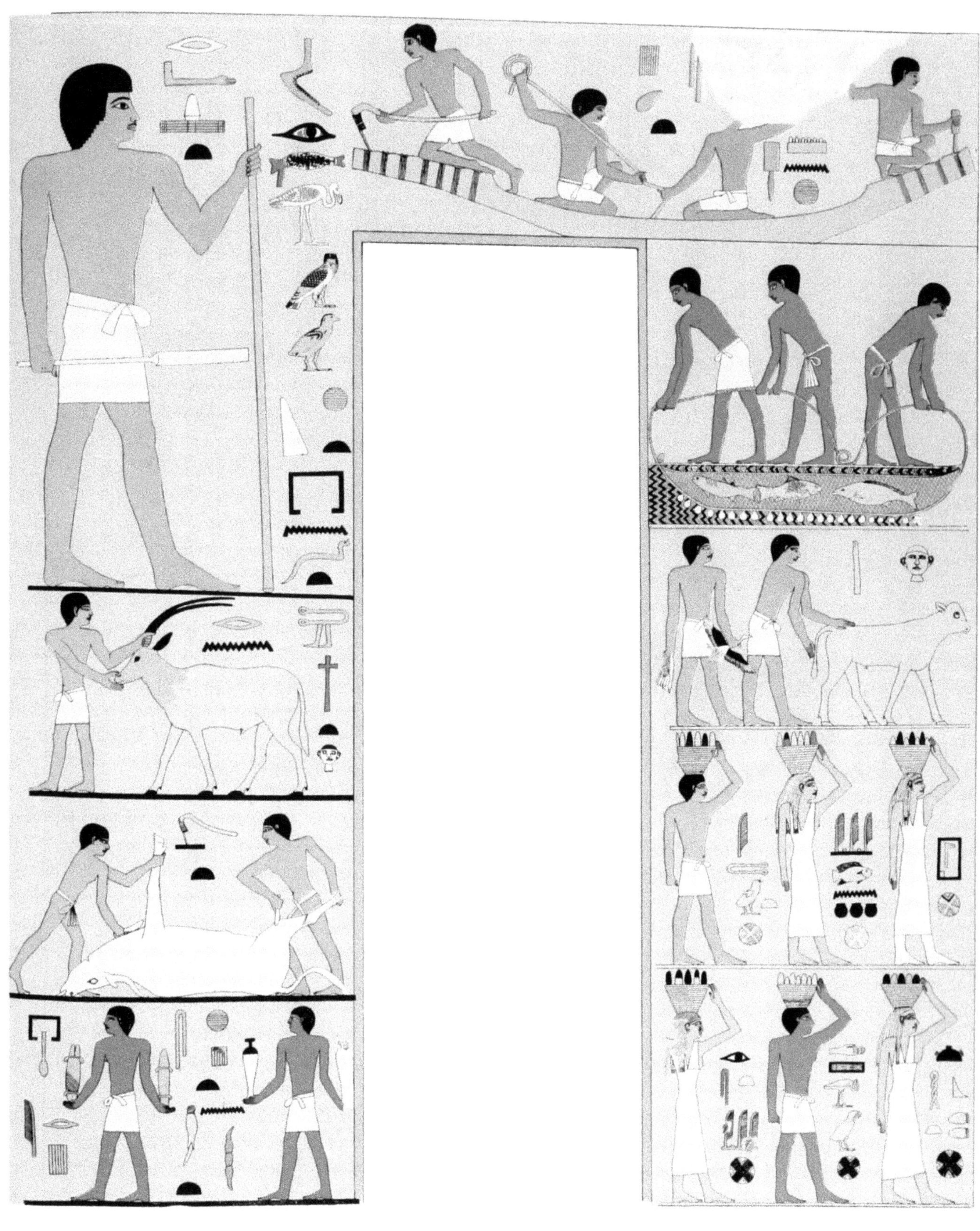

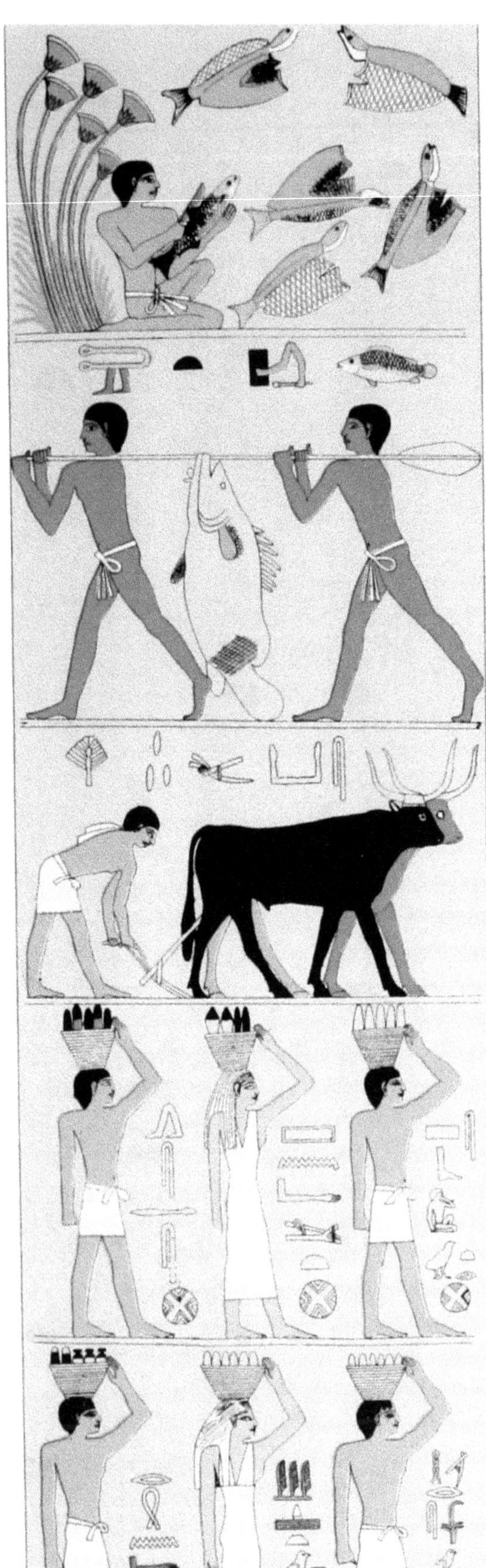

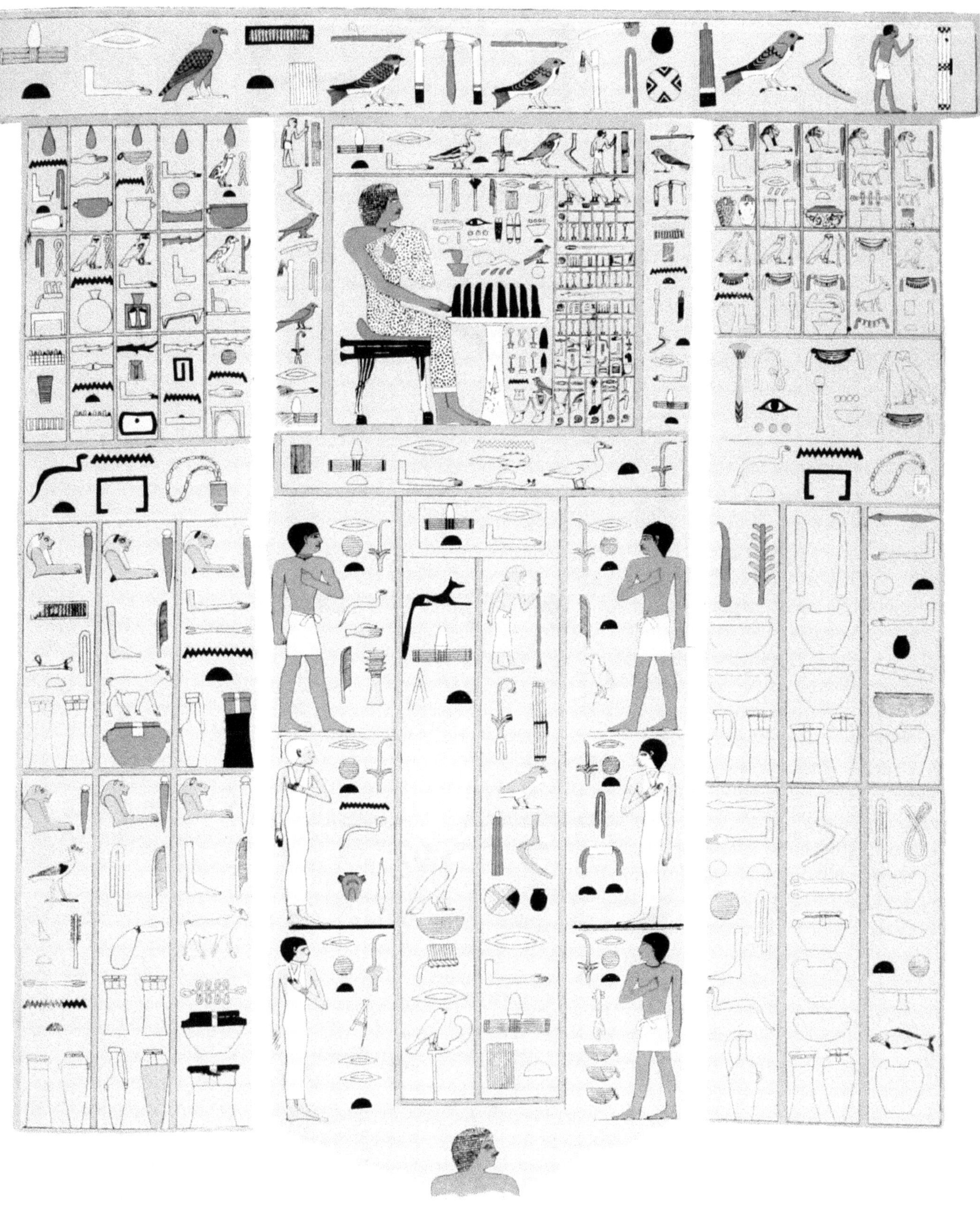

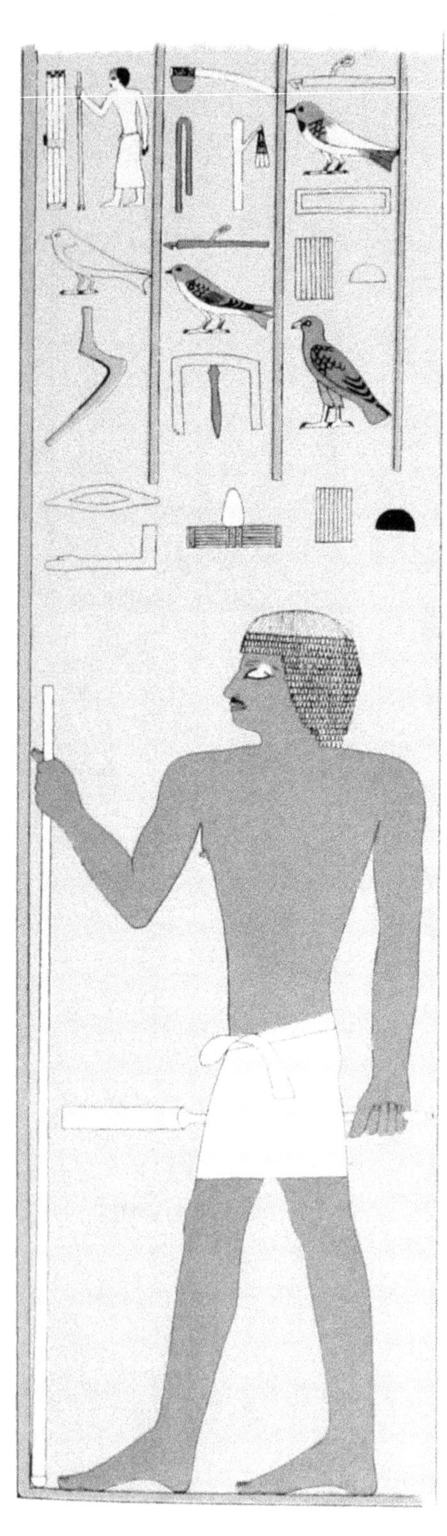

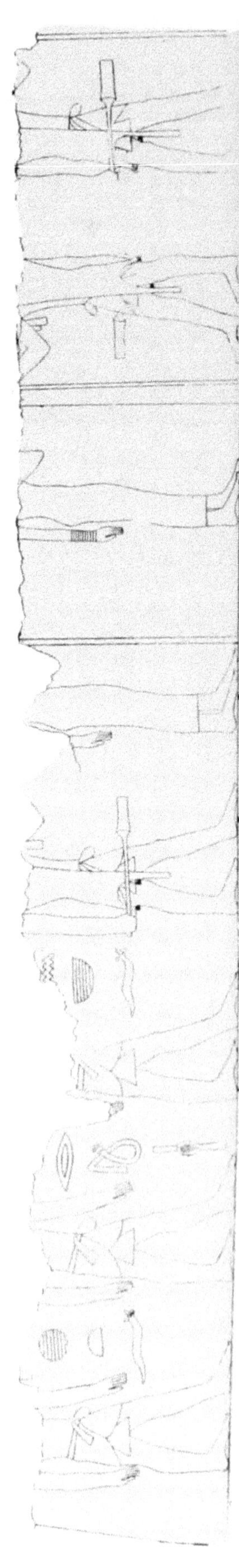

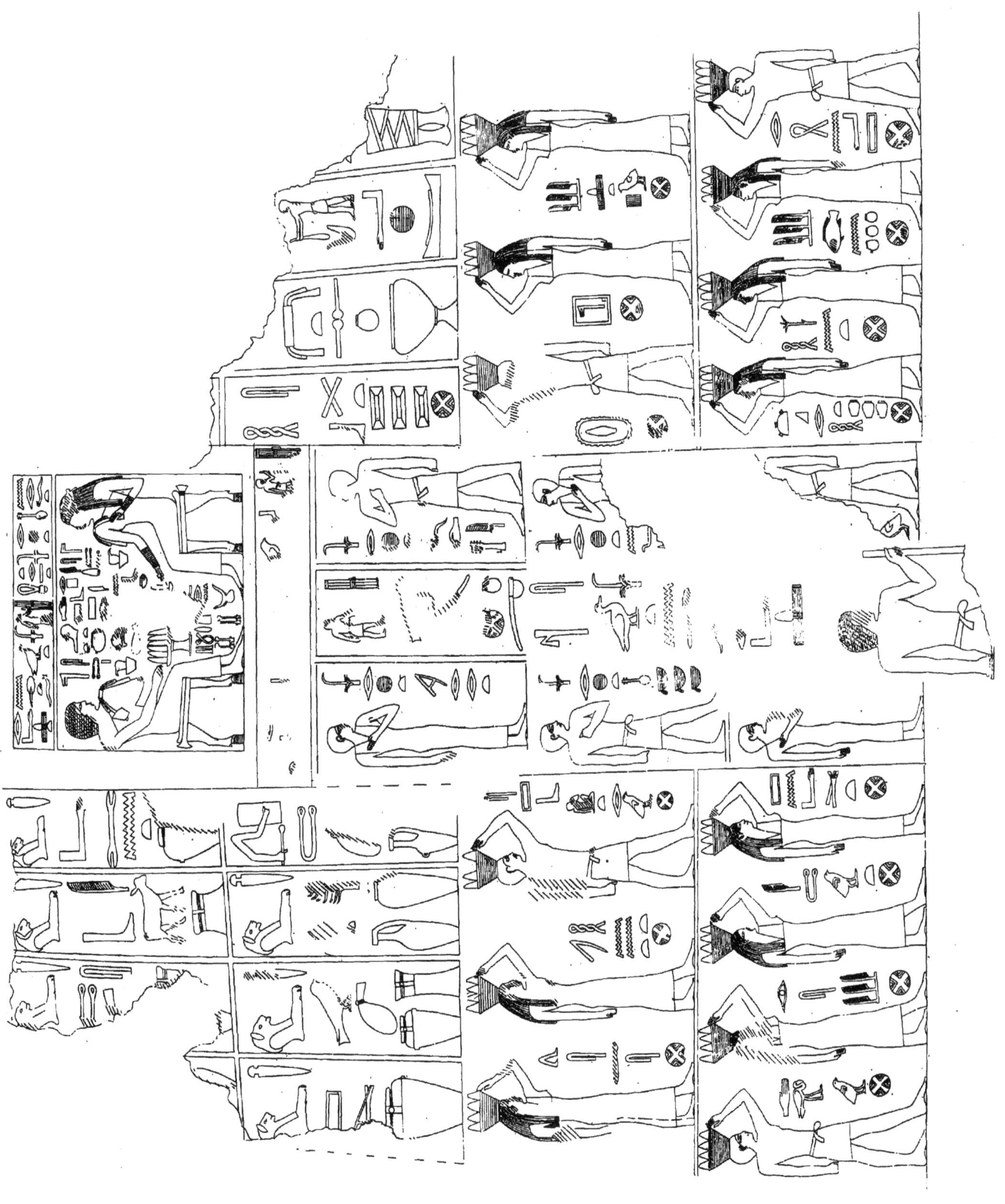

CONTINUED BELOW

CONTINUED ABOVE

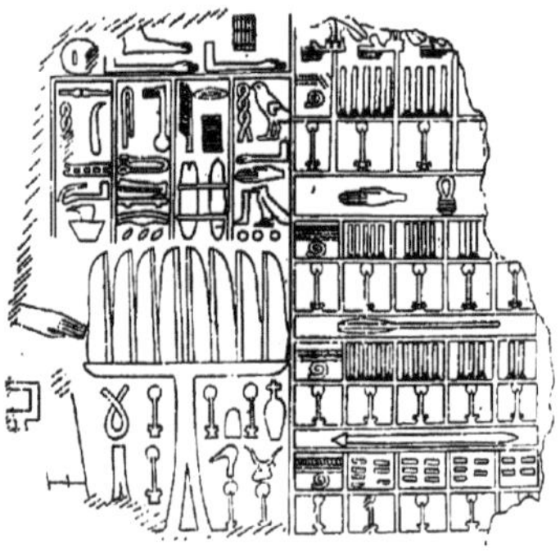

STELE OF HEKNEN.

PORTION OF LINTEL, FROM MASTABA No. 7.

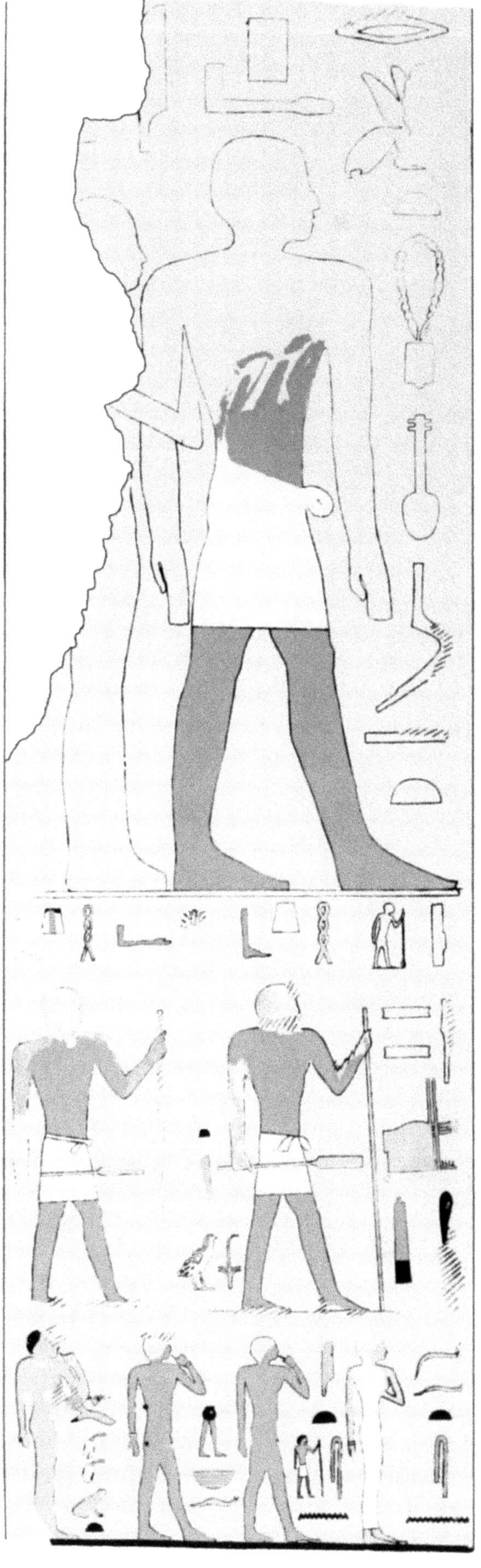

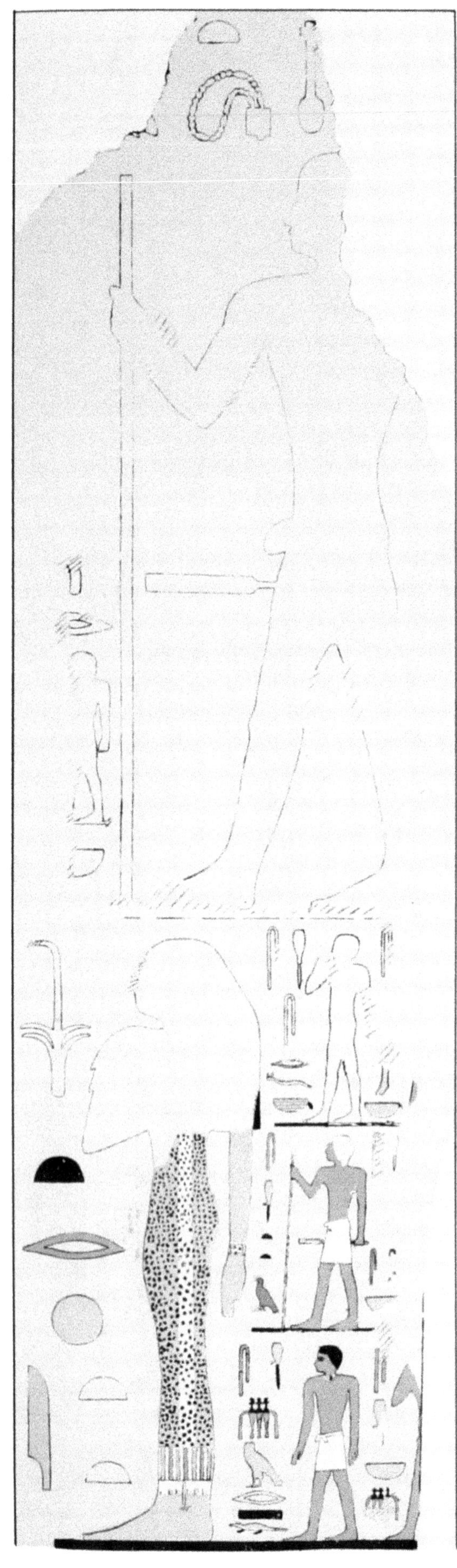

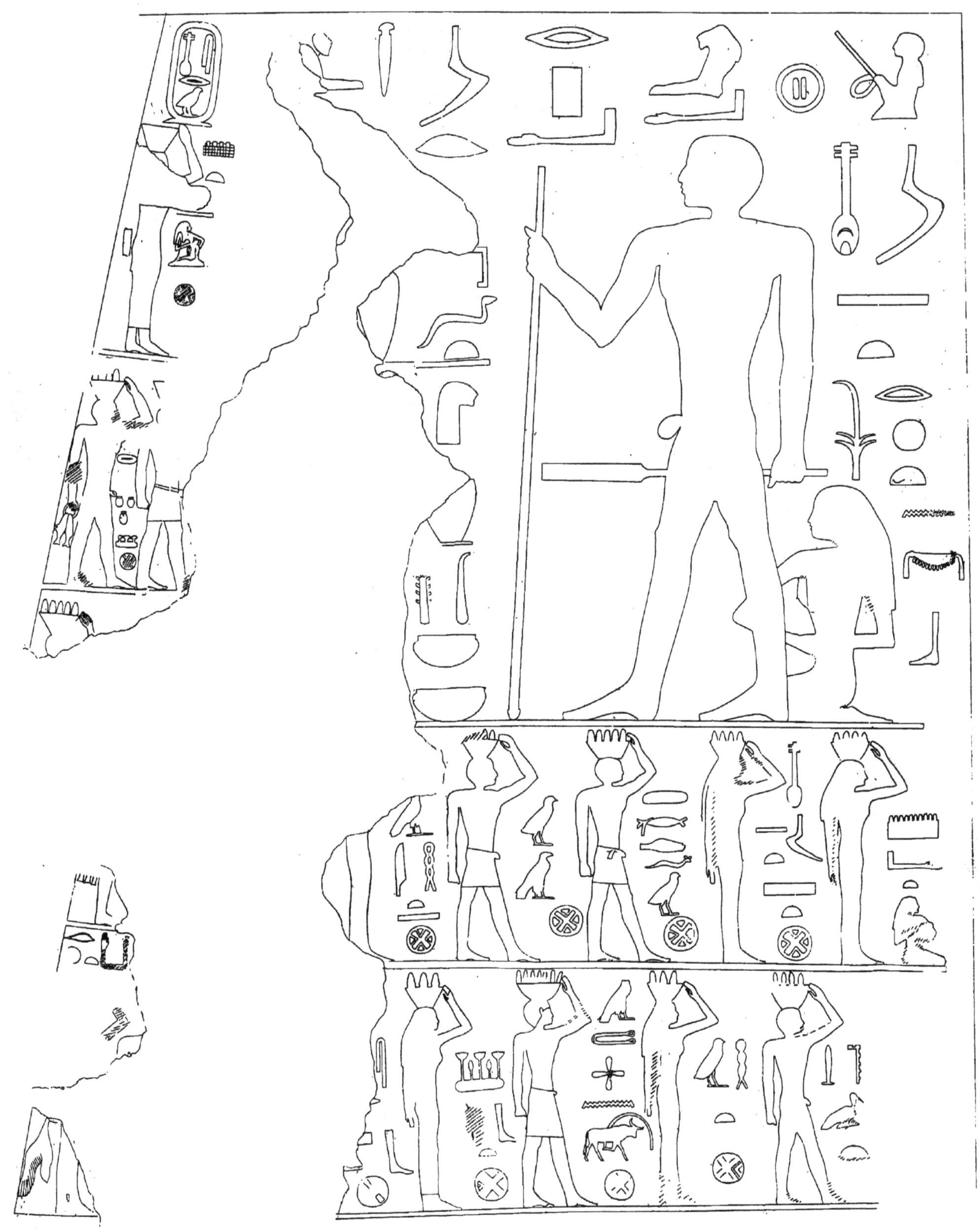

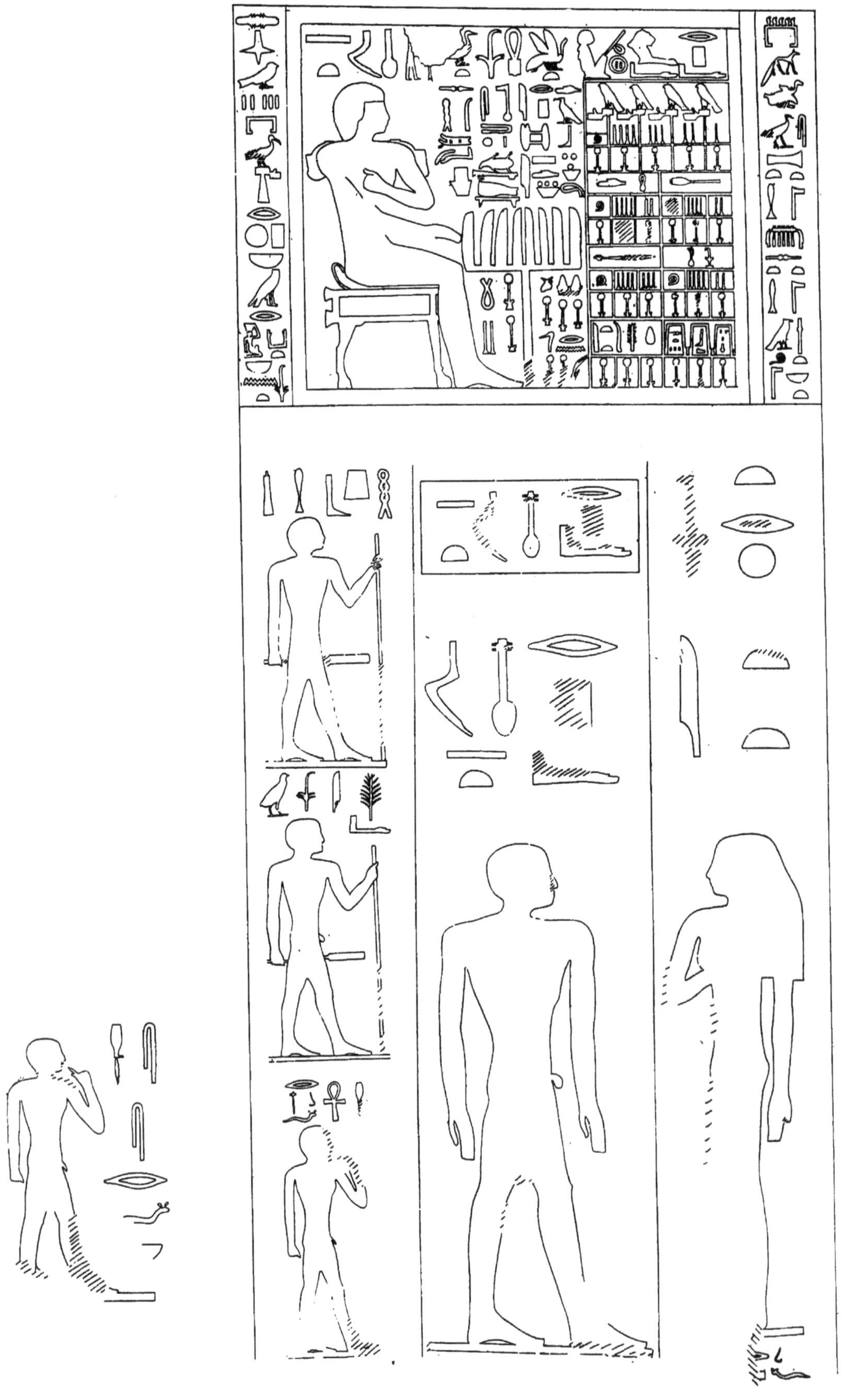

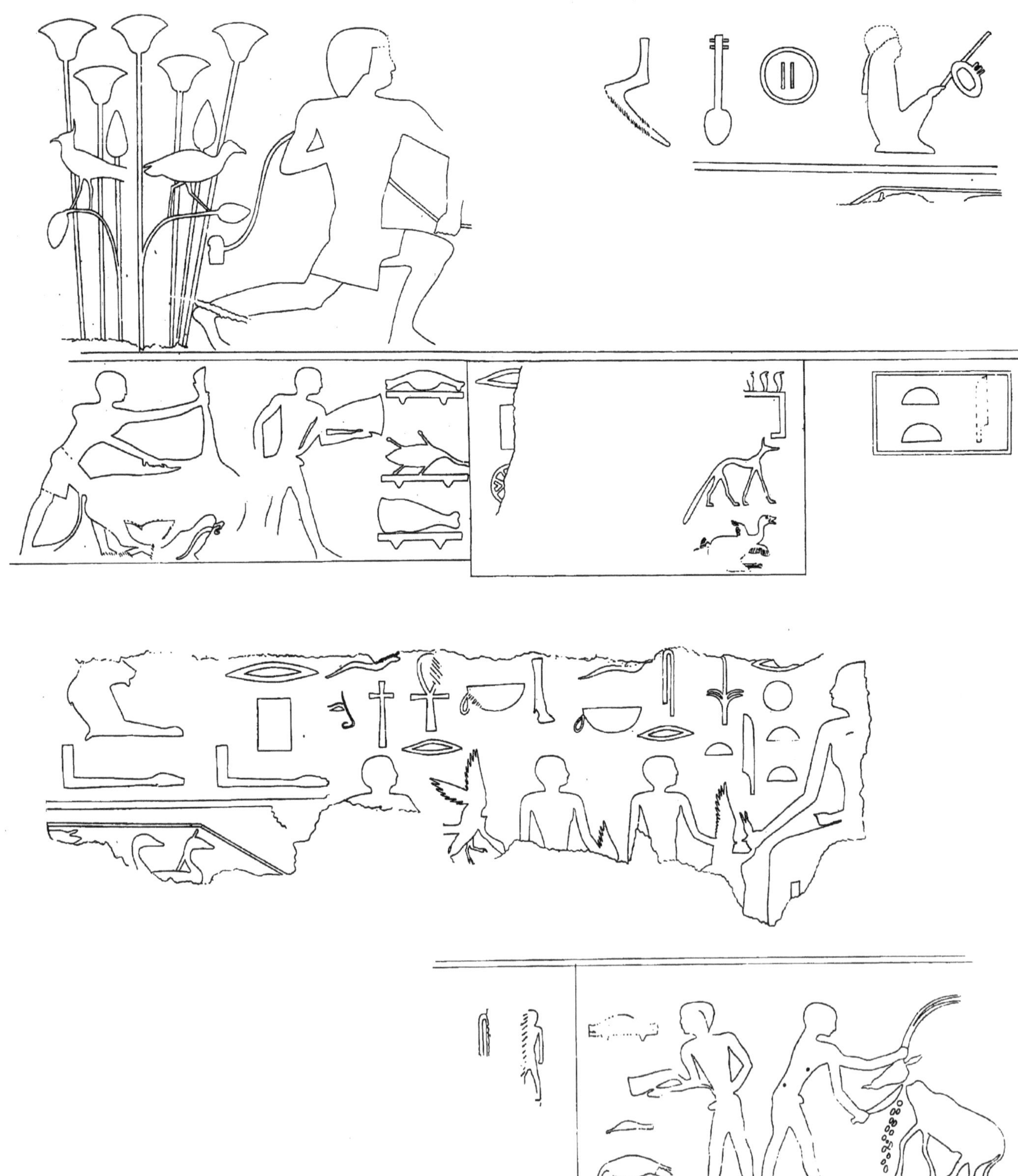

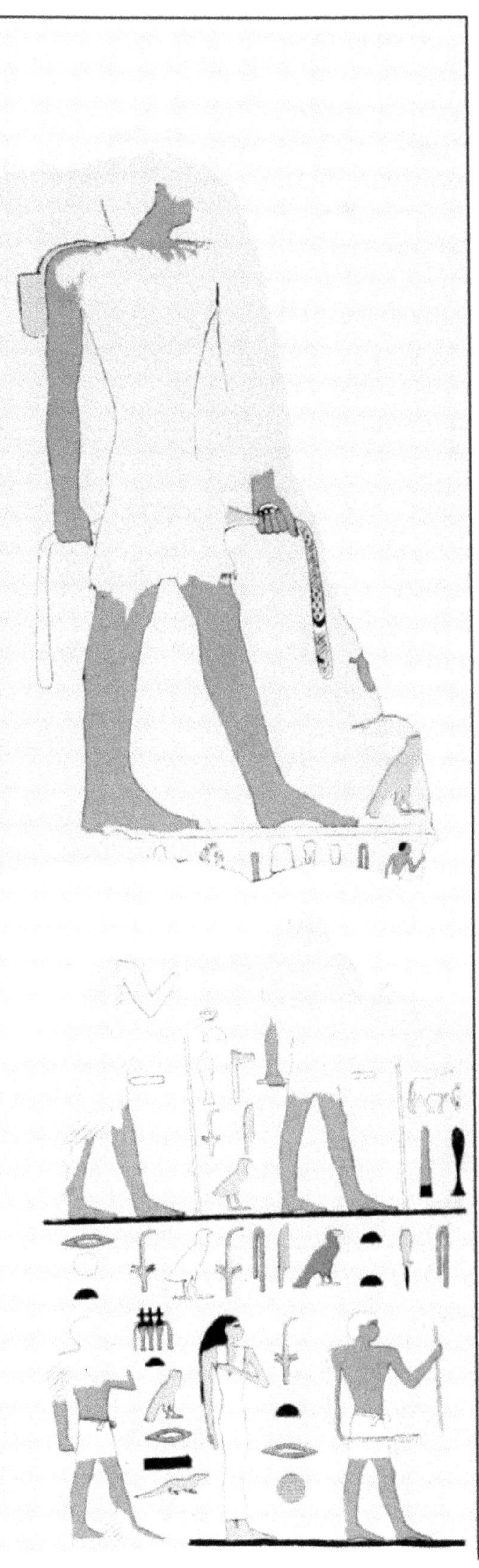

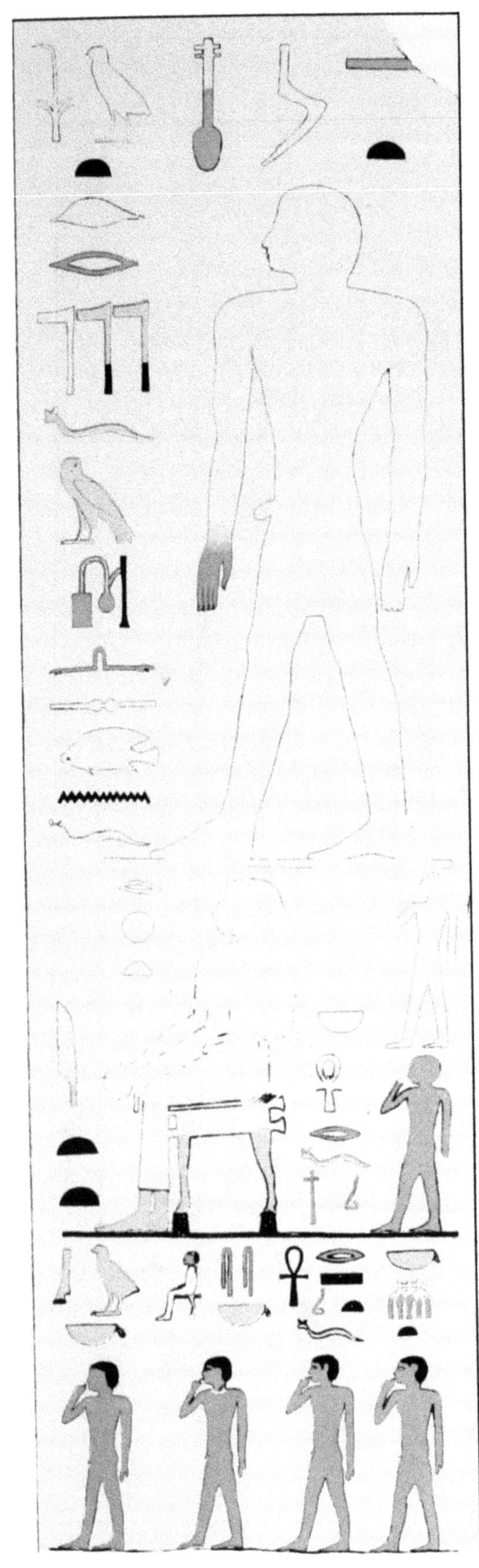

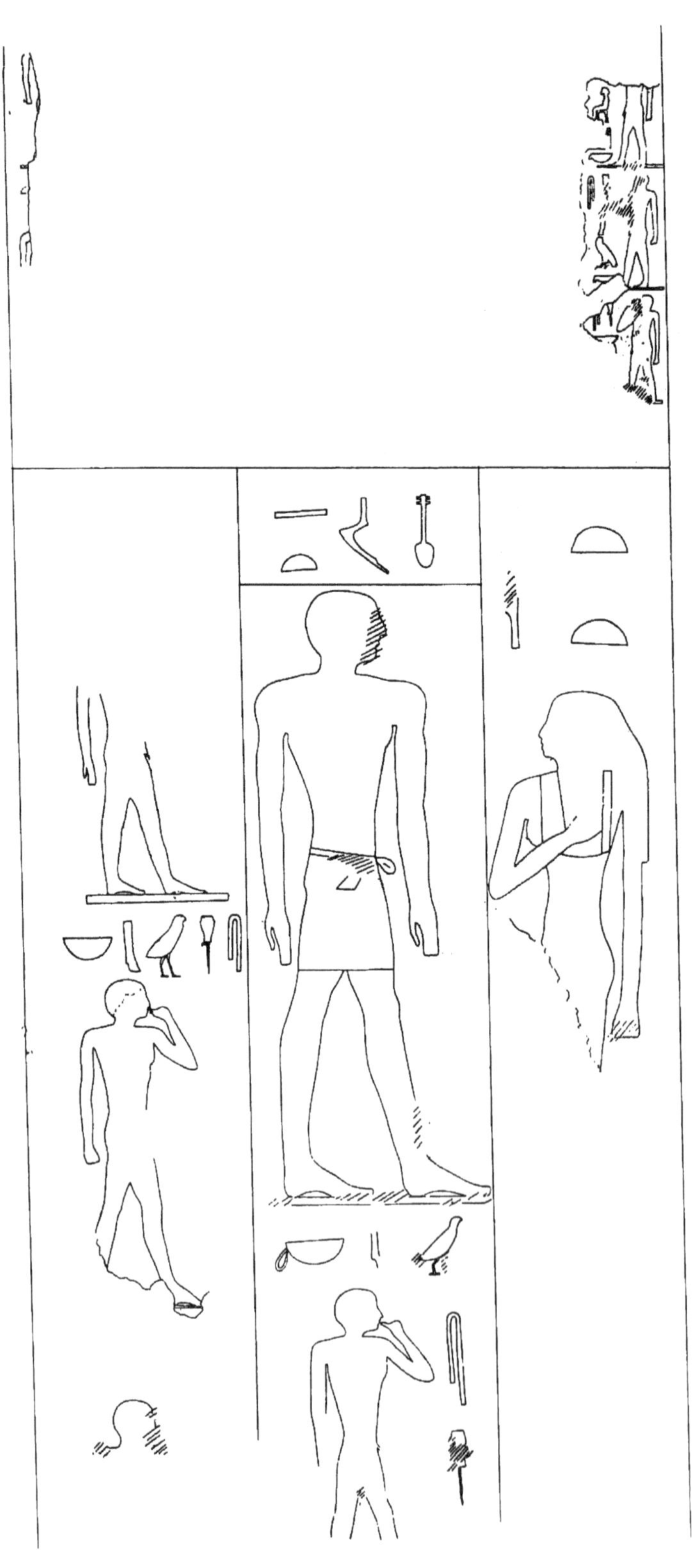

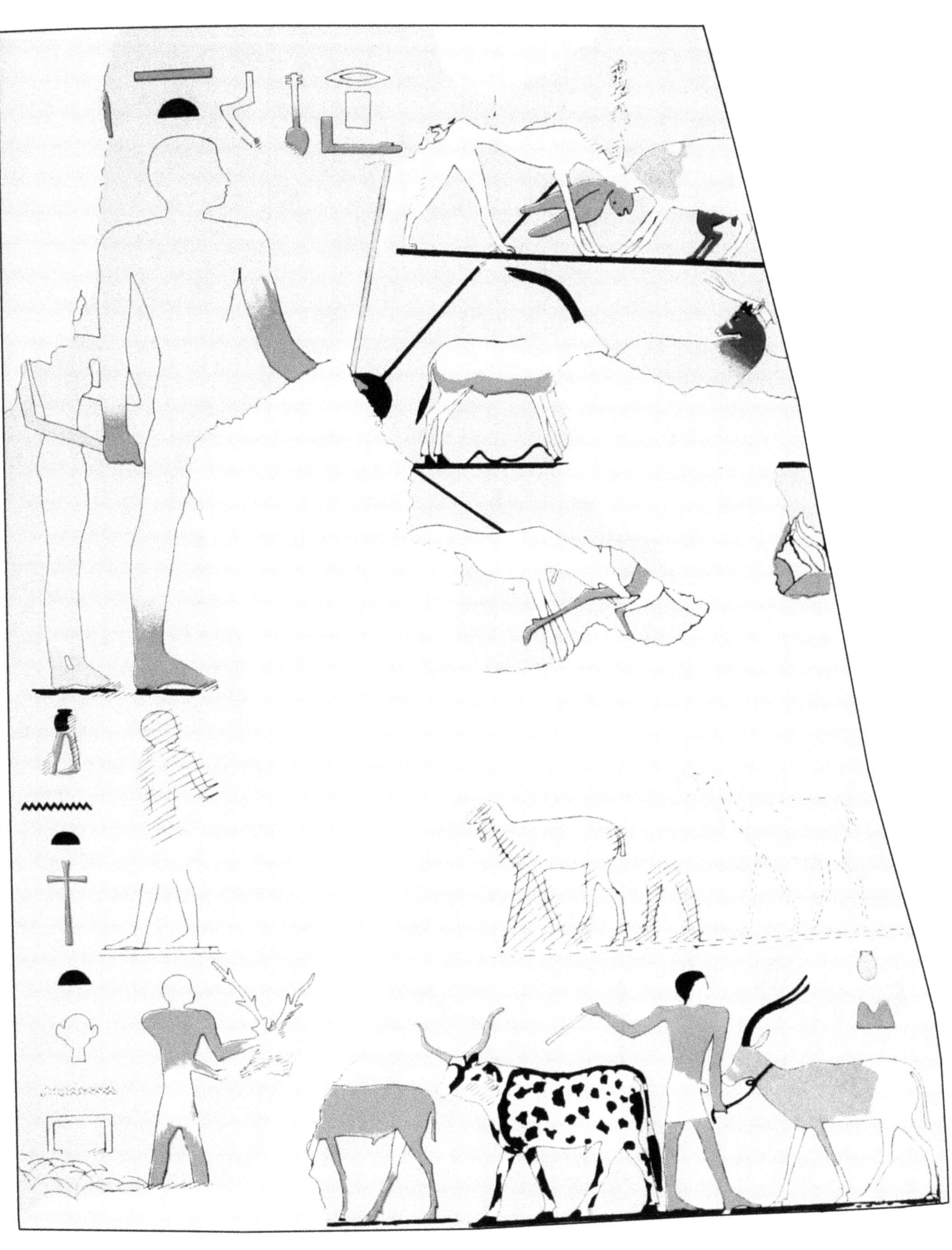

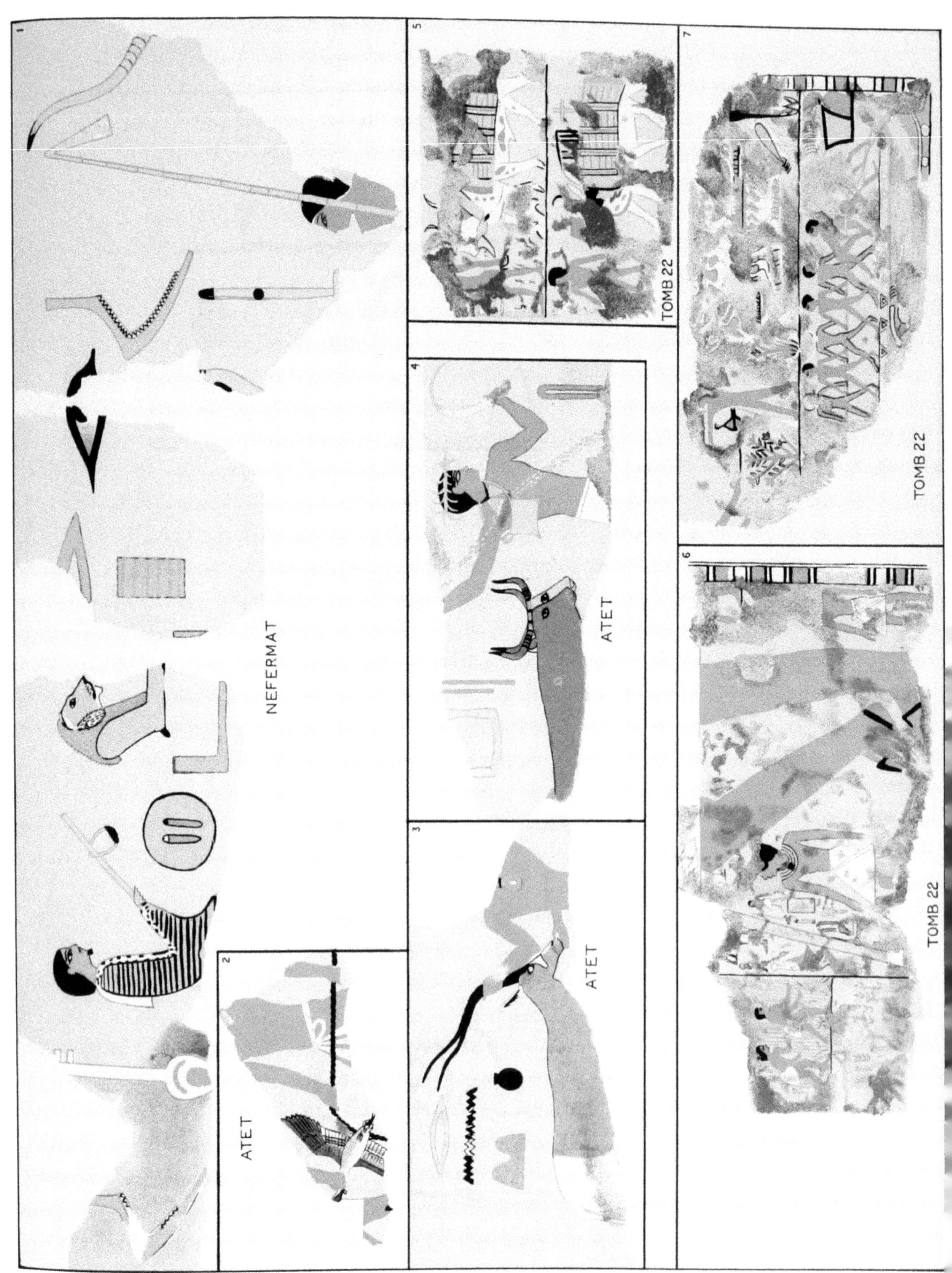
1
NEFERMAT
2
ATET
3
ATET
4
ATET
5
TOMB 22
6
TOMB 22
7
TOMB 22

TEMPLE

1 Limestone.

2 Limestone.

3 Blue glaze.

4 Grey Limestone

5 Limestone

6 Black Serpentine

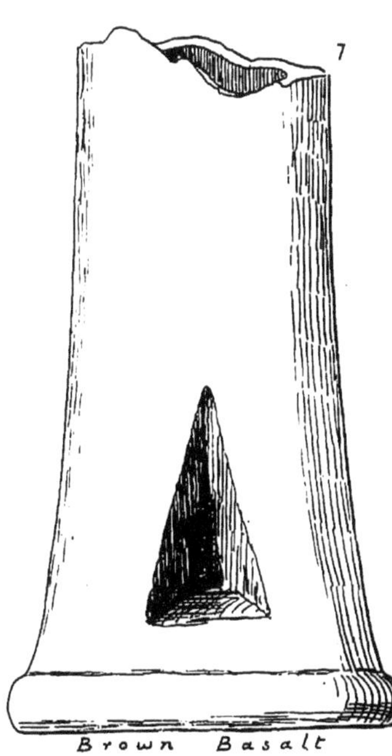
7 Brown Basalt

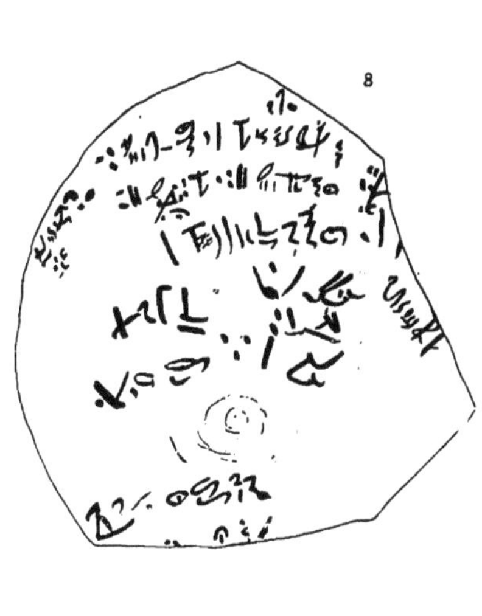
8

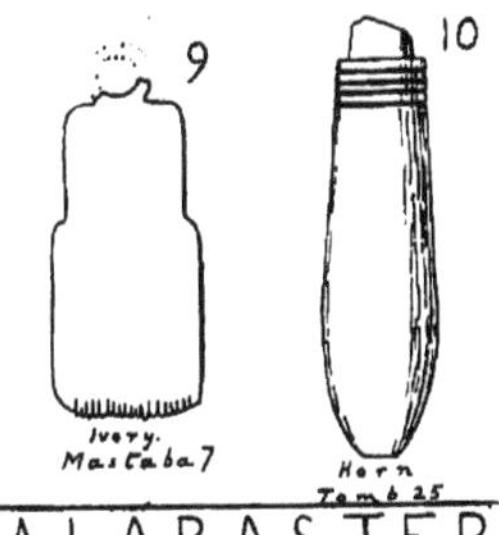
9 Ivory. Mastaba 7

10 Horn Tomb 25

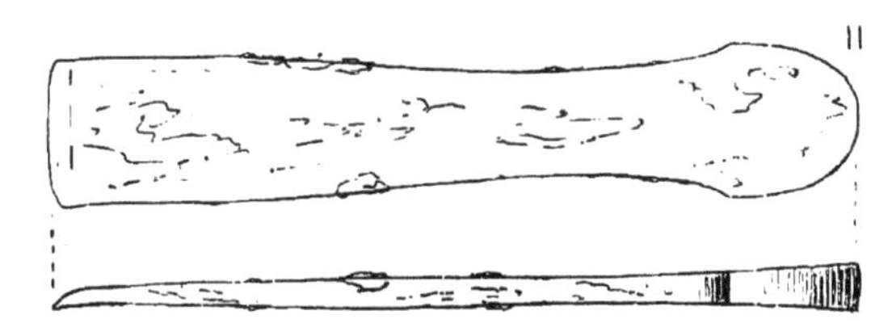
11 Copper Adze. Well of Rahotep. No 6.

12 Copper Saw, chip-ground N. of No 17

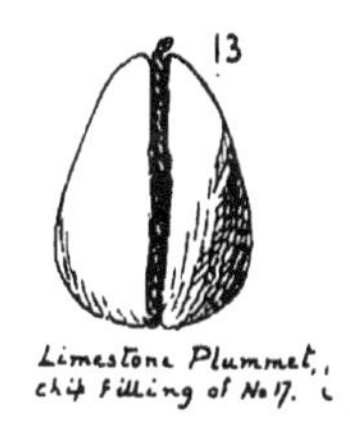
13 Limestone Plummet, chip filling of No 17.

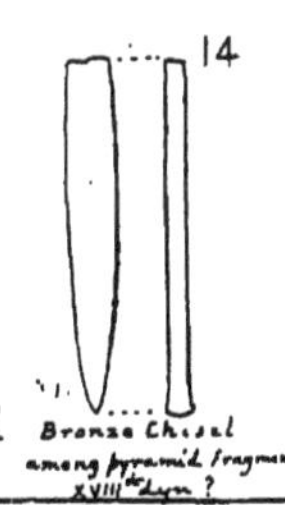
14 Bronze Chisel among pyramid fragments XVIIIth dyn.?

ALABASTER AND POTTERY BOWLS, FLINTS, &c, MASTABA No. 8.

15 Alabaster

16 Red Pottery

17 Shell containing colour (Chessylite)

18, 19 Copper Needles.

W. M. F. P.

Worked Flints, from the surface.

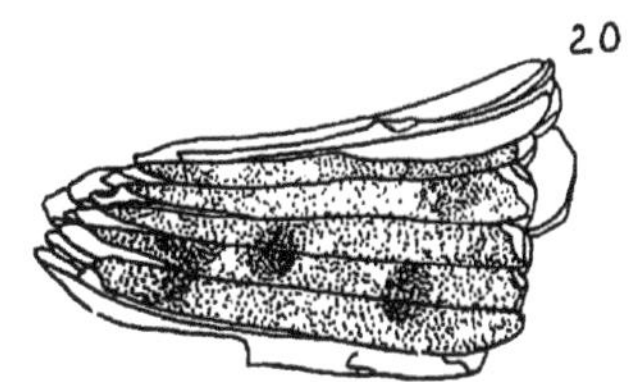
20

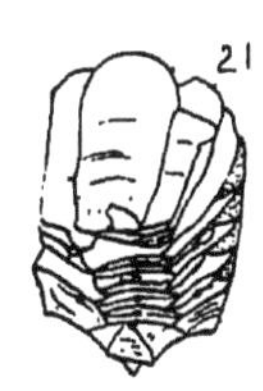
21

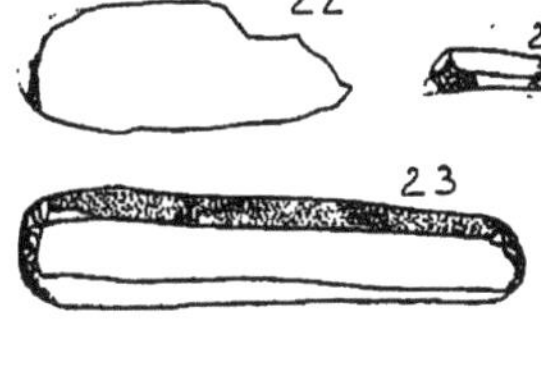
22, 23, 24, 25

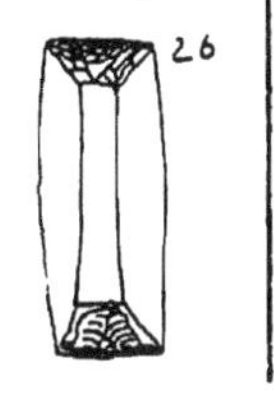
26

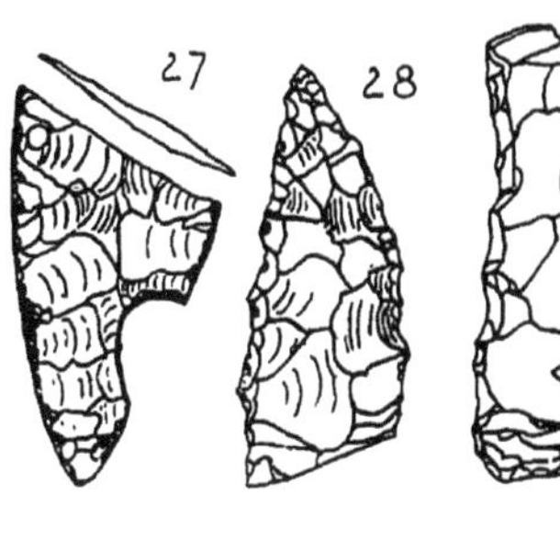
27, 28, 29

F. C. J. S.

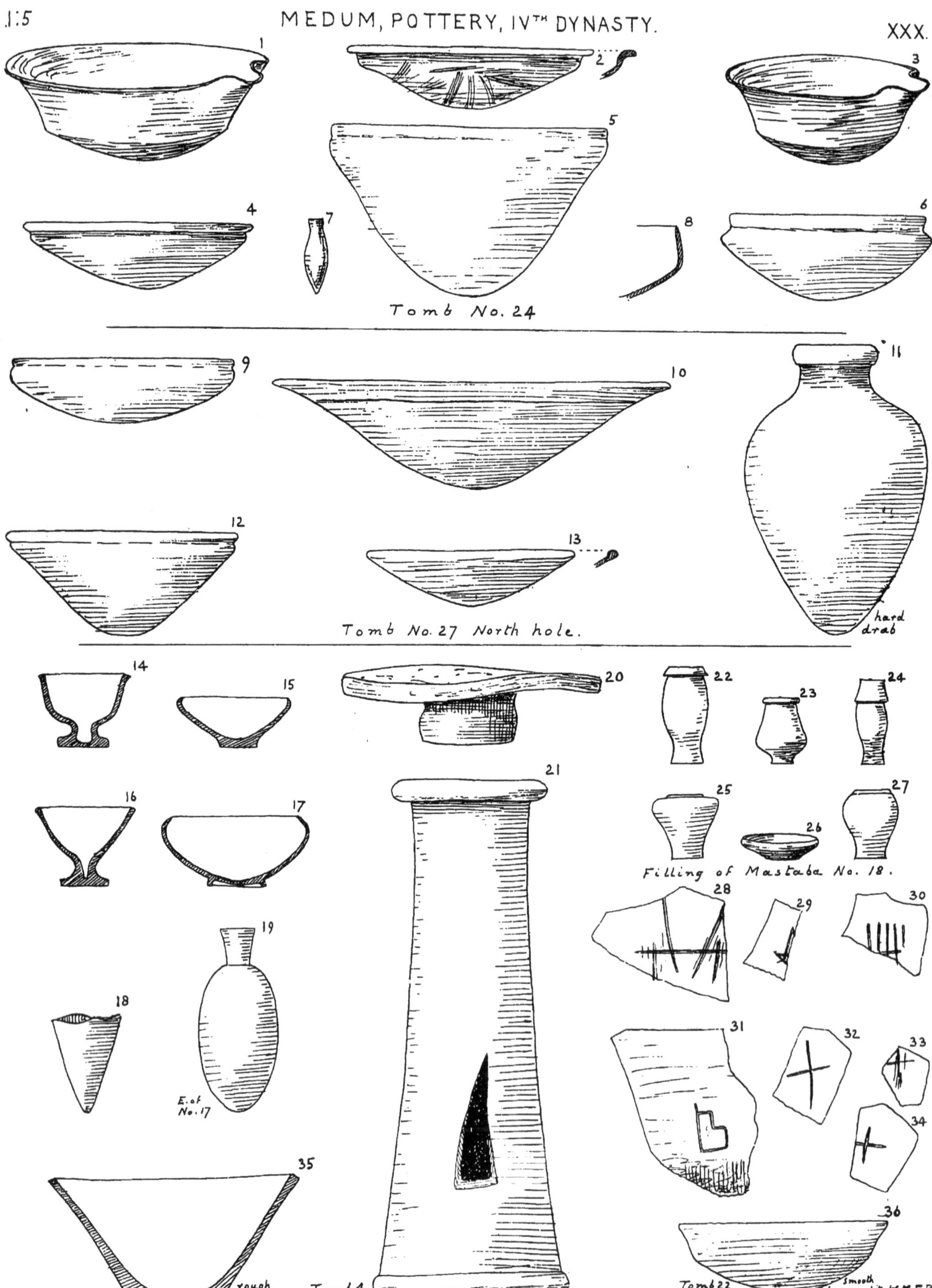
1
2
3
4
5
6
7
8
Tomb No. 24
9
10
11
12
13
hard drab
Tomb No. 27 North hole.
14
15
16
17
18
19
E. of No. 17
20
21
22
23
24
25
26
27
Filling of Mastaba No. 18.
28
29
30
31
32
33
34
35
36
Tomb 22
rough brown
Tomb 4
Tomb 22
smooth browny whit. W. M. F. P.

MEDUM, POTTERY, IVth DYNASTY.

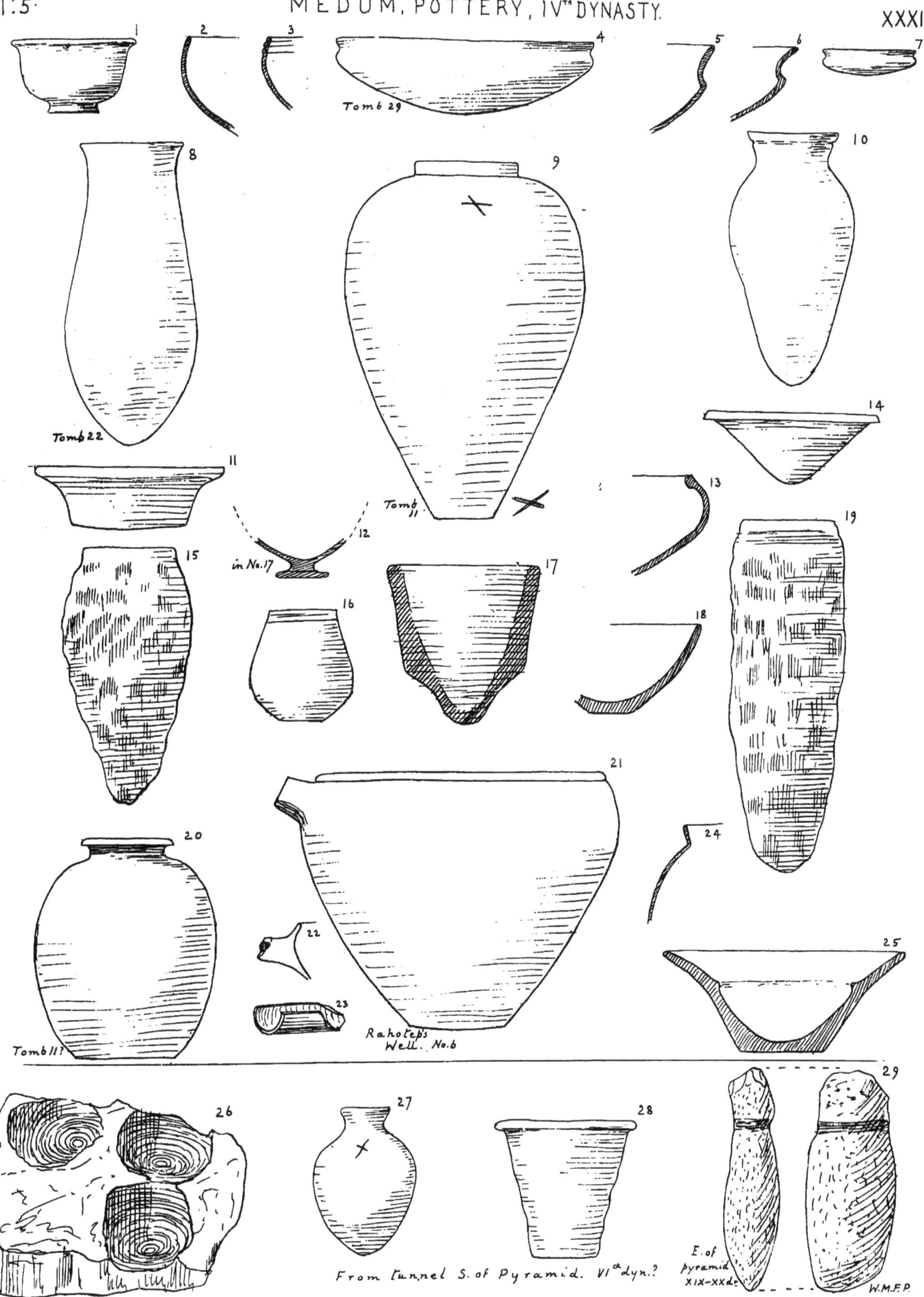

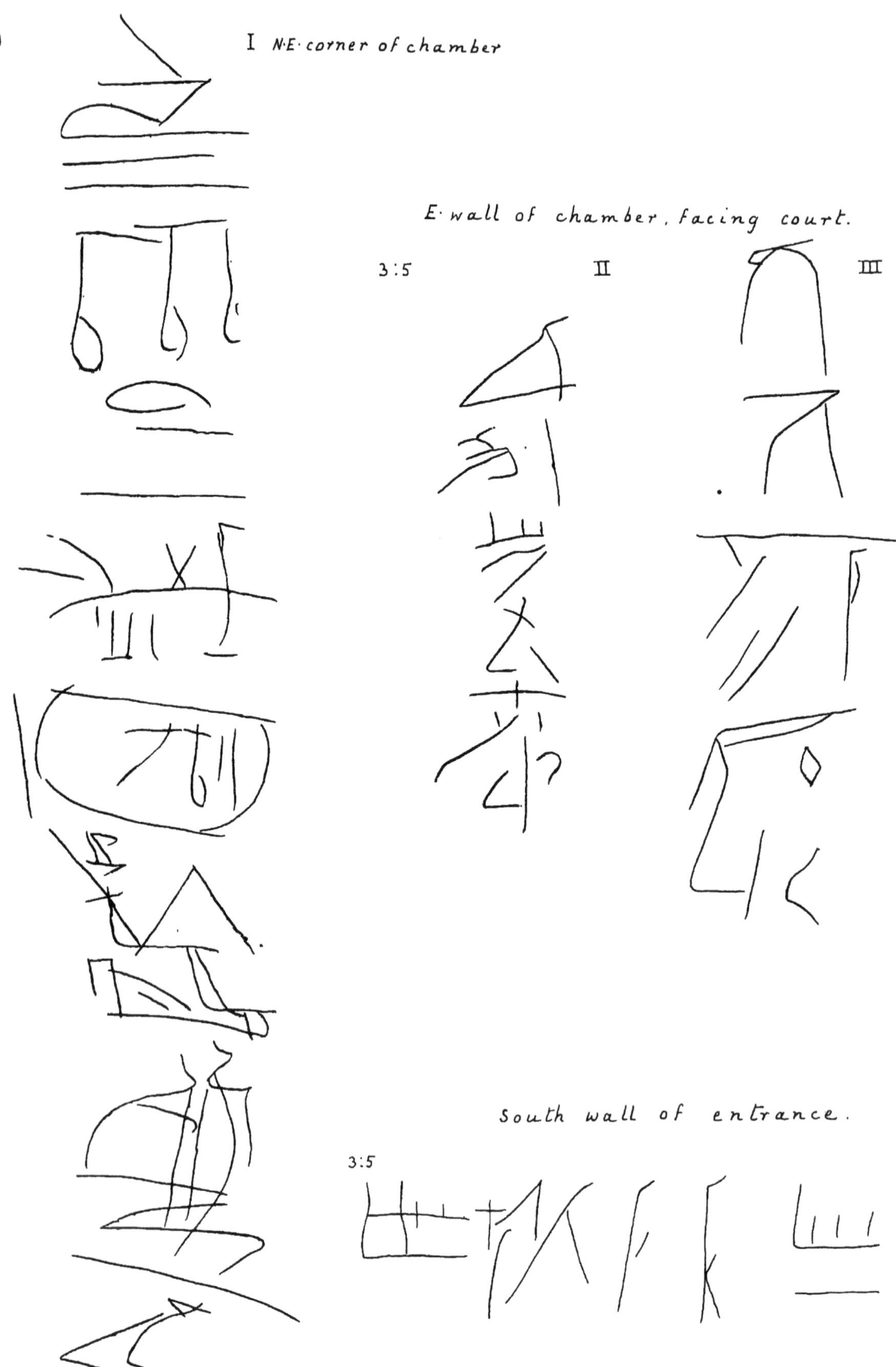
3:10
I N·E· corner of chamber
E· wall of chamber, facing court.
3:5
II
III
South wall of entrance.
IV.
3:5
WMFP

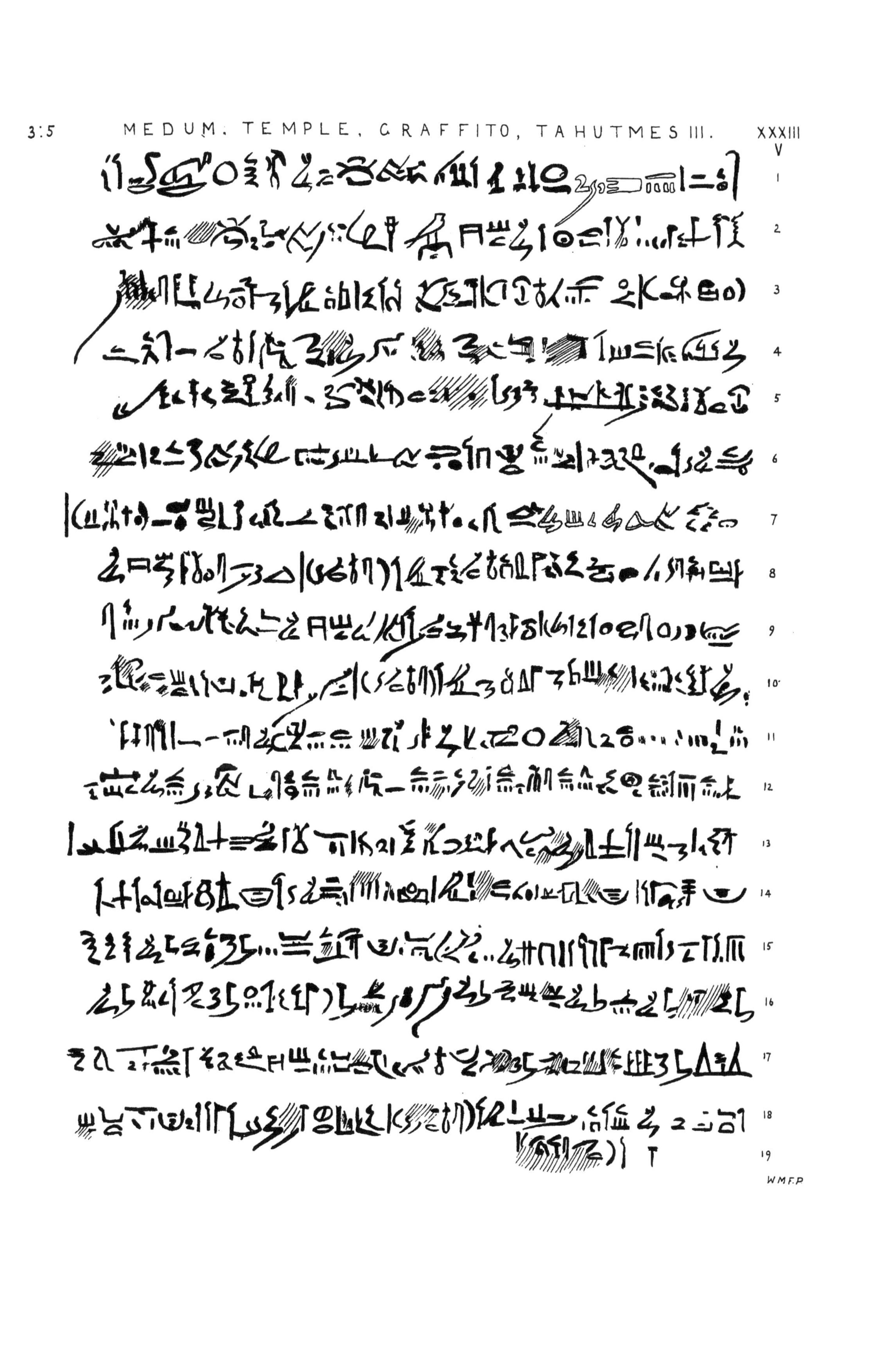

W.M.F.P.

VI

1

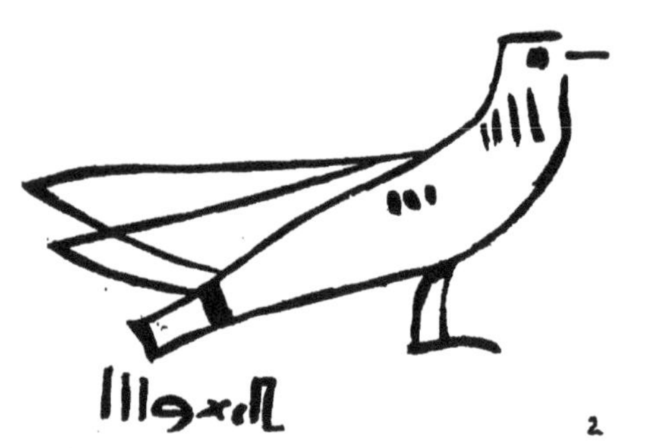

2

VII

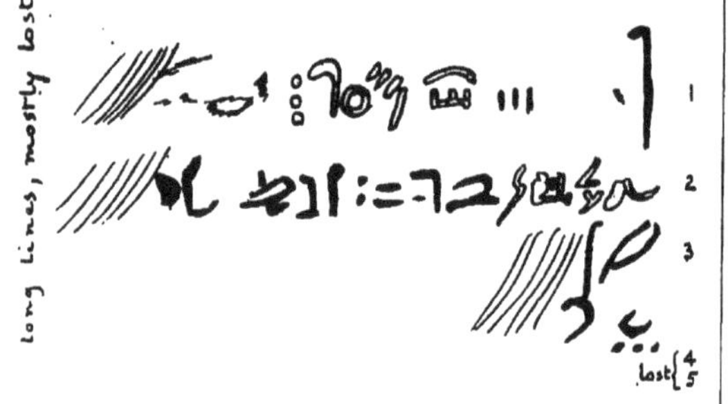

VIII

1
2
3
4
5
6
7 blank
8 blank
9 blank
10 blank
11
12
13 end

IX

1
2
3 } on roof of door.

X

XI

W.M.F.P.

XII

1

2

3

4

5

6–10 quite illegible

XIII

XIV

1

2

joint

3

end

4

XV

1

end

2

XVI.

1

2

3

4

5

W. M. F. P.

XVII

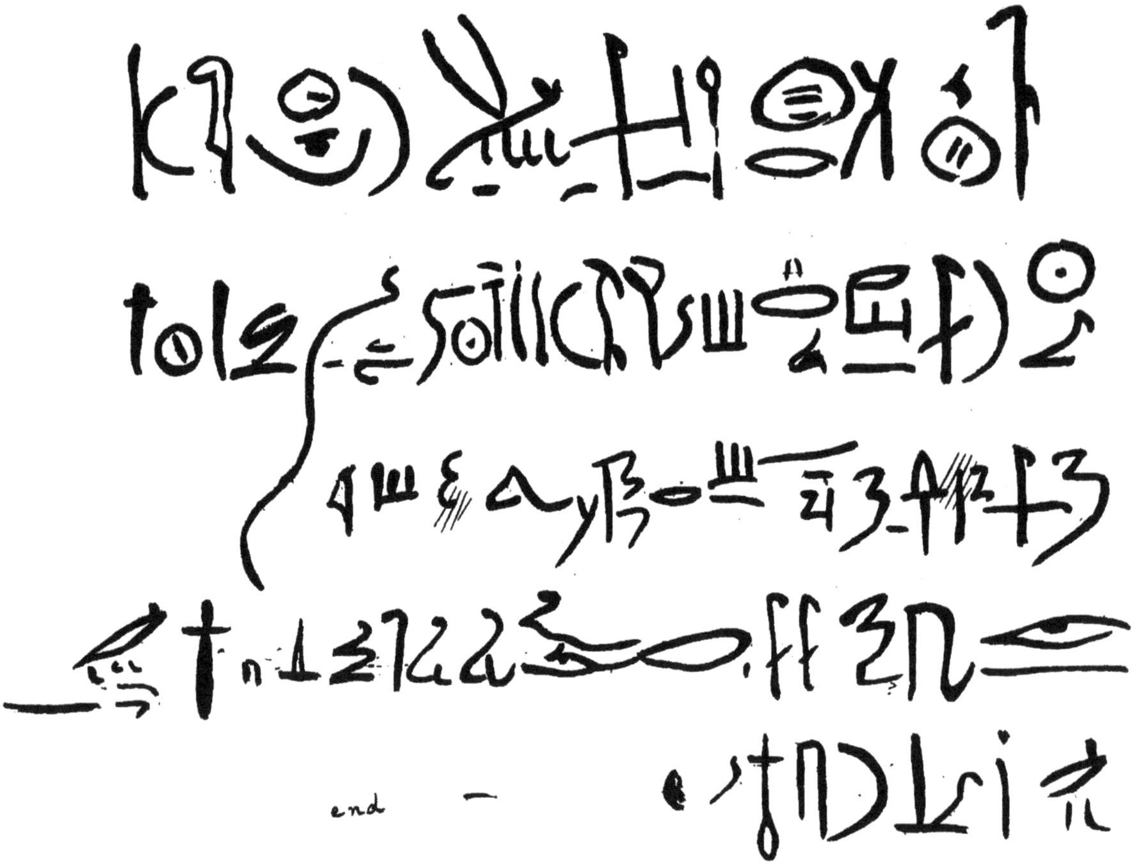

1

2

3

4

end 5

XVIII

1

2

3

end 4

At extreme top of wall. XX

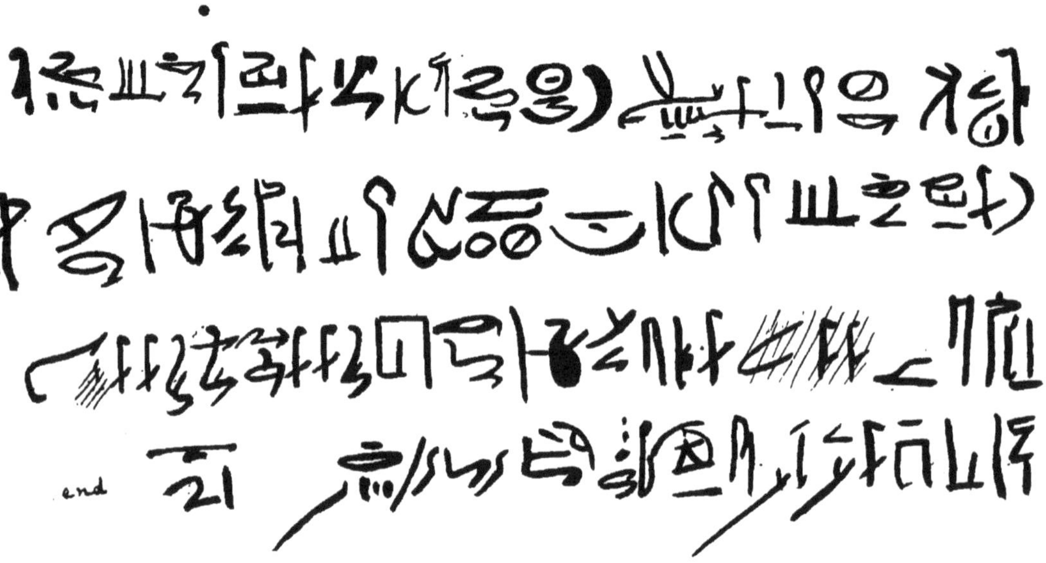

Trials of signs, isolated: preliminary to writing V. 1. XIX

1 2 3 4 5 6 7

W. M. F. P.